Qualitative Research

SAGE was founded in 1965 by Sara Miller McCune to support the dissemination of usable knowledge by publishing innovative and high-quality research and teaching content. Today, we publish over 900 journals, including those of more than 400 learned societies, more than 800 new books per year, and a growing range of library products including archives, data, case studies, reports, and video. SAGE remains majority-owned by our founder, and after Sara's lifetime will become owned by a charitable trust that secures our continued independence.

Los Angeles | London | New Delhi | Singapore | Washington DC | Melbourne

Qualitative Research

Analyzing Life

Johnny Saldaña
Arizona State University

Matt Omasta
Utah State University

Los Angeles | London | New Delhi
Singapore | Washington DC | Melbourne

FOR INFORMATION:

SAGE Publications, Inc.
2455 Teller Road
Thousand Oaks, California 91320
E-mail: order@sagepub.com

SAGE Publications Ltd.
1 Oliver's Yard
55 City Road
London EC1Y 1SP
United Kingdom

SAGE Publications India Pvt. Ltd.
B 1/I 1 Mohan Cooperative Industrial Area
Mathura Road, New Delhi 110 044
India

SAGE Publications Asia-Pacific Pte. Ltd.
3 Church Street
#10-04 Samsung Hub
Singapore 049483

Acquisitions Editor: Helen Salmon
Editorial Assistant: Chelsea Pearson
eLearning Editor: Katie Ancheta
Production Editor: Kelly DeRosa
Copy Editor: Alison Hope
Typesetter: C&M Digitals (P) Ltd
Proofreader: Susan Schon
Indexer: Joan Shapiro
Cover Designer: Gail Buschman
Marketing Manager: Susannah Goldes

Brief quote on page xxi is from p. 206 from *The Search for Signs of Intelligent Life in the Universe* by Jane Wagner. Copyright (©) 1986, 1990 by Jane Wagner Inc. Reprinted by permission of HarperCollins Publishers.

Printed in the United States of America

Library of Congress Cataloging-in-Publication Data

Names: Saldaña, Johnny, author. | Omasta, Matt, 1980- author.

Title: Qualitative research: analyzing life/Johnny Saldaña, Arizona State University, Matt Omasta, Utah State University.

Description: First Edition. | Thousand Oaks : SAGE Publications, Inc., 2017. | Includes bibliographical references.

Identifiers: LCCN 2016037493 | ISBN 9781506305493 (pbk.: alk. paper)

Subjects: LCSH: Social sciences—Research—Study and teaching (Higher).

Classification: LCC H62.S31865 2016 | DDC 001.4/2—dc23
LC record available at https://lccn.loc.gov/2016037493

This book is printed on acid-free paper.

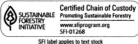

Certified Chain of Custody
SUSTAINABLE FORESTRY INITIATIVE
Promoting Sustainable Forestry
www.sfiprogram.org
SFI-01268
SFI label applies to text stock

17 18 19 20 21 10 9 8 7 6 5 4 3 2 1

Brief Contents

List of Displays   xvii

Preface   xxiii

Acknowledgments   xxvii

About the Authors   xxix

PART I—ANALYZING QUALITATIVE DATA

Chapter 1—Introduction: Analyzing Life   3

Chapter 2—Analyzing Field Sites   29

Chapter 3—Analyzing Documents, Artifacts, and Visual Materials   63

Chapter 4—Analyzing Interviews: Preparing, Conducting, and Transcribing   89

Chapter 5—Analyzing Interviews: Condensing and Coding   117

PART II—ANALYZING THE FRAMEWORK

Chapter 6—Analyzing Qualitative Methodologies   141

Chapter 7—Analyzing Qualitative Research Design   165

Chapter 8—Analyzing Research Ethics   191

PART III—ANALYTIC ASSEMBLAGE

Chapter 9—Analytic Synthesis: Condensing, Patterning, and Unifying   213

Chapter 10—Analytic Synthesis: Understanding, Interpreting, and Theorizing   245

Chapter 11—Analytic Write-Ups   283

Chapter 12—Analytic Presentations   317

Chapter 13—Closure: Leading an Analytic Life   335

Appendix—Three Representative Articles in
Qualitative Research   341

Glossary   411

References   423

Index   431

Detailed Contents

List of Displays   xvii

Preface   xxiii

   The Organization and Through-Line of the Book   xxiii

   The Coauthors' Approach   xxiv

   To the Instructor   xxv

Acknowledgments   xxvii

About the Authors   xxix

PART I—ANALYZING QUALITATIVE DATA

Chapter 1—Introduction: Analyzing Life   3

   Learning Objectives   3

   Introduction   3

   Developing Fundamental Qualitative Analytic Skills   3

      Condensing large amounts of data   4
      Noticing patterns in textual and visual materials   7
      Unifying seemingly different things   10
      Understanding social processes of human action, reaction,
         and interaction   12
      Interpreting the routines, rituals, rules, roles, and relationships
         of social life   15

   On Qualitative Data Analysis—and Life   23

   Closure and Transition   24

   Resources for an Introduction to Qualitative Analysis   25

   Analytic Exercises   25

   Sample Data for Analysis   26

Chapter 2—Analyzing Field Sites   29

   Learning Objectives   29

   Introduction   29

   On Culture   30

   Observation Settings   32

      Finding a place and space   32
      Access   33

The Observer's Frames 34

Lenses, filters, and angles for fieldwork 34
Observer membership roles 36
Purpose-driven observations 37

Field Notes 38

Written documentation of analytic observations 38
Front matter 39
The setting 39
Jottings and write-ups 40
Observer's comments 43
Time stamps 44

Technical Matters of Fieldwork and Field Notes 45

Audio- and video-recording 45
Fieldwork clock hours 47
Field note files 48

Analyzing Observations of Social Life 50

Reflecting on action, reaction, and interaction 50
Reflecting on routines, rituals, and rules 51
Reflecting on roles and relationships 53
Analytic memoing of field notes 54

Closure and Transition 57

Resources for Participant Observation 58

Analytic Exercises for Participant Observation 58

Sample Field Notes for Analysis 58

Chapter 3—Analyzing Documents, Artifacts, and Visual Materials 63

Learning Objectives 63

Introduction 63

On Values, Attitudes, and Beliefs 64

Analyzing Manifest and Latent Contents 66

The Materials and Meanings of Human Production 67

Analyzing Documents 68

Collecting materials 69
Analyzing attention 70
Analyzing identity 72

Analyzing Artifacts 73

Analyzing belonging 74
Analyzing symbolism 76

Analyzing process   78

Analyzing extensions   79

Analyzing Visual Materials   81

Analyzing collaboratively   82

Analyzing evocation   83

The Routines, Rituals, Rules, Roles, and Relationships in Documents, Artifacts, and Visual Materials   85

Closure and Transition   86

Resources for Analyzing Documents, Artifacts, and Visual Materials   87

Analytic Exercises for Documents, Artifacts, and Visual Materials   87

Sample Photograph   88

Chapter 4—Analyzing Interviews: Preparing, Conducting, and Transcribing   89

Learning Objectives   89

Introduction   89

Types of Interviews   89

Surveys and structured interviews   90

Semi-structured interviews   92

Unstructured interviews   92

Focus groups   93

Participant Selection   95

Sampling methods   95

Number of interviews   97

Interview Preparation, Scheduling, and Arrangements   101

Audio- and video-recording equipment   102

Asking Questions   103

Interview protocols   104

Phrasing the inquiry   108

Maintaining the conversation   111

Transcribing   113

Basic documentation principles   114

Topic summaries   116

Closure and Transition   116

Analytic Exercises for Interviewing   116

Chapter 5—Analyzing Interviews: Condensing and Coding   117

Learning Objectives   117

Introduction   117

Interview Condensation   117

Analyzing Interviews Through Codes and Coding   120

In vivo coding and analytic formatting   121
Process coding   126
Values coding   128
Emotion coding   129

Closure and Transition   131

Resources for Interviewing   132

Analytic Exercises for Interviewing   132

Sample Interview Transcript   133

PART II—ANALYZING THE FRAMEWORK

Chapter 6—Analyzing Qualitative Methodologies   141

Learning Objectives   141

Introduction   141

Theoretical Premises of Qualitative Research   141

Ontology and epistemology   141
Interpretation   142
The constructivist nature of qualitative inquiry   142
Paradigms   143
An example of quantitative research   143
An example of qualitative research   144

A Rationale for Qualitative Research   145

Selected Methodologies of Qualitative Research and Analysis   146

Ethnography   147
Case study   148
Grounded theory   150
Phenomenology   151
Content analysis   153
Action research   155
Evaluation research   156
Autoethnography   158

Mixed Methods   159

On Genres   162

Closure and Transition   163

Resources for Analyzing Qualitative Research
   Methodologies   163

Analytic Exercises for Qualitative Research
   Methodologies   164

Appendix Readings   164

Chapter 7—Analyzing Qualitative Research Design   165

Learning Objectives   165

Introduction   165

Researching and Analyzing the Topic   166
   Focusing the study's topic   166
   Writing the purpose statement   168
   Writing the rationale   169

Analyzing the Literature   170
   Initial searches   171
   Organizing and managing the literature   172
   Consulting mentors, experts, and peers   173
   Unifying the literature   173

Research Questions   174
   Developing research questions   175

Site Selection   178

Participant Selection   178
   Sampling   179

Data Collection Methods   180

Data Analysis Methods   181

Presentation Modes   182

Timeline Design   183

Conceptual Frameworks   184
   Examples of conceptual frameworks   185

Closure and Transition   188

Resources for Analyzing Qualitative Research Design   188

Analytic Exercises for Qualitative Research Design   189

Outline for a Qualitative Research Proposal   189

Chapter 8—Analyzing Research Ethics   191

Learning Objectives   191

Introduction   191

The Rules of Research   192

Consent   192

Confidentiality   193

Comprehensive information   194

Communication   195

Conflict-free research   195

Institutional Review Boards   196

What is human subjects research?   197

Review types and timelines   198

IRB applications   199

Researcher and Participant Relationships   205

Analyzing Ethical Ambiguity   206

Closure and Transition   208

Resources for Research Ethics   208

Analytic Exercises for Research Ethics   209

PART III—ANALYTIC ASSEMBLAGE

Chapter 9—Analytic Synthesis: Condensing, Patterning, and Unifying   213

Learning Objectives   213

Introduction   213

On Synthesis   213

Condensing Large Amounts of Data   215

Analyzing relevant text   215

Codes and coding   216

Descriptive coding and subcoding   217

Dramaturgical coding   219

Versus coding   222

Found poetry   224

Patterning Textual and Visual Materials   225

Categories   226

Themes   230

Unifying Seemingly Different Things   235

Concepts   235

Propositions   237

Matrices and tabular displays   239

Mixed methods   242

Closure and Transition   244

Analytic Exercises for Analytic Synthesis   244

Chapter 10—Analytic Synthesis: Understanding, Interpreting, and Theorizing   245

Learning Objectives   245

Introduction   245

Understanding Social Processes of Human Action, Reaction, and Interaction   245

Assertions   245
Vignettes   251
Diagrammatic displays   252

Interpreting the Routines, Rituals, Rules, Roles, and Relationships of Social Life   255

Analytic meta-memos   255

Theorizing   257

Four properties of a theory   257
Elements of a theory   259
Constructing theory: Life learnings   260
Constructing theory: An analytic review   261

CAQDAS   268

On Credibility and Trustworthiness   271

Closure and Transition   273

Resources for Analytic Synthesis   277

Qualitative data analysis   277
Technology for qualitative data analysis   278

Analytic Exercises for Analytic Synthesis   278

Sample Data for Analytic Synthesis   278

Chapter 11—Analytic Write-Ups   283

Learning Objectives   283

Introduction   283

Stylistic Approaches to Research Writing   283

Analytic and formal   284
Descriptive and realistic   286
Confessional   287
Impressionist   289
Interpretive   291
Critical and advocacy   292
Literary narrative   294
Collaborative and polyvocal   296
Dramatic   298

Poetic   300
Other writing and presentation styles   302

On Writing About the Major Elements of a Study   303
Writing is prewriting   304
The research design as a preliminary report outline   304
Something to say   306
The evidentiary warrant   307
Point of view   308
Write easy, not hard   309
On citations and references   310
On titles, abstracts, and searches   310

Journal Article Submission and Publication   312

Closure and Transition   313

Resources for Analytic Write-Ups   314

Analytic Exercises for Write-Ups   314

Sample Abstracts for Analysis   315

Chapter 12—Analytic Presentations   317

Learning Objectives   317

Introduction   317

Paper Presentations   319
Roles of participants   319
Protocols and etiquette   319
Slide design   321
Types of slides   323

Poster Presentations   324

Dramatic/Staged Readings   326

Presenting Data Effectively   328
Ground plans   328
Word clouds   328
Photos and videos   330
Diagrams/models   331

Professional Networking   333

Closure and Transition   334

Resources for Presenting Qualitative Research   334

Analytic Exercises for Presentations   334

Chapter 13—Closure: Leading an Analytic Life   335

Learning Objectives   335

Introduction   335

Learning More About Qualitative Research   335
   Key book and journal publishers   335
   Key Internet resources   336
   Key organizations and conferences   337
On Professional Development   338
Analysis as a Lens, Filter, and Angle on Life   338
Closure   339
Resources for Leading an Analytic Life   339
Analytic Exercises for Leading an Analytic Life   340

Appendix—Three Representative Articles in
Qualitative Research   341
  Introduction   341
  "On the Bus With Vonnie Lee: Explorations in Life History and
    Metaphor," by Michael V. Angrosino   343
  Discussion Topics and Activities for "On the Bus
    With Vonnie Lee"   354
  "Nightmares, Demons, and Slaves: Exploring the Painful
    Metaphors of Workplace Bullying," by Sarah J. Tracy,
    Pamela Lutgen-Sandvik, and Jess K. Alberts   355
  Discussion Topics and Activities for "Nightmares, Demons, and
    Slaves"   387
  "'They Think Minority Means Lesser Than': Black Middle-Class
    Sons and Fathers Resisting Microaggressions in the School,"
    by Quaylan Allen   388
  Discussion Topics and Activities for "They Think Minority Means
    Lesser Than"   410

Glossary   411

References   423

Index   431

List of Displays

Figure 1.1—This abstract artwork possesses unity (original in color).   10

Figure 1.2—This couple is engaged in action, reaction, and interaction.   13

Figure 1.3—A holiday initiates rituals with decor that symbolize the event's meaning.   16

Figure 1.4—Humans interact through their roles and relationships.   21

Figure 1.5—The individual in social interaction experiences a tightly interwoven nucleus of action, reaction, and interaction patterns within the interrelated five Rs.   22

Figure 2.1—A culture or what is cultural is constructed and interpreted by the researcher.   31

Figure 2.2—An open-ended setting has varying pools and flows of social action.   33

Figure 2.3—A fieldworker's positionality has a lens, filter, and angle, comparable to a camera.   35

Figure 2.4—Fieldworkers observe people in action, reaction, and interaction.   38

Figure 2.5—A pencil sketch ground plan of an elementary school's visual art classroom.   41

Figure 2.6—A screenshot from V-Note video analysis software (courtesy of Brandon Emig, BREMIG LLC/V-Note, www.v-note.org).   46

Figure 2.7—Excerpts from a fieldwork observation log.   49

Figure 2.8—Fieldworkers observe people in their roles and relationships.   52

Figure 3.1—Infer or interpret what might be going through the wife's and husband's minds. (Photo by Matt Omasta.)   66

Figure 3.2—This glass paperweight has a symbolic representation by its owner. (Photo by Johnny Saldaña.)   77

Figure 3.3—A screenshot from Transana video analysis software. (Courtesy of David K. Woods, the Wisconsin Center for Education Research/Transana, www.transana.org.) 82

Figure 3.4—A representational image from a weight-loss workbook. (Photo by Matt Omasta.) 84

Figure 3.5—A representational image from a weight-loss workbook. (Photo by Matt Omasta.) 84

Figure 3.6—Two university students engaged in conversation in a lounge. (Photo by Matt Omasta.) 88

Figure 4.1—Surveys generally pose prestructured, close-ended questions to participants. 91

Figure 4.2—Focus groups require an expert facilitator to manage quickly shifting conversations and equitable contributions from all participants. 94

Figure 4.3—How does a person without a home survive the harsh winters of New York City? 98

Figure 4.4—Researchers must analyze how the physical space might affect the participant or interview. 100

Figure 4.5—Researchers take measures to ensure participant anonymity and confidentiality of information. 103

Figure 4.6—A researcher's interview protocol for people with diabetes. 105

Figure 4.7—The researcher guides the interview in a way that best serves the overall research question of the project. 111

Figure 4.8—By transcribing their own interviews, researchers initiate a deep cognitive understanding of their data. 115

Figure 5.1—A movie theatre employee treats guests cordially. 124

Figure 5.2—Values, attitudes, and beliefs are a tightly interrelated system. 128

Figure 5.3—An emotional arc, derived from a participant's interview transcript. 131

Figure 6.1—Rebekah Nathan (2005) studied university culture in *My Freshman Year.* 148

Figure 6.2—The Emotional Timeline of September 11, 2001 (Back, Küfner, & Egloff, 2010). 154

Figure 6.3—An Excel spreadsheet displays both quantitative and qualitative survey data.   161

Figure 6.4—The Lifelong Impact study examined the influences and affects of high school theatre and speech participation.   162

Figure 7.1—A qualitative researcher can investigate a homeless family's experiences.   168

Figure 7.2—The central research question serves as a focal point that holds the related research questions.   176

Figure 7.3—A visual model for a conceptual framework (Wallace & Chhuon, 2014).   187

Figure 8.1—Maintaining confidentiality is an essential trait of qualitative researchers.   194

Figure 8.2—Certain populations are considered vulnerable by IRBs.   199

Figure 8.3—Researchers must keep all data private and secure.   201

Figure 8.4—A template for an informed consent letter.   204

Figure 9.1—The relationship between antecedent conditions, mediating variables, and outcomes.   238

Figure 9.2—A matrix of "lifelong impact" across high school graduates from the 1950s to 2000s.   240

Figure 10.1—The key assertion derives from assertions and subassertions.   247

Figure 10.2—A model in progress of HIV test anxiety.   253

Figure 10.3—Eight categories of "home" and two participants' contrasting responses.   264

Figure 10.4—Four variables of "home" and their components.   266

Figure 10.5—A screenshot from Quirkos Software (courtesy of Daniel Turner, Quirkos Software, www.quirkos.com).   269

Figure 10.6—A screenshot from Dedoose Software (courtesy of Eli Lieber, SocioCultural Research Consultants LLC/Dedoose, www.dedoose.com).   270

Figure 10.7—A screenshot from INTERACT® Software (courtesy of Ursula Heldenberger, Mangold International/INTERACT®, www.mangold-international.com).   271

Figure 10.8—A summary of analytic methods profiled in Chapters 9 and 10. 273

Figure 11.1—Adolescents benefit from extracurricular activities in athletics and the arts. 285

Figure 11.2—Finley and Finley (1999) developed poignant narratives about homeless youths. 294

Figure 11.3—Hanauer (2015) poetically represents a U.S. soldier's experiences in the second Iraq war. 300

Figure 11.4—Dance utilizes the body as an expressive instrument of lived experiences. 303

Figure 11.5—Create and work in ideal conditions for research writing. 310

Figure 12.1—An effective cover slide for a presentation. (inside back cover)

Figure 12.2—An alternative cover slide for a presentation. (inside back cover)

Figure 12.3—A pie chart with carefully considered color choices. (inside back cover)

Figure 12.4—A pie chart with randomly selected color choices. (inside back cover)

Figure 12.5—A PowerPoint text comparison slide. 323

Figure 12.6—A scene from a research-based reader's theatre script. 326

Figure 12.7—A Room Arranger 2D bird's-eye ground plan view of a classroom. 329

Figure 12.8—A Room Arranger 3D ground plan view of a classroom. 329

Figure 12.9—A word cloud of term frequencies. 330

Figure 12.10—A PowerPoint photograph slide. 331

Figure 12.11—A diagram of interacting factors, drawn with NVivo software. 332

. . . at the moment you are most in awe of all there is

about life that you don't understand,

you are closer to understanding it all

than at any other time.

Jane Wagner (1986), *The Search for Signs of Intelligent Life in the Universe*, p. 206

Preface

Qualitative Research: Analyzing Life introduces readers to methods of conducting field-based inquiry in natural social settings.

The Organization and Through-Line of the Book

The coauthors take a unique approach to the organization of this textbook. Unlike the majority of methods works, we promote that it's important to learn the craft of qualitative research before students learn the art of it. Thus, Part I of this book acquaints readers with ways of collecting qualitative data through methods such as participant observation; documents, artifacts, and visual materials; and interviews. Part II discusses the elements of research design, while Part III focuses on the synthesis and presentation of research.

This title also differs from other introductory textbooks in qualitative inquiry by emphasizing analysis throughout the research endeavor rather than toward the latter stages of it. Most research methods texts place data analysis chapters in the latter third or fourth of the book. We begin with qualitative data analysis in Chapter 1, and that thematic thread is woven throughout each chapter that follows. The reason for this approach is that analysis is one of the most elusive processes to students of qualitative inquiry. Unlike quantitative approaches, there are no standardized formulas or algorithms to generate answers. Qualitative inquiry relies on multiple heuristics (open-ended methods of discovery during inquiry) to construct researcher insights about social life. We therefore provide several ways to analyze empirical materials collected during all stages of the study.

This first chapter of Part I begins with an overview and discussion of five basic analytic skills we believe all qualitative researchers should possess. Chapter 2 describes methods of observing participants in natural social settings. Chapter 3 outlines analytic methods for documents, artifacts, and visual materials. Chapters 4 and 5 address the most frequent method for collecting qualitative data: interviews.

Part II then segues into research design. Chapter 6 provides an overview of major qualitative research methodologies. Chapter 7 outlines design factors to consider before fieldwork begins. Chapter 8 discusses the ethics involved in research with human participants.

Part III delves into research representation and presentation. Chapters 9 and 10 focus on analytic synthesis, while Chapter 11 provides an overview of the writing styles of qualitative research reportage. Chapter 12 offers guidelines for sharing research, and Chapter 13 offers resources for continued development as a qualitative researcher.

We include three exemplary qualitative research articles as an appendix. A glossary of terms concludes the text. This book has a companion Web site hosted by SAGE Publications that includes such features as downloadable interview transcripts, supplemental readings, glossary flashcards, and PowerPoint slides for instructors at **study.sagepub.com/saldanaomasta.**

The Coauthors' Approach

Saldaña and Omasta bring to this project their experiences as theatre artists and educators at all levels. Our training as actors, directors, playwrights, and educators has given us not only a performative lens, but also a deep human awareness of life. Practitioners of theatre must have perceptive insight into people's character to represent them truthfully in written play scripts and live on stage. We are taught to delve deep into motivations, emotions, and interaction through improvisational studio methods and in detailed analyses of scripted works. We have been studying life in its broadest sense for decades, and that has given us an advantage when we transfer those skills to the demands of qualitative inquiry.

However, we take a dramaturgical approach to research only when appropriate, because a study's design must be constructed around the goals of the project and the questions of interest, among other factors such as available time and resources. We bring to this book an analytic lens on life because it's what we've been trained to do. We are no different from those who study psychology, sociology, anthropology, education, communication, and health care. Even areas such as technology, business, and government require that their practitioners know about the intricate dynamics of social interaction. We are all acting, reacting, and interacting with life through what we label the five Rs: our routines, rituals, rules, roles, and relationships.

The coauthors acknowledge that life is complex, yet answers to our most pressing problems can actually be quite simple; they're just very difficult to realize. Since all of us have individual value, attitude, and belief systems, each of us has our own agendas, our own causes to fight for, and our own axes to grind. Sometimes we are unified by an issue that brings us closer together as a community; other times we are highly divided over an issue because of our multiple and conflicting opinions. Life is complex, and people are complicated. *Qualitative Research: Analyzing Life* hopes to provide readers with ways to observe and make sense of the social world in all its rich and complicated complexity.

Johnny Saldaña
Matt Omasta

To the Instructor

This approach to methods of qualitative research departs from the conventional order of topics and subtopics found in virtually all introductory textbooks in the subject. Thus, the curriculum sequence of *Qualitative Research: Analyzing Life* diverges from the traditional ways instructors most likely learned the subject themselves and the way they currently teach it to their students.

This alternative sequencing has been field tested in graduate seminars at Arizona State University, and it provided students valuable working knowledge of data collection methods first, enabling them to later understand how these methods service research design and the role they play in selected methodologies of qualitative inquiry (ethnography, grounded theory, phenomenology, etc.). Also, qualitative data analysis is too formidable a topic to reserve exclusively toward the latter portion of the curriculum when most students are fatigued and their "brains are full." Thus, analysis in this textbook is introduced from the very beginning in order to build students' analytic skills cumulatively as chapters and learning experiences progress throughout the course term.

We acknowledge that this model of teaching qualitative research methods can provoke some cognitive dissonance in instructors used to presenting the multiple topics of qualitative inquiry in a particular order. Change is hard, particularly for teachers accustomed to their established and signature ways of working. But we encourage colleagues to explore this new approach to the subject with students. In fact, consider how you yourself might implement an action research project, evaluation research study, case study, or autoethnography about your personal experiences with different teaching methods and an alternative curricular paradigm of qualitative research methods instruction. Nonetheless, we offer that for those who need a more traditional curricular sequencing of topics for their course, begin with Part II's chapters, then proceed to Part I, and conclude with Part III.

Acknowledgments

The coauthors thank Helen Salmon, acquisitions editor at SAGE Publications, for her encouragement to write this book and for her nurturing support throughout its development; and Eve Oettinger, Jade Henderson, Susannah Goldes, Gail Buschman, Chelsea Pearson, Katie Ancheta, Kelly DeRosa, Alison Hope, and Anna Villarruel of SAGE for their preproduction guidance;

Daniel Turner of Quirkos Software, Ursula Heldenberger of Mangold International/INTERACT®, Brandon Emig of BREMIG LLC/V-Note, David K. Woods of the Wisconsin Center for Education Research/Transana, and Eli Lieber of SocioCultural Research Consultants LLC/Dedoose, for screenshot contributions;

Colin Anderson, for assistance with interview transcriptions;

Sherre Barnes, Keri Holt, Preston Grover, Cameron Mumford, Kimberly Lamping, Nicole Martineau, Ryan Martineau, and Ashley Pyle for data contributions from fieldwork;

Extended excerpts from "Theatre of the Oppressed With Children: A Field Experiment," "Survival: A White Teacher's Conception of Drama With Inner-City Hispanic Youth," "Lifelong Impact: Adult Perceptions of Their High School Speech and/or Theatre Participation," and "The Reader's Theatre Script for 'Lifelong Impact: Adult Perceptions of Their High School Speech and/or Theatre Participation,'" from *Youth Theatre Journal* reprinted by permission of the American Alliance for Theatre and Education (AATE), www.aate.com, and by permission of the publisher Taylor & Francis Ltd, www.tandfonline.com;

Brief quote in frontispiece from p. 206 from *The Search for Signs of Intelligent Life in the Universe* by Jane Wagner. Copyright (c) 1986, 1990 by Jane Wagner, Inc. Reprinted by permission of HarperCollins Publishers.

Saldaña extends his gratitude to his research instructors and colleagues for their inspiration, mentorship, and collegial support: Tom Barone, Mary Lee Smith, Amira De la Garza, Sarah J. Tracy, Harry F. Wolcott, Norman K. Denzin, Yvonna S. Lincoln, Mitch Allen, Patrick Brindle, Jai Seaman, Ray Maietta, Ronald J. Chenail, Leo A. Mallette, Patricia Leavy, Joe Norris, Laura A. McCammon, and Matt Omasta.

Omasta thanks all those who have shaped his work as a scholar and practitioner, including Robert Colby, Bethany Nelson, Drew Chappell, Nicole Adkins, Dani Snyder Young, Laura A. McCammon, and Johnny Saldaña.

About the Authors

Johnny Saldaña received his BFA and MFA degrees in drama education from the University of Texas at Austin, and is Professor Emeritus from Arizona State University's (ASU) School of Film, Dance, and Theatre in the Herberger Institute for Design and the Arts. He is the author of *Longitudinal Qualitative Research: Analyzing Change Through Time* (AltaMira Press), *The Coding Manual for Qualitative Researchers* (third edition, SAGE Publications), *Fundamentals of Qualitative Research* (Oxford University Press), *Ethnotheatre: Research From Page to Stage* (Left Coast Press), *Thinking Qualitatively: Methods of Mind* (SAGE Publications), coauthor with the late Matthew B. Miles and A. Michael Huberman for *Qualitative Data Analysis: A Methods Sourcebook* (third edition, SAGE Publications), and the editor of *Ethnodrama: An Anthology of Reality Theatre* (AltaMira Press). His methods works have been cited and referenced in more than 4,000 research studies conducted in more than 120 countries.

Saldaña's research in qualitative inquiry, data analysis, and performance ethnography has received awards from the American Alliance for Theatre and Education, the National Communication Association (NCA) Ethnography Division, the American Educational Research Association's (AERA) Special Interest Group on Qualitative Research, and the ASU Herberger Institute for Design and the Arts. He has published a wide range of research articles in journals such as *Research in Drama Education, Multicultural Perspectives, Youth Theatre Journal, Journal of Curriculum and Pedagogy, Teaching Theatre, Research Studies in Music Education,* and *Qualitative Inquiry,* and has contributed several chapters to research methods handbooks.

Matt Omasta is associate professor and Theatre Education Program Director at Utah State University. He received his BA from Ithaca College, his MA from Emerson College, and his PhD from Arizona State University. He is the author of *Play, Performance, and Identity: How Institutions Structure Ludic Spaces* (Routledge), *Playwriting and Young Audiences* (Intellect), and numerous articles in journals including *Research in Drama Education: The Journal of Applied Theatre and Performance, Youth Theatre Journal, Theatre for Young Audiences Today, Theatre Topics,* and the *International Journal of Education and the Arts* among others.

Omasta's work has been recognized by honors including the Founders' Award from the Educational Theatre Association, the Lin Wright Special Recognition Award and the Research Award from the American Alliance for Theatre and Education, and the Arts and Learning Special Interest Group (A & L SIG) Dissertation Award from the American Educational Research Association (AERA).

Analyzing Qualitative Data

Introduction: Analyzing Life

Introduction

Analysis (all bolded terms appear in the glossary) is the through-line for this introduction to qualitative research because we believe it's one of the least emphasized and thus most misunderstood facets of social inquiry. Rather than some obligatory front matter that discusses why research is important or that surveys the history of the field, we instead focus on developing analytic skill sets as the first activity in the first section of this first chapter. It is important to develop these foundational skills early because the better researchers are at them from the very beginning, the better prepared they'll be for managing and reflecting on **data** collected throughout the study. Most qualitative data are documentation of what people say, do, write, and create. How analysis integrates with other essential research-related matters will be discussed as chapters progress.

Developing Fundamental Qualitative Analytic Skills

Five of the most fundamental yet critical analytic skills qualitative researchers and data analysts employ are

1. Condensing large amounts of data;

2. Noticing patterns in textual and visual materials;

3. Unifying seemingly different things;

4. Understanding social processes of human action, reaction, and interaction; and

5. Interpreting the routines, rituals, rules, roles, and relationships of social life.

Learning Objectives

After reading and reviewing this chapter, researchers should be able to

1. Define analysis and qualitative research,

2. List and describe five basic qualitative data analysis skills, and

3. Discuss how analysis is a continuous process throughout a qualitative research study.

Qualitative analysis is an active process with one's mind and body to find patterns in data and to articulate their interrelationships. It draws on your ability to synthesize the various facets of what you have observed and to reconfigure them into new formulations of meaning.

Let us offer some brief explanations and a few simulation exercises to acquaint beginning researchers with these necessary skills. First, purely for introductory purposes, we define **qualitative research** as an umbrella term for

> a wide variety of approaches to and methods for the study of natural social life. The information or data collected and analyzed is primarily (but not exclusively) non-quantitative in character, consisting of textual materials such as interview transcripts, field notes, and documents, and/or visual materials such as artifacts, photographs, video recordings, and Internet sites, that document human experiences about others and/or one's self in social action and reflexive states. (Saldaña, 2011b, pp. 3–4)

If human experiences are the primary focus for investigation, then the analysis of human actions and their meanings should be the primary focus of our research.

Condensing large amounts of data

Qualitative researchers work with large collections of purposely collected narrative and visual data, sometimes labeled **empirical materials**. Condensing large amounts of data is a necessary analytic task because a writer cannot report to readers absolutely everything gathered during the investigation. We present selected facets of the inquiry that we determine to be the most important for others to know, and that provide sufficient evidence for the case. Also, an individual researcher or even a multiple-member research team cannot possibly keep every single **datum** (the singular form of data) coherently organized and accessible in their heads. The human mind, even with the help of computers, can retain only so much information. Our brains are hardwired to summarize and symbolize vast amounts of information in order to work more efficiently. "This ability to digest large amounts of information by breaking it into smaller pieces is how our brains turn information into knowledge" (Duhigg, 2016, pp. 245–246). Qualitative data analysis capitalizes on how humans naturally think.

We use the board game *Three for All!* as a playful analogy for what we do with qualitative data analysis and for developing your analytic skills. A round of *Three for All!* presents three clues to a player, and not only must she guess the answers to the clues, but she must also determine what the three answers share in common. For example, below is a clue for a word or phrase we're prompting you to say out loud:

> "You put two, sometimes four slices of bread in this thing and push the handle down to make the bread hot and crispy."

Hopefully you said "toaster." What you just did was condense a long description into a shorter form. You took a 23-word datum and assigned it a one-word symbolic representation, or a **code**. Here's another clue; determine what we're describing:

> "You put liquids and stuff in this thing and then push a button and it swirls fast and mixes everything up."

You might have thought of a "food processor." And while that response would be correct, given the information or data we gave you, it's not the most appropriate answer or code because it's not what we originally had in mind. So, we'll have to provide additional information and more reflection time to steer you toward a more appropriate response:

> "You make drinks like margaritas and milk shakes and smoothies in this thing."

Perhaps your next answer is "blender." That would be the better response or code. The lessons: sometimes both responses or perspectives can be valid, sometimes you need to consider multiple options before selecting the most appropriate one, and sometimes certain condensed forms of meaning are better or more precise than others.

Here's a third clue/datum:

> "You put ground coffee and water in this thing and it heats up and it makes a hot beverage."

But we have made an error. We weren't supposed to say the words "coffee" or "makes" in our clue because, according to *Three for All!* rules, we're not allowed to say the actual answer in our description. But it's too late to take it back. You've been given an advantage with our description and you give us the correct answer: "coffeemaker." But this is a teachable moment. There will be times when the symbol or code you create for a datum can employ a word or two from the datum itself. This is a method called **In Vivo Coding** (discussed further in Chapter 5). Sometimes, the people we interview provide rich insights with their own words, better than the researcher could ever compose.

A round of *Three for All!* provides you with three different clues, and you must generate a separate answer for each prompt. Condense these sets of data into shorter codes:

1. "This has got Matthew, Mark, Luke, John, Genesis, and Revelation in it": _____

2. "This has a lot of words in alphabetical order along with their definitions in it": _____

3. "This has a lot of names of people who live in a city, their home addresses, numbers, area codes, and it's got yellow pages in it": _____

Do you want the correct answers now to make sure you got them right? We could provide them, but that's not always how qualitative data analysis works. If you are working as an individual researcher when you condense large amounts of data into shorter forms, you must rely on your own best judgment to determine if you've gotten it right. Two or more researchers might work collaboratively on coding the data to better ensure consistency of interpretations—a form of **intercoder agreement**. Sometimes you can go back to the person who originally supplied the data to offer your condensed interpretations for feedback and verification as a **participant check** but, more often than not, you take responsibility for your analytic coding assignments. If you feel confident with your choices, that's a good intuitive sign. Nothing is set in stone—you can always revise the code later if new information suggests a reanalysis of your initial assignments is in order.

Analyzing life, in part, sometimes consists of symbolizing or condensing what people say about their perceptions and experiences into essences. Just as with the *Three for All!* example above, what word or words would you use to capture the meaning of each of the following interview quotations from several participants? Try to go beyond the topic, usually phrased as a noun, and label the content as an action-oriented **Process Code** or gerund (a gerund is an "-ing" word/phrase such as reflecting, praising accomplishments, complaining about pain):

1. "You can't trust politicians. Once they get elected, they go back on their campaign promises and do the opposite of what they said they'd do. And it's just to get votes, they don't really care about people.": _____

2. "Being a parent is hard. You're worried about your children, even when they're fully grown and on their own, you still want to know if they're doing OK. You can e-mail and Facebook all you want, but you still need to see it in their faces, you know?": _____

3. "I'm paying about $500 a year in co-pays for prescription medications. I looked at the total and thought, 'When did that happen? When did I start needing so much medicine to live my life?'": _____

You might have found it quite difficult to find just the right Process Codes to symbolize the essences of these quotations. Unlike quantitative research with its standardized formulas to generate numeric answers, qualitative inquiry relies on researcher creativity and **heuristics**—methods of discovery—to generate comparable findings. Solid quantitative reasoning relies on statistical accuracy. In qualitative research, precision rests with our word choices.

In sum, an essential qualitative data analytic skill is the ability to condense large amounts of data into briefer summarized forms. Condensed data do not always have to take the form of codes; other summative forms such as categories and sentence-length themes are possible. Also, summary can range from condensing a 30-page interview transcript into 10 pages of the most important or relevant passages, to analyzing only a 5-minute segment of a 30-minute video because the excerpt seems to capture the richest portion of the total social interaction. More on these analytic principles will be discussed later. For now, let's examine a second critical skill.

Noticing patterns in textual and visual materials

Patterns are human constructions and concepts: we notice repetition in human actions and thus label them as routines, rituals, or rules. Roles and relationships (e.g., parent–child, customer–salesperson, citizen–government) also maintain repetitive actions according to function and purpose. This repetition or pattern-making, assuming it consists of constructive purposes, helps humans feel secure and provides a sense of social order and continuity to daily life. People do most things over and over out of need, habit, adherence to tradition, responsibility, socialization, or because the routine has proved to generate successful results. Sometimes, though, patterns can consist of bad habits or destructive actions such as addiction to illegal drugs or constant belittling of a spouse. But noticing these is important, too. When individuals are aware of what's working and what isn't, they can hopefully take positive action to rectify the wrongs and make a better self and world. Noticing patterns gets researchers closer to finding answers about the human condition—that is, why we do the things we do.

Let's return to the *Three for All!* game to review pattern construction. In the most recent round, we prompted you to respond with this clue: "This has got Matthew, Mark, Luke, John, Genesis, and Revelation in it." Hopefully the clue and your background knowledge were sufficient enough to generate the answer, "the Bible." One answer or datum is a good thing, but reliable or credible conclusions cannot be drawn from just one facet of knowledge. Thus, we need more observations and answers to construct a pattern in progress.

The second clue prompts, "This has a lot of words in alphabetical order along with their definitions in it." Again, hopefully the clue and your background knowledge were sufficient to generate the answer, "a dictionary." A pattern, as we define it, starts to form when something repeats more than twice in the data. Thus, your goal in the game is to start formulating what the Bible and a dictionary might have in common—the characteristics or qualities they share. Your mind is imaging them and reflecting on their constituent elements or **properties**: they both have bound pages with words on them, for example. You also might brainstorm answers such as, "They're online books" or "They're reference books." But as you reflect on how or what they might have in common, you conclude that the Bible is not considered a reference book, so you eliminate that answer as a possibility—for now. And, yes, they are both accessible online through several platforms, but they are also published in hardback and paperback formats. More information is needed since the more repetitions, the more stable the pattern.

You now reflect on the third clue or datum: "This has a lot of names of people who live in a city, their home addresses, numbers, area codes, and it's got yellow pages in it." You have the answer but soon realize it might go by different names, from the colloquial "phone book" to the more formal "telephone directory" or even the overtly stated "yellow pages." You keep all of these in mind for now. A specific name might or might not matter at this point, but at least you feel confident that you have the gist.

You now have comparable forms of data that occur more than twice, so you reflect on your three different answers: the Bible, a dictionary, and a telephone directory. The next goal of *Three for All!* is to propose what these three things have in common. In other words, what is the pattern that seems to emerge? Remember that several answers can all be correct in one way or another, but some answers and often just one of them, in your best judgment, might be more appropriate or credible than others. You could offer that what the Bible, a dictionary, and a telephone directory all have in common is that they all have pages, or that they're all accessible online, or that they're all things you can read, or that they all contain numbers, and so on. But the most seemingly appropriate answer you decide to put forth is, "They're all books."

If you came to that conclusion or deduction fairly quickly, that's good. But what might have seemed like an obvious answer actually took a lot of cognitive processing to formulate. Your mind went through some sophisticated mental operations to arrive at the answer, and it's important to know what some of these processes are because they'll play a role as you continue qualitative analytic work. Briefly, three of these operations are as follows.

Induction is open-ended exploration of a problem, going into an inquiry to learn as you go, formulating answers as more information is compiled. Every sentence-length clue you received in the *Three for All!* simulations above prompted you to think inductively. Much of qualitative research is inductive inquiry or **analytic induction**, because researchers generally begin with open-ended questions for investigation rather than fixed hypotheses to test. Think of induction as on-the-job training in which one learns more and gets better at the tasks each day.

Abduction examines an array of possibilities in order to select the most likely, plausible, or best possibility. Any time you had more than one alternative, option, or answer to consider while playing *Three for All!* (e.g., a food processor or a blender; a phone book, telephone directory, or yellow pages) you exercised abductive thinking. Qualitative inquiry considers a range of participant perspectives and experiences, including the unexpected and anomalous. Researchers look at the totality of data to consider different possibilities for interpretation and, after careful analysis, put forth the one(s) that seem(s) most likely.

Deduction is a culminating process and product, derived from inductive and/ or abductive thinking. It is the conclusion drawn after considering all the evidence or data (e.g., "They're all books"). Deductions come in various forms: some are summative statements like assertions, propositions, and theories. But deductions can also consist of smaller summaries (toaster, blender, coffeemaker) that accumulate into a more comprehensive deduction (they're all small kitchen appliances).

After reading each *Three for All!* clue, you employed inductive thinking through your reflections on their contents. When you mentally brainstormed the possibilities of what they all shared in common, you utilized abductive thinking. And when you formulated what the three things had in common, you were thinking deductively by constructing a pattern that unified them. Unifying or finding relationships among and between data is another essential analytic skill, discussed next.

Unifying seemingly different things

When you play *Three for All!*, the goal is to unify three things according to what they have in common. If our three prompts to you are: butter, ice, and candle, what property do they share? They all melt.

Figure 1.1   This abstract artwork possesses unity (original in color).

©iStockphoto.com/Manuela Krause

Another facet of qualitative data analysis is constructing relationships between different condensed forms of data and the patterns observed. This goes beyond finding what different things have in common: it's also unifying them in some way through the analysis and description of their **interrelationship** or how they connect. **Unity** is a design principle in which seemingly disparate things or elements harmonize. Unity is an aesthetic that suggests, "These things belong together, go together, or work together." Qualitative research reports should also attempt to present a feeling of unity in their presentation. An abstract portrait (see Figure 1.1) can at first appear as a random, chaotic arrangement. But the artwork possesses unity because the varying shapes are all nonrealistic, fluid, and graphically bold.

Sometimes what unifies elements of a research study is that they are all distinct yet interrelated facets of the same experience or **phenomenon**. One of Saldaña's (1997) ethnographic studies documented a White, female, beginning school teacher's experiences at a predominantly Hispanic school. Three main challenges she faced as a novice educator were (1) unfamiliarity with the young people's Spanish language, (2) the ethos or culture of inner-city youths, and (3) the gangs that maintained an active presence in the neighborhood. Language, ethos, and gangs were three major elements that contributed to and unified the experience of *cultural shock* (DeWalt & DeWalt, 2011) of this novice teacher's indoctrination into the profession.

Sometimes unity is achieved by connecting elements of an **analytic story-line** together. Qualitative researchers place great stock in process, meaning the trajectories of human action. This might include marking the phases, stages, and/or cycles of the patterns observed. As an example, Saldaña conducted fieldwork in elementary schools to observe young people's emotional intelligence (Goleman, 1995). Children's understanding of and vocabulary for emotions progresses from a core understanding at approximately ages six and seven of such basic feelings they identify as happy, sad, mad, sly, sneaky, excited, and so on. Though one might expect a cumulatively smooth trajectory of emotional development as children grow older, that is not the case. Around age nine, most children go through emotional ambivalence, a developmental stage in which they experience new and complex emotions such as guilt, angst, and so on, yet they do not have the vocabulary to identify and thus describe their feelings. One child might say she experienced "a different kind of happy—a floating happy" to describe euphoria. By ages 11–12, their emotional vocabulary expands greatly to include such nuanced feelings they identify as caring, proud, confident, embarrassed, regretful, apprehensive, distraught, and envious. This developmental story of their *emotional literacy* compares various stages to illustrate change. Emotions unify this analytic story-line.

Another way unity is achieved in research is finding a central or **core category** that functions as an umbrella for all of the study's constituent elements. Kathy Charmaz, a key writer of grounded theory (explained in Chapter 6), explored how serious chronic illness affects the body and the identity of self. A core category she identified from her interviews with the physically impaired was *adapting*. Her analysis below explains the story or trajectory of adapting (a core Process Code) to physical impairment through time:

> By adapting, I mean altering life and self to accommodate to physical losses and to reunify the body and self accordingly. Adapting implies that the individual acknowledges impairment and alters life and self in socially and personally acceptable ways.

> Bodily limits and social circumstances often force adapting to loss. Adapting shades into acceptance. Thus, ill people adapt when they try to accommodate and flow with the experience of illness. . . . After long years of ignoring, minimizing, struggling against, and reconciling themselves to illness, they adapt as they regain a sense of wholeness, of unity of body and self in the face of loss. (Charmaz, 2009, pp. 155–156)

Social life can be messy and complex. Unfortunately, the short form of an academic research article might not always permit a detailed explanation of the complex messes people sometimes get into. That's why the skills of condensing, patterning, and unifying are necessary for research write-ups. Researchers don't have to present watered-down accounts of field experiences for research reportage, but they do need to put forth the major headlines or findings.

Researchers must also acknowledge that life's contradictions do not always enable a neatly unified analysis, and some issues are so complex that they require book-length narratives to describe the necessary, tightly interwoven details. Unity does not mean tying things up in a neat little satin bow. A coarse hemp rope full of knots and frays looks unattractive but still possesses unity.

Qualitative analysis requires that researchers know how to analyze people and their lives. Social life, in its broadest sense, is composed of action, reaction, and interaction.

Understanding social processes of human action, reaction, and interaction

Action is what a person does (e.g., thinking, speaking, and moving). **Reaction** is response to an action—to someone else's or one's own action or given circumstances. **Interaction** is the collective back-and-forth sequences of action and reaction. These three terms and concepts constitute the cyclical process of humans engaged with social life. And a researcher's ability to perceptively observe and inquire about these processes provides her with rich data for intensive and, hopefully, insightful analysis. Clarke, Friese, and Washburn (2015) offer that people within social worlds are "groups with shared commitments to certain activities, sharing resources of many kinds to achieve their goals and building shared ideologies about how to go about their business. They are interactive units, worlds of discourse, bounded not by geography or formal membership but by the limits of effective communication" (p. 140).

When an action occurs in everyday life, fieldworkers observe it and make note of its meaning—that is, its reason, motive, drive, purpose, objective, goal, intention, and so forth. Reactions suggest much about how people perceive and respond to others and the world around them and, like actions, offer a window into their values, attitudes, and beliefs. Even thoughts kept inside the mind (imagining, fantasizing, meditating) are considered actions and reactions because they are purposive. Look at Figure 1.2 and infer what's happening between the two people. A popular folk saying goes, "Life is 20% what happens to you, and 80% how you react to it." Lieberman (2013) scientifically supports this by asserting that our social brains are hardwired for reciprocity and influence by others.

Figure 1.2 This couple is engaged in action, reaction, and interaction.

©iStockphoto.com/BartCo

Interactions, or collective exchanges of actions and reactions, compose units or **moments** for analysis. Researchers infer and interpret the sometimes hidden, subtextual agendas within and between humans as they act, react, and interact. They also infer and interpret broader social meanings about these moments of interaction patterns. It is a complex interplay of communication that observers attempt to understand through psychological, sociological, anthropological, and even dramaturgical (i.e., theatrical) lenses, filters, and angles—that is, the way each researcher perceives the social world.

Below is a narrative example of a moment of social interaction. It is set in a restaurant on an early Friday evening. Two male customers approximately in their fifties are seated in a booth and a female server, approximately in her mid-twenties, is assigned to them:

SERVER: *(walking by the table carrying a tray of dishes)* Hi, I'll be with you two gentlemen in just a minute, OK?

CUSTOMER 1: OK. *(approximately two minutes pass)*

SERVER:	*(returns to table, smiling)* OK, thanks for waiting. Can I get you two started on some drinks? *(she sets down two paper napkins on the table)*
CUSTOMER 1:	Yes, and I think we're ready to order too, if we may.
SERVER:	Certainly, let's do it! *(opens and writes on her order pad)* What can I get you?
CUSTOMER 2:	Can I get the club sandwich, extra mayo on the side, and instead of fries, can I get coleslaw instead?
SERVER:	*(writing in her pad)* Certainly. And to drink?
CUSTOMER 2:	What kind of flavored ice teas do you have?
SERVER:	We have green, tropical, and raspberry.
CUSTOMER 2:	I'll take tropical, no lemon.
SERVER:	*(writing in her pad)* No lemon, OK. *(to other customer, smiling)* And for you?
CUSTOMER 1:	I'll have water, a Diet Coke, and the stuffed corn tortillas.
SERVER:	*(writing in her pad, cheerily)* OK, sounds good! Any appetizers to start with?
CUSTOMERS 1 and 2:	No.
SERVER:	*(smiling)* All right, I'll get this order sent to the kitchen for you right away. Thanks! *(she takes the menus from the table and leaves)*

To some, this might seem like a mundane, insignificant passage of dialogue exchanged between a restaurant server and customers. But to selected social researchers, the interaction is rich with meaning, as analyzed below. We offer that when we look at social action, reaction, and interaction (and notice the unity of those three terms), researchers can examine and analyze them through interrelated components we label the five Rs: routines, rituals, rules, roles, and relationships (notice the unity and pattern of alliteration in those five terms). Though all five work together in intricate interconnectivity, each one merits its own discussion.

Interpreting the routines, rituals, rules, roles, and relationships of social life

The complexity of action, reaction, and interaction cannot always be neatly categorized into five separate facets for analysis, but they serve as an introductory foundation for focusing a researcher's lens, filter, and angle on social life.

Routines When researchers look at the properties of life qualitatively, they examine what patterns of action and reaction reoccur. **Routines** are actions that take care of the everyday business of living, symbolize our self-cultivated and socialized habits, and meet our human need to create a sense of order. Some believe that everyday, mundane, trivial routines are not worthy of investigation. But these particular patterns of social interaction can hold particular significance for a particular study. Humans do things over and over again for a reason, even if that reason could be perceived as irrational or self-destructive. And remember too that instability and inconsistency can be considered patterns of action.

The server in the dialogic restaurant moment above more than likely has an established introductory routine for her job: greet customers, take their drink orders, return with their drinks, take their food orders, submit their food orders for preparation, and so on. And even though the customers might be visiting this restaurant for the very first time, there is a generalized routine or **schema** established from their previous dining experiences at other establishments: wait to be seated, review the menu, place drink and food orders with the server, and so on. This socialized pattern organizes the business of a public routine.

But life does not always go smoothly, and humans must often deal with disruptions to patterned routines. Notice that within the expected interaction routine at the restaurant, selected moments were breached. The server expected to take just the drink orders first, but the customers wanted to take care of their food order at the same time. Other minor breaches occurred, such as side dish substitutions, which the server seemed cheerily willing to accommodate. Her gracious reactions to the disruptions of her routine suggest that she was willing to assume a compliant role during the interaction to create a pleasant dining experience for the customers. On the other hand, the accommodation to take both drink and food orders at the same time might have been secretly to her advantage because it would save time. Thus, her accommodation was not an acquiescence of power, but a mutual agreement to beneficially speed the routine. Another interpretation, however, might hold that the server did indeed lose power, masked by her cheery performativity or emotional labor (Hochschild, 2003). In other words, she is paid to look happy and make customers feel satisfied.

Research gets enriched not only from examination of routines, but also from the breaches or conflicts that interrupt the flows of daily life. We learn much from how people handle, avoid, and prevent the glitches that come their way. We also learn much from an awareness that people's routines can be repeated without question, prompting the researcher to reflect on the purpose or futility of these action patterns. As life is analyzed, observe what people seem to be doing again and again and, perhaps more important, explore just why they are engaging in consistent action patterns.

Rituals When researchers explore life qualitatively, they also look for the occasional nonroutine or nonmundane moments of action that seem to suggest meaningful importance, either to the participants or to the observer. This is a subjective interpretation: what is considered routine to one person could be deemed a **ritual** to another. Everyday life is occasionally punctuated with the special, significant, or the sacred—that is, the patterned ceremonial event. These events or symbolic moments hold personal or cultural importance as they mark or affirm a tradition, an occasion, an achievement, a transition, a remembrance, or fulfillment. Lakoff and Johnson (2003) assert, "There can be no culture without ritual" (p. 234). Figure 1.3 illustrates how a holiday initiates rituals with decor that symbolize the event's meaning.

People usually associate rituals with formal gatherings such as worship services, graduation ceremonies, weddings, and the like. But rituals can also exist in the daily or weekly routines of a brief prayer before a

Figure 1.3 A holiday initiates rituals with decor that symbolize the event's meaning.

©iStockphoto.com/David Sucsy

meal, a happy hour with friends every Friday afternoon, an exchange of gifts, or brisk morning runs through the neighborhood. A ritual transcends the routines of everyday matters because of the pattern's **significance** it holds for the individual or group. Rituals are status-passages that demarcate transitions of some kind, usually through processes such as separation, reversal, cleansing, challenging, changing, or celebration. "These observances provide a form of performative punctuation in the passage of mundane time and the life-course" (Atkinson, 2015, p. 87).

Dining out might be considered not just another meal but also a ritual to some, because for most people it does not happen frequently and thus is considered a special event. But dining out might also be a routine for others because it might occur at predetermined, expected times—for example, every Friday night or every Sunday afternoon. Qualitative significance is subjectively attributed onto something by the participants and/or the researcher. If the overall action of dining out is a ritual, then the event is made up of smaller acts or micro-rituals— for example, the ritual of escorted seating to a table, the ritual of a friendly opening greeting by the server, the ritual of scanning the menu and selecting the "sacrifice," and so on. And though tipping is not required, it is a customary ritual in certain contexts, a token of thanks. Anthropologists have written much about the concept of ritual, ranging from cultures in developing countries to urban lifestyles, and from everyday matters to coming-of-age ceremonies. As it's used in this book, the word *ritual* means significant routine—that is, patterns of human action endowed with special meaning by its participants and/or from the researcher's interpretation.

As life is observed, discern whether a social pattern of action should be interpreted as a routine or a ritual. Rituals provide rich, self-contained nuggets for qualitative analysis. They lend insight into the value, attitude, and belief systems of the individual, group, or culture, and bring us closer to comprehending that which is symbolic, significant, and meaningful.

Rules Most routines and rituals can be influenced to some extent by the **rules** set in place. When researchers look at life qualitatively, they examine how tacit frames of acceptable social conduct or formal rules and laws are followed—or breached. Each society creates expectations, codes, and regulations for daily conduct, a process called **socialization**. This includes everything ranging from such benign behavior as waiting in line, to respecting the property of those who own it. Individuals also have their own rules for daily living, a personal code of ethics or a moral compass for action, reaction, and interaction with others. Those who do not conform to the socially established order of things might be perceived by the majority as deviant and stigmatized as outcasts. But rules are culturally and socially specific: what is unacceptable conduct in one setting or context might be completely appropriate in another setting or context.

Rules are based on traditions, morals, and value, attitude, and belief systems. Their origins stem from sources as diverse as religious writings to current legislative needs as a society evolves (e.g., same-sex marriage, Internet security, international terrorism). Even digital tools are laden with rules. Facebook, Twitter, Yik Yak, and other social media require that users adhere to policies regarding appropriate language and images, along with structural rules such as length of postings or a user's minimum age. Rules, in their broadest sense, maintain social order and are designed usually to keep people and property safe from harm. Rules are an important part of the glue that holds a society together. But oppressive rules also exist, as does the abusive and discriminatory enforcement of such rules by those who overreach their authority. In addition, not everyone will agree with a particular law in place. As a colloquialism goes, "Not everything that is legal is ethical, and not everything that is ethical is legal."

In the restaurant scene above, there are few formal laws in place dictating the kind and quality of customer and server interactions. There are, however, social expectations that servers will show respect toward paying customers, and customers will respect the decorum of the establishment ("No shirt, no shoes, no service"). There are formal regulations and laws in place in many countries for restaurant employee health, sanitary conditions, proper food storage and preparation, and so on. Customers are also bound by acceptable forms of conduct in a public setting, and an obligation to pay for food served to them and consumed. Although nothing is formally on the books (in the United States, at least) for gratuities that must be offered to servers, there are sociocultural traditions in place that encourage customers to tip servers according to the quality of service received (e.g., 15% for satisfactory service, 20% for very good service). The routine or ritualistic act of dining out is rife with rules.

Infractions of rules lead to a breakdown of the social order yet sometimes to positive outcomes. Traditions unquestioningly followed can lead to oppressive and even destructive consequences. Those who challenge the status quo often do so to create better life conditions or to initiate social justice. However, rules are about values systems, and conflicts can easily arise when one social segment's set of rules does not harmonize with the values system of another social segment. These rules refer to everything from a nation's constitution, to a teacher–student relationship, to unquestioned hegemony, to fascist police states, to Robert's Rules of Order.

Much of the academic literature refers to **power** as the grand construct that influences and affects social life. Authoritative mandates restricting human actions can come from social institutions such as national and local government agencies, to people such as parents and older siblings. Power can also include a person's "cops in the head" (Boal, 1995), meaning indoctrinated messages learned throughout one's life about expected conduct and individual self-perception (e.g., "Real men don't cry," "I'm not attractive," "There's nothing I can do about it"). Some researchers maintain their lenses, filters, and angles on social life to investigate how those with and without power affect roles and relationships such as between men and women, White Americans and African Americans, and government and big business. Rules, in their broadest sense, are just one facet of power, yet analyzing how they influence humans serves as a manageable way of understanding the complexity of power.

As you observe and analyze life, document what rules guide the actions, reactions, and interactions of participants in their particular social settings. Determine what seems to be conditioned adherence to ways of working, formal organizational policies and procedures in place, and individual values systems influencing and affecting relationships.

Roles When researchers look at life qualitatively, they examine human actions determined, to some extent, by the **roles** people play. Roles are the assumed or attributed actions, personas, and characteristics of individuals. Erving Goffman's (1959) groundbreaking sociological classic, *The Presentation of Self in Everyday Life*, proposed that humans perform in accordance with how we wish to be perceived by others. But others might perceive us in different ways according to how they interpret such factors as our physical appearance, speech, and personality.

At any given moment, each one of us plays one or more roles that possess various levels of **status** or position. In the military, privates respect and follow the orders of those with the rank of sergeant and lieutenant. Adult parents and teachers usually assume a higher status or power position over children and adolescents. Many men, knowingly or unknowingly, assume authority over women. Children assume dominant roles over others when they act as bullies. Roles emerge from individuals' personalities or **identities**, a complex concept discussed more fully in later chapters.

Roles are realized and enacted through particular routines, rituals, and rules of conduct. The restaurant scene above features two general, different roles: the customer and the server. Each role carries with it a socially constructed set of expectations—for example, expectations that the server will interact with customers in ways that will create a pleasant dining experience. Likewise, customers are expected in their roles to dine without disturbing other patrons with offensive actions such as loud profanity in a family restaurant. There are other general expectations such as common courtesy by customers toward the server—although some customers assume a more dominant role over someone whom they perceive in a subservient role. In this case, two White, senior, male customers interact pleasantly with a White, younger, female server. But depending on each of the three individuals' ages, genders, sexual orientations, races/ethnicities, nationalities, social classes, religious backgrounds, political affiliations, and family structures—let alone personalities—the scene could have unfolded in a variety of ways.

Organizations and institutions also play roles in social life. For example, a restaurant chain's primary role is to provide food service. A political party's primary role is to govern a nation in accordance with its ideological beliefs. The health-care system's primary role is to treat the ill and maintain people's wellness. But a critical lens, filter, and angle on these institutions can reveal how their rules affect their roles. Certainly, the health-care system provides essential support to patients in need, but the rules of its organizational structure can influence whether its role is charitable or profit driven. The pharmaceutical industry in the United States promotes its public role as the creator of innovative medicines to make people's lives better. But the news media, in their role as social informants, often presents investigative reports that the pharmaceutical industry's private role is also to generate exorbitant profits for its executives and shareholders. Institutional roles can be multiple and conflicting, yet remember: their rules and relationships with society are established by people.

As you observe and analyze life, pay attention to the roles humans assume (or are assigned) and the accompanying actions that seem to correspond with them. Pay particular attention to the dynamics of status and rule-making/rule-breaking during interactions between people. Detect how a role is composed of particular facets of character that together constitute a perceived identity.

Relationships When researchers look at life qualitatively, they examine how people act, react, and especially interact with each other in various social contexts. **Relationships** vary in quality, depending on the attitude one holds toward another person, group, or institution. The closeness to or distance from others is perceived by the individual, and the degree of belonging says much about the culturally constructed sense of community, family, group, membership, and so on. And relationships are dynamic, meaning they "are multiple, can be fluid, and change at different rates" (Pink et al., 2016, p. 107).

The roles people assume, to a significant degree, influence and affect the types of relationships they have with others, who are also in their own roles with their own perceptions of relationship status. Students assembled in a classroom with a teacher will jointly construct relationship dynamics that can vary from intimidating and toxic, to impersonal and businesslike, to nurturing and joyous. The people's perceptions of a nation's leaders will also influence and affect a citizenry's attitudes toward and interactions with their government, and establish an **ethos** or cultural pulse. Examine Figure 1.4 and describe the inferred relationship dynamics between the two people in the photo.

Figure 1.4 Humans interact through their roles and relationships.

©iStockphoto.com/Yagi-Studio

In the restaurant scene above, the interactions between the customers and server seem perfunctory yet pleasant. Exceptions to the menu rules were requested, not demanded. The server appears to cultivate a relationship that accommodates the desires of the diners, affirming any requests and changes in protocol. With roles come expectations, and the pleasantries of the server seem obligatory, yet they initiate courteous, interactive responses or reactions from the customers, who were not required to be polite but were motivated to do so by her positive demeanor and acquiescence.

Robert V. Kozinets (2015) offers that digital technology has reconfigured both our live and online relationships into "networked individualism" in which we are connected rather than embedded in social groups. The Internet is a "new neighborhood" where home and work, and the public and private are intertwined. Social memberships are now partial rather than permanent, with more specialized peer-to-peer relationships. "Networked individuals move easily between relationships and social settings to construct their own complex identities, depending on their passion, beliefs, lifestyles, professional associations, work interests, hobbies, media habits, subcultural inclinations and other personal characteristics" (p. 48). As relationships are investigated, reflect on how the digital technology most people use every day influences and affects the quality of an individual's connections and networks.

Interaction is how relationships get constructed. They are collective chains of actions and reactions in which people in roles conduct routines and rituals in accordance with rules for living. Not every social interaction is equitable, however. People have different goals and objectives for themselves and for others. These complex interaction patterns are what qualitative researchers attempt to discover in order to answer why we do the things we do. Figure 1.5 is our best attempt at visually illustrating the individual in social context—a tightly interwoven nucleus of action, reaction, and interaction patterns within the interrelated five Rs.

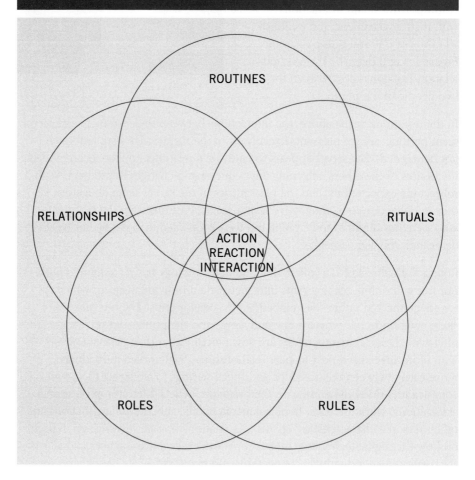

Figure 1.5 The individual in social interaction experiences a tightly interwoven nucleus of action, reaction, and interaction patterns within the interrelated five Rs.

As researchers observe human action as it naturally occurs around them (and this includes action online), or listen to people recounting their experiences and perceptions during an interview, they stay attuned to their collective interactions happening in the moment or as they recall them. Not only do fieldworkers carefully document their back-and-forth exchanges, but they analyze those exchanges for their explicit and implicit meanings. How one person relates with others reveals much about his own role identity and values, attitudes, and beliefs.

On Qualitative Data Analysis—and Life

Research methodologist Michael Quinn Patton (2015) posits, "Because each qualitative study is unique, the analytical approach used will be unique" (p. 522). We frontload readers with this principle early because many students in research courses seek, and probably also need, explicit procedures for the "correct" way to conduct qualitative data analysis. Although it is possible to make errors that deviate too far from accepted practices, there really is no one "right" way to analyze qualitative data.

Nevertheless, there are some established guidelines and methods available for this mode of inquiry. The analytic methods chosen depend on several factors, including the forms of data collected (discussed in Chapters 2–5), the methodological genre employed and the types of research questions posed (discussed in Chapters 6–7), the types of participants studied and the parameters for investigation (Chapter 8), and a variety of other matters including the researcher's own comfort level with particular analytic approaches (Chapters 9–10) and the form a final presentation takes (Chapters 11–12). Analysis does not start after all the data have been collected. Analysis is an ongoing process from beginning through end of an inquiry. Remember that qualitative researchers work inductively, constructing questions when a topic first emerges for possible investigation, then constructing answers as fieldwork progresses, data emerge, and the report is composed.

Though we emphasize qualitative data analysis from the very beginning of this book, we cannot possibly cover everything there is to know about the subject in just one chapter. Instead, we distribute throughout this text methods of analysis as they relate to the particular topics discussed. Think of analysis as a through-line—that is, a thematic thread that weaves throughout the research endeavor or extended experience. It is our goal that each chapter cumulatively builds within readers a series of techniques and skills. We prefer not to think of these collected strategies as a toolkit or recipe book. Instead, we think of these methods collectively as a compendium of analytic knowledge, a repertoire of analytic skills, or even a mental rolodex of methods accessed on an as-relevant basis (Saldaña, 2015).

As for analyzing life, we acknowledge that that is a formidable task, especially in an era when buzzwords such as *complexity, messiness, ambiguity, uncertainty,* and *troubling the data* appear in selected philosophical approaches to inquiry. Psychologists, sociologists, anthropologists, historians, artists, poets, playwrights, and everyday citizens of the world have been trying to analyze life ever since people could conceptualize that something puzzling about human existence needed to be answered. One would think that with the millennia of knowledge we've accumulated as a species that people would have figured out how to live ideally by now. But the human race has still not "gotten it right." There are too many unanswered questions about life, too many unsolved problems, and too many unresolved issues.

Research is one way of reflecting deeply on the human condition, and there are multiple methods to help gather the information needed to make substantive insights and revelations. But we also acknowledge that methods alone are insufficient. We take counsel from case study methodologist Robert E. Stake (1995), who wisely offers that "Good research is not about good methods as much as it is about good thinking" (p. 19). It is our hope that this book might help readers sharpen the thinking skills needed to analyze life in its multifaceted complexity.

CLOSURE AND TRANSITION

The qualitative researcher and data analyst should possess five fundamental skills. She or he

1. Condenses large amounts of data;

2. Notices patterns in textual and visual materials;

3. Unifies seemingly different things;

4. Understands social processes of human action, reaction, and interaction; and

5. Interprets routines, rituals, rules, roles, and relationships of social life (the five Rs).

These analytic skills will be utilized as additional techniques for qualitative inquiry are learned. They serve the researcher through all phases, stages, and cycles of the process, from literature reviews through fieldwork observations, and from research question development through final write-up.

Qualitative Research: Analyzing Life takes a pragmatic stance toward investigation. We believe it's important for novices to know the craft of research before they tackle the art or design of it. Thus, the next chapter focuses on what is considered one of the primary ways many researchers learn about the social world: observing people in patterns of action, reaction, and interaction in natural settings as they go about their routines, rituals, rules, roles, and relationships.

RESOURCES FOR AN INTRODUCTION TO QUALITATIVE ANALYSIS

The following resources will offer you additional guidance for an introduction to social inquiry:

Abbott, Andrew. (2004). *Methods of Discovery: Heuristics for the Social Sciences.* New York: W. W. Norton & Co.

Dobelli, Rolf. (2013). *The Art of Thinking Clearly* (Nicky Griffin, Trans.). New York: Harper.

Saldaña, Johnny. (2015). *Thinking Qualitatively: Methods of Mind.* Thousand Oaks, CA: Sage.

ANALYTIC EXERCISES

1. Visit the Remote Associates Test Web site and complete several exercises to develop your pattern recognition skills: www.remote-associates-test.com/

2. In one household room, list up to 30 things you see that have patterns to them or on them (e.g., stripes on a pillow, pleats on a curtain), objects that are multiple (e.g., 25 books shelved horizontally), and overall organizational patterns (e.g., all furniture pieces pushed against the wall).

3. Visit a public social space such as a movie theatre lobby, fast food restaurant, or shopping mall. Simply observe and listen for approximately 15 minutes to the actions, reactions, and interactions of people. Stay particularly attuned to how people react to someone else's dialogue in conversation.

4. Write a list of your typical activities done throughout an average week (a minimum of 30 different actions). Separate the list into three columns: actions you consider routines, actions you consider rituals, and as the center column, actions that are both or variable (i.e., it depends). Reflect why you consider the actions in the ritual column ritualistic, and why the central column's contents are variable.

5. Visit a public social space such as a movie theatre lobby, fast food restaurant, or shopping mall. Look for any posted signage that explicitly state rules of conduct in the space (e.g., "No smoking," "Only service animals allowed"). Then observe what forms of tacit (i.e., socially understood) rules of conduct are exhibited by people in the space.

6. Compose a list of five people you know and have periodic face-to-face contact with; vary the people you list by age, relationship, gender, ethnicity, and so on. Assign two to three role labels to each person (e.g., Lisa: woman, African American, mother). Reflect on your own roles and relationship dynamics when you interact with each of these individuals.

SAMPLE DATA FOR ANALYSIS

Below is an excerpt from an interview with Colin, a former employee of a movie theatre discussing his job responsibilities. (Additional portions from the complete interview will be discussed in later chapters. The complete transcript can be downloaded from the book's companion Web site at study.sagepub.com/saldanaomasta.) Read and reflect on the transcript excerpt and apply one or more of the five fundamental analytic skills to these data. Possible applications include

- Condensing large amounts of data: Condense this excerpt to one third its length, selecting and retaining only the most salient passages. Or underline, circle, or highlight the most significant words/phrases to you to compose an initial set of In Vivo Codes.

- Noticing patterns in textual and visual materials: Identify what occurs or what is discussed more than twice in this data excerpt.

- Unifying seemingly different things: Interrelate the different patterns observed in the data.

- Understanding social processes of human action, reaction, and interaction: Describe what forms of action and reaction the participant takes, and what types of interactions occur.

- Interpreting routines, rituals, rules, roles, and relationships of social life: Identify one or more of these five facets as discussed by the participant.

INTERVIEWER: In general, at that particular job, how did you personally approach customer service? In terms of policies and what you actually did, what were your mind-set and actions in terms of customer service?

COLIN: Sure. I am very adamant on customer service. Cleanliness is a big thing. I mean, they trained us on all these things, but even my own values and practices kind of seep through. I was always very apologetic. I like to keep the policies, and even though there were managers that had conflicting thoughts, I tried hard to be accommodating to whoever was supervising me.

INTERVIEWER: Was there ever a time when you were unable to give a customer something they wanted or meet a request of theirs because it conflicted with a policy? A time where somebody wanted something and you were not able to provide that?

COLIN: Absolutely. Absolutely. So, our drinks specifically were nonrefillable, and there were many guests who came back and said, "Can I have a refill?" or, "Oops. I spilled this drink. Could I get a refill?" and because of policy we can't. Because that's just what they tell us to do. We can't give refills on drinks, even if they spill them.

INTERVIEWER: Can you think of any specific examples of a time where somebody came back and said that, and how you responded?

COLIN: Sure. What comes to mind, actually, was it was a group of teenage girls, and they had bought a large drink and a large popcorn—and large popcorns get refills, but not drinks—and right after ordering it, almost three feet away, the girl dropped her drink, and it went scattering. And they came up, and they were like, "Oh my goodness. Can I get a refill?" Because of policy, I had to say, "Unfortunately, we don't do refills. I could sell you another drink." And they were a little discouraged because they were thinking about the drink on the ground, and they felt like it was an accident. They luckily didn't push anything too much. I think they got a medium drink after that, but they were a little discouraged by the fact that I couldn't just refill their spilled drink.

INTERVIEWER: Any other times? Any other situations where somebody asked way beyond that? Where a customer was more dissatisfied by that?

COLIN: I mean, it was a policy that lots of employees had issues with because it wasn't consistent. Some employees let them have it, and so there was one time when—not with me, but the person next to me—where he came back for a refill, and he made this big fuss about how, "The last time I was here, I had refills. This is garbage. Let me talk to your assistant manager." And we went and got the manager, and the manager explained and apologized, saying they couldn't give them a refill. But it never got violent. It was just very loud noises. It was very disgruntled kind of yelling.

INTERVIEWER: How did the customer feel at the end of the situation, do you think? What did they express?

COLIN: That's a good question. I do not know the ending of that story. All I know is that they didn't get what they wanted, and they made a big fuss, and then they went back to the theatre. That's all I've heard. They might have done more afterwards, but . . .

INTERVIEWER: In general, do you have any thoughts on how you personally might have navigated any differences between a customer's expectation—what they wanted—and the policies? What were some of your thoughts on that topic?

COLIN: Well, that's tough because they advertise customer service first, but then some of the policies are more on the business side and less on the customer's side. So how I, I always try to be cordial. I always try to approach the circumstances, try to do everything I possibly could, based on the policies, but due to the fact that I am employed and getting paid by them, I made sure to keep the policies of selling, and not giving refills, and making sure that you're checking ID for seventeen and younger, and so forth.

INTERVIEWER: What do you think about policies like that? For example, the girls who spilled their drink in front of you, and it was clear they spilled it and didn't drink it. How do you think if you were the employer, if you were the person making the decision, how would you have handled that?

COLIN: That's a good question. I would first have to analyze the situation. I'd have to see how many people are around because, like, if there were lots of people around and you gave out a free refill, even though it went against your policy normally, other people might use that excuse to get more drinks, which I could see on the business end not being good. But, in their scenario, where nobody was around, I don't think it would have taken that much just to refill them, or even get a new cup and just not charge them, considering it was an accident. It was a clear accident. You saw it happen, and, you know, things like that happen.

Analyzing Field Sites

Introduction

One of the best ways to analyze life is to observe it in all its rich detail. **Participant observation** is the researcher's method for watching and listening to people act, react, and interact in natural social settings, most often during everyday matters but sometimes during special circumstances. As humans go about their lives, researchers analyze people's movements, conversations, and environments to discern what, how, in what ways, and/or why they do the things they do. Their routines, rituals, and rules are documented for reference and analysis, along with interpretations of their roles and relationships with one another.

Systematic participant observation has its roots in anthropology when different world and national cultures were studied in the early 20th century and documented in writing and sometimes photography and film (Brinkmann, Jacobsen, & Kristiansen, 2014). The goal of these studies was to present just enough rich data to give readers a sense that they were there at the sites themselves. The traditions of those early methods have evolved, but the basic goal remains the same: to observe and analyze humans as they live their lives in a variety of social settings.

Participant observation is not necessary for every qualitative study. In fact, most qualitative research with adults uses interviews to obtain participant perspectives (Roulston, deMarrais, & Lewis, 2003, p. 646). But studies whose topics or research questions focus specifically on the dynamics of human interaction, or settings where interviewing is not possible with those observed, lend themselves to this data collection method. Nevertheless, participant observation can be conducted in conjunction with interviews and other data collection procedures to enhance

Learning Objectives

After reading and reviewing this chapter, researchers should be able to

1. Describe methods of conducting and documenting observations of social life in natural settings,

2. Demonstrate familiarity with participant observation of social life, and

3. Explain the analytic processes involved with field notes.

the total data base or **data corpus**. Sometimes what participants offer during interviews contradicts what they say and do in natural contexts. This leads researchers to more carefully analyze and reconcile the discrepancies. Participant observation can also stimulate topics or specific questions for continued fieldwork and interviews at a later time.

Two new terms require brief explanation here: method and methodology. A **method** is how you go about doing something. A **methodology** is why you're going about it in a particular way. The "how to" ways of participant observation are described below and include techniques such as writing field notes and recording audio and/or video of natural life. The "why" of participant observation is to provide the researcher a real-time, uncensored view of the social world to more credibly analyze how humans go about their lives. Permissions processes for and the ethics of conducting participant observation will be discussed in Chapter 8. In this chapter, we focus on method.

On Culture

Culture and its related terms—subculture, microculture, counterculture, and so on—are a bit slippery to explain. Even anthropologists have no consensus; hundreds of definitions for the core term exist, and the culture concept today is perceived as unstable, random, and unpredictable (Kozinets, 2015, pp. 6, 10). Many descriptions, however, include knowledge as a key component of what culture is: "*knowledge* that is learned and shared and that people use to generate behavior and interpret experience. . . . It is social knowledge, not knowledge unique to an individual" (McCurdy, Spradley, & Shandy, 2005, pp. 5–6; emphasis in original). Culture is not a static "thing" that can be observed directly. Rather, it is an ever-evolving process, system, abstraction, concept, and even performance. Culture is constructed and interpreted by the researcher through observing a group of people's particular actions and words, social practices and routines (i.e., their norms and traditions), tacit or hidden rules for conduct, and rituals and ceremonies that produce and reproduce what the group "is" during a particular span of time (Chirkov, 2016; Duhigg, 2016; Gobo, 2008). We characterize culture broadly as the participants' site-specific ways of working and living with others:

> As individuals we have multiple affiliations, whether voluntary or not, with different groups of people. Our types of belonging shape and are shaped by our social interactions with [others]. Researchers observe the particular forms of acting, reacting, and interacting that

happen in particular settings in order to document in what ways
these occur. The composite combination of unique interactions and
the values, attitudes, and beliefs embedded within them help us
identify and formulate what is "cultural" about the specific site and
its members. (Saldaña, 2015, p. 101)

To clarify the sometimes hazy difference between society and culture, the latter
is part of the former. Charon (2013) defines a **society** as "a social organization
of people who share a history, a culture, a structure, a set of social institutions,
usually a language, and an identity" (p. 340).

One of the ways a fieldworker describes a culture is through what anthropologist
Clifford Geertz (1973) promoted as **thick description**, an approach that does
not imply lengthy narratives but a written
interpretation of the nuances, complexity,
and significance of a people's actions.
By focusing on the details of what we
experientially witness, we can reflect on and
hopefully render an account that provides
insightful knowledge for readers about a
social group's interrelationship dynamics.
C. J. Pascoe's (2007) ethnography, *Dude,
You're a Fag: Masculinity and Sexuality in High
School,* explores not just male homophobia,
but also the spectrum and interplay of
heterosexuality, homosexuality, gender, race,
bodies, sex, identity, and their interwoven
ritual performance and reproduction in high
school culture.

Figure 2.1   A culture or what is
cultural is constructed
and interpreted by the
researcher.

©iStockphoto.com/bst2012

Researching a people's five Rs offers a
template for documenting unique aspects
of their ways of life, and participant
observation is a most suitable method for
conducting **ethnography**, the study of a
culture. Ethnography is not the sole focus
of this book, but the fieldwork components
described below offer guidance for research
in that genre, discussed further in Chapter 6.
In this chapter, classroom culture is profiled
through examples.

Observation Settings

Participant observation happens somewhere, and it is the "where" (and people populating that "where") that provides optimal opportunities to gather data to inform a research study. If one's topic is teaching and learning, a classroom is an ideal site. Health-care studies might observe patients in hospitals, clinics, or in their homes. For studies of immigration issues between the United States and Mexico, observations of border patrol agents working in California, Arizona, New Mexico, and/or Texas might be in order. Recent studies in qualitative inquiry have even explored the technological worlds of online gaming and social media as digital cultures. Perhaps the site itself intrigues you and motivates an extended study, as the street vendors on New York City sidewalks did for sociologist Mitchell Duneier (1999). A setting of natural social action, reaction, and interaction provides rich moments for observation and analysis.

Finding a place and space

Sometimes the physical setting itself is important, and other times it's the specific people who just happen to be living or working in a particular setting that determines where researchers go. Regardless, first look for and scout out possible locations for fieldwork. **Fieldwork** is the research act of observing social life in a specific setting and recording it in some way for analytic reference. Being a fieldworker, or "in the field," is a researcher's placement and immersion among particular people in a particular environment for close examination.

Public places such as shopping malls and restaurants have large collections of people, but they are clustered in smaller groups without a single focus of attention for everyone. These open-ended settings require the researcher to continually scan and mingle among the crowd to observe the varying pools and flows of social action. Ambient noise and multiple simultaneous conversations can also make listening difficult. Large gatherings like concerts and sporting events, or smaller settings like offices, however, are close-ended with a central and more purposeful focus for attention by the participants and are thus generally easier to observe and document. However, some close-ended settings like small elementary school classrooms can have a myriad number of activities to document. Fewer people does not always make participant observation easier, but the collective or majority reactions to a central point of action are easier to take in.

Most people interact in a number of different settings. For example, a child's social worlds usually include her or his home, a school bus, several classrooms, a lunchroom, a playground, stores, streets, friends' houses, parks, perhaps extracurricular activities in a commercial gym or soccer field, and so on. One female researcher observed and interviewed a female adolescent as a case study at the student's school, a community center where she took classes, and in the teenager's bedroom, which gave the researcher a unique opportunity to look at the furnishings, decor, and mementos she collected.

Figure 2.2 An open-ended setting has varying pools and flows of social action.

©iStockphoto.com/Memitina

Access

This brings up the topic of **access** for participant observation—a researcher's ability and permission to observe at a particular site. A female researcher in a teenage girl's bedroom was possible because she received permission from the girl's mother. But a male researcher might not have received such access. Access comes from **gatekeepers**—people with the authority to grant permission and facilitate the researcher's entry into a particular field setting. Adult gatekeepers at school might include its principal, teachers, and parents. Even children themselves might function as gatekeepers if the leader of a clique approves and supports (or doesn't) a fieldworker's presence among his circle of friends. Gatekeepers can sometimes be key participants themselves because they can either consent to or reject the researcher's presence in their lives. Publicly accessible spaces such as coffee shops do not have gatekeepers but they do have rules: anyone who enters must display proper dress and decorum and, more often than not, must patronize the business by purchasing something.

At field settings requiring gatekeeper review, researchers should meet with those individuals and explain the purpose of their study. They should present themselves professionally yet humbly as people who value the opportunity to learn from an experience and to benefit others who could be interested in their research topic. They must negotiate any understandings, ways of working, and restrictions (e.g., no review of filed paper documents, no intrusive distractions to participants during work). Students observing for a research methods class project should openly admit that and offer that the field experience is part of their educational development since their primary goal is to learn about, from, and with others. Some settings require that fieldworkers maintain some sort of credential like a fingerprint/security clearance card or successful completion of a volunteer training program before they work with particular groups. Written and signed letters of agreement explaining the project guarantee fewer misunderstandings and miscommunications between the researcher and the site's primary gatekeepers.

The Observer's Frames

Participant observers bring who they are into the field site. And they must adopt various roles, positions, and perspectives as they watch others conduct their lives. This section explores some of the frames or stances of the observer herself in relation to the participants and the purpose of the study.

Lenses, filters, and angles for fieldwork

Participant observation data bases will consist of both narrative and visual materials, but what does one specifically look for or at? Researchers are like cameras and their eyes like **lenses**. The way researchers perceive social life can be influenced and affected by their own significant demographic attributes such as gender, age, race/ethnicity, sexual orientation, socioeconomic class, and/or occupation. Lenses might also consist of the particular research methodology or disciplinary approach employed for a study (educational, sociological, psychological, etc.).

Cameras also have **filters** covering their lenses that let certain wavelengths in and keep others out. The filters that cover a researcher's lens might consist of a set of personal values, attitudes, and beliefs about the world, formed by her unique personal biography, learned experiences, and individual thinking patterns. Researchers' identities as human beings will influence and affect what they observe in the field site since we tend to interpret others' experiences based on our own. Filters also consist of particular theoretical perspectives or **standpoints** within a discipline—for example, feminist, critical, emancipatory. Some educators, for example, might place more emphasis on schooling as guided by sets of national standards, while others prefer more student-centered and individualized instructional designs.

Cameras are also placed at particular **angles**, suggesting not just panoramic and close-up views, but also a researcher's relational **positionality** as a peripheral, active, and/or complete member, in addition to her interpretations of social action she sees and hears at the **micro-** (local and particular), **meso-** (cultural, national, or mid-range), and/or **macro-** (global, universal, or conceptual) **levels** of life. Researchers zoom in and out throughout the course of observations to get varied perspectives of the social scene, varying from insider to outsider, from intimate to distant, or from emotionally invested to neutrally detached.

Figure 2.3 A fieldworker's positionality has a lens, filter, and angle, comparable to a camera.

©iStockphoto.com/David Hills

The lenses, filters, and angles of one's personal worldview work in conjunction with one's research topic and questions to help guide and focus the fieldwork observations. A female researcher and a male researcher will observe and interpret a women's support group differently. A gay man and a heterosexual fundamentalist Christian man will observe a gay pride festival in very different ways. An older Hispanic and a young African American will interpret U.S. immigration issues differently, and so on. This is not to suggest that researchers with particular demographic backgrounds are more competent or better qualified to observe the nuances of social action among similar people; on the contrary, sometimes an outsider to a social group can perceive things that an insider takes for granted. Researchers should, however, always consciously reflect on how their standpoint and positionality influence and affect what is interpreted through their lenses, filters, and angles.

Subjectivity, the researcher's personal and unfettered perspective, is virtually unavoidable in qualitative research. It is a human dimension that is both an advantage and liability to the fieldworker. Subjectivity permits us to respond to data in ways that generate emotion-laden and meaningful interpretations about the social world. But if research consists solely of subjective opinions, first impressions, gut feelings, and personal biases, the work loses credibility with audiences. A respectful balance between facts and feelings is necessary to ensure a trustworthy account of the investigation. An honest disclosure of the researcher's lenses, filters, and angles, in addition to some of the methods we describe below for field note analysis, better guarantee a more substantive report.

Observer membership roles

Adler and Adler (1987) identify three researcher positions or membership roles for participant observation: peripheral, active, and complete. With a **peripheral role**, the researcher maintains a fly-on-the-wall stance, literally off to the side of what he or she sees and hears, not participating directly in any activities observed. The researcher is witnessing and documenting social life as it occurs. Some methodologists refer to this role as naturalistic observation rather than participant observation. This role serves best when it is important to focus attention exclusively on interaction as it happens, or when one must maintain an unobtrusive presence.

With an **active role**, the researcher takes a stance midway between peripheral and complete roles. The researcher in an active role occasionally participates in the action of the field setting. This provides firsthand experience in what participants are doing, such as office work in a corporate setting. The participation is not full-time but instead is part-time to permit other necessary researcher tasks such as document review or peripheral observation.

With a **complete role**, the researcher is a co-participant personally immersed in the social world studied. He or she lives the same experiences as those observed for a lengthy duration. An example might be an educator who both teaches her class and observes the children at work for a research study on learning. Another example is Barbara Ehrenreich's (2001) riveting account of her stories as a minimum wage earner in *Nickel and Dimed: On (Not) Getting By in America*. Ehrenreich took on such complete roles as a restaurant server, housecleaner, and big box store clerk to learn firsthand about the types of work people in these positions do and their meager wages for living.

Ehrenreich also assumed a **covert role** for her fieldwork—that is, she did not inform all the people she worked for that she was documenting her (and their) experiences for research and investigative journalism purposes. Such disclosure might have restricted her access to the sites and prevented her from learning the behind-the-scenes intricacies of minimum wage work. Most compelling, her complete participation in the tasks of server, housecleaner, and store clerk with their degradation and unlivable salaries provided her irrefutable details about the lower-class condition.

Covert participant observation has been conducted about studies such as mundane factory work, university dorm life, sexual activity in men's restrooms, drug abusers, and biker gangs. A covert position provides access to hidden facets of social life like illegal activities. It is a strategic choice when the phenomenon of interest cannot be studied as in depth through other methods like interviews. This can sometimes have embarrassing and even dangerous consequences for the researcher if participants discover they were being observed by an outsider. And if a researcher's study is subject to institutional review by a university, for example, her oversight committee might not permit covert research due to ethical concerns and liability concerns.

A researcher's role as a peripheral, active, or complete member during fieldwork should be the one that offers the best angle or perspective on social life, and gives her the best insight into the phenomenon studied. See Pink et al. (2016) for newer digital ethnographer roles such as remote and virtual (p. 134).

Purpose-driven observations

The researcher also uses the purpose of the study and its accompanying research questions as a frame for what gets painted in the life picture. If the goal of one's research is to study customer-clerk communication in retail stores, her observations focus primarily on these two roles as they converse, not necessarily on customers shopping on their own as they walk through store aisles. But listening to conversations among clerks themselves in the store's private break room might also provide insightful awareness on what people in these roles say out of customers' earshot. Also, the interactions between sales clerks and customers will vary greatly from dollar stores to high-end department store chains. A single question can lead researchers to multiple but comparable sites to compare participant actions, and this generates a more substantial data base for analysis.

One's research question might suggest that the lens of observation focus on a particular person as a case study, such as a teacher. Limiting observations to her classroom is certainly a viable choice, but to get a broader perspective of a teacher one would need to observe her interactions with colleagues in a variety of sites such as a faculty lounge, with her principal at an area faculty meeting in the school library, with her children's parents in the school office, with her students on a field trip, and even—with permission—with her family in her home after school hours, as Tracy Kidder (1989) did during a year-length study of a fifth-grade teacher. As with multiple sites about the same research topic, researchers should observe a case or the same group of people in multiple social settings for a more three-dimensional rendering of the participants' lives.

Figure 2.4 Fieldworkers observe people in action, reaction, and interaction.

©iStockphoto.com/Christopher Futcher

The first days of fieldwork can be overwhelming. Even with a specific research agenda, the dizzying array of social life happening can be too much to take in. Fortunately, it does get easier with time. New researchers find their bearings and settle in after a few days and have a clearer sense of purpose for observations.

Field Notes

Memory is a sometimes unreliable substitute for credible, tangible evidence. Social life is filled with such meticulous detail that no one can keep all that happened recorded accurately in his mind. Observations are best documented in some way through writing and/or visual methods for recall and analytic reference. Field notes accomplish these goals; as some researchers staunchly attest, "If it's not in the field notes, it didn't happen." There is no standardized way to take field notes, but we offer methods that have worked best for us.

Written documentation of analytic observations

Field notes are most often for the researcher's eyes only, a private data base of observation experiences. Thus, they can range from sketchy, handwritten journal entries to detailed narratives typed on a laptop. What a researcher chooses to share from them through publication or presentation is her choice. But we offer that the better written one's field notes, the better their data for reflection and analysis.

Some researchers prefer to handwrite their initial, real-time observations, then transfer and elaborate on them with a desktop computer. Others prefer to type observations directly into a program on a laptop as they watch and listen as a step-saving method. Depending on a fieldworker's setting, he might not have access to electric power or battery life when needed, and the sound of laptop typing/clicking could distract participants at the site. Also, his particular site or membership role might not permit him to take field notes as he's participating in the social action of interest. Thus, he documents his observations and experiences later, preferably as soon as possible while the memories are fairly fresh in his mind. Regardless of how or when one takes field notes, there are some specific ways we offer to write them.

Front matter

Document the day and date, specific location of the observations, and start and end time of fieldwork at the beginning of each day's or section's notes. Though it will come after the observations and analytic reflections have been conducted, caption or headline the specific field note set with a descriptive or evocative title: "First Day Observations," "Having a Bad Hair Day," "A Glimmer of Hope," or "What Was He Thinking?" Most often helpful to also note are any necessary participant demographics such as the number of males and females, ethnic ratios, age ranges, and so on if those data might be pertinent to the research agenda or analysis. A field note heading might look like this:

> January 21, 2014 (Tuesday)—"Group Murals"
>
> Escobar School, Art Classroom/Studio, 9:00–9:40 A.M.
>
> Period 2 Art Class (Carol and 22 3rd grade children—13 girls, 9 boys, all Hispanic [2 boys absent today for testing])

The setting

The first time observations occur in a particular setting, narratively describe and, if equipment is available and permission is granted by gatekeepers, photograph the site for analytic reference and embed the photo in field notes. Descriptions of the setting needn't be so detailed that the photograph becomes irrelevant. Highlight general points such as amount of space, organization, maintenance, and key items, as pertinent. Document the setting in neutral ways first, using factual descriptors to identify salient features such as architecture, furnishings, and so on. Then record sensory experiences and visceral impressions. Odors are particularly noticeable in some environments, and wall colors and lighting can influence and affect participant dynamics. Some researchers even consider the site itself an active participant with a distinctive character or **geo-identity,** as it's currently termed.

Below is an excerpt from a set of field notes Saldaña took while observing at an inner-city, elementary magnet school for the arts. This brief narrative describes a visual art classroom:

> The entire classroom smells of wax crayons. Tables and chairs look slightly worn but well maintained. North wall windows allow natural light to stream in.

Rack labels by the entry door: "Detention Forms," "Attendance Files."

On display on the south wall are laminated collages, laminated still lifes in colored pencil. On the shelved counter beneath are plastic tubs with teachers' names on them to keep student class work together.

Various media supplies are moderately organized in the east wall's four gray cabinets: paper bags, paper plates, construction paper, white paper, colored paper, crayons, markers, colored pencils, scissors [child and adult sizes], etc. One cabinet door's handle is broken from overuse. Another door is dented in, making it look slightly warped.

Multiple posters are posted on the cabinet doors: "The ABCs of Happiness," "Classroom Rules," "Earth: one house, many rooms," "De todas las cosas que llevas prestas, tu expresion es la más importante," "My Declaration of Self Esteem," "I am me," "Fire Drill Rules."

Despite the walls painted "institutional white," the room has a sense of warmth where children's creativity is valued through "ordered fun."

It is also helpful if a **ground plan** or bird's-eye view of the field site is hand-drawn to label and assess its accommodation of furnishings, spatial relationships, and foot traffic. This might or might not be useful in future analyses, but it helps to have it in your beginning notes for reference (see Figure 2.5). Some prefer to use software for drawing a ground plan, but we find that, for personal field notes, hand drawing it with basic shape templates to approximate scale goes much faster. Finished and cleaned ground plans are appropriate for publications and presentations. Also, some environments such as classrooms might periodically rearrange furnishings for the particular action needed. Simply document what is a typical day's layout of the space, with any special notes placed in the margins.

Jottings and write-ups

Social action, especially in some sites like school classrooms, happens quickly. When we observe, we create **jottings** or brief, hastily handwritten notes with simple descriptions of action and participant quotes (one of the most neglected items of a beginning researcher's field observations). Jottings are used as an outline for more-elaborated notes made on the researcher's own time.

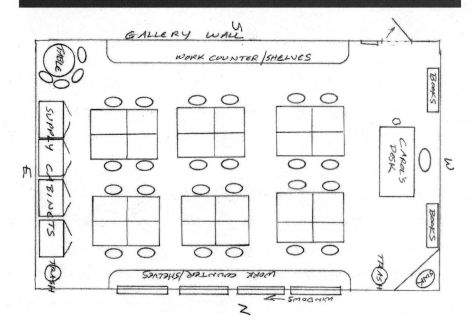

The actual handwritten field notes themselves are illegible to most other readers, but a direct transcription of the jottings Saldaña wrote as he observed a teacher's classroom is below. Note the use of shorthand (C for the teacher, Carol; Ks for kids) and the use of quotation marks to indicate what was spoken by participants in this "messy" sketch of social action:

> C holds up mural "Let me show you what another class did"
>
> C raises hand, Ks do; 1 boy claps
>
> "The people at your table are the people in your group—you will work on a mural"
>
> Ks get poster boards
>
> 3–4 children tables
>
> Ks speak English Spanish as they work
>
> C walks, help tape
>
> "Work together as a team."

More walking

"Now you have to decide what kind of mural you're going to make"

Kids talking, C "You can talk but quietly, OK?"

Girl: "Dónde poner el sky?"

C, "Good job, guys."

This 93-word set of spontaneous jottings was cleaned up and enhanced later that day into a 232-word field note narrative passage or **write-up** (with an additional 172 words of interpretive commentary, discussed later). The jottings jogged Saldaña's memory of what he saw and heard, which enabled him to better detail the classroom action he observed. This shorthand helps observe efficiently and trigger later recall. Notice the straightforward, descriptive, present-tense language used to document the social scene, and the occasional insertion of what participants actually said, in quotes:

> Carol shows her class a sample mural: "Let me show you what another class did." She holds up four sheet-sized poster boards taped together for one lengthy mural that a small group developed and colored. Carol raises her hand to get the children quiet and the children raise their hands and stop talking. One child responds with a clap, but Carol says that response is for another class. She continues: "The people at your table are the people in your group—you will work on a mural."
>
> One student from each table group is asked to come to the front of the classroom to pick up poster board sheets. During small group work (3–4 children at each table), all children switch back and forth between English and Spanish but the predominant language in small group work is Spanish. Carol walks around the classroom and helps groups tape their four pieces of poster board together. Carol says, "Work together as a team. . . . Now you have to decide what kind of mural you're going to make. . . . You can talk but quietly, OK?" In one group, a girl holds the poster board sheets together while a boy tapes them. One girl asks her team in Spanglish: "¿Dónde poner el sky?" ["Where do we put the sky?"] Carol continues walking among the children and says to them, "Good job, guys." . . . [observations continue]

We strongly recommend transferring and/or enhancing jottings into field notes as soon as possible. Many research methodologists recommend finishing them on the same day observations are made while the memories are still fresh. Some even advise not conducting any additional observations until a day's field notes have been completed.

Observer's comments

Bogdan and Biklen (2007) recommend the addition of **observer's comments** (OCs) throughout field notes. Broadly speaking, OCs are a way of separating the researcher's feelings from the facts. They document the subjective impressions of what's going through a researcher's mind and can serve as analytic jottings of the observations in progress. OCs might also consist of relevant sidebars or follow-up reminders for fieldwork. The purpose of OCs is to provide a forum for interpreting participant subtexts and researcher reflections on the social action witnessed.

As an example, below are the field notes of Carol's art class with indented and italicized OCs interspersed throughout them. OCs should get inserted whenever your researcher's instinct feels the need to comment on a particular passage or memory. As an additional formatting tactic, anything actually spoken by participants is bolded to separate the three forms of data:

> Carol shows her class a sample mural: **"Let me show you what another class did."** She holds up four sheet-sized poster boards taped together for one lengthy mural that a small group developed and colored.
>
> > *OC: Not a bad little piece of art! I'm impressed with what third graders can do. Take a picture of it later for my notes.*
>
> Carol raises her hand to get the children quiet and the children raise their hands and stop talking. One child responds with a clap, but Carol says that response is for another class.
>
> > *OC: That was funny! But it's bad teaching practice for a school to have so many different management techniques in place for children—no wonder he was confused about what to do.*
>
> She continues: **"The people at your table are the people in your group—you will work on a mural."**
>
> > *OC: I hate working in small groups, but I guess that's me as an adult. Children need to learn how to get along.*

One student from each table group is asked to come to the front of the classroom to pick up poster board sheets. During small group work (3–4 children at each table), all children switch back and forth between English and Spanish but the predominant language in small group work is Spanish.

OC: I appreciate how Carol's not being strict on "English only" in her classroom. It's a nice inclusive way of working. I wonder what the music teacher's stand is on this—talk to him later.

Carol walks around the classroom and helps groups tape their four pieces of poster board together. Carol says, **"Work together as a team. . . . Now you have to decide what kind of mural you're going to make. . . . You can talk but quietly, OK?"**

OC: Nice side-coaching on her part. She seems relaxed, in control.

In one group, a girl holds the poster board sheets together while a boy tapes them. One girl asks her team in Spanglish: **"¿Dónde poner el sky?"** ["Where do we put the sky?"]

OC: I haven't heard Spanglish all that often thus far from children at this school. Keep your ears open for this as I go on.

Carol continues walking among the children and says to them, **"Good job, guys."**

OC: "Good job" is so overused—even teachers themselves make fun of that phrase when they shop-talk together at professional development workshops.

OCs can be inserted during jottings, as field notes are written-up, or later as they are reviewed and thoughts enter the researcher's mind. Most OCs are interpretive commentary at a rudimentary level of analysis and can be considered somewhat as warm-ups for analytic memo writing, discussed later in this chapter.

Time stamps

If time is or becomes a critical variable in your study, add time stamps in the margin of your written field notes. Time stamps note the beginning, ending, and duration of specific moments or chunks of action. An example from the art class field notes is condensed below:

9:00 A.M.	Attendance and announcements.
9:04 A.M.	Carol shows her class a sample mural: "Let me show you what another class did." . . . She continues: "The people at your table are the people in your group—you will work on a mural."
9:07 A.M.	One student from each table group is asked to come to the front of the classroom to pick up poster board sheets.
9:09–9:17 A.M.	During small group work (3–4 children at each table), all children switch back and forth between English and Spanish. . . . Carol continues walking among the children and says to them, "Good job, guys."

Time stamping field notes can reveal surprises such as how long it takes certain actions to occur, or how much necessary time is devoted to (or wasted on) selected aspects of daily life. Research studies in education, for example, have noted through such methods the often inequitable balance between teacher-centered instruction and learner-centered activity. Minute-by-minute time stamping is not always necessary for qualitative fieldwork, but it is most appropriate when the processes of social action suggest that their duration influence and affect participant reactions and interactions in some way. Be cautious of letting boredom or impatience with fieldwork skew perceptions of the passage of time. Time stamping keeps fieldworkers grounded in how long it actually takes for things to happen.

Technical Matters of Fieldwork and Field Notes

We now address a few technical matters that researchers should consider in their on-site observations, write-ups, and data management.

Audio- and video-recording

Digital technology has made the visual and aural documentation of fieldwork quite easy. Some field researchers audio- and/or video-record the field site's action while concurrently writing jottings. Later, they flesh out their field notes while listening to or watching the recording to more accurately document what participants said and did. Recordings become particularly indispensable when studies focus on conversations between participants or their physical mannerisms and movement with others through space. Figure 2.6, a screenshot from V-Note software, is just one of several programs that can access recorded video, enabling the analyst to later transcribe, code, and annotate the data. V-Note is available in desktop and iPad editions for field researchers.

Figure 2.6 A screenshot from V-Note video analysis software (courtesy of Brandon Emig, BREMIG LLC/V-Note, www.v-note.org).

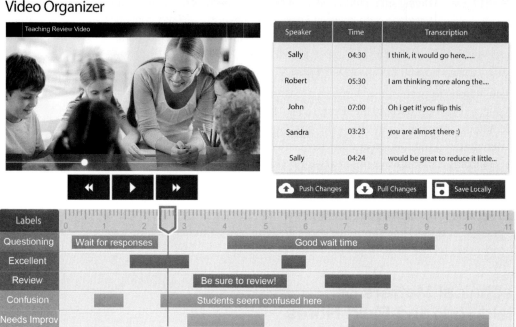

Participants should always be made aware of when their actions and voices are being recorded, but gatekeepers and participants might not permit recording out of self-consciousness or for privacy purposes. The presence of a digital video camera might also intimidate or unduly influence and affect the natural actions of participants (though some eventually become accustomed to its continuous use over time). If permitted, stationary camera placement should be off to the side and angled to capture as much general action as possible, or strategically focused on an area of immediate interest. Handheld recording devices such as a mobile phone or tablet permit the researcher to walk around to pan and scan the setting's action as needed.

We have found that occasional audio-recording serves well for participant observation documentation. One out of every seven to ten clock hours of

Figure 2.7 Excerpts from a fieldwork observation log.

DAY/DATE	TIME BLOCKS	CLOCK HOURS	LOCATION	OBSERVATION
Thu., Feb. 2	8:00–9:45 a.m.	1.75	Martinez School Neighborhood	Neighborhood Homes, Streets
Thu., Feb. 2	9:45–10:00 a.m.	0.25	Martinez School Main Office	Literature Rack, Office Matters
Mon., Feb. 6	7:45 a.m.–3:00 p.m.	7.25	Nancy's Classroom	Periods 1–7, Lunch, Occasional Conversations with Nancy
Tue., Feb. 7	7:45–11:00 a.m.	3.25	Nancy's Classroom	Periods 1–3
Wed., Feb. 8	7:45–10:00 a.m.	2.25	Nancy's Classroom	Prep Time, Periods 1–2
Wed., Feb. 8	10:00–11:00 a.m.	1.00	Nancy's Classroom	Interview 1 with Nancy
Thu., Feb. 9	8:15–10:00 a.m., 12:00–1:00 p.m.	2.75	Nancy's Classroom	Periods 1–2, 5
Thu., Feb. 9	1:00–1:30 p.m.	0.50	Martinez School Auditorium	School Assembly
Mon., Feb. 13	11:50 a.m.–12:55 p.m.	1.00	Nancy's Classroom	Period 5
Tue., Feb. 14	7:50 a.m.–12:50 p.m.	5.00	Nancy's Classroom	Periods 1–5, Guest Artist
Thu., Feb. 23	8:45 a.m.–12:30 p.m.	3.75	Linder School Auditorium	Speech Tournament
Fri., Feb. 24	8:50 a.m.–12:00 p.m.	3.00	Linder School Auditorium	Speech Tournament
Mon., Feb. 27	11:45 a.m.–12:45 p.m.	1.00	Martinez School Main Office	Interview with Principal
Wed., Mar. 1	11:50 a.m.–1:00 p.m.	1.00	Nancy's Classroom	Period 5
Thu., Mar. 2	3:25–4:30 p.m.	1.00	Martinez School Library	Faculty Meeting

Analyzing Observations of Social Life

There are several methods for analyzing qualitative field note data. Two of them will be discussed in this chapter: reflection and analytic memo writing.

Qualitative researchers do a lot of thinking, and **reflection** is personal, mental immersion in the data, their meanings, and the study as a whole. **Reflexivity** is individual reflection on one's relationships with the data, the participants, the nature of the study, and even with one's self as a researcher. Think of reflection as looking outward, and reflexivity as looking inward. Both of these play a critical role when the researcher as an analytic instrument mulls over the data and their implications.

Some researchers document their thinking in the form of written journals, as supplemental field note entries, or even as recorded conversations with the participants as they shop talk about the study. We have found that personal and private quiet time to focus exclusively on the data and to reflect on "what it all means" is the best way to achieve some sense-making and meaning-making about life as it was observed. Reflection's goal is to consolidate or to join together the disparate thoughts in one's mind into a coherent whole. And though reflecting is analyzing, it does not always lead to a well-articulated analytic outcome. We cannot teach readers how to think, but we can offer some general things to consider in this regard.

Reflecting on action, reaction, and interaction

Remember that one of the analytic tenets of this text is to observe people in action, reaction, and interaction. Briefly, this suggests you conduct your observations and reflect on them with these general goals in mind:

- Analyze what people want or want others to do;
- Analyze how people *react* to their own actions, their given circumstances, or to what is said and done to them; and
- Analyze strings of action and reaction that compose significant interaction moments.

Now consider the following questions as an exercise in analytic reflection:

- Focusing on Carol, the elementary school visual art teacher, what did she want and want her students to do throughout the course of the moment documented in the field notes?

- How did both Carol and the children *react* to each other's actions throughout the moment?

- How would you characterize the interaction dynamics between the art teacher and her students during this particular moment?

Your responses hopefully take you beyond mere repetitive description and into the minds of the participants. Carol wanted the children to work in small groups to create group murals. But perhaps you inferred that Carol also wanted to carefully manage her students' behavior through attention-getting tactics, physical proximity, and positive reinforcement. The children's collective hand raising reaction to Carol's hand signal suggests an effective classroom management strategy at work. As for the interaction dynamics between teacher and students, they seem pleasant and organized, and Carol does not distance herself but mingles among the children as they work, suggesting either on-task monitoring and/or concern for her children's progress. However, also noticeable is that Carol speaks to her primarily Spanish-language children only in English. Unknown at this point is whether she does so deliberately to enhance their English-learning skills, or whether she is deficient in Spanish.

Notice that much of the analysis depends on your ability to **infer** or to fill in the blanks and elaborate on given field note details. Even if you're not in education, the narrative was hopefully just enough to give you a sense of being there by recalling your own elementary school experiences. This was also an artificial exercise since you did not observe the action firsthand and take the field notes yourself. Visual and aural memories of the nuanced actions from Carol and her students would be fresher in the fieldworker's mind since he was actually there. He also has knowledge of Carol's ways of working with her other art classes, affording him the ability to compare this class with her younger and older groups. Nevertheless, the purpose of this section is to emphasize that observing and analyzing actions, reactions, and interactions are just some of the primary goals of fieldwork.

Reflecting on routines, rituals, and rules

Social life consists of everyday routines peppered with the occasional ritual, all occurring within and driven by sets of rules. When conducting participant observation, reflect on the routines, rituals, and rules suggested by people's actions, reactions, and interactions. This analysis brings researchers closer to determining the patterned and significant in people's lives.

Figure 2.8   Fieldworkers observe people in their roles and relationships.

©iStockphoto.com/Chris Schmidt

Return to the field note excerpt of the art teacher's interaction with her class. What do you infer are the routines of this teacher and the students? What do you assume (given the moment you have to work with) are the actions that most likely happen in this particular classroom on a regular basis? The teacher's specific instructions for art projects and her walking among students during independent work might be routines, as is the Spanish-language conversation among students during independent group work. Though not in the field notes, other classroom routines consist of actions such as taking attendance and cleaning the tables for the next class's use.

Now consider the rituals (as you interpret them) that seem to suggest significance because of their occasional use. To the observer, the art-making is one ritual because it consists of tribal (i.e., small group) creation and effort. It is also ritualistic because each small group's microculture (i.e., collective decision-making process of its membership) will be embodied and exhibited in an artifact.

Finally, reflect on what known and tacit rules operate in this classroom. Observe socialized habits, actions of compliance, and the exhibition of power by the participants. Perhaps one of the most apparent rules is the teacher's raised hand to signal the class that quiet and attention are needed. A tacit or socialized rule is the children's automatic acceptance that the people sitting at their table compose their assigned small group. Though not in the field notes, a poster hangs in the classroom that lists specific student expectations and consequences for misbehavior ("Be respectful and kind toward others," "Keep your hands and feet to yourself").

Reflecting on roles and relationships

Routines, rituals, and rules are what people do. Roles and relationships generally hone in on who people are, based on and exemplified by what they do. As researchers observe social life, they infer the roles or characteristics people assume (or are endowed with by others) and how their statuses influence and affect relationships. Analyses of these components of social life tend to focus on the qualities of individuals—aspects such as their emotions, values, attitudes, and beliefs. A person's actions, reactions, and interactions in particular circumstances or moments also say much about the quality of that person, as do the routines they establish, the rituals they take part in, and the rules they create and adhere to (or breach).

When observing life, attribute descriptive characteristics to people in their roles. It's one thing to be "a teacher." But it's more accurate to say "a White novice teacher" and even more precise to identify her as "a White novice teacher whose pedagogical focus seems centered around classroom management more than the content of her art lessons with elementary school children at this point in her career." For describing and analyzing relationships, more-evocative language seems in order to articulate the back-and-forth, give-and-take nature of the interactions: "Carol is an artist learning the craft of teaching. She exhibits a professional yet motherly demeanor with her students, rendering a carefully managed, secure environment for creative expression."

Fieldworkers should always stay open to the surprising, intriguing, and disturbing of social settings (Sunstein & Chiseri-Strater, 2012, p. 115). As an example, Saldaña once accompanied another novice teacher he was observing to her car in the parking lot after school. He casually glanced inside her automobile as they continued talking and noticed the floors and seats fully covered with junk food wrappers. He later learned that this teacher suffered from an eating disorder, compounded by the stress of her new job. Life is not always mundane, smooth, and conflict-free. Fieldworkers will often find the anomalous moment or unexpected incident that throws the sometimes tedium of participant observation off balance. These glitches are rich opportunities for further exploration and can be compared against the patterns of regularity documented thus far. Their appearance in the social world can signal an underlying and unresolved issue, a hidden agenda at work, or simply a new and undetected pattern thus far. These also provide opportunities to observe how participants handle moments of disruption, which reveal much about the dynamics of their roles and relationships.

The reflections above focused on thinking. Now we discuss writing about thinking.

Analytic memoing of field notes

An **analytic memo** is an extended researcher commentary stimulated by field notes (and other data such as documents and interview transcripts). Think of memos as sites for researchers to "dump their brains" freely in their own words about what they've observed. They are reflective narratives that expand and expound on observations by taking researchers' thinking and writing up a notch. With memoing, researchers attempt to transcend the descriptive of their field notes and venture into richer analytic connections and insights.

"What is going on here?" or "What is happening here?" serve as open-ended prompts for reflection after observing a slice of natural social life. But those questions can seem too broad for some to tackle at first and suggest summary rather than synthesis, so 12 more-specific prompts are provided to help focus initial analyses (Saldaña, 2016). During or after field notes have been composed, the researcher reflects on and writes about

1. The participants' actions, reactions, and interactions;

2. The participants' routines, rituals, rules, roles, and relationships;

3. How the researcher personally relates to the participants and/or the phenomenon;

4. Emergent patterns, categories, themes, concepts, and assertions;

5. The possible networks and processes (links, connections, overlaps, flows) among the patterns, categories, themes, concepts, and assertions;

6. An emergent or related existent theory;

7. Any problems with the study;

8. Any personal or ethical dilemmas with the study;

9. Future directions for the study;

10. The analytic memos generated thus far (called meta-memos);

11. Tentative answers to the study's research questions; and

12. Passage drafts for the final report of the study.

If writing is thinking, then composing a memo is a processual form of analysis. Writing the memo condenses real-time, lengthy observations into richer passages of meaning. To some research methodologists, analytic memos are the transition techniques between data collection and the final report.

Examples of Analytic Memos A memo is stimulated most often by the particular contents of a set of field notes. Reflection on what actually happened keeps researchers grounded in the realities of the setting while transcending them to higher or deeper levels of meaning—a compound form of reflection we label **highdeep thinking**. The art class field note excerpt serves as an example of how to compose memos about the phenomenon of interest: a White novice teacher's experiences with inner-city Hispanic youths.

We find it best to compose the memo first, then determine which one(s) of the 12 prompts might have been addressed. This is because memos, like front matter for field notes, should be labeled with their date of composition and a representative title that captures both the content and the focus of the analysis. Below is one memo that zooms in on a pattern of action, reaction, and interaction observed in Carol's teaching. Note their informality and unabashed honesty:

January 21, 2014

REACTION PATTERNS: CLASSROOM (MIS)MANAGEMENT

Carol's "on your feet" work is relaxed and controlled with this class, but Periods 3 and 6—the classes from hell—are when she lets the children's erratic energies get to her and she picks up on their vibe. I've often said that a visiting or one-class-at-a-time teacher inherits the classroom culture of another teacher's children. Carol's best efforts to manage Periods 3 and 6 are thwarted by their home teacher's poor management styles.

Part of Carol's solution may just be continued professional development and on-the-job learning. She's trying to use the same management techniques—a pattern of teaching—with every single class, when a class-by-class management approach may be needed. I wonder if it's my place to offer that suggestion to her. She may take offense to it or be embarrassed, but my intentions are to help her out. I even caught myself giving a stern look to some boys in Period 6 when they were horsing around and they stopped and got back on task. If a pattern isn't working, it's got to be changed. Rules just aren't meant to be broken—they're meant to be revised.

This next memo focuses on the interactions and relationships observed between the participants:

January 22, 2014

RELATIONSHIPS: WHITE TEACHER/BROWN STUDENTS

Interesting is how Carol seems to see the two-language classroom as a "given." She doesn't enforce an English-only policy of any kind; she speaks however she can (her knowledge of Spanish is very limited) and lets the students speak however they feel comfortable. Perhaps visual art to her is a "universal language" that binds them together. What children create with their hands is important. She praises their process and products. There's also a valuing of their original ideas. She didn't mandate what the content of their murals should be— she left that decision to the group, empowering them with creative choice, something children have very little of these days.

Memos should incorporate observational evidence such as participant quotes or descriptive moments of interaction to support the researcher's analytic constructions. This memo tackles the primary research purpose of the study:

January 23, 2014

RESEARCH QUESTION: A UNIVERSAL LANGUAGE

The purpose of this study is to determine in what ways a White novice teacher instructs a predominantly Hispanic school population. Carol, as the case study, is still focused on the routine expectations and demands of teaching as a profession. The language barrier between her and her students has compounded some of the difficulties she has communicating with them. But the universal language of a smile and pleasant, affirming voice ("Good job, guys") seems to have created a loving relationship between most of them. She's rarely seated at her desk while children work; she's continuously roaming the classroom and dialoguing with them. Perhaps Carol, as a visual artist, relies on images to communicate her teacher self. I've noticed how strongly gestural she is with her hands in front of a class, but less so with teacher colleagues.

Memos serve as a transitional data base, of sorts. They transform the raw data of fieldwork into more condensed forms. The collective memos then become the new material for the analyst's synthesis and highdeep reflections on the phenomenon of interest. The process is one way to transcend the local and particular of a site and to progress toward more general and transferable meanings.

An occasional **meta-memo** integrates the accumulated memos to date to compose an even richer composite of the field experience. Like the game *Three for All!* described in Chapter 1, the meta-memo below brings the reflections from January 21, 22, and 23 together (CLASSROOM (MIS)MANAGEMENT, WHITE TEACHER / BROWN STUDENTS, and A UNIVERSAL LANGUAGE) to think about what they might have in common—that is, to pattern and unify them:

> January 24, 2014
>
> META-MEMO: UNIVERSAL AND UNIQUE COMMUNICATION
>
> It seems it doesn't matter what language they speak—children are children. And when teachers from one culture work with children from different cultures, the universals must be found. These universals consist of nonverbal affirmations, vocal tones of pleasantry and respect, comfortable proximity, and communication through a medium—like visual art—that transcends language barriers.
>
> But all classes are not the same. Each classroom is a subculture unto itself. Some are composed of smooth routines, and others are composed of disruptive rule-breaking. A universal pattern of classroom management techniques does not translate from one classroom subculture to another. The subtle dialects must be discerned and new vocabulary learned to communicate and create a more productive mini-social world.

For more on the intricacies of analytic memo writing, see Emerson, Fretz, and Shaw (2011) and Saldaña (2016).

CLOSURE AND TRANSITION

Participant observation is just one primary way to analyze life. Its advantages include documenting social actions as they naturally happen, and utilizing the researcher's mind to reflect on and interpret their meanings. Across time, researchers' collective experiences with fieldwork accumulate to help them infer and inductively analyze social patterns and their interrelationships.

People create and use products of varying kinds. The next chapter focuses on analyzing the documents, artifacts, and visual materials of our social worlds.

RESOURCES FOR PARTICIPANT OBSERVATION

The following resources will offer you additional guidance for methods of participant observation and field note analysis:

DeWalt, Kathleen M., and Billie R. DeWalt. (2011). *Participant Observation: A Guide for Fieldworkers,* 2nd edition. Lanham, MD: AltaMira Press.

Emerson, Robert M., Rachel I. Fretz, and Linda L. Shaw. (2011). *Writing Ethnographic Fieldnotes,* 2nd edition. Chicago: University of Chicago Press.

Sunstein, Bonnie Stone, and Elizabeth Chiseri-Strater. (2012). *FieldWorking: Reading and Writing Research,* 4th edition. Boston: Bedford/St. Martin's.

ANALYTIC EXERCISES FOR PARTICIPANT OBSERVATION

1. Locate an interior public space (e.g., a shopping mall, restaurant, department store, gym) where a moderate number of people gather for a particular purpose. Sit and/or walk around and observe the actions in the space for 20 minutes without taking any field notes; simply watch and listen. Then, go to a private place to work and write or type out as much as you can recall from the observation experience.

2. Do the same exercise as 1 above, but write down jottings as you observe. Then, go to a private place to work and flesh out the field notes and add periodic OCs.

3. Do the same exercise as 2 above, then compose three separate analytic memos triggered by your field notes, and finally compose a meta-memo about the three.

4. Draw a ground plan of one room in your current residence or a portion of the indoor site you observed for exercise 1. In a separate narrative, describe the general look or geo-identity of the setting.

SAMPLE FIELD NOTES FOR ANALYSIS

Excerpts from a set of Saldaña's field notes on observing a junior high school drama teacher, Nancy (a fictitious name or **pseudonym** to protect the participant's identity), and her class are included below. Note the use of personal shorthand (N = Nancy, G = girl, B = boy), the italicized and indented OCs, and the bolded quotes. This observation was audio-recorded but only notable passages were transcribed.

Review the field notes and compose three to five separate analytic memos based on what you infer and interpret from the action described.

February 28, 2005 (Monday)—"Collaboration"

Escobar School, Drama Room, 11:50 A.M.–1:00 P.M.

Jr. HS Theatre Class (Nancy, 9 Hispanic girls, 5 Hispanic boys, all 8th graders)

Before 12:00 noon class, a few students start to enter the room.

N: "Who's a dancer in the jukebox scene?"

G: "Ms. N. what are we doing here today?"

N: "I don't know, I thought we'd just hang around."

OC: *Friendly banter, the kind she's noted for.*

There is a discussion on the cheerleading competition from last week. **N: "Hey, I think we did a good job on that . . . our girls did really good."** Students begin standing around N's desk. N continues to ask individuals, **"OK, whoever's in the jukebox dance needs to go to dance. Are you in the dance? If you're in the dance you're supposed to go to dance."** 2 Bs bounce balls by the desk.

N: **"We have to work on *La llorona*."**

G: **[in an anglicized dialect] *"La horona."***

N: **"Is anyone here in the jukebox dance?"**

B: **"I am."**

N: **"No you're not."**

B: **"I am, I think."**

N: **"You don't know if you are?"**

About seven students are clustered around N's desk.

OC: *Students could be talking to peers away from the teacher but they gravitate around her. That's a sign of love/like.*

Class begins on time. **N: "The rest of us let's put two tables in a big square and sit together. Move it, move it."** Students connect two tables and move chairs around the table format and sit.

OC: *Tables shifted for each period reflect the flexibility of N.*

Jose comes in late. **N: "Where were you, Jose?"** He explains that he was in the playground. **N: "No, I need to have a pass before I'll let you in this class."** He leaves.

A five-page, two-sided first draft outline of *La llorona* is distributed to the class around the table. There is no pagination on the script, they are not collated, and the first and last pages of the script are on opposite sides of the same page. N has a stapler and gives students explicit instructions on which page is first so it can be laid face down with other pages following.

> OC: N usually has her act together. I wonder if her illness for the past two days kept her from having this text prepared?

N: "This is the script so far." A student comments on the typos. **N: "OK, so I can't type. . . . We are going to read through this. . . . There are some places where it needs narration. . . . If you were these characters, on stage, what would you add to the script? You have to think how would these people speak. They wouldn't say, 'Hey homie.'"** The group laughs.

Jose returns to the classroom. He has no pass. There is a 30-second discussion about his tardiness. Jose states that the playground monitor told him he had 15 minutes left before the next class. **N: "Didn't you get the clue when everyone else came in . . . that you should come in?"** She insists that Jose get a pass from the monitor. He leaves.

> OC: Nancy is firm about the procedure. Although Jose tries to state his case, he does not back-talk to Nancy rudely but acquiesces.

> OC: Refer to play script artifact for text.

N reads the opening stage directions from the script. N says they're going to use tin luminarias with Christmas tree lights in them because they can't use candles on stage. She continues reading stage directions. There are marimba and guitar music playing. She explains the term *crescendo* as "gets louder" for the group.

> OC: N's script starts off with a bang. There's a nice mood set and theatricality to it.

> N: **"Does that kind of give you an idea of what we're starting with? So we start off with these *La llorona* figures. They're going to have these white streamers on them and they're going to be moving, and we won't be able to see their faces but we'll see these things moving and then we'll hear the chimes."**

> OC: N has already conceptualized some of the staging of the piece. Again, time efficient, thinking through things ahead of time.

N assigns people to read selected lines although there are no dialogue indicators on the play script. The opening scene is the set-up for a birthday party. N asks, **"OK, what can we add in there** because this is a surprise party for this girl, let's say she's 13 or 14. What else can you say? 'Surprise, Happy Birthday, Maria.' What else would her friends say to her?"

> OC: *This script is a framework, yet she's allowing students to give input—to flesh out and take ownership of the piece. Even though there's a product as an ultimate goal, N is still concerned with improvisational process.*

G: "It doesn't sound right."

N: "What doesn't sound right?"

They discuss the age of the person having the birthday. N asks the group, "**What age should we make her in** *La llorona*? **15? OK, we need to add something in Spanish, OK? I know you guys know Spanish.**" One girl says, "**I don't.**" A few students share "**Feliz cumpleaños.**" N asks them how cumpleaños is spelled; N: "**I know how to spell 'Feliz.'**" She writes it in her script.

Jose comes in with his pass and gives it to Nancy. He joins the group and N asks him to share a script with someone so time won't be wasted collating another.

> OC: *Time again.*

N reads a line from the play: "**Maria, the most beautiful of all girls in the world, just like the Maria of** *La llorona*." A G says it's a "**corny line.**" N: "**What should we change that to?**"

> OC: *N states no offense at a student's honesty, but instead asks for an alternative line. Open, accepting.*

One G is confused and thinks the birthday girl is the character of *La llorona*. N explains the character will be playing her in the play-within-a-play. A student asks who will be playing the character. N looks through her papers. One student laughingly says "**Soledad.**" N: [jokingly] "**Soledad. Ran away.** *La llorona* **went to the river.**" [students laugh]. N: "**Sonia is gonna be the** *La llorona* **of the rap version.**" A student asks if there will be two stories. N asks them to get back on the script for an alternative line. She explains how the transition should be subtle. N: "**We just can't go, 'Let's do the play of** *La llorona*!' **and start doing the story on stage.**" She explains how the transition is to work.

N asks how the next line is to be spoken; N: "**OK, who can read this in Spanish because I don't know what I wrote, Mrs. Garcia told me.**" The students read, "*La Llorona* **era muy linda.**" N: "**What does that mean?**" A few students translate for her and there is banter.

A B thinks another line is not right: "**You have grown up to become a beautiful young woman.**"

N: "OK, so what can we put for her dad? If it sounds funny what could we put?"

B: "'Cause Mexican dads, they don't say that."

The Bs jokingly suggest other things. N: "OK if your dad was on the off-chance telling you you're beautiful, how would he say it.?" Gs giggle. N: "I know, it's a stretch, it's a stretch." Girls offer some lines.

N: "How would he say it in Spanish? What's a term of endearment in Spanish, like 'beautiful.'"

B: "Que linda estan, mi hija."

G: "Yeah, like that!"

N: "What is that?"

B: "I don't know."

OC: *He probably does and doesn't. Sometimes there's catch phrases that you know are appropriate but don't know the exact translation.*

[field notes continue]

CHAPTER 3

Analyzing Documents, Artifacts, and Visual Materials

Introduction

This chapter explores how qualitative researchers analyze the material and digital products people create and use. The analytic emphasis in Chapter 2 was placed on researcher reflection through techniques such as observer's comments (OCs) and analytic memo writing. Those same techniques will be applied to new data forms, and to additional analysis methods for narrative and visual empirical materials.

Qualitative researchers should spend some slices of time analyzing the many things humans own, create, and use on a regular basis, as suggested by the research topic or questions. The products in and of environments are inseparable parts of social worlds. Fieldwork attunes researchers not just to people's actions, but also to what they work with, play with, need, and treasure. A focus on **material culture** heightens researcher awareness of the objects people accumulate across time. Each artifact evokes within its viewer a possible story of its history, or an explanatory purpose for its presence. These stories and explanations accumulate into a larger picture of a participant's local world, and suggest a variety of emotional and affective human meanings connected to the objects. Social analysts have suggested contemporary life is lived in a **digital culture** or **visual culture**, meaning that the ubiquity of images found in digital technology is now an everyday part of many people's lives. Professional research organizations dedicated to visual analysis such as the International Visual Sociology Association (www .visualsociology.org) have recently emerged. Kozinets (2015) examines **netnography**, the study of online cultures and the virtual worlds of cyberspace in *Netnography: Redefined*.

This chapter includes separate discussions about documents, artifacts, and visual materials such as photographs and video.

Learning Objectives

After reading and reviewing this chapter, researchers should be able to

1. Discuss the qualities attributed to the materials of human production, and

2. Apply selected methods for analyzing narrative and visual materials.

But you cannot always separate each format neatly when you're analyzing, say, Facebook pages—a digital document with texts and embedded photographs viewed on the artifact of a mobile phone. The best recommendation is to examine these material products through both their individual, constituent elements, and as a total representation of human production.

On Values, Attitudes, and Beliefs

Since many material objects are not just things but also potentially rich symbols of meaning, a discussion of three key interrelated concepts is in order since these concepts play an essential role in the analysis of documents, artifacts, and visual materials (as well as human interaction): values, attitudes, and beliefs. Each concept has a different meaning, but for clarity they combine into what will be referred to as a **values system**.

A **value** is the importance someone attributes to herself, another person, a thing, or an idea. Values are the principles, moral codes, and situational norms people live by (Daiute, 2014, p. 69). Saldaña (2016) perceives value as an intrinsic process: "The greater the personal meaning [of something to someone], the greater the personal payoff; the greater the personal payoff, the greater the personal value" (p. 131). Today, many people view Facebook as a valuable Internet resource for the expression of significant moments from their lives and for maintaining instantaneous, electronically mediated communication with family and friends. Facebook provides meaning to most individuals because of its community-generating experience. The payoff of accessing the site is feeling better informed and connected to friends and loved ones. The value of Facebook is enhanced for its users through frequent access several times a day.

An **attitude** is the way someone thinks and feels about himself, another person, thing, or idea. Think of attitudes as evaluative perceptions and sets of cumulative reactions, reflecting the beliefs people learn through time (Shaw & Wright, 1967, p. 3). For example, whenever something on Facebook strikes a person in a positive way, he might click the Like button to inform the post's author that she has posted something he likes and affirms. His attitude about the original post (or his reaction toward the individual poster's action) and/or its previously posted comments, might motivate him to add a supplemental comment as an attitudinal remark.

A **belief** is part of a system that includes interrelated values and attitudes, as well as personal knowledge, experiences, opinions, prejudices, morals, and other interpretive perceptions of the social world. Wolcott (2008) reinforces that beliefs are embedded in the values attached to them. The content that users post on Facebook, especially if they are shared memes of quotable quotes or affirming messages (e.g., "How others see you is not important; how you see yourself means everything"), reflect their beliefs about life and living it.

Values, attitudes, and beliefs are formed, perpetuated, and changed through social interactions and institutions, and our cultural and religious (if any) memberships (Charon, 2013). Pools of Facebook friends most likely share comparable values systems. However, people often value some friends more than others since they hold varying attitudes toward the spectrum of people they know because of identical to opposing beliefs about matters such as politics, social issues, and current events. Sociological theories such as differential association posit that people's values are influenced by the groups they interact with most intensively, suggesting that people's values systems are not fixed constructs but are rather malleable and ever-evolving processes (Rubin & Rubin, 2012, p. 132), though they tend to become more firmly fixed as people age. Values, attitudes, and beliefs can be analyzed separately but not without reference to the other systems' concepts. In fact, it is sometimes quite difficult to discern whether a participant's statement is a value, an attitude, or a belief. This conundrum reinforces the intricate interconnectivity of a total values system.

Values, attitudes, and beliefs themselves are not intrinsic to documents, artifacts, and visual materials such as photographs. Rather, humans endow the material objects with meaning, based on how they're perceived and interpreted. The value of an antique is not in the object itself, but in the value humans attribute to it because of its age, rarity, historic connections, condition, aesthetics, availability, and other factors such as its allure and demand by collectors, which determine not just its monetary value, but also its personal value.

Yet, an object does not have to be expensive to be treasured. A handwritten thank-you card from a close, personal friend might not be worth anything to anyone else, but to the recipient it is a beloved artifact that symbolizes a deep, enduring relationship. Values, attitudes, and beliefs about the person who gave the card are transferred onto it by the one who received it. But even the most seemingly mundane document/artifact such as a driver's license can be assigned a range of meanings based on the holder's values system. An older adult can perceive the license as an obligatory, legally required card that helps the holder conform to the rules of driving on public roads, and serves as a necessary item for airline travel and identity confirmation. But an adolescent receiving his first driver's license probably perceives it as a significant rite of passage (i.e., ritual) toward adulthood that suddenly changes the teenager's self-perception (i.e., social role). Prior (2004) attests, "Our identities are supported and altered by various forms of identification" (p. 88).

In sum, when analyzing documents, artifacts, and visual materials, explore the attributed values, attitudes, and beliefs about them from the participants' perspectives. Also, as will be discussed in future chapters, recognize that people maintain a values system toward other people, and not just toward objects.

Analyzing Manifest and Latent Contents

Manifest refers to what is readily observable in the material—its apparent and surface content. **Latent** refers to what is hidden within or inferred about the material—the subtexts interpreted by the observer. Analysts explore the manifest and latent (or overt and covert) contents of documents, artifacts, and visual materials in order to describe their physical properties and assess their symbolic meanings.

A careful analysis of the manifest, constituent elements of an object might bring researchers closer to understanding the latent. In other analyses, the holistic impression one gets from a document, artifact, or photograph triggers a host of associated memories and experiences. These triggers endow the item with reads or takes (i.e., intuitive reactions about the manifest) that quickly lead toward the latent. Figure 3.1 is a photograph of a young married couple. Look at each person's face and infer or interpret what might be going through each one's mind. Now look at the woman and man's body postures and physical relationship, and infer and interpret how each one feels about the other. We could offer our own reads or takes about the couple in this photo, but it is your own interpretations that matter here. However, the first impression you got from the image should be substantiated by supporting evidence. What specific visual details in the photo led you to your inferences about their interrelationship?

Content analysis and **discourse analysis** are only two of the established methods for scrutinizing the manifest and latent of narrative and visual texts. Quantitative content

Figure 3.1   Infer or interpret what might be going through the wife's and husband's minds. (Photo by Matt Omasta.)

analysis (Krippendorff & Bock, 2009; Weber, 1990) is generally a systematic analysis of material that primarily counts the number of times particular words, images, or ideas appear in a set of data. Inferences and interpretations of quantitative results are then applied to assess any particular meanings to the material. Qualitative content analysis (Schreier, 2012) extends beyond counting to assess thematic features and concepts suggested by the data.

Discourse analysis (Altheide & Schneider, 2013; Gee, 2011; Rapley, 2007; Willig, 2008) examines not just the contents (what) but also the contexts (how) of narrative and visual texts. Discourse analysis focuses on selected nuances of language, conversation, and images to assess how elements such as vocabulary, grammar, intonation, topics, and so on work together in intricate combination to impart meaning about human relationships and big-picture ideas such as culture, identity, politics, and power. Content analysis targets the manifest by counting in order to get to the latent, but discourse analysis targets the latent from the very start by examining not how many but, rather, what kinds of words or images are used to convey something. Content analysis informs a researcher that automobiles are one of the products featured most frequently in primetime network television commercials. Discourse analysis informs the researcher how truck commercials generally employ hypermasculine visual action, vocabulary, and deep resonant voice-overs (e.g., "Guts. Glory. *Ram*.") to target and appeal to a particular market of male consumers.

Qualitative researchers examine people's discourse not just in documents and media materials but also in life: discourse occurs during participant observation, as well as during the analytic scrutiny of conversations and interview transcripts. It is a way of not taking everything at face value, of reading between the lines, interpreting subtexts and embedded meanings, detecting hidden agendas, digging underneath to reveal the covert, reading psychological clues, peeling back the layers, and assessing subliminal tactics that persuade or motivate us to action. We do not mean to imply that everything or everyone has something to hide, but there are subtleties and nuances that should not be overlooked. Qualitative researchers relish details, because in them lie stimuli for constructing richer meanings about life.

The Materials and Meanings of Human Production

A theory posits that the products people create are extensions of the human body. For example, fingernail clippers are extensions of teeth, a carpet is an extension of skin and hair, a camera lens is an extension of an eye, an audio speaker is an extension of a mouth and vocal cords, and so on. Original material products also hold their designers' creative and aesthetic preferences for form and function. Walk through a retail clothing store and notice the wide array of shirts and blouses for sale and the infinite combinations possible with fabric textures, colors, logos, motifs, fit, drape, and so on. When consumers are able to purchase clothing items that appeal to them, they adopt the designers' aesthetic values and ascribe their own intrinsic values onto the clothing such as "the clothes are fancy," "comfortable," or "trendy." Clothing, too, is an extension of the human body—nicknamed "the second skin" (Horn & Gurel, 1981)—and reflects the wearer's persona and the desired presentation of self to others (Goffman, 1959).

The products people create also reflect their value, attitude, and belief systems. Humans write things, which transfer their thoughts and ways of thinking onto paper or digital formats. People decorate walls and rooms, which suggests not only what's available but also what's important and beautiful to them. Some professions build things, which reflect the craft, training, and standards of the manufacturers. Other professions deal primarily with creating and communicating original ideas, and the products of those ideas embody their creators' imaginations. As the design folk saying goes, "We are what we make; we make what we are."

When analyzing life, consider what participants own, create, and maintain. The things in people's lives are not only extensions of their bodies, but are also extensions of their minds and identities. Anthropologists have long known that the artifacts of a culture symbolize the values system—the ethos—of the people who created them. That same principle applies to an individual's everyday social environment and the products of and in that world.

Analyzing Documents

Language is a symbol system that conveys messages to readers and listeners. Particular words in particular combinations expressed by the writer or speaker are intended to communicate a particular intent. But other individuals might interpret the sender's original message in a completely different way. Much has been written about transactions with texts, and we could devote this entire book to that topic alone. Instead, we focus on the qualitative researcher as an interpreter of narratives written by others. In this section we explore **documents**, in their broadest sense, as forms of textual and sometimes visual communication. Documents can consist of materials such as business or organizational hard-copy letters and e-mails; printed newspapers and magazines; Internet Web sites and digital modes of communication (e.g., tweets, Facebook posts, text messages, blogs); books in various formats; print advertisements and circulars; and personal materials written by participants in the form of journals, diaries, poetry, and so on.

Documents are social products that reflect the interests and perspectives of their authors (Hammersley & Atkinson, 2007, p. 130) and carry "values and ideologies, either intended or not" (Hitchcock & Hughes, 1995, p. 231). Official documents in particular are "site[s] of claims to power [and] legitimacy" (Lindlof & Taylor, 2011, p. 232). Analyzing the values system suggested by documents through manifest readings and interpretations of their latent content and discourse are the primary foci for this section. More systematic quantitative methods of textual analysis can be accessed from related sources (e.g., Franzosi, 2010; Krippendorff, 2013; Wilkinson & Birmingham, 2003).

Collecting materials

We recall an anecdotal factoid that says that 90% of all filed paper documents for business purposes are never accessed or referred to again. We have no statistical data about comparable frequency of saved and deleted electronic communications and files, but we speculate that the number of reopened documents is also strikingly minimal. The good news is that these amassed materials are a rich repository of data for analysis. But since one of the key analytic skills of a qualitative researcher is to condense large amounts of data, it is not necessary to gather anything and everything in print at the field site.

Pay particular attention to how forms of written language are used in the participants' social worlds—that is, what do they read and write (if anything)? Workplace ethnography, for example, examines partly how business is conducted and accomplished through written communication. Educational ethnography in particular examines what teachers and students write and read, and the administrative materials of schooling that permeate each day such as official forms, records, and data bases. Some documents are considered confidential for personal or legal reasons, so the researcher should respect the limitations of access.

Upon entering the field site, just one of your many initial tasks is to scout the setting for documents that are written and read—both frequently and rarely. If possible, maintain a copy as part of your own records (e.g., one brochure from many copies available in a health-care clinic's literature rack). When only one copy of something important exists, make a hard copy or scan/digitally photograph the document. There are a number of mobile apps for this task that can also covert the images into a PDF. Sites such as Dropbox or Google Drive can serve as repositories for the data. A researcher also takes cognitive ownership of one-of-a-kind texts when she herself handwrites or types them directly into her field notes.

For larger documents available electronically, request or download a copy. Bookmark and regularly access all field- or participant-related Internet sites (e.g., home pages, PDFs, Facebook accounts). It might be helpful to save or print copies of Web pages when you first visit them since they can be deleted or updated with completely different content the next time you access them. Failing to create a physical or virtual copy the first time could mean losing the data permanently. The same applies to Facebook and other social media accounts: users can delete or modify content at any time. You might not read or analyze everything you collect, but the materials are there on an as-needed basis.

Below, we offer two analytic frames for documents: how they capture attention, and how they embody the identities of their writers.

Analyzing attention

When analyzing a document's contents, there are several researcher lenses, filters, and angles for interpreting it. One of the first tasks for the researcher to examine is how it gets the reader's attention. In other words, analyze what strategies the writer uses to maintain a reader's focus on and engagement with the text. The attention-getting tactics employed can reveal the creator's objectives or goals, knowledge of rhetoric (i.e., persuasion), values system, and presumptions of authority or expertise. Reflection on these aspects offer a critical examination of the document's latent contents—its discourse.

Print advertisements are certainly in the business of attention-getting through such strategies as large fonts, eye-catching images, triggers to positive emotions (e.g., happiness) or negative emotions (e.g., fear), and so on. But what about noncommercial documents? As an example, below is a text excerpt from a weight-loss workbook developed and distributed by a health insurance company for its clients (Cigna, 2012, pp. 18–19). This self-help material, titled *A Healthier Point of View: Living at a Healthier Weight*, offers readers information and guidance for proper diet, nutrition, and exercise. One section on snacking includes this advice:

BE SNACK SMART

A midmorning or midafternoon snack can help boost your energy and satisfy your hunger until the next meal. If you choose well, your snacks can contribute to your recommended daily intake from each food group. Snacking is not bad as long as you use judgment and moderation.

Snack smart by choosing snacks that provide the calories and nutrients that fit with your eating plan. Include them as part of your daily calorie allowance, and limit portions to one serving.

What types of snacks do you tend to eat? Try to think of some healthy snacks to replace the less healthy ones.

Instead of . . .	Try . . .
Potato chips	Popcorn (no butter/salt)
Ice cream	Frozen yogurt
Candy	Nuts or sunflower seeds
Chocolate bar	Granola bar
Nachos	Celery sticks or baby carrots with hummus

Analytic memos, explained in Chapter 2, are certainly one approach to inquiry about textual materials. But a variant of OCs helps focus on the constituent elements of attention-getting strategies employed in the document. Simply list or bullet point the specific ways the writer achieves a particular objective, how the writer persuades its reader, what values system operates in the material, and what authority or expertise is suggested. For an anonymous document, the analyst can speculate on its possible authorship. Likewise, researchers can reflect on the document's targeted readership and how its author writes with a particular audience in mind. This item-by-item method makes the analyst more aware of the nuances of rhetoric, especially when direct quotes from the document are used as supporting evidence. A few analytic bullet points about the above workbook text include the following:

- "Be snack smart" is a short proverb that's easily remembered.

- The reader is reassured that snacking is not bad, lessening the dread of not eating to lose weight.

- There are several conditions listed throughout, placing responsibility on the reader/dieter: "If you choose well," "as long as you."

- Frequent parameter-like word choices appear to reinforce minimal amounts of eating: "recommended," "allowance," "moderation," "daily," "fit," "limit," "no."

- The healthier options are listed on the right side of the page, subliminally suggesting they're the right (i.e., correct) snacks to eat.

The collection of bullet points can be woven into a more coherent narrative for an analytic write-up.

An item-by-item list of attention-getting tactics is just one approach to documents. It serves well for discourse analyses and studies that examine values systems in written materials.

Analyzing identity

Another method for analyzing a document, particularly when its origin and creator are unknown, is to profile its writer. By profile, we mean to reflect on the possible identity of its creator(s). But even when an analyst knows who wrote the document, profiling its elements can generate a better understanding of the participant. Note that we do not refer to profiling in its negative sense, meaning to stereotype, but instead as an investigative method to analyze the contents and contexts of narratives.

If we operate under the assumption that the document a person wrote is the product of her thinking, then the document should suggest something about its writer's identity—not who she is, but how she perceives herself. What are things you can deduce about the person who created the document, based on what you infer from the document's appearance and content? There might be some clues in the text that permit a researcher to infer demographic factors such as the writer's gender, age, and so on. The vocabulary and narrative style could suggest something about the person's education level. An analyst can also infer something about the writer's ways of working. What do such things as the layout, color choices, and/or font tell you about this person's work ethic? Since the writer's values system can be found embedded in the document, the researcher can make inferences regarding what she finds important.

Hager, Maier, O'Hara, Ott, and Saldaña (2000) conducted focus group interviews with high school teachers to gather their perspectives on a forthcoming state-issued standards document for their class instruction and curriculum planning. The teachers themselves had little to no input on the standards and performance objectives drafted by the state department of education, which listed no specific names of contributors or committee members. Teachers could not identify the standards writer(s) by name but they speculated on general characteristics of their developers, which included who and what they were (and were not):

- The entry-level standards were not developmentally appropriate for young children, suggesting writers who were not teachers who were experienced with youths.

- The higher-level standards set unrealistic expectations for adolescents, suggesting writers who did not teach on a daily, long-term basis in high schools.

- The discipline-based premise of the document suggested writers who were unfamiliar with the needs of rural and Native American districts' vocational curriculum mandates.

- Selected phrases in the document (e.g., "reflect the conditions of their time and place," "analyze and interpret how technological and scientific advances," "Greek drama, French classicism") suggested writers who taught at the university level rather than at K–12 levels.

These premises suggested that the author(s) of the standards were most likely well-educated, possibly older university faculty who did not maintain frequent contact with elementary and secondary educators or their students, and writer(s) who seemed to push their particular approach to the discipline through autocratic means. Gender could not be deduced, but it was speculated that the writer(s) were most likely White due to the primarily Eurocentric contents and token multiculturalism in the document. The cell-by-cell matrix formatting of the standards suggested writers who valued conformity, linearity, and systematic approaches to education, rather than the open-ended, site-specific, and signature curricula promoted by teachers.

The study by Hager et al. (2000) used the standards document as a prompt for participant interviews. Likewise, a researcher might share a document that intrigues him with a participant and ask her about its contents, relevance, influence, and so on. If she is unfamiliar with the document and can speak freely about it, he might get some rich first impressions that hone in on the spontaneous read of it. Jointly dialoguing about the material could build a cumulative understanding of its contents and the identities of its writers.

Analyzing Artifacts

The term **artifact** is to be interpreted broadly here, and does not usually refer to the stereotypical view of an ancient, worn down relic buried underneath layers of dirt. Artifacts include any object made by humans (handmade or manufactured) or natural object that can be touched and handled. Artifacts are the things people use for their daily routines and rituals. They range from this book you're reading to the chair you're sitting on. A home is filled with artifacts such as furniture, decor, and smaller functional objects such as televisions, lamps, bowls, and so on. Artifacts refer to both the materials necessary to get work done and the items considered ornamental or decorative. Artifacts are also residual traces of human presence such as trash left on the ground, or other **unobtrusive measures** or evidence of past activity such as footprints left in the dirt, a teacher's writings that remain on a classroom white board, spray-painted graffiti, or a Web browser's history of previous sites visited.

Qualitative researchers observe and record artifacts included in environments, making special note of items that seem to suggest particular meaning to either the researchers or the participants. Researchers employing participant observation should pay occasional attention to the material objects used by participants. Some might be used frequently out of utilitarian necessity, while others gather dust as they rest untouched. A few might stand out if researchers infer they are souvenirs or mementoes of some kind that could hold emotional value by their owner. Artifacts have stories—origins, histories, moments, reasons—about how they were collected, created, inherited, and/or purchased. Since artifacts can't speak for themselves, researchers need to infer their history or use them as conversation pieces with participants to learn more about the relationship between objects and humans.

Since researchers cannot collect and keep one-of-a-kind artifacts from field settings in data bases, digitally photograph key items for additional reflection and meaning making. There's also nothing wrong with old-school methods such as hand drawing a quick sketch of an item when photography is not possible. Below we offer four analytic frames for artifacts: analyzing how they belong, their symbolic connotations, their processes, and how they are extensions of human beings.

Analyzing belonging

In this section we discuss the particular assemblage of objects in a setting we broadly refer to as a place where people and things "belong." Belonging occurs in homes, workplaces, retail stores, outdoor areas, hospitals, prisons, and so on. There might or might not be feelings of comfort, neatness, safety, or community in these spaces, but those are aspects or values that merit discernment and analysis.

Some people put careful thought into the visual appearance of each room in their homes and the strategic location of each artifact. Others, often for financial reasons or space limitations, assemble miscellaneous objects that are primarily functional and utilitarian. Some workplaces limit decoration to promote efficiency, while other organizations permit employees to create how their own workspaces look with personal items such as family photographs and stress-relieving toys. Retail businesses arrange their products and design their spaces to promote product access and sales. Airports are designed to handle thousands of travelers daily with concerns for their safety and security, along with necessary objects such as luggage, tickets, and boarding area seating. Outdoor sporting events include the equipment necessary to play the game; within athletic arenas, spectators often hold signage, food and drink items, and assorted memorabilia to show their team support.

In other words, each social space is a specific place where things in it generally belong. One analytic task is to survey the things in fieldwork sites to reflect on their ways of belonging. This is where the analytic skill sets of discerning unity and relationships come into play. One needn't conduct an extensive written inventory of each and every item in a space, but the guiding principle to apply to an analysis is, "What is the first and general impression we get about this environment, and what details within it lead us to that impression?" The details most often refer to the collection of artifacts in the setting. For example, a shelf in Omasta's university office holds seemingly unrelated odd things such as a five-year-old dried pineapple, a pasta sauce jar with a butterfly in it, an elegantly framed fake leaf, and a placard from the United States Holocaust Memorial Museum in Washington, DC. At first glance, this random assemblage makes absolutely no sense in the space until one learns that these different things do indeed belong together and belong in his office: they are all personally treasured mementoes of play productions Omasta directed.

Spaces most often contain a logic—an organization and management—to the items within them. It is important to identify not just what's in a setting but also why those items are there. Put simply, what are the artifacts for? What function do they serve? Analyzing their purpose can bring an understanding of their perceived value, and especially the attitudes and beliefs held toward them. Even merely decorative items serve functions. There are, of course, sometimes anomalous things in settings that seem oddly out of place. But considering these is also part of the analytic exercise. Their presence offers researchers opportunities to speculate or inquire about their purpose or the participant's logic of placement.

Just as a researcher can dialogue with participants about a document, she should dialogue with them during an interview about a significant artifact as if it were a conversation piece, pointing out the item and asking about its history, purpose, and meaning to its owner—and especially why it's located in a particular place. Certainly researchers can learn much more about a space's occupants and its artifacts by having participants give them a guided tour of the site, accompanied with questions and answers about significant items that attract their visual attention. After the tour, it can be worthwhile to ask, "What are three things in this space that you would most likely try to save in the event of a fire? Why?" The participant's choices suggest a hierarchy of value, again signaling the values system that could be at work.

Analyzing symbolism

Anthropologists explore the symbolism of and in a culture's artifacts. The assumption is that a people's ethos—their values systems—are embodied in the objects they create:

> Symbols . . . are human constructions and condensed attributions of specific associations, memories, and meanings. They consolidate various properties into a single representative entity. The function of a symbol can range from practical utility (e.g., shorthand) to maintenance (of customs and traditions) to aesthetic achievement (in literature and the arts). Symbolizing may be our brain's way of creating order and making meaning from disparate pieces of information. It consolidates various parts into a significant whole. (Saldaña, 2015, p. 66)

Artifacts' meanings can be inferred through a process of historic research and interpretive insight. Analyzing symbolism enables discernment of what an object presents (the manifest) and represents (the latent) to its creators, owners, and/or viewers.

Berger (2014), in *What Objects Mean: An Introduction to Material Culture*, examines the smartphone as a technological artifact of modern culture. Through various theoretical lenses (e.g., developmental, sociological, psychological), he posits that the device symbolizes everything from a surrogate for human contact to the multitasking minds of humans themselves. Selected products, such as the latest Apple iPhone, are symbols of status. The ability to text message, especially among adolescents, symbolizes social connection and identity affirmation in an era of social and cultural alienation. Berger offers varied interpretations in his analytic essay, reinforcing that there are more than one way to decode the symbolism of an object. A researcher's disciplinary interests and experiential knowledge will influence and affect how she perceives an artifact, and participants themselves hold varied meanings toward a single object. Researchers should therefore gather a spectrum of perceptions to learn about people's relationships with artifacts. Interview questions and prompts might include the following:

- Tell me how you got this [artifact].

- What is this [artifact] used for and how often?

- How important is this [artifact] to you?

- What three words or phrases would you use to describe this [artifact]?

- How might this [artifact] be part of you?

People can also attribute specific symbolic significance and meaning to an artifact that is not readily observable in the object. This is when the artifact's story, as told by the owner–participant, reveals aspects such as history, purpose, and value. For example, in Saldaña's home office there sits a glass paperweight on a bookshelf (see Figure 3.2). Someone new to the space might first assume that the object is merely a decorative item, perhaps even a gift, purely for aesthetic purposes. But the paperweight's history is that it previously belonged to a former faculty colleague who died of AIDS in the mid-1980s. This beloved professor kept a collection of more than 20 paperweights in his office as decorative mementoes. When he passed, the executor of his estate informed us he wanted certain faculty members to each inherit a paperweight as a remembrance of him. Thus, the artifact has sentimental value attached to it. Its purpose is to remind—to maintain tangible evidence of a particular human life, and to occasionally evoke memories of that life from its owner. Analyze not just what artifacts are, but also what they symbolically represent.

Figure 3.2 This glass paperweight has a symbolic representation by its owner. (Photo by Johnny Saldaña.)

Analyzing process

Since artifacts are not just things but are also stimuli for human action, reaction, and interaction, one analytic strategy is to identify key items as gerunds ("-ing" words). Transform what the items actually are into what they do or are used for, from the mundane to the conceptual:

- Pencil → writing, erasing
- Book → reading, learning
- Picture of a loved one in a frame → remembering, honoring
- Wall calendar → keeping track, marking time
- Mobile phone → staying connected, digitizing life

Assembling the artifact gerunds related to the participant and the sites they inhabit provides a list of what happens in those spaces—the actions and reactions of interactions between people and their objects. Review this list of gerunds suggested by artifacts in a doctor's waiting room:

- Managing appointments (receptionist's counter with sign-in sheets, pens, business cards)
- Managing bodies, comforting clients (chairs)
- Cautioning (posted signage about patients' responsibilities for referrals, x-rays, blood work, etc.)
- Informing, preparing (brochures about medical equipment, hospices, transportation, etc.)
- Cleansing the environment (a portable air purifier)
- Entertaining, occupying time (TV set to CNN, assorted magazines)
- Decorating, filling the space (artwork on walls)

These gerunds and gerund phrases are Process Codes—summative, symbolic representations of larger data. Simple observable activity (e.g., reading, playing, watching TV, drinking coffee) and more general conceptual action (e.g., struggling, negotiating, surviving, adapting) can be coded as such through Process Codes. The processes of human action can be "strategic, routine, random, novel, automatic, and/or thoughtful" (Corbin & Strauss, 2015, p. 283). **Process Coding** is appropriate for all forms of qualitative data, and particularly for studies that search for the routines and rituals of human life, and the actions and reactions that occur as we deal with conflicts or problems to solve.

The observable, manifest action of people in the doctor's clinic space is waiting (comprising constituent actions such as reading magazines, watching TV, filling out forms, looking at watches, talking to others, accessing mobile phones, etc.). But there are also latent actions within patients consisting of emotional processes such as worrying, regulating impatience, raising spirits, comforting a spouse, and so on. The analytic task here is to discern how the human actions within the space and the artifact actions within the space interrelate. How does one action set unify with the other?

Reflecting and synthesizing are the most suitable heuristics for arriving at an answer. In the example above, three of the seven bullet-pointed processes could be chosen to represent what the artifacts were doing: managing, regulating, and caring. For example, we could posit that the portable air purifier was managing the indoor environment, regulating air quality, and caring for patients' respiratory health. We could also posit that the cautionary signage about patients' responsibilities was managing administrative matters, regulating proper procedures for insurance coverage, and caring for patients' complete medical records and history.

Since unity is the analytic goal in this particular case, researchers next attempt to codeweave the three processes by composing an **assertion**—a declarative, summative statement that synthesizes various observations, supported by confirming evidence from the data corpus (discussed further in Chapter 10). **Codeweaving** integrates the primary codes of interest into a brief narrative to analyze their interrelationship. One assertion that could be put forth about the doctor's office artifacts and the patients using them is as follows:

> This clinic's waiting room is a site where patients' pre-appointment emotions are managed through a balance of regulating the administrative matters of health care with temporary, time-filling comforts of human care.

Analyzing the processes of artifacts enables you to observe them not just as inanimate objects around the participants, but also as materials integrated with human action.

Analyzing extensions

The beginning of this chapter discussed how the products people create are extensions of human beings—their bodies, minds, and actions. Analyzing the possible extensions of a field setting and key artifacts at the site could provide some insight into the participants who inhabit it:

> The environments we establish for ourselves may also embody who we are. Spaces have a macro "look" and "feel" to them based on the collective assembly of its micro details of specific items, organization, maintenance, cleanliness, lighting, color, and other design elements. When I walk into a new space, the primary analytic task that runs through my mind is, "Tell me something about the person or people who work/live here." (Saldaña, 2016, p. 61)

A popular saying about the secrets people keep and the lives they've led goes, "If these walls could talk . . . ." Researchers can capitalize on that concept as an analytic strategy. What would a field setting's walls and artifacts say if they really could talk? Researchers can anthropomorphize them and write "in role" from the objects' point of view. If the products humans create are extensions of human beings, they can be endowed with human qualities. A field note reflection as an extended memo about a doctor's office waiting room might read like the following:

> Please, come in and sit down. The chairs are deliberately comfortable to make you feel relaxed and at ease. If the wide variety of magazines doesn't amuse you as you wait for the doctor, look at my large aquarium and get lulled and soothed as you wait to learn if you have just a cold or a terminal illness. And don't forget to browse all the informational literature about your health and well-being in the literature rack—we care. We're sorry if the TV's news programming, always set to CNN, doesn't entertain you, but we take things seriously here. The room is moderately lit and decorated in neutral colors to calm you—and look: potted plants all around let you know we value life in all its forms. This place is spotless because we're professionals here. And we expect you to maintain a sense of decorum as well: as the posted sign says, "Please turn off all cell phones in the waiting room."

This same strategy can be applied to key artifacts in a setting. In this example, a stethoscope in the doctor's office "talks":

> I am the ears of the doctor. She places me against your chest and back to listen carefully to your heartbeats and breathing. In a way, I'm also her eyes since she cannot see directly inside your torso,

but the sounds I pick up clue her as to what might be happening inside your heart and lungs. I'm almost always draped around her neck and shoulders—an invaluable tool of the trade.

The purpose of analyzing a key artifact's extensions is to better understand its qualities and intrinsic values, as perceived by self or others.

Analyzing Visual Materials

People rarely photograph at random. Instead, they purposefully select particular moments to document visually because they are important and meaningful in some way. A photograph, as an extension of the human body, is a cognitive memory of what was visually experienced. But the photo also embodies the photographer's values system. In addition, viewers, who were not present when the photo was taken, interpret meaning from the photo through their values-laden reading of its contents. Pezzarossi (2015), reflecting on 19th-century tintype technology and popularity, observes that the functions of portraiture in the past have not changed all that much for 21st-century purposes. People take selfies today as a vehicle to explore their personal identities, to express desires and fantasies, and to make durable their presentations of self for future memory.

Visual analysis (Margolis & Pauwels, 2011; Spencer, 2011; Thomson, 2008) consists of a variety of methods for studying material products, landscapes, architecture, photographs, video, digital media, and artwork, from children's drawings to public sculptures. Analytic methods range from documenting the principles of design seen in the visual work (e.g., the use of line, color, texture, composition), to the fundamentals of content analysis, to the arts-based rendering by the researcher of participant portraits, to the intricate frame-by-frame microanalysis of video. Figure 3.3 shows a screenshot from Transana, a video coding and analysis software package. The windows illustrate the audio track components alongside the visual images and codes.

Though highly systematic methods have been profiled by other writers for analyzing the visual, we offer that researchers should place more trust in their intuitive reactions first, followed by a more formal review of how those responses came to be, which then supplement the initial responses with a possible reanalysis of the work. In other words, analyzing the visual (like analyzing narrative) is a reverberative process. Researchers look at the visual image and get a first impression. Then they reflect on that impression and carefully reexamine the image to consider what elements in it support or disconfirm their initial read. They then return to the image with those analytic musings in mind to consider

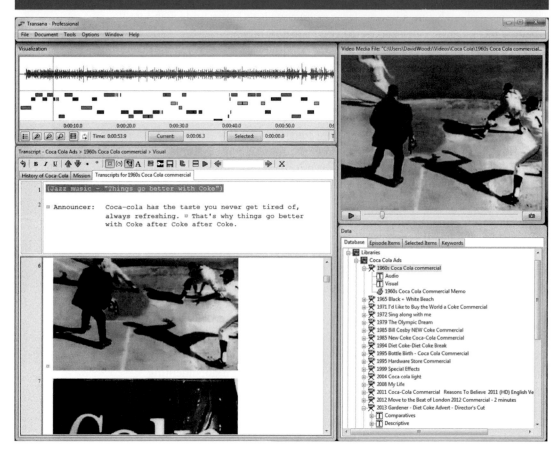

Figure 3.3 A screenshot from Transana video analysis software. (Courtesy of David K. Woods, the Wisconsin Center for Education Research/ Transana, www.transana.org.)

how they and the work newly interact. As with social life, visual analysis is action, reaction, and interaction.

We offer two analytic methods for visual materials: analyzing video collaboratively, and analyzing what photographs evoke.

Analyzing collaboratively

Sometimes researcher-initiated video is used for occasional documentation of fieldwork. It is not the video technology itself that is analyzed, but rather the social action captured on it. One of Saldaña's studies examined a video of children in participatory play with adults. He watched the video with a research assistant and both of them took individual written notes about what they observed, comparable to field note taking. They stopped the sixty-minute video every ten minutes to discuss and compare their observations thus far to note any similarities and to share anything their individual captures might have missed. If necessary, they reversed the video to confirm an analytic insight or to clarify a disagreement about their findings. Their reflections in-between each 10-minute segment enabled them to shop-talk and come to a consensus about how the children interacted with adults. The exchange and development of ideas between two researchers—**dyadic analysis**—was richer than either of them could have generated on their own (Saldaña, 2016, p. 63).

The analytic methods for video are actually quite comparable to Chapter 2's recommendations for analyzing field sites. The advantage with video recording is the ability to view and scrutinize the nuances and details of short, social moments repeatedly for **microanalysis**. Heath, Hindmarsh, and Luff (2010) offer exceptional guidance for video in qualitative research. They promote collaborative viewing with participants, colleagues, and stakeholders to better guarantee the trustworthiness of observations and thus findings. The methodologists support an analytic inductive approach that favors "the ways in which social action and interaction involve the interplay of talk, visible and material conduct" (p. 9). Paulus et al. (2014) also offer state-of-the-art technological guidance in *Digital Tools for Qualitative Research*. Altheide and Schneider (2013) and Berger (2012) provide recommendations for analyzing commercial broadcast videos such as newscasts and fictional works like dramas and situation comedies.

In a way, researchers' video analysis is comparable to a video camera/player's functions. Their eyes can zoom in and out to capture the big picture as well as the small details. When necessary, they can freeze the frame, play a portion in slow motion, or loop a section to replay continuously in order to scrutinize the details of social action. Their written analysis of video is like the translation subtitles or DVD soundtrack commentary that accompanies the original footage.

Analyzing evocation

Since visual analysis is a tacit, intuitive process, researchers should place analytic emphasis on what is first evoked within them as they look at an object or image. Subjective first impressions are documented in writing to note their initial interpretive read. For example, we reviewed a weight-loss workbook (Cigna, 2012) quickly to get a general idea of its contents. When we examined the document, our eyes naturally gravitated toward the full color images included throughout (see Figures 3.4 and 3.5 for comparable photos from other noncopyrighted sources). We jotted down the thoughts and emotions first evoked within us:

Figure 3.4   A representational image from a weight-loss workbook. (Photo by Matt Omasta.)

Figure 3.5   A representational image from a weight-loss workbook. (Photo by Matt Omasta.)

Positive, upbeat, happy people! The goal is to make the reader think that weight loss, eating right, and exercise are fun. There's no pain, no dread, just people of all ages and all ethnicities leading happy, healthy, fulfilling lives.

Next we conducted more-careful and more-systematic reviews of the photographs to assess the legitimacy of those first impression jottings. A simple content (counting) analysis reveals that

> 51 full photographs of people and/or food images appear throughout the 82-page document. Of these 51 photographs, 15 feature people exercising (running, bike riding, swimming, etc.), and 14 exhibit people interacting with food in some way (preparing, eating, shopping, etc.). Of these 29 photos with people, 3 of them show either a neutral face or faces not in view of the camera. That leaves 26 photos (50% total) of people in various poses of exercising or eating—and all of them with smiles on their faces or in mid-laughter. No one appears exceptionally obese or physically strained, and no perspiration appears on the skin or clothing of those

exercising. Five ethnic groups of people are included (White, Hispanic, Asian, Black, and one ethnicity we are unable to identify), ranging in age from young children to the elderly with an equal balance of males and females. The photos are professional, posed model shots, not captures of everyday people doing everyday things. The photo credit at the end of the document states: "All models are used for illustrative purposes only."

After this basic content analysis, we conducted a discourse analysis—that is, a more-interpretive and more-critical read of the latent contents after we have examined the manifest contents. This again is a reverberative act—returning to the initial jottings, photos, and content notes for additional reflection on what is evoked, and how and why:

> The goal of the weight loss workbook is to inform and persuade its readers to live a healthier lifestyle through proper diet and exercise. The discourse of the photos suggests that, no matter what your age, gender, or ethnicity, exercise can be a pleasurable activity that leads to happiness. But the reality—for many if not most people—that exercise can be a physically demanding activity which makes some individuals grimace in pain or strain, is missing from the photographs. (When was the last time we saw anyone smile as he did push-ups? The workbook cover features this image.) Such negative imagery can dissuade sedentary readers from giving exercise a try. Thus, through positive reinforcement, the photos subliminally suggest that various forms of physical activity are not effortful but enjoyable. (And they can be for the physically fit, but those people are not the workbook's targeted readership.) The workbook smartly notes in large type: "Although increasing your physical activity will require hard work and dedication, the benefits you gain will far outweigh the amount of effort you put in."

More systematic methods for photographic analysis are available. But for visual images that supplement or accompany primarily narrative texts, we believe that open-ended interpretations of photographs and illustrations are most appropriate.

The Routines, Rituals, Rules, Roles, and Relationships in Documents, Artifacts, and Visual Materials

There is action when a person or organization creates a product, as well as action that emerges from someone who reads, handles, or views the product. That person also reacts to the product as she interacts with it. Analyzing how the five Rs work through documents, artifacts, and visual materials still comes into play, because the principles are applicable not just to people but also to things in the social world.

Some documents are created to establish relationships with their readers. The weight-loss workbook is intended as a user-friendly product to break the user of bad routines and to establish new, healthier ones. It even attempts to generate new exercise rituals such as walking or running. The weight-loss workbook expresses rules through what to eat and what not to consume. The reader assumes that the document (created by people with special knowledge) plays an authoritative role as expert in health, fitness, and well-being.

Many routines and rituals employ necessary artifacts for their completion. Some material products, like surgical equipment, should only be used (a rule) by those in certain roles, such as health-care professionals. Every video watched has an audience of some kind—a relationship between media and a viewer. The five Rs are woven throughout analyses of documents, artifacts, and visual materials. Integrating them into an examination of attention, belonging, or evocation enriches insights regarding the things humans make, buy, and use on a regular basis.

A current analytic theme in some academic circles is consumption—that is, critical analysis of the excessive material production of first-world cultures and the obsessive drives for purchase and ownership found in people from those cultures. Visualize the blocks-long lines of customers waiting outside big box stores the day after Thanksgiving, and crowds of holiday shoppers in malls the week before Christmas, and the notion of consumption is clear. Think of how documents such as sales coupons, the artifacts of gifts in display windows, and the barrage of seasonal television advertising inundates and motivates a populace to buy. The discourse of consumption is a fascinating lens, filter, and angle to examine how the five Rs play out with material products and media.

CLOSURE AND TRANSITION _____

Keep in mind that the analytic frames described above are interchangeable. Analyzing attention and identity are not just limited to documents—they can also be applied to artifacts and photographs, just as analyzing symbolism and process can be applied to documents and video. We have not directly addressed the forms of visual representation and presentation of data that are more creative and arts-based, such as participant-created collages and photovoice (Butler-Kisber, 2010; Knowles & Cole, 2008), but these too can be analyzed with several of the methods profiled above.

In the next two chapters, we focus on the data collection method used most frequently for qualitative research: interviewing participants and analyzing transcripts.

RESOURCES FOR ANALYZING DOCUMENTS, ARTIFACTS, AND VISUAL MATERIALS

The following resources will offer you additional guidance for methods of analyzing documents, artifacts, and visual materials:

Altheide, David L., and Christopher J. Schneider. (2013). *Qualitative Media Analysis*, 2nd edition. Thousand Oaks, CA: Sage.

Berger, Arthur Asa. (2012). *Media Analysis Techniques*, 4th edition. Thousand Oaks, CA: Sage.

Berger, Arthur Asa. (2014). *What Objects Mean: An Introduction to Material Culture*, 2nd edition. Walnut Creek, CA: Left Coast Press.

Heath, Christian, Jon Hindmarsh, and Paul Luff. (2010). *Video in Qualitative Research: Analysing Social Interaction in Everyday Life*. London: Sage.

Kozinets, Robert V. (2015). *Netnography: Redefined*, 2nd edition. London: Sage.

Pink, Sarah, Heather Horst, John Postill, Larissa Hjorth, Tania Lewis, and Jo Tacchi. (2016). *Digital Ethnography: Principles and Practice*. London: Sage.

ANALYTIC EXERCISES FOR DOCUMENTS, ARTIFACTS, AND VISUAL MATERIALS

1. Access the Internet home page of a major national commercial retailer. Analyze the home page's contents (texts, images, layout) for its attention-getting strategies.

2. Read a day's Letters to the Editor section of a local newspaper. Describe the values systems of respondents based on how they address various issues and your interpretation of their language.

3. Select an artifact from your own living space that has personal meaning to you. Anthropomorphize it to compose a brief monologic account from the point of view of the artifact.

4. Go through the artifacts contained in a kitchen or bathroom. Select a few manufactured objects and speculate how they are extensions of the human body.

5. If you belong to a social media site, scroll through a day's posts and content analyze the visual images uploaded by your friends. Also examine the discourse of selected memes.

6. Brainstorm a list of what some people collect (e.g., baseball cards, coins, refrigerator magnets). Discuss with a peer why humans maintain collections of artifacts.

7. Read and examine a personal legal document of some kind (e.g., birth certificate, passport, rental agreement, terms of service, etc.). Reflect on the routines, rituals, rules, roles, and relationships suggested by the document.

SAMPLE PHOTOGRAPH

Figure 3.6 shows two university students engaged in conversation in a lounge. Review and analyze the image for its manifest and latent contents using one of more of the methods discussed in this chapter.

Figure 3.6 Two university students engaged in conversation in a lounge. (Photo by Matt Omasta.)

CHAPTER 4

Analyzing Interviews: Preparing, Conducting, and Transcribing

Introduction

Chapters 2 and 3 discussed how qualitative researchers analyze field sites, documents, artifacts, and visual materials to infer information about people. Perhaps the most commonly used method for qualitative inquiry, however, is the **interview**. During an interview, a researcher asks participants directly about their personal experiences related to the study's topic; their values, attitudes, and beliefs; their knowledge or understanding of various topics; or any other matters pertinent to the study. While researchers must continuously engage in analysis during and after an interview, the researcher's role changes because participants are able to answer questions explicitly. Of course, participants might not always answer questions directly or honestly, but during interviews researchers need not rely entirely on inference making. On the other hand, because they are actively engaged in conversations with their participants, researchers must exercise different skill sets such as understanding appropriate interview protocols, maintaining the conversation, and constantly analyzing responses in order to determine what question would be most appropriate to ask next.

Types of Interviews

Almost any interaction in which a researcher and participant engage in conversation or a dialogic series of questions and answers can be considered an interview, whether the interview takes place in person, over the phone, through an online video chat program such as Skype, or by other means. Most interviews

Learning Objectives

After reading and reviewing this chapter, researchers should be able to

1. Compare different types of interviews and evaluate which is most appropriate for a given research study,

2. Describe qualitative sampling methods, including procedures for selecting the type and number of participants appropriate for a particular study,

3. Devise interview protocols, and

4. Conduct and transcribe semi-structured interviews.

are conducted live, although some take place **asynchronously** (e.g., through e-mail exchanges). A significant advantage to live interviews is that they permit the researcher to analyze responses as participants speak and, in many types of interviews, permit the researcher to ask follow-up questions, change the course of inquiry, or otherwise steer the conversation in ways that can potentially generate richer responses from participants.

Some participants might prefer e-mail interviews since that medium allows them to fully process a question, think about their answers, type them up, revise them if they don't accurately reflect their views, and then send them to the researcher. In such cases follow-up questions might be possible, though in general respondents do not want to engage in lengthy e-mail correspondence, which limits researchers' abilities to fully explore a topic. Yet e-mail interviews can save the researcher a great deal of time.

In all types of interviews, researchers must be aware of how power dynamics affect an interview. The researchers and participants might come from different backgrounds in terms of gender, sexual orientation, race/ethnicity, socioeconomic status, and so on. While it may not be possible to change this, researchers should be aware that interpersonal dynamics will likely affect any type of interview; we encourage researchers to make efforts to create as equitable a relationship as possible.

We now discuss four general forms and approaches to interviews, colloquially described in qualitative inquiry as "conversations with a purpose."

Surveys and structured interviews

Not all interviews employ qualitative research methods. One of the most basic types of interview is a **survey**, a highly structured interaction in which researchers pose a predetermined series of either close-ended or open-ended short response questions that do not vary between participants. The usual goal of such surveys is to gather data for quantitative analysis. Political polls are excellent examples of surveys, and can pose either close- or open-ended questions. For example, a pollster might ask, "Which of the following issues matters most to you as you consider who you will vote for in the upcoming election: the economy, education, the environment, military conflicts, or tax rates?" In this case, the respondent has only five options from which to select, which the pollster records, then enters into a data base for statistical analysis. Many mixed-methods studies today combine qualitative and quantitative components. Qualitative interviews do not, however, generally include or consist of close-ended questions.

A very similar type of interview does include a qualitative component when questions are open-ended. For example, the pollster could ask a slightly modified version of the question above: "What issue matters most to you as you consider who you will vote for in the upcoming election?" In this case, the participant would need to generate her own response, and while she might give a simple answer such as "the environment," she might also say, "That's a tough question, and I'm not sure how to answer. I mean, as a mother I obviously care about the quality of my kids' education, but at the same time I'm very upset about the war taking place in the Middle East, and it's hard needing to do more with less money these days."

In this case, the pollster/researcher would need to code the respondent's answer, perhaps using Values Coding (discussed in Chapter 5), to condense the data into what is most salient. The researcher might easily determine that the data can be coded or summarized with the terms *education* and *military conflicts* (answers to the close-ended version of the question), but the last part of the response is trickier. "It's hard needing to do more with less money these days" could mean several things: the respondent could be referring to the economy in general but might be referring to taxes if they had recently increased, or she could be referring to a personal situation such as the loss of a job and income. Thus, while this type of survey does employ the qualitative method of coding, it is problematic in that it does not always present the researcher with a clear picture of the participant's values, attitudes, and beliefs. Because the survey questions are predetermined and unchanging between participants, the pollster cannot go back and ask for more detail or nuance but must systematically proceed to the next question.

Figure 4.1 Surveys generally pose prestructured, close-ended questions to participants.

©iStockphoto.com/pink_cotton_candy

Semi-structured interviews

One of the most commonly used methods in qualitative inquiry is the **semi-structured interview**, and this chapter focuses on this type. As the name implies, these interviews have a degree of structure but also offer researchers significant latitude to adjust course as needed; researchers make such adjustments as a result of their in-interview analysis. To analyze during an interview means to attend carefully to both the participants' answers (or nonanswers) and other indicators such as vocal tone and body language.

When preparing for semi-structured interviews, researchers should develop a complete, detailed list of questions that covers all the topics they wish to discuss with the participant. The questions should be presented in a coherent, logical order that will help the participant naturally move from one question to the next. It is often wise to begin with simpler questions to orient the participant to the interview and build rapport with the interviewer before delving into detailed, complex, or sensitive questions. In cases where the interviewer is unable to predict particular respondents' answers, but the answers will necessarily redirect the flow of the interview, he or she can prepare multiple sets of follow-up questions to ask depending on any given participant's response. Special forms of semi-structured interviewing such as **oral history** require that questions focus on soliciting certain types of responses such as personal, lived experiences with period details in structures such as story-based, historic narratives.

In other cases, a respondent might say something that sparks a new line of inquiry in the researcher's mind. When this occurs the researcher should analyze whether it would be worthwhile to develop a new set of questions during the interview to follow up on this new idea, or if the overall study would be best served by sticking to the line of inquiry determined in advance. In all cases, researchers must be active listeners and co-participants in the process, as opposed to structured interviewers who simply ask a question, record the response, and move on to the next question regardless of the participant's response.

Unstructured interviews

Sometimes the most useful way to collect data from a participant is to enter into an informal conversation with her with little structure at all beyond the general scope of inquiry. This approach might be appropriate when researchers are just beginning to explore a topic about which they have little knowledge, perhaps because only insiders to a particular group or culture are familiar with it. A researcher might begin a study with **unstructured interviews** to gain rapport by offering participants greater control over the topics discussed to see what the participants are interested in discussing that could inform other aspects of the study.

Saldaña conducted multiple, brief, unstructured interviews during his fieldwork in a middle school. There were five minutes of time between classes when students moved from one classroom to the next. During that time, he asked the teacher he observed two or three short questions related to the class he had just seen (e.g., "How do you think the class went?" "Michael seemed out of sorts today. Is something going on with him?" "Did the students accomplish what you wanted them to?"). All of these responses were documented in his field notes as moments of unstructured interview data for later reflection and analysis. Some researchers nowadays use text messaging, Yik Yak, and other social media with participants for brief, spontaneous electronic conversations as unstructured micro-interview data.

When conducting unstructured interviews, researchers sometime begin with little more than, "Please tell me about . . . ." Their goal thereafter is to listen carefully to what the participant has to say. The researcher could ask clarifying questions, ask the participant to share more about a particular topic, or perhaps ask him to explore tangential topics. But while the researcher's goal is always primarily to listen, that goal is especially important during unstructured interviews.

Focus groups

Focus groups were originally designed by marketing researchers to assess consumers' preferences and habits. The group interview method has expanded over time to include adolescents, women's support groups, teachers, and other populations to address topics ranging from job satisfaction to politics to social issues. Focus groups require an expert facilitator to manage the quickly shifting conversations among a number of people in one room and to ensure equitable contributions from all participants. It is an intriguing approach to research that illustrates how people in conversational interactions exchange and build on each other's ideas. Focus groups are not meant as time-efficient methods for data collection but rather as forums for multiple voices and perspectives to be discussed and shared.

Sometimes it is beneficial to interview a group of participants at the same time in a setting where they can hear each other's responses and engage in conversation, rather than strictly responding to the question posed by the interviewer. This approach can be particularly useful when a researcher wants to analyze the dynamics of a group to see how it functions as a whole, rather than the responses of group members in isolation. While individual semi-structured interviews can allow respondents to talk about how they perceive the group to function, a focus group allows researchers to witness for themselves how the group interacts, at least in the context of the focus group itself.

Focus groups, ranging from as few as 2 to as many as 12 participants, also potentially help individual respondents remember things that they might not have alone. For example, one group member might tell a story about a particular event, which prompts several other group members to recall their own experiences about the event. Similarly, one group member might recall particular details about a topic of inquiry that others affirm or refute. A group member might even change her response, realizing it did not align with what happened, based on information provided by the others.

Of course, this also points to a problem with focus groups. There are times when group members change their responses—not because someone triggered a memory, but rather because they desire to conform or be seen as part of the group. Imbalances in social power in a group can also lead participants to provide less-than-authentic responses. Sometimes these power imbalances are obvious and a researcher can easily analyze the group's composition to identify the problem and change it. For example, if a group is going to discuss the quality of a particular workplace, it would be unwise to have five workers as well as their immediate supervisor in the same group. Other times the researcher might be unable to predict group dynamics. If the supervisor is removed from the group above, one person might still be more popular and therefore have more social capital in the group, swaying others to follow her lead. At times this can be desirable if the researcher is studying how workers act in the presence of their supervisor or an influential peer. But in any case, researchers need to pay close attention to how the participants interact, analyze those interactions, and adjust the interview if necessary.

Figure 4.2 Focus groups require an expert facilitator to manage quickly shifting conversations and equitable contributions from all participants.

©iStockphoto.com/Stuart Jenner

Participant Selection

All studies are unique and require varying numbers of different types of participants from different populations; there are no universal rules that apply to all studies. Before beginning the participant selection process, researchers should ask themselves, "In order to explore my research question, do I need to interview anyone at all?" While most qualitative studies involve interviews, not all do or should. Bringing live participants into a study complicates it on many levels, so although interviews are a powerful method, they should be used only if they will genuinely advance inquiry, not simply because most qualitative studies include them.

If a study does indeed require interviews in order to gain insights from participants firsthand, researchers must consider whose perspectives would be most valuable to ascertain (both in terms of particular populations and specific individuals within them), how those people will be selected, and how many people should be interviewed in order to gain a complete picture of the experiences being analyzed.

Sampling methods

Once researchers have determined that they need to interview individuals for their study, they must next identify who those individuals will be. These people are referred to as the **sample** of participants—the person or group of people who will contribute to the study. While they are often drawn from different segments of society and therefore possibly espouse values, attitudes, and beliefs similar to those of others from that segment, they are not necessarily representative of that segment in the sense traditionally used in quantitative research. Researchers cannot conclusively determine that their perspectives are indeed shared by others. It is important to note that **sampling**, the parameters and procedures used for selecting the specific participants for a study, in qualitative research is quite different from procedures used in quantitative research in general: the methods of each methodology are unique to the paradigm. Furthermore, the sample of participants might evolve over the course of a study as researchers realize they need additional participants to provide new perspectives to confirm or disconfirm developing assertions or theories.

Before selecting a sample, researchers should consider if they will be selecting participants from a single site, or if their study would benefit from interviewing and analyzing data collected from multiple locations. When all participants are drawn from a single site, researchers conduct **within-case sampling**. This can be conducted whether the sample is limited to a single person or to a single group, such as a member of a particular baseball team or nurses working a particular shift in a particular unit of a particular hospital. In general, when working with a small number of participants it is wise to interview them multiple times at different points as determined by the research questions.

Studies can sometimes be made more robust by employing **multi-case sampling**, which allows researchers to analyze whether particular findings hold true only at a particular site or more broadly. Multi-case approaches to the example above might include interviewing players from multiple baseball teams, from players of different sports, or nonplayers including managers, coaches, fans, or even stadium custodial staff, depending on the specific research question. The study of nurses could include nurses from different shifts, different units within the hospital, multiple hospitals, or different nursing specialties (e.g., hospice, geriatric, oncology). In all cases, the decision about which approach is best is driven by the research question, not by any particular gold standard. Researchers must therefore constantly analyze their study's questions, the data they hope to obtain, and (later in the study) the data they have already collected in order to determine the best approach to sampling for the given study.

The easiest but most problematic sampling method is **convenience sampling**. As the name implies, this involves selecting participants with whom researchers have easy access. For example, those working or studying in university settings often find it relatively easy to form samples of students, given the large number of them present within a geographically bounded area. But convenience samples can be problematic due to a number of factors. They are sometimes relatively homogenous (i.e., not diverse), and they often have direct or indirect relationships to the researchers. A study exploring Americans' perceptions of religious issues could be quite biased if all the individuals interviewed were roughly between the ages of 18 to 24 and living in the same location with a shared academic affiliation. It is highly unlikely that a sample composed of such individuals would represent the broader American population. Furthermore, students participating because they know the researcher (student or professor), or will receive extra credit, might alter their responses based on these dynamics.

Most qualitative research employs **purposive sampling**, in which participants are deliberately selected because they are most likely to provide insight into the phenomenon being investigated due to their position, experience, and/or identity markers (e.g., demographics such as gender, race/ethnicity, health status). These participants might be known to researchers or their colleagues in advance, or they might be recruited. Researchers might recruit participants by approaching an organization constituted by the types of people required for the study. For example, researchers conducting a study exploring care for the elderly sometimes approach retirement communities to see if they would assist in finding participants. In some cases, there is no organization where potential participants would meet; in such cases researchers might even advertise for participants that meet certain criteria. Researchers hoping to investigate certain populations, especially those that are otherwise difficult to locate, might employ **snowball sampling**, a method in which participants are asked to recommend other similar participants to take part in the study in order to gain a larger pool of participants than the researcher originally had access to.

Miles, Huberman, and Saldaña (2014) describe how purposeful selection requires researchers to establish both boundaries and conceptual frames in order to purposively select participants effectively. **Boundaries** physically limit a project's scope of inquiry—for example, the amount of time available to conduct a study, access to the population being analyzed, and limits to the geographic area a researcher can travel to. While boundaries are concerned primarily with physical limitations, **conceptual frames** help researchers "uncover, confirm, or qualify the basic processes or constructs that undergird" their studies (Miles et al., 2014, p. 31). An example of a conceptual frame is a study on a phenomenon such as gratitude. It is not specific types of people who must be sought to participate, but rather an array of people who can speak to the concept under investigation.

A specific type of purposive sampling is **theoretical sampling**, often employed later in a qualitative study and based on the theory that has been developed to date; it is particularly useful in the development of grounded theory. Marshall (1996) notes, "Theoretical sampling necessitates building interpretative theories from the emerging data and selecting a new sample to examine and elaborate on this theory" (p. 523). With this type of sampling, researchers are seeking participants they hope will be able to confirm (or disconfirm) the patterns that have emerged from the data to that point.

Additional sampling methods will be discussed in Chapter 7.

Number of interviews

A number of insightful, well-regarded qualitative studies involve only a single participant; others involve hundreds. The number of participants and the number of interviews per interviewee required for a study depends on its research question. Consider the following possible research questions for studies related to homelessness; each one would potentially benefit from different numbers and types of participants:

1. How does a person without a home survive the harsh winters of New York City?

2. What factors do people without homes in New York City believe contribute to their circumstances?

3. How do residents of New York City regard those living without homes?

A researcher exploring the first question above could potentially generate rich data by interviewing a single participant living without a home in New York City. The researcher would likely interview the participant multiple times throughout the year (assuming the researcher could locate him) and use a number of other qualitative analytic methods such as those described in the previous chapters. A final report that synthesized material from interviews along with detailed field notes from the researcher's observations of the participant's daily activities and analysis of artifacts from the participant and the environment could effectively speak to the research question.

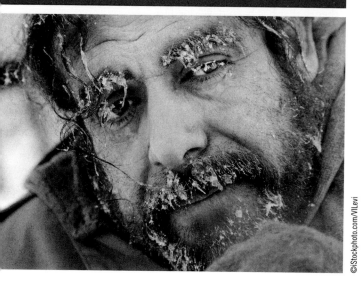

Figure 4.3   How does a person without a home survive the harsh winters of New York City?

©iStockphoto.com/ViLevi

This approach would not be appropriate, however, for an investigator exploring the second research question ("What factors do people without homes in New York City believe contribute to their circumstances?"). While a single participant could give one view on the circumstances that led to her living without a home, it would be irresponsible to assume that her views reflected those of all other people in comparable situations. Tackling the second research question would require interviewing a larger number of people.

There are several things to consider when determining the most appropriate number of participants required. The first is the principle of **triangulation**, which involves considering data from at least three different sources to help ensure more dimension to the data. This might mean interviewing three separate individuals about a phenomenon, interviewing one person at three points in time, comparing interviews with other empirical materials such as field notes, documents, and so on. Researchers could analyze data from these various sources to determine whether any patterns or themes emerge consistently across them. Assuming that the three participants were independent (did not know each other, lived in different areas, etc.), researchers could possibly make warranted assertions about the research question if the participants' responses harmonized.

Similarly, researchers could identify ways in which participants' views diverged. Either way, it would be wise for researchers to consider interviewing additional participants if their goal was to answer a question intended to gain the perspectives of a large group, as the second research question suggests. Researchers might continue interviewing additional participants until they reached data saturation—the point at which additional data do not contribute any additional learnings. Saturation generally happens when the researcher has determined what major trends appear in the data, and each new interviewee simply continues to affirm the already established salient findings.

The second question raises another point: not all research questions are best handled through qualitative approaches alone. While clearly much could be learned from interviews as described above, researchers using this approach alone could not claim that their data were generalizable or transferable to other contexts. **Generalizability** is a term from quantitative research that refers to the assumption that the findings from a particular group of study participants can be generalized to the entire population the participants represent. That is, provided that a quantitative study is appropriately designed, if 75% of participants in the study hold a particular belief, 75% of the larger population should also hold that same belief (plus or minus a certain percentage).

Qualitative research cannot be generalized in this fashion because it does not follow the sampling procedures of quantitative research such as the random selection of participants. So even if qualitative researchers investigating the second question found that every person they interviewed believed the most significant factor contributing to their situation was the mayor's apathy about their plight, the researchers could not claim that this finding was generalizable. To do so would be to claim that each and every person without a home in New York City believed the mayor's apathy was the most significant contributing factor. Since it is highly unlikely that this is true, and since the qualitative study would be employing quantitative terminology, most readers would find the study suspect. The findings from the qualitative study could, however, serve as the basis for a larger mixed-methods study.

The third research question ("How do residents of New York City regard those living without homes?") also calls for multiple participants because it asks what views people in New York City hold about people living without homes. This question requires that a variety of people be interviewed. While the participants in question two (people without homes) would likely be interviewed for the third research project as well, it would be inappropriate to interview these participants exclusively because they represent only one segment of the New York City population. Researchers pursuing question three would likely want to know what people living with homes and particular groups within that category think about those living without homes.

Figure 4.4   Researchers must analyze how the physical space might affect the participant or interview.

©iStockphoto.com/JackF

To answer this question, purposive and theoretical sampling approaches would be critical. For example, in addition to people living without homes, researchers would want to identify and purposefully select a variety of types of people with homes, most likely from a variety of socioeconomic, political, and religious backgrounds. In addition, there might be specific individuals that researchers logically determine should be interviewed (e.g., the director of the city's housing authority, leaders of both secular and religious organizations operating food banks, legal clinics or other social services for people without homes, or representatives from the police department). After conducting many interviews and analyzing the data, the researchers might determine they had reached a point of data saturation, or they might realize they need to conduct additional interviews, in which case they would likely employ theoretical sampling, seeking out specific individuals to confirm or disconfirm their theories in progress.

Interview Preparation, Scheduling, and Arrangements

Once participants for a study have been identified, researchers must attend to logistical matters such as determining where the interview will take place and how interviews will be scheduled. Researchers must analyze how the physical space might affect the participant or interview. For example, conducting an interview at a coffee shop might make sense in many ways due to its convenience and relaxed atmosphere, but there is likely to be quite a bit of ambient noise that will make transcription more difficult. A quiet location is ideal.

It is rare to find a neutral space; nearly any site selected will have connotations for the interviewer and participant. For example, a study might be exploring a work-release program for prison inmates who are allowed to leave the prison several days a week to work a job, but must return to the prison each weekend until they have served their sentences. Researchers could schedule interviews with the inmate participants at several places: in the prison itself, at their workplace during a lunch hour, at the researcher's university, at the participant's home, and so on. Participants will likely feel different levels of comfort in the various settings, and this could very well affect their responses. Unfortunately, researchers can never know with certainty how different contexts will affect the participant, and should be careful about making assumptions. While researchers might speculate that a participant would feel far more comfortable in her home than in the prison, the opposite would be true if the inmate is embarrassed to be with her family in light of the situation. Furthermore, whereas a university conference room seems like it would be a neutral setting, the sterile, unfamiliar environment might have status connotations the researcher did not anticipate.

Given these complications, researchers have several options. They might interview a variety of participants in a variety of settings, or a single participant in multiple settings, and then reflect on how their responses changed (or not) based on context. In some cases, researchers will not have a choice at all: for example, prison officials might require that the interviews take place at the physical institution as part of their agreement to participate. Other times, researchers can try to schedule interviews in the most convenient place for the participant as a courtesy or even to secure their agreement to participate. In a study Omasta conducted regarding an educational theatre program based in Washington, DC, but with partnerships in surrounding states, he conducted numerous interviews at the theatre itself with staff and young people in the program, but also traveled to schools and district office buildings throughout the region to ensure school officials could be included, since many of these individuals could not leave their schools or offices during the workday. Regardless of where an interview takes place, researchers should note in their final reports any impacts they suspect the venue might have had on the interview.

When scheduling interviews, researchers should be as organized and respectful of their participants' time as possible. Based on what researchers know about their participants, they must determine when they are likely to be available, how much time they can likely give to the project, and how the researchers' schedules can accommodate multiple interviews, possibly over an extended period of time.

In general, researchers should schedule interviews at times that are most convenient for participants, even if those times are less convenient for the researchers. Participants in many qualitative studies are uncompensated, and making the process as easy for them as possible might motivate them to be more helpful during the interview itself. When a large number of participants need to be scheduled, it can be useful for the researcher to create a grid of all open times in advance; the researcher can tell participants what times are available so they can pick a convenient time. There are also a number of free online tools such as Doodle (www.doodle.com) or Fasterplan (www.fasterplan.com) that can be used for this purpose that researchers should consider using when scheduling interviews with a number of participants.

In cases when participants are interviewed over time, researchers should consider the relevant benchmarks in the participants' lives and schedule interviews accordingly. For example, in the study investigating how a person without a home can survive harsh winters in New York City, it would be prudent to schedule initial interviews before the winter to learn what the participant has done in the past and/or plans to do in the future, several times during the winter, and again in the spring (assuming, of course, that the unhoused person can be located across this time span). These interviews would likely be combined with other analytic tools such as participant observation and artifact analysis as the researcher follows the participant over time.

As for the proper length of an interview, there are no fixed guidelines, though most researchers indicate that their time with adults ranged from 60 to 90 minutes per session. Very young children can be interviewed for 15 minutes in one sitting, with older children in 30-minute time blocks and adolescents from 30 to 60 minutes in length. The length of the interview should be negotiated between the researcher and participant to provide a comfortable block of time for data collection while respecting the participant's personal schedule.

Audio- and video-recording equipment

Whenever possible, it is advisable to record interviews so there is a tangible record of the discussion that researchers can refer back to in case they have questions about what was said. Recordings are a solid form of evidence for the qualitative data base but should not serve as a replacement for the researcher's note-taking. Writing down key points as participants say them, along with analytic jottings and ideas for new questions, is critical throughout the process and can help keep researchers engaged. It is also possible for a digital recording to fail, so researchers might unexpectedly need to rely on their notes.

Figure 4.5   Researchers take measures to ensure participant anonymity and confidentiality of information.

©iStockphoto.com/ryasick

Today's technology provides a variety of accessible hardware and software tools for audio and video recording. Cell phones, iPads, and laptops are usually equipped with recording programs. Skype video interviews can also be recorded, and **synchronous** online interview chats can be downloaded and printed for analysis. We strongly advise that interviewers test all equipment or Internet connections before the interview to ensure a successful recording, and to have sufficient power charges or electrical access for hardware.

For one-on-one interviews, audio recording is generally sufficient and less obtrusive. While many participants probably anticipate a small audio recorder, some might be put off by a video camera in the room. However, if analysis of a participant's nonverbal communication is important, video recording the interview is vital so that the researcher can analyze body language and facial expressions later. Video recording is particularly helpful with focus groups, as this makes it much easier to identify who is speaking at any given time. While focus groups might be audio recorded only, there is a distinct possibility that the researcher or other transcribers will misattribute quotes during the transcription process.

Asking Questions

A key component of well-designed interview-based qualitative studies is the **interview protocol**. More than a list of questions, this document guides interviewers (whether they be principal investigators for a project or research associates hired to assist with interviewing) through all stages of their interaction with the participant from the moment they meet until they part.

No two interview protocols will be the same because their content is highly dependent on the specific research questions a study investigates. The following section provides general guidelines for developing interview protocols including many of the elements frequently included in protocols, but they should not be considered prescriptive rules to be followed precisely in every study. We also provide a sample interview protocol that was used to administer an interview included at the end of Chapter 5.

Interview protocols

Interview protocols generally begin by the interviewer introducing herself to the participant, reviewing any **informed consent** or permissions paperwork required, answering any questions participants have, confirming the amount of time available for the interview, and ensuring they sign all the appropriate forms. If the participants' only interaction with the researcher takes place at the interview, the protocol itself should begin with a script for introducing the informed consent form, affirming important points such as the voluntary nature of their participation and requesting their signature if they wish to proceed. In some cases, including the example we introduce below, the participants will already have completed the informed consent paperwork at an earlier stage in their participation (e.g., when they complete a preinterview survey to provide basic information about themselves). In these cases, it is still wise for a protocol to remind the participants about some of the basics of the consent they gave, such as the voluntary nature of their responses.

Although the nature, number, and form of questions vary for each study, interview questions should always be grounded in the larger research question. Interview questions will often move from the general to the specific and, in semi-structured interviews that permit follow-up questions, they can sometimes go back and forth since specific questions follow up on the first general question before moving on to the second general question. Additional guidelines for crafting questions appear in the following section.

Galletta and Cross (2013) suggest a model for semi-structured interviews, particularly for collecting oral histories, comprising three segments. The opening segment "create[s] space for a narrative grounded in participant experience" (p. 47), the middle segment explores "questions of greater specificity" (p. 49), and the concluding segment "revisit[s] the opening narrative, important theoretical connections, and move[s] toward closure" (p. 51). While not all semi-structured interviews will follow this pattern, considering interviews as stories or narratives with beginnings, middles, and endings corresponding to the sections Galletta and Cross suggest can be a useful framework.

Most interview protocols usually contain the following at a minimum:

- An opening script
  - Introduce the interviewer and build rapport
  - Review informed consent materials
- A list of questions that should guide the conversation
  - Build from general to specific questions
- A concluding script

A sample interview protocol appears in Figure 4.6. Note the main sections of the protocol described above. This protocol was used for a case study concerning diabetes; the transcript of the full interview using this protocol is included at the end of Chapter 5. Compare the protocol to the transcript and note the ways in which the researcher followed and deviated from the protocol in response to the participants' answers and comments throughout the interview.

Figure 4.6 A researcher's interview protocol for people with diabetes.

DIABETES STUDY INTERVIEW PROTOCOL

STUDY RESEARCH QUESTION:

How do people with diabetes understand the condition, and how does it affect their lives?

Begin with the introductory script below, followed by the questions in the order presented. Be sure to familiarize yourself with all italicized directions before beginning the interview.

Hello, my name is (INTERVIEWER NAME). Thank you for taking the time to talk to me today. Before we begin, do you have any questions about the informed consent form that you completed earlier?

(Continued)

Figure 4.6 (Continued)

If the participant has questions, be sure to address them, using the actual form they signed to clarify. Once this is complete, or if they have no questions, continue.

To be sure that we have an accurate record of today's conversation, I am going to supplement my notes by audio-recording our interview, is this okay?

If the participant objects, explain that unfortunately you are unable to continue with the interview. If possible, have the Principal Investigator speak to the participant. If the participant is not willing to continue, thank her or him for their time and conclude the interview. If the participant agrees that the interview may be audio recorded, thank her or him and continue.

Today is (DATE/TIME), and I am speaking with (PARTICIPANT). I am going to be asking you a few general questions. If there is anything you do not feel comfortable answering or that you do not know the answer to, that is not a problem; just let me know, and we can skip that question.

1. In your own words, how would you describe diabetes to someone with no experience and limited knowledge of the condition?

   Consult the Pre-Interview Survey to determine the age at which the participant was diagnosed with diabetes. If the participant was diagnosed at age ten or earlier, ask question two and the corresponding follow-up questions. If they were diagnosed at age eleven or later, ask question three and the corresponding follow-up questions.

2. At what point do you recall learning about diabetes as you were growing up?

   a. What do you recall learning about the condition when you first learned about it?

   b. Do you remember learning different things about diabetes at different times in your life?

   c. From what sources did you learn about diabetes?

   d. Do you ever recall receiving conflicting information from different sources?

      If participant indicates "yes," ask:

      i. How did you decide what information was most accurate?

3. You indicated that you were diagnosed with diabetes at age *(see pre-interview survey)*.

   a. What do you recall (if anything) knowing about diabetes before you were diagnosed?

   b. How do you recall feeling and reacting when you were first diagnosed with diabetes? What questions did you have?

   c. What do you recall learning about diabetes shortly after you were diagnosed?

d. From what sources did you learn about diabetes?

e. Do you ever recall receiving conflicting information from different sources?

   If participant indicates "yes," ask:

   i. How did you decide what information was most accurate?

4. In your experience, how much do people who do not have diabetes understand about the condition?

5. What are some different ways that people react if they find out you have diabetes?

   a. *Possible prompts for follow-up:*

      i. How do you feel about these reactions?

      ii. How do you respond to these reactions?

6. In the time since you were diagnosed, are there any ways in which diabetes has affected the way you live your life?

   a. *Possible prompts for follow-up:*

      i. Have you experienced shifts in terms of how you feel, physically and/or emotionally?

      ii. Have there been any other tangible tasks that are part of your life that weren't before?

      iii. Have your interactions with others changed at all?

7. Do you imagine that your life would be significantly different if you didn't have diabetes, or do you think that it would be fairly similar?

   a. *Possible prompts for follow-up:*

      i. In what ways?

      ii. Why not?

8. Is there anything you think the general public does not know about diabetes, or living with diabetes, that they should?

9. Is there anything else you would like to share about diabetes?

   Thank you so much for taking the time to talk with me today. I and everyone on our research team really appreciate your help. If you have any questions in the future, please feel free to contact us using the information on the paperwork we gave you earlier. Thank you again!

Phrasing the inquiry

When designing research questions, researchers should consider what they want to know in terms of their larger research question, then analyze what is most important to learn from the specific participant(s) they will interview. Time is valuable and often limited, so researchers should consider what data they can obtain from other sources (e.g., a review of documents/artifacts, participant observation) before writing their questions. For example, in the case of the study regarding work-release prisoners, researchers might be able to gain detailed information about the participants' schedules by examining prison documents, or learn about the physical arrangement of an inmate's cell by visiting it in person. If so, it would not be particularly productive to ask questions such as "What is your schedule like, hour by hour?" or "Please describe the physical layout of the cell you occupy at the prison," unless a specific goal of the project was to examine the participants' actual perceptions of what could be considered to be factual information. This might be the goal of some studies, but if such data are only tangential to the primary research question, it is not worth spending limited time asking about topics that are interesting but potentially low yield in terms of useful data.

Once researchers have determined what type of data they wish to collect from interview participants, the next step is to actually compose the initial questions (though when using a semi-structured interview format, questions can evolve or be added/dropped throughout the course of any given interview). Although there is no one correct formula for developing interview questions, there are several guidelines that often help strengthen questions. To begin, all questions should stem from the overarching research question of the study. Most research questions are sufficiently broad so as to allow for a number of subquestions. Some of the overarching research questions might manifest as actual questions posed to participants, and many will simply be guiding frameworks that must be addressed through a series of questions with participants.

In most semi-structured interviews, the goal is to have participants share as much information as possible with minimal direction from the interviewer. As such, strong questions tend to be open ended so that participants can interpret the questions and share the ideas that come to their minds (e.g., "What were some of the questions you remember having when you first learned you had diabetes?"). Even if there are very specific things researchers want to inquire about within the context of a broader question, it might be best to hear if the participant addresses those issues on her own when the open-ended question is asked. It is always appropriate to compose potential follow-up questions that are more specific that researchers can use on an as-needed basis. There might be times when researchers can predict possible answers participants might offer and prepare two different questions that could be asked in response to participants' answers/situations. Some questions could also lend themselves to particular follow-up questions that might or might not be appropriate to ask, based on how a participant responds. These probes for further information can also be included in the interview protocol (see examples in Figure 4.6).

Questions should enable participants to speak comfortably, honestly, and freely about the topic of inquiry. To help ensure this, researchers should avoid two types of queries: leading questions, and questions to which there is an obviously desirable response. Questions of either nature heighten the potential for **social desirability bias** or **participant compliance**, which essentially means that participants tell researchers what they want to hear. Avoiding leading questions can be more difficult than it seems, especially because researchers (like all people) can be unaware of their own biases. Some leading questions are obvious while others are subtler. Consider the following questions that researchers might ask as part of a study assessing American citizens' views of international economics:

1. It is well established that the United States is the greatest contributor to the international economy. What are some of the main reasons you think this is the case?

2. Why is the United States the greatest contributor to the international economy?

3. What factors do you believe contribute most to the United States' leading role in the international economy?

4. What is your perception of the United States' role in the international economy?

The first question begins as a statement, followed by a prompt for participants to affirm it; this is not really a question at all. The second and third questions are subtler versions of the first. With either question, researchers will never know if the participant believes the positive things they say about the United States' role in the international economy, or if they are simply telling the researchers what they clearly want to hear. The final question differs significantly from the first three by asking respondents about their perceptions without suggesting that the researcher would prefer a particular response.

While not technically leading questions, other queries can easily result in social desirability bias when they ask participants about well-established social norms, especially in particular contexts. Social norms are always changing, sometimes quite swiftly. Before the summer of 2015, most politicians in the state of South Carolina (where the Confederate flag flew at the state capitol) vehemently rejected any notion of removing it, despite decades of protest by those who believed it symbolized racism. But within weeks of a mass-shooting at an African American church in which one of the victims was a state senator, several politicians who had expressed a steadfast belief that the flag must stay abruptly changed their minds. The South Carolina governor and prominent national leaders called for removal of the flag; after large majorities of both houses of the state legislature voted in favor of that proposal, the flag was removed. With that in mind, there can be times when researchers might benefit from asking questions that seem to have clear socially desirable responses, but they should exercise caution when doing so.

In many cases, researchers will be meeting participants for the first time at an interview, and for that reason it is important that questions are phrased professionally yet in a way that might help build rapport. As mentioned above, however, all researchers have biases, and that can sometimes affect the questions they ask and thus the data they collect in detrimental ways. Consider the following questions that all theoretically seek to gain the same information from a participant in the prison work-release study:

1. Given the terrible crimes you have committed, why do you think you are entitled to participate in the work-release program?

2. As a criminal, why do you think you deserve to participate in the work-release program?

3. Why do you believe you merited inclusion in the work-release program?

4. What factors do you believe played a role in your selection as a participant in the work-release program?

The researchers' bias against the inmate/participant is most blatant in the first question, which begins not with a question but with an attack ("Given the terrible crimes you have committed") and other baiting language such as "entitled." Such a question could cause a participant to end the interview immediately. Even if she did answer, any response she gave would be influenced by her knowledge that the researcher likely did not have her best interests in mind.

While the second question has a slightly less abrasive tone, it still begins with an attack ("as a criminal"), and the use of the term *deserve* could put a participant on the defensive. The third question might seem ideologically neutral but it retains a subtler, more-nuanced balance by employing the term *merited,* which might force the participant to defend her selection for inclusion in the program. The fourth question, while still about the individual participant's participation, shifts the focus from making her defend her selection to greater forces (the prison or other officials) by asking about "factors" and referencing her "selection," which is more-neutral language.

Maintaining the conversation

Once researchers have gone through the opening script of an interview protocol and asked the first question, their most important job is to listen attentively, constantly analyzing the data the participant provides and jotting notes as to how that will affect the interview moving forward. If something stated is unclear or confusing, write a note to ask a follow-up question. If the participant raises a point or idea that was unanticipated but pertinent to the research question, write a note to ask more about that.

Figure 4.7 The researcher guides the interview in a way that best serves the overall research question of the project.

©iStockphoto.com/Steve Debenport

Researchers also write personal impressions of what the participant is saying. What does she seem to value and what are her attitudes about it? Should you ask a follow-up question to further explore her beliefs about that topic? Does something a participant says eliminate the need to ask planned questions later in the interview? Does the participant seem to be answering the questions honestly? If not, why might she give a dishonest answer? Is there another question that you could ask to readdress the issue in a way the participant might be more open to answering? The main point is that a researcher's job is not simply to record the information given and move on (as in a structured interview/survey), but rather to analyze information as it is received and to guide the interview in a way that best serves the overall research question of the project.

One of the clearest and most concise sets of guidelines for interviewing was developed roughly a century ago by Elton Mayo, who examined issues related to the industrialization of workplaces and, as part of his project, interviewed workers. The enduring relevance of his guidelines warrants presenting them here:

1. Give your whole attention to the person interviewed, and make it evident that you are doing so.

2. Listen—don't talk.

3. Never argue; never give advice.

4. Listen to:

   a. What he wants to say.

   b. What he does not want to say.

   c. What he cannot say without help.

5. As you listen, . . . from time to time summarize what has been said and present for comment (e.g. "Is this what you are telling me?"). Always do this with the greatest caution, that is, clarify but do not add or distort.

6. Remember that everything said must be considered a personal confidence and not divulged to anyone. (Mayo, as cited in Brinkmann, 2013, p. 8)

These recommendations, of course, must be interpreted in light of the circumstances of any particular study. Mayo's sixth recommendation, for example, might or might not be relevant based on the informed consent arrangement between researchers and participants. As discussed earlier, there might be cases when it is acceptable to divulge what is said in an interview, but only if the participant fully understands and approves this ahead of time.

Nevertheless, these guidelines largely hold true. The first few are quite straightforward: actually listening to each participant is paramount, and demonstrating that you are checking in (by asking questions as suggested in Step 4, to simply nodding and making eye contact) will help participants feel that they are valued and that what they have to say matters. Participants are much more likely to go into detail and provide helpful information if they believe that it will actually be useful to others in some way.

When considering the things Mayo lists in Step 4, researchers must not only listen to the words participants speak, but also to places they hesitate, while simultaneously reading their body language. There are many things participants will share freely, but not everything: some topics are sensitive and controversial. Participants might not want to discuss these at all, in which case researchers must either decide to respect that and avoid the subject, or perhaps find a gentler way to approach the topic that the participant is comfortable with.

In terms of "what [the participant] cannot say without help," researchers must walk a careful line. It is never appropriate to ask a leading question or to directly prompt a participant (e.g., "It seems like you want to tell me about issues with your mother"), since this could lead the participant to simply agree (even if she wasn't trying to communicate what was suggested), or it could upset the participant if she thinks the researcher is pushing too far. On the other hand, restating something a participant has said and asking for clarification would be appropriate (e.g., "Earlier you said that the day with your mother did not end well. Would you feel comfortable telling me more about that?"). Morse (2012) cautions that research topics on health and illness quite often generate strong emotional responses from participants during interviews and crying is the norm, not the exception. Sensitive interviewers must be ready for any unanticipated emotional distress that arises from participants and offer sympathetic support without judgment.

In all cases, treat participants with respect, acknowledge their contributions, and analyze the ways in which the data they have shared with you informs your larger research question.

Transcribing

Once an interview or large number of interviews has been recorded, they must be transcribed or written out verbatim. While researchers could always consult an audio or video recording of an interview later in the research project, it is much faster to consult a written record of the interview in a searchable document than to locate the exact moment on a digital recording that a participant told a particular story or shared important data.

Basic documentation principles

To be of any value, a **transcript** must be accurate. Accidentally changing or omitting a single word can significantly alter the meaning of data that a participant provided. Consider the difference between "I do enjoy hunting" and "I don't enjoy hunting." Given that these sentences have exactly opposite meanings, it might seem that nobody would ever confuse them, but such errors happen more often than one might think. After all, "do" and "don't" are very similar, and a researcher trying to transcribe hundreds (or even just dozens) of hours of interviews could easily make this mistake. For this reason, we recommend that transcripts always be double-checked, preferably by a person other than the original transcriptionist. Time consuming as these tasks might be, they can save a great deal of headaches down the line and preserve the integrity of a study's data.

While the transcription process can be tedious, there are resources available to make the process easier and more efficient. Researchers who simply cannot afford the time to transcribe interviews themselves might be able to delegate this task to research assistants or, if they do not have access to assistants, they might be able to hire an outside firm to do the work for them. Numerous services are available through agencies online and, particularly in larger cities, in person. Depending on the amount of data researchers have to transcribe, outsourcing transcription can save days or even weeks of their time. The trade-offs for saved time, however, are usually money and (almost always) accuracy. Since most transcriptionists were not involved with conducting the interviews, they can lack the context to interpret certain complex data accurately; also, some external transcriptionists might be less invested in a project than researchers. Thus, while it is always important to verify transcript accuracy, this can be even more important when hiring others to assist with this portion of the project.

Fortunately for researchers transcribing their own interviews, technology has advanced the field far beyond the days of manually playing a tape recording, stopping it, typing up what was heard, and then restarting the tape. A simple Internet search will retrieve a few products that attempt to convert voice to text automatically such as iTalk, Google Docs (Tools/Voice Typing), and Dragon NaturallySpeaking (though the researcher must carefully monitor such transcription). While we do not recommend any particular software or other package, researchers should be able to find one that suits their needs with a bit of online research.

We strongly advise DIY (do-it-yourself) transcription. The researcher as the interviewer has firsthand knowledge of the interactions that occurred and the participant's demeanor, and ultimately holds the greatest investment in the project. By transcribing their own recordings, researchers initiate a deep cognitive understanding of every word spoken and gain embodied ownership of their data. The task can seem laborious: it can take three to five hours or more to transcribe a one-hour interview. But the payoff is rich and detailed awareness of the participant's experiences and perspectives for more-insightful analysis. Transcribing one's own interviews also permits a researcher to add "stage directions" that only she would be aware of (e.g., noting that a participant stared at the ground before answering a question, or looked about anxiously). These notes can be added to the transcript in italics to give those reading the transcript a better overall picture of what happened during an interview session.

A growing number of software programs attempt to automate the transcription process by detecting what people in a recording are saying and using voice recognition technology to produce a transcript, similar to the way that many smartphones now have digital assistants that process commands, transcribe dictated text messages, and so forth. These programs vary in terms of their reliability, but are growing more sophisticated with time. While such software might save time, we recommend that researchers transcribe their own data in order to reexperience and analyze it. Researchers using digital transcription should also very carefully review the work for errors, which can be common at this stage as technology continues to evolve.

Figure 4.8 By transcribing their own interviews, researchers initiate a deep cognitive understanding of their data.

©iStockphoto.com/edfuentesg

Topic summaries

As researchers transcribe interviews, it can be helpful for them to pause after each major section of the interview, or whenever the interview topic shifts substantively, to add a title that succinctly describes that portion of the interview (e.g., "Symptoms," "Diabetes Resources," "Counting Carbs"). Researchers can also add a few sentences further describing the content, especially if the interview segment is particularly long. This can both reinforce in the researcher's mind what major topics were discussed and allow her to reflect on the interview through the process of summarizing it. Eventually the interview will be condensed significantly, but topic summaries simply serve as brief descriptors of portions of narrative text. It is important to demarcate topic summaries by indenting them, setting them in the margins, using a different font, and so on, so that it is clear they were added after the fact and are not part of the actual interview.

CLOSURE AND TRANSITION

This chapter provided foundation content for preparing, conducting, and transcribing the qualitative semi-structured interview. The next chapter illustrates a full interview in analysis, in addition to other methods for analyzing participant responses. Bibliographic resources for interviewing and sample data are provided in Chapter 5.

ANALYTIC EXERCISES FOR INTERVIEWING

1. Generate a research question that could be explored through interviews with members of the general population (e.g., about relationships, technology, or politics), and draft an interview protocol that could be employed in the study.

2. Using the interview protocol you developed, conduct an audio-recorded 15- to 20-minute interview with a colleague, friend, or stranger, after first explaining that it is for a class project, that you will not be using the data for any research study, and that you will erase the recording once you are finished with the exercise.

3. Transcribe the interview you conducted for the previous exercise. As you do, write topic summaries and perhaps jottings or analytic memos.

4. Review your transcript from the exercise above for accuracy. Consider times you diverged from the interview protocol (if any) and how these deviations helped you further explore your research question. If they did not help you explore, think about how you got off topic and what you might do to avoid this in the future.

CHAPTER 5

Analyzing Interviews: Condensing and Coding

Introduction

Just as researchers analyze data as they are spoken during interviews, they also analyze data when they are transcribing. In fact, this is an ideal time for informal analysis because researchers are once again dealing with every word the participant spoke, but this time without the participant present, which allows time to study particular passages in depth. While formal analysis also takes place after transcribing, when researchers are steeped in the data as they both hear and type it, insights can arise that the researchers should note so they can return to it later. It is entirely appropriate to write jottings or analytic memos while transcribing, either in a separate document or even as OCs on the transcript itself. Such comments should usually be transferred to a separate document later in order to produce a clean transcript for review by other researchers or by the participants themselves if the researcher employs participant checks in which participants verify the accuracy of the transcript.

This chapter discusses two primary methods of interview transcript analysis: condensing and coding. We also provide a full interview transcript for reference and analytic exercises.

Interview Condensation

Unless the interviews are extremely short, there are usually too many data in an interview transcript to effectively use for analytic purposes. This is especially true with long interviews or even brief interviews with many participants. As such, following transcription and transcript verification most researchers begin the process of **interview condensation** to reduce the length of the

Learning Objectives

After reading and reviewing this chapter, researchers should be able to

1. Condense semi-structured interviews, and

2. Analyze interviews using multiple coding methods.

interview, usually to approximately one third of its original length, by focusing on the more salient data presented, eliminating extraneous and tangential comments unrelated to the research questions of interest (Seidman, 2013).

One way to begin is by reducing the text of each question to the minimum needed to clearly communicate what was asked. The words of the interviewer are far less significant than those of the participant in traditional interviews, so these should be made as concise as possible. Next, focus on removing redundancies, such as when a participant says the same thing twice or more using different words unless, in the context of the particular study, such repetition is important. For example, if a respondent says something four times to deliberately emphasize its importance, this is worth noting. On the other hand, if the participant simply seems to be trying to find the right words and stumbles (e.g., "Actually that's not what I mean. I meant to say . . ."), only the latter sentence might be retained if the researcher believes the original sentence is less meaningful. Words such as *um, like,* and other verbal debris can generally be removed, as can false starts to sentences. While deleting a participant's words to condense data is appropriate, researchers should never change or add language to clarify what they think a participant meant to say or how they think the participant would have said something more concisely. While it is acceptable to change an interviewer's questions for maximum brevity, the participant's words should remain unchanged if they still appear in the condensed interview.

A full transcript of a brief interview with a participant in a diabetes study is included at the end of this chapter. The total transcript is 2,379 words, so an ideal condensed length would be approximately 800 words. Below is a condensed version of the transcript from the first few questions and answers up to the general question, "You mentioned maintaining a healthy diet and exercise. Are those things you have to make changes in your life to accommodate?" This section of the transcript contains 878 words and would ideally be reduced to just 300 words. Go to the full transcript at the end of this chapter and read through the answer to the specific question above, then return here to read a condensed version of that same transcript that runs 299 words, then compare the full and condensed versions. Notes on how the interview was condensed follow the sample.

March 26, 2015, at 4:30 p.m., Sarah.

INTERVIEWER: Describe diabetes.

SARAH: Type I diabetes is when your pancreas no longer makes insulin; you need insulin to open up your cells to allow sugar to be processed by your cells. If you don't have insulin, your cells can't process sugar, you don't have any energy, and it affects your brain. You have to take insulin. You have to operate as your own pancreas to administer insulin to yourself, to process food and to get energy.

INTERVIEWER: What did you previously know about diabetes?

SARAH: Very little. That it was something people had, and you had to take shots.

INTERVIEWER: How did you feel when diagnosed?

SARAH: I was relieved because it explained unusual feelings I had been having; usual symptoms. I was losing a ton of weight, going to the bathroom all the time, constantly thirsty, and really tired. All of a sudden that made sense. It was unexpected, but not devastating.

INTERVIEWER: What questions did you have?

SARAH: What is the treatment going to be? Are there any long-term negative effects? I learned it's a pretty treatable disease. You have to learn to manage how much insulin you need to take based on your food, so you have to learn to count how many carbs are in any meal you eat. If you eat a healthy diet and exercise, it's pretty easy to keep a handle on. Long-term effects are if you don't take care of it. You can go blind, get neuropathy.

INTERVIEWER: How do you count carbohydrates?

SARAH: There's books that give you the carb counts of basic foods. You get good at reading labels. You can always look it up, there's apps on phones.

INTERVIEWER: Any changes to maintain a healthy diet and exercise?

SARAH: No.

The first round of condensation was straightforward. First, all introductory material and discussion of informed consent procedures were deleted, as these were not relevant to the research question. Pleasantries on the part of the interviewer (e.g., "Thank you" and "Please tell me about . . .") were deleted, as were transition words (e.g., "first," "next") as was text that is implied even when absent (e.g., "In your own words, . . .").

The participant in this particular interview regularly began but then rephrased sentences, making deletions easier. Also, placeholder language when the participant was thinking, such as "So, yeah, I'd . . ." was easily removed, as were extraneous afterthoughts (e.g., "and that sort of thing"). Wordy sentences were condensed:

"Basically, you kind of end up where you don't have any energy"

became

"You don't have any energy"

The point is still clearly communicated using the participant's words but with only 5 of them instead of 12.

After the first pass, the second round of condensation was more difficult because it entailed removing potentially useful data. Researchers must remember that all data are potentially useful, yet they must also remember their overarching research question and analyze which data are most likely useful for their particular study. Researchers hesitant about data condensation should also remember that they still have the full transcript of each interview available. The condensed versions simply help them identify the most salient data and themes. As always, some researchers find it helpful to write jottings or analytic memos during the process of interview condensation, since insights are likely to emerge as they decide what is most important to include.

Interview condensation is not appropriate for studies in conversation and discourse analysis since verbatim texts are necessary for those two approaches. We also recommend that interview transcripts from child and adolescent participants not be condensed to preserve their authentic language and voices for developmental research.

Analyzing Interviews Through Codes and Coding

Chapter 1 proposed that when researchers took clues in the form of sentences and transformed them into shorter meanings (e.g., "You put two, sometimes four slices of bread in this thing and push the handle down to make the bread hot and crispy" = toaster), you were doing a form of coding. More formally, a code in qualitative data analysis is

most often a word or short phrase that symbolically assigns a summative, salient, essence-capturing, and/or evocative attribute for a portion of language-based or visual data. The data can consist of interview transcripts, participant observation field notes, journals, documents, open-ended survey responses, drawings, artifacts, photographs, video, Internet sites, e-mail correspondence, academic and fictional literature, and so on. The portion of data coded . . . can range in magnitude from a single word to a full paragraph to an entire page of text to a stream of moving images.

In qualitative data analysis, a code is a researcher-generated construct that symbolizes or translates data (Vogt, Vogt, Gardner, & Haeffele, 2014, p. 13) and thus attributes interpreted meaning to each individual datum for later purposes of pattern detection, categorization, assertion or proposition development, theory-building, and other analytic processes. Just as a title represents and captures a book, film, or poem's primary content and essence, so does a code represent and capture a datum's primary content and essence. (Saldaña, 2016, p. 4)

Coding is symbolizing—the condensation of a datum into a richer, more compact form of meaning. Researchers code qualitative data primarily to create more-manageable units to help expedite analysis. But it is also a process that stimulates thinking and reflecting on the data's essences. The method has over a half century of use in qualitative inquiry but is just one way, and not the only way, to analyze data. Below we introduce some fundamental coding processes, and continue with additional methods and other analytic approaches in Chapters 9 and 10. Though we discuss them as four separate methods—In Vivo Coding, Process Coding, Values Coding, and Emotion Coding—researchers can strategically mix and match them as needed during first and future coding cycles.

In vivo coding and analytic formatting

We introduced In Vivo Coding briefly in Chapter 1. This coding method utilizes the participant's own language as a symbol system for qualitative data analysis. The researcher reviews interview transcripts and other participant-generated texts to cull words and phrases that seem to stand out, as if they deserve to be italicized, bolded, underlined, or highlighted for visual emphasis; or if they might be vocally stressed by the participant if spoken aloud. In vivo is Latin for "in that which is alive," suggesting that codes extracted from data originate organically and possess a living quality unto themselves.

As an example, below is an excerpt from an interview with a movie theatre employee discussing customer service expectations at his job. We present it with his most salient words (as we interpreted them) in bold font. Notice that only the participant's responses, not the interviewer's questions, were considered. Our choices for these words and phrases came after multiple readings of the interview transcript, and consist of a pared-down number after our first impressions were reconsidered. Other researchers might consider other words and phrases in this excerpt just as suitable for In Vivo Codes, and their choices could be just as valid. Coding is not a precise science; it is primarily an interpretive act by each individual researcher:

INTERVIEWER: In your own words, what were the official policies of the theatre regarding customer service to the best of your knowledge?

COLIN: The **official policy** would be, "Clean, efficient, fun, movie theatre experience for every guest." Or customer. We called them "**guests**" because that was just what they told us to call them instead of "customers." But yeah, no. **Clean, fast, easy, fun**.

INTERVIEWER: Were there any policies specifically on how you should interact with customers—or guests, in your case?

COLIN: Very **cordially**, of course. One of the things in training was always be the **first to apologize** if anything goes wrong. **Never blame** the guest—or customer—be **concise and clear** with them about what they have to offer.

INTERVIEWER: In your view, did your employer's official policies on customer service align with their actual practice in terms of customer service?

COLIN: That's a good question. Probably, for the most part, no. I think, for the most part, we were **true in word**, but when it came to application, I'd guess **only about forty percent** of the employees or managers actually took that part of the policy serious.

Before turning to the analysis of the In Vivo Codes, we review some recommendations for formatting data and analytic work.

We advise that researchers format narrative data for coding as we've illustrated below. Place the interviewer's text in brackets since it will not be coded. Align the text to the left half to two thirds of the page, leaving a right-hand column for the codes, which are capitalized to distinguish them from regular text. Divide the data into **stanzas** or units with a line break between them when a noticeable topic shift occurs; this is to better manage the data corpus and to make researchers aware of changes in a participant's narrative trajectory. Handwrite on hard copy or type into a text editing program ascending superscript numbers at the beginning of a datum to be coded, and place a corresponding number followed by the code in the right-hand column. In Vivo Codes (unlike other codes) are placed in quotation marks to remind the researcher that they originated from the participant. The interview excerpt above now appears thusly:

[INTERVIEWER: In your own words, what were the official policies of the theatre regarding customer service to the best of your knowledge?]

COLIN: The [1] official policy would be, "Clean, efficient fun, movie theatre experience for every guest." Or customer. We called them [2] "guests" because that was just what they told us to call them instead of "customers." But yeah, no. [3] Clean, fast, easy, fun.

[1] "OFFICIAL POLICY"

[2] "GUESTS"

[3] "CLEAN, FAST, EASY, FUN"

[INTERVIEWER: Were there any policies specifically on how you should interact with customers—or guests, in your case?]

COLIN: Very [4] cordially, of course. One of the things in training was always be the [5] first to apologize if anything goes wrong. [6] Never blame the guest—or customer—be [7] concise and clear with them about what they have to offer.

[4] "CORDIALLY"

[5] "FIRST TO APOLOGIZE"
[6] "NEVER BLAME"
[7] "CONCISE AND CLEAR"

[INTERVIEWER: In your view, did your employer's official policies on customer service align with their actual practice in terms of customer service?]

COLIN: That's a good question. Probably, for the most part, no. I think, for the most part, we were [8] true in word, but when it came to application, I'd guess [9] only about forty percent of the employees or managers actually took that part of the policy serious.

[8] "TRUE IN WORD"
[9] "ONLY ABOUT FORTY PERCENT"

Figure 5.1   A movie theatre employee treats guests cordially.

Our formatting recommendations are not standardized or required. They are simply ways we've found helpful to our own analytic process. Researchers using Excel software for their analysis can place each stanza of data into an individual column cell, with codes placed in adjoining cells in the next column. Researchers using computer software specifically designed to assist with qualitative data analysis (discussed in Chapter 10) will find that formatting requirements vary according to product.

In Vivo Coding is a good method to first learn how to code because it requires that researchers scrutinize data closely and pay meticulous attention to every word the participant says. It also makes first attempts at coding easier since the participant, in a way, has already done some of the work by supplying the codes. Researchers simply select from the text the most salient symbols. We advise, however, that researchers use In Vivo Coding economically. Complete sentences as codes can be cumbersome, and overusing the method can cause the number of codes to proliferate and overwhelm when it comes time for further analysis. Also, In Vivo Coding is not the only method available, so researchers should not rely on it as a default approach to initial data analysis.

Chapter 9 will illustrate how codes can be synthesized in various ways for analytic work. In this section we focus on how codes serve as prompts or triggers for reflection on the deeper meanings they evoke. Part of qualitative analysis is open-ended reflection—documenting what's going through the researchers' minds as they review the data and reflect on any initial interpretive work like coding. Consider three analytic memo topics outlined in Chapter 2:

- The participants' routines, rituals, rules, roles, and relationships

- How you personally relate to the participants and/or the phenomenon

- Emergent patterns, categories, themes, concepts, and assertions

First, review a cluster of five sequential codes from the movie theatre employee's transcript:

"CLEAN, FAST, EASY, FUN"

"CORDIALLY"

"FIRST TO APOLOGIZE"

"NEVER BLAME"

"CONCISE AND CLEAR"

Chapter 1 introduced the game *Three for All!* in which players had to determine what three words or phrases had in common. With these five In Vivo Codes, try playing *Five for All!* by considering how these five codes interrelate in some way according to one or more possible analytic memo topics:

- These codes relate to workplace policies. Write a memo (approximately one to two paragraphs in length) about how they are comparable to rules, and how the employee's role with them establishes guest relationships.

- Write a memo about a similar situation in which you yourself had to exhibit cordiality, to be the first to apologize, or to be concise and clear with someone else.

- Write a memo about how the five In Vivo Codes constitute a pattern, category, or theme of some kind. Reflect on what they all have in common.

Don't feel bound by these recommended topics. Write about anything in the data that is surprising, intriguing, or disturbing (Sunstein & Chiseri-Strater, 2012, p. 115).

Analytic memo writing remains grounded in the data if researchers integrate some of the codes and participant quotes into their personal narratives as evidentiary support. One example memo reads,

> May 1, 2016
>
> PATTERNS: "CLEAN, FAST, EASY, FUN"
>
> The code "CLEAN, FAST, EASY, FUN" seems like policy shorthand that employees memorize as a mnemonic to remind them of how they should do their jobs. Even the phrase itself is "clean, fast,

easy, fun" to say aloud. The phrase seems to embody the four codes that follow, suggesting that not just janitorial work but also customer interactions must be "CLEAN, FAST, EASY, FUN." Like the illusion of the movies they show, their employee roles are Hollywood performances by good actors in front of the paparazzi. "We were true in word, but" not everyone on staff follows the rules for good public relations. Perhaps the stress of the job or lack of role modeling by management contributes to this outcome, just as a poor film director results in poor performances on screen.

Memo writings are first draft analyses that concretize researchers' thinking processes and serve as foundations for continued analytic work.

Process coding

Process Coding, briefly introduced in Chapter 1, uses gerunds ("-ing" words) as codes. The purpose of the method is to identify forms of participant action, reaction, and interaction as suggested by the data. Some methodologies of qualitative inquiry emphasize that analyzing human action is key to discerning the conditions, contexts, causes, consequences, and other dynamic processes of life. Process Coding has also been labeled Action Coding (Charmaz, 2008).

We return to the movie theatre employee's interview data to illustrate that the same passages of text can be coded in different ways, which can thus lead to different analytic insights. Process Codes describe in realistic or conceptual terms what participants are doing or what is happening, either within the stories they tell or within the experiences they relate. Here are just a few examples as we propose them. We include only the participant's texts below. Also notice that Process Codes tend to be applied less frequently than In Vivo Codes:

COLIN:	[1] The official policy would be, "Clean, efficient, fun, movie theatre experience for every guest." Or customer. We called them "guests" because that was just what they told us to call them instead of "customers." But yeah, no. Clean, fast, easy, fun. . . .	[1] STREAMLINING SERVICE
COLIN:	[2] Very cordially, of course. One of the things in training was always be the first to apologize if anything goes wrong. Never blame the guest—or customer—be concise and clear with them about what they have to offer. . . .	[2] ACQUIESCING TO GUESTS

COLIN: That's a good question. [3] Probably, for the most part, no. I think, for the most part, we were true in word, but when it came to application, I'd guess only about forty percent of the employees or managers actually took that part of the policy serious.

[3] NOT WALKING THE TALK

Just three codes cannot initiate a complete analysis. The entire transcript's full set of Process Codes would be needed for that. But what we illustrate here is the repeated use of the code NOT WALKING THE TALK, which appeared eight times in our first cycle of coding the movie theatre employee's entire interview. In Vivo Codes are so unique that they might not appear more than once during a cycle of coding. But other methods, such as Process Coding, could generate repeated codes because there is regularity in human affairs—routines and patterns of action—and thus the researcher will probably notice this regularity in the data as well. Below are four excerpts (from a total of eight) from the employee's complete interview that we assigned the code NOT WALKING THE TALK:

1. COLIN: I think, for the most part, we were true in word, but when it came to application, I'd guess only about forty percent of the employees or managers actually took that part of the policy serious.

2. COLIN: They pushed us very much that we needed to sell large popcorn, large drinks with every single transaction, but then they said, "Don't push merchandise." . . .

3. COLIN: So, sometimes there was conflicting in the sense that they wanted us to push sales, but they also didn't want us to push and be impolite to guests, so I think sometimes those two kind of conflicted.

4. COLIN: Well, that's tough because they advertise customer service first, but then some of the policies are more on the business side and less on the customer's side.

Code frequency can suggest regularity, but frequency is not always an indicator of significance. Nevertheless, eight NOT WALKING THE TALK codes cannot be ignored, so this becomes an important trigger for further analysis.

Since Process Codes suggest action, we also encourage researchers to embody each code as a form of kinesthetic experience and analysis. Gesturally or with his whole body, a researcher enacts movements that interpret the codes. For example, ACQUIESCING TO GUESTS might be represented by bowing down at the waist while spreading his hands. NOT WALKING THE TALK might be interpreted by looking away with an indifferent facial expression as he holds a palm up to suggest the saying, "Talk to the hand." Novice researchers might find this a bit awkward at first, but it is a legitimate heuristic to gain deeper understanding of the codes' symbolic and subtextual meanings.

Values coding

Chapter 3 introduced the concepts of values, attitudes, and beliefs—collectively called a values system. As a reminder, a value is the importance people attribute to themselves, other people, things, or ideas, and the principles, moral codes, and situational norms people live by. An attitude is the way people think and feel about themselves, other people, things, or ideas—evaluative perceptions and sets of cumulative reactions, reflecting the beliefs they've learned through time. A belief includes interrelated values and attitudes, and personal knowledge, experiences, opinions, prejudices, morals, and other interpretive perceptions of the social world. Values, attitudes, and beliefs can be discerned and analyzed separately but not without reference to the other system's concepts (see Figure 5.2).

Values Coding of an individual's values system notes which one of the three concepts (attitudes, values, and/or beliefs) the participant overtly states, or how the researcher infers and interprets it from the data. It is sometimes quite slippery to determine whether a datum represents a value, attitude, or belief, though it supports the tight interrelationship between and among them. We use the following symbol system as part of the coding method:

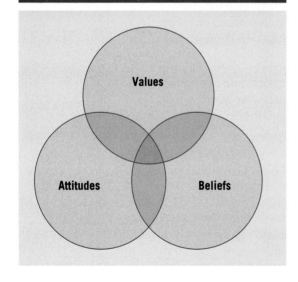

Figure 5.2 Values, attitudes, and beliefs are a tightly interrelated system.

- V: _____ [VALUE]

- A: _____ [ATTITUDE]

- B: _____ [BELIEF]

As an example of Values Coding, we return to the interview of the movie theatre employee, who was asked to give some final thoughts on the subject of customer service from his perspective:

COLIN: [1] From that of an employee's, specifically of a   [1] B: CUSTOMER
movie theatre, it was hard, particularly towards the   SERVICE IS "HARD"
end. [2] What disgruntled me as an employee the most   [2] A: TORN IN TWO
was the fact that we were selling and trying— . . .   DIRECTIONS
not to take advantage of guests—but getting money
from them and charging really expensive—the
business side—but also trying to be accommodating
and the face of customer service. [3] You might gripe   [3] A: HATES
about a guest, but as soon as a guest is there we put   INSINCERITY
on this facade that things are good. It just seems
kind of two faced and kind of cheesy. [4] I understand   [4] V: BUSINESS
why it happens, but it's just unfortunate that that   INTEGRITY
has to be the case, that we have to play two fronts,
that of a business making money and ripping people
off, and then also making sure they are happy and
that they are coming back for more.

Analysis of Values Codes can proceed by examining all value, attitude, and belief codes separately, then exploring their interrelationship by memoing how the beliefs are embedded in the values, how the person's attitudes reflect his beliefs, how his values influence his attitudes, and how the three work together as a composite values system.

Values Coding is appropriate for virtually all qualitative studies, but particularly for those that explore cultural values, identity, intrapersonal and interpersonal participant experiences and actions in case studies, oral history, critical ethnography, psychology, and sociology. Values Coding is applicable not only to interview transcripts and participant-generated materials such as journals, diaries, and social media entries, but also to field notes in which naturalistic participant actions are documented. Using multiple sources, in fact, corroborates the coding and enhances trustworthiness of the findings since a participant's statements about what his values, attitudes, and beliefs are might not always be truthful or harmonize with his observed actions, reactions, and interactions (Saldaña, 2016, pp. 131–132).

Emotion coding

Goleman (1995) defines an emotion as "a feeling and its distinctive thoughts, psychological and biological states, and range of propensities to act" (p. 289). **Emotion Coding** labels the emotional states experienced or recalled by the participant, or inferred by the researcher about the participant. Emotions are present in virtually everything a person does, and they offer insightful windows into the person's mind, assuming we have inferred and interpreted with some degree of accuracy how that person is feeling. Hundreds of words exist for emotions, yet sometimes metaphors, similes, and other descriptors are used to express them—for example, the codes "LOSING MY MIND," "I WANTED TO HIDE," "ON CLOUD NINE." When a participant uses evocative language such as this, In Vivo phrases function as intriguing Emotion Codes.

For example, we present the same passage of data used to illustrate Values Coding—again, to reinforce that the same data can be coded/analyzed in different ways, thereby gaining different insights into the participant's experiences. We should also reinforce that Emotion Coding happens not just with a written transcript, but also from the presence and memories of the researcher during the live interview, and from listening to the audio recording repeatedly for nuances in the participant's vocal tone, rate, volume, and other subtextual dynamics, cluing the analyst to additional emotional layers. Consider the emotion codes assigned to this passage, noting that In vivo emotion codes are enclosed in quotation marks, while researcher-generated codes are not.

COLIN: [1] From that of an employee's, specifically of a movie theatre, it was hard, particularly towards the end. [2] What disgruntled me as an employee the most was the fact that we were selling and trying—not to take advantage of guests—but getting money from them and charging really expensive—the business side—but also trying to be accommodating and the face of customer service. [3] You might gripe about a guest, but [4] as soon as a guest is there we put on this facade that things are good. It just seems kind of two faced and kind of cheesy. [5] I understand why it happens, but it's just unfortunate that that has to be the case, that we have to play two fronts, that of a business making money and ripping people off, and then also making sure they are happy and that they are coming back for more.

[1] "HARD"

[2] DISGRUNTLEMENT

[3] "GRIPE"
[4] "TWO FACED"

[5] REGRETFUL

One approach to analyzing Emotion Codes is to plot an **emotional arc** or trajectory as a participant progresses through a story or experience. For stage and

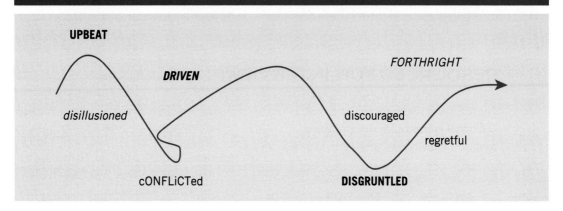

film performance, actors are trained to reveal their characters' emotional journeys through time by transforming from one emotional state to another as the action of the script suggests. Real life is no different, because people shift from one emotion(s) to another as our lives progress through action, reaction, and interaction. Core emotions are plotted in a diagram to illustrate their change and intensity. Rich text formatting and font sizes and styles can even be incorporated to enhance the arc. Figure 5.3 illustrates our interpretations of the movie theatre employee's emotional arc as he describes his job conflicts and tensions during the interview. This diagram becomes a stimulus for analytic reflection and memoing.

Emotion Coding is appropriate for virtually all qualitative studies, but particularly for those that explore intrapersonal and interpersonal participant experiences and actions, especially in matters of social relationships, reasoning, decision-making, judgment, and risk-taking. The subject is intricately complex, so explore the literature from various disciplines of study to assess the conceptual frameworks, operating definitions, and theories regarding emotions.

CLOSURE AND TRANSITION _____

Part I has addressed methods for gathering, generating, and initially analyzing qualitative research data, with a particular focus in this chapter on analyzing semi-structured interviews. The coding methods discussed above are useful not only for transcripts, but also for exploring a wide variety of qualitative data.

In Part II, we focus on research methodologies and designs that will incorporate many of the methods discussed to this point, illustrating how they can be contextualized with particular studies driven by specific research questions.

RESOURCES FOR INTERVIEWING

The following resources will offer you additional guidance for designing and conducting interviews with participants:

Brinkmann, Svend. (2013). *Qualitative Interviewing*. New York: Oxford University Press.

Brinkmann, Svend, and Steinar Kvale. (2015). *InterViews: Learning the Craft of Qualitative Research Interviewing*, 3rd edition. Thousand Oaks, CA: Sage.

Galletta, Anne, and William Cross. (2013). *Mastering the Semi-Structured Interview and Beyond: From Research Design to Analysis and Publication*. New York: New York University Press.

Josselson, Ruthellen. (2013). *Interviewing for Qualitative Research: A Relational Approach*. New York: Guilford.

Roulston, Kathryn. (2010). *Reflective Interviewing: A Guide to Theory and Practice*. London: Sage.

Seidman, Irving. (2013). *Interviewing as Qualitative Research: A Guide for Researchers in Education and the Social Sciences,* 4th edition. New York: Teachers College Press.

ANALYTIC EXERCISES FOR INTERVIEWING

1. Condense the interview below from the participant with diabetes beginning where the sample condensation stopped. (The complete transcript can be downloaded from the book's companion Web site at study.sagepub.com/saldanaomasta.) Begin with the question, "Going back to how you learned about diabetes, what sources did you learn about the condition from? Where did you learn about diabetes once you were diagnosed?" and continue through the end. The original text you will condense is 1,501 words, so your goal is to condense the interview to about 500 words.

2. Choose a section of about 300 words from the sample interview below. Consider which two of the four coding methods discussed above (In Vivo, Process, Values, or Emotion Coding) would be most appropriate for analyzing the text, then code it twice using both of your selected methods. Compare the results and consider how the different coding methods employed helped reinforce each other or provided divergent analytic insights.

SAMPLE INTERVIEW TRANSCRIPT ⸻

SELECTED DATA FROM PREINTERVIEW SURVEY:

Participant ID: A-67

Pseudonym: Sarah

Diabetes Type: Type 1

Gender: Female

Age: 33

Age Diagnosed: 27

INTERVIEW TRANSCRIPT (FULL)

INTERVIEWER:	Hello, my name is Matt. Thank you for taking the time to talk to me today. Before we begin, do you have any questions about the informed consent form that you completed earlier?
SARAH:	No, thank you.
INTERVIEWER:	To be sure that we have an accurate record of today's conversation, I am going to supplement my notes by audio-recording our interview, is this okay?
SARAH:	Yes.
INTERVIEWER:	Thank you. Today is March 26, 2015, at 4:30 p.m., and I am speaking with Sarah. Thank you for taking the time to talk to me today. I am going to be asking you a few general questions. If there is anything you do not feel comfortable answering or that you do not know the answer to, that is not a problem; let me know, and we can skip that question.
SARAH:	Excellent.
INTERVIEWER:	First, in your own words, how would you describe diabetes to someone with no experience and limited knowledge of the condition?
SARAH:	So, Type I diabetes is when your pancreas no longer makes insulin, and you need insulin to open up your cells to allow sugar to be processed by your cells. So if you don't have insulin, your cells can't process sugar, and basically you kind of end up where you don't have any energy, and it affects your brain, and that sort of a thing. So you have to take insulin. They

have synthetic insulin you can take, so you sort of have to operate as your own pancreas to administer insulin to yourself, to process food and to get energy.

INTERVIEWER: Thank you. You indicated you were diagnosed with diabetes six years ago . . .

SARAH: Yes.

INTERVIEWER: What do you recall (if anything) knowing about diabetes before you were diagnosed?

SARAH: I knew very little about it. So . . . yeah, I'd . . . Typically, in the past, it'd be something you'd be diagnosed with as a child or in adolescence, so I knew, you know, that it was something people had, and you had to take shots, but that was about all I knew about it.

INTERVIEWER: How do you recall feeling and reacting when you were first diagnosed with diabetes? What questions did you have?

SARAH: I was . . . First I was relieved because it explained a lot of the . . . unusual sort of feelings I had been having. The usual symptoms, you know.

INTERVIEWER: What were some of those feelings or symptoms?

SARAH: I was losing a ton of weight, I was going to the bathroom all the time, I was constantly thirsty . . . I had all the classic symptoms, and I was really tired. So, all of a sudden, all of that made sense. And yeah, it was a little bit of a learning curve. I had a lot to learn. But it was also—So yeah. It was unexpected, but not devastating, or anything like that.

INTERVIEWER: What were some the questions you remember having when you first learned you had diabetes?

SARAH: My first question was, so what is the treatment going to be? Are there any, sort of, long-term negative effects? Those were sort of the main . . . the main questions.

INTERVIEWER: What did you learn about those questions? The treatment and any long-term negative effects?

SARAH: I learned that it's pretty easy, it's a pretty treatable disease. And basically, you have to learn how to manage how much insulin you need to take based on your food, so you learn how many carbs . . . you have to learn to count how many carbs are in any meal you eat. Basically, you also learn it's very treatable and that you just . . . if you eat a healthy diet and exercise, it's pretty easy to keep a handle on. It's not a particularly disruptive disease, at least in my experience. And then, long-term effects are if you don't take care of it . . . yeah, you'll have long-term effects. You can go blind, you can get neuropathy where you can't feel your fingers or toes, and that can be dangerous if you don't take care of it. Basically, it's just a disease you need to keep on top of.

INTERVIEWER: How do you learn to do some of the things, like counting carbohydrates?

SARAH: So, there's all kind of books that you can get that give you the carb counts of basic foods, fast foods, those sorts of things. Then you just get really good at reading labels. Luckily, there's labels on pretty much everything. And then, after a couple of months, you pretty much . . . I've discovered most people eat the same things most of the time. When you're not eating the same things, you can always look it up, and there's all kinds of apps on phones now, and stuff. So it's pretty easy to look things up and develop a sort of working knowledge of how many carbs there are and stuff. It takes time. It's doable.

INTERVIEWER: You mentioned maintaining a healthy diet and exercise. Are those things you have to make changes in your life to accommodate?

SARAH: No. I was already pretty good about getting exercise, and then, like everybody else, I go through phases where I'm lazier than others, but on the whole that wasn't necessarily a big change.

INTERVIEWER: Going back to how you learned about diabetes, from what sources did you learn about the condition? Where did you learn about diabetes once you were diagnosed?

SARAH: So, when I got diagnosed, the doctor's office and the hospital gave me a big pack of, you know, "Your first year with diabetes." "Tips about diabetes." There's a lot of great Web sites. The American Diabetes Association has a great Web site. There's a . . . shoot. I think it's called Juvenile Diabetes Research . . . has a really good Web site. And they refer you. They have all kinds of exhaustive lists on information from the Web site and books you can read. And then there's . . . American Diabetes puts out a magazine called *Diabetes Forecast*, and you can get all kinds of information there. Finding information was pretty easy.

INTERVIEWER: How many of those resources do you think you actually looked at when you were . . .

SARAH: Did I look at? A lot of them, just because I'm academic, so you know, I do the research. So, I would say for sure the American Diabetes Web site and the one that starts with a "J" that I can't remember off the top of my head. And then there were a couple of really good books. I looked at one that had a really good title called, like, *Being Your Own Pancreas*, or something like that. And then there's a *Diabetes for Dummies* book. My mom also loaded me up with books. So, yeah, I had no end to books. In fact, there were almost too many of these sources. You reach a certain point where you . . . they're all sort of repeating the same things and answering the same questions.

INTERVIEWER: Actually, brings me to my next question. Do you ever recall receiving conflicting information from different sources?

SARAH: Nope. It was pretty consistent across the board. The thing I found to be wary of were there's a lot of Web sites I found that were support group Web sites where you'd get people talking about their own experiences, and sometimes those could get a little questionable, sometimes. Again, those are just individuals, not doctors, talking about it, so I kind of steered clear of some of those. But yeah, on the whole it was consistent, reliable, and yeah.

INTERVIEWER: In your experience, how much do people who do not have diabetes understand about the condition?

SARAH: I find it varies. It's a little bit confusing because there's Type I diabetes and Type II diabetes, and there's not a lot of understanding what the difference is. To be honest, since I don't have Type II, I'm not sure I even understand Type II, though Type II is often caused by, you know, if you're overweight, or you don't exercise, or you're older. That's where Type II is more associated with that. So there's confusion that there are different types, and some people think that if you have diabetes you can't ever eat any sugar. That seems to be the other big misconception. You can eat sugar. You just have to dose, give yourself more insulin if you eat a lot of sugar. And yeah, like any person should be eating a ton of sugar anyway. So that seems to be the main . . . I think people know more about it, but what they know about is Type II, which is different from Type I.

INTERVIEWER: What are some different ways that people react if they find out you have diabetes?

SARAH: They're usually afraid about dietary restrictions, or they don't want to give me something that I can't eat. That's usually the reaction I get. "I'm so sorry. I served you dessert with dinner." But, yeah I'm pretty . . . I don't have any food restrictions. I just have to just know how many carbs are in something, so that's usually the main concern.

INTERVIEWER: How do you respond to these reactions?

SARAH: I usually just try to put them at ease, you know. It's ultimately my responsibility to take care of it, not you. And if I eat sugar I'm not going to die, so that kind of thing.

INTERVIEWER: Since you were diagnosed six years ago, are there any ways in which diabetes has affected the way you live your life?

SARAH: Yeah, I just have to be more aware of what I eat, is the main concern. You know, the main thing you have to be worried about is having a low blood sugar. That's when you can have effects, and that can affect your driving, and it can affect your judgment, and that sort of thing. I just have to make sure I always have a snack in my bag to ward off . . . Luckily, if you have a low blood sugar, all you have to do is eat something with carbs in it, so it's really easy to treat. Those would be sort of . . . Yeah, being aware of food, and always having a snack.

INTERVIEWER: Have there been any other tangible tasks that are part of your life that weren't before?

SARAH: Yeah, again, it's mostly just I have to be aware, double check my blood sugar if I'm going to go exercise really strenuously or if I'm going on a long road trip, or something. It's just making sure I check my sugar level.

INTERVIEWER: How do you do that?

SARAH: You just stick your finger and draw some blood. And then you've got this blood sugar reader that you have to test. So you've always got your little testers with you. So, I guess you have to be a little more organized and aware, which is a challenge for me as a disorganized person. Again, it's a pretty manageable disease.

INTERVIEWER: Do you imagine that your life would be significantly different if you didn't have diabetes, or do you think that it would be fairly similar?

SARAH: It would be pretty similar. The one thing it does is that it's another kick to the butt to eat healthy and be active, and that sort of thing, so I'm probably better about that than if I didn't, but I wouldn't say it's super . . . that it changed my life in radical ways.

INTERVIEWER: Is there anything you think the general public does not know about diabetes, or living with diabetes, that they should?

SARAH: I think it's probably good to know about the dangers of having a low because sometimes if I'm having a low blood sugar I can't always tell. The people who I spend a lot of time with, if I'm going on a trip or something, I'll usually alert them to what the . . . but I don't think that's something the general public needs to know. Type II diabetes, it's more important for people to have an awareness of, you know, not eating a lot of sugar and trying to be generally active, and I think with Type II it's a lot more important because that's something . . . No one knows what causes Type I. It's sort of luck of the draw. It can't be avoided, but Type II can be avoided. So that one I think is a little bit more important for the public to be aware of.

INTERVIEWER: Is there any specific information that you think would be useful for people to know?

SARAH: And I think it's stuff that's out there already, you know. Like, don't eat a ton of sugar, and, you know, try to be active. All that sort of stuff that goes with being a healthy person. And I think that there's . . . I think that people have a pretty good awareness about, you know, that those are things to avoid. So yeah, once you get Type I, if you get Type I, it's pretty easy, like I said. It's pretty easy to educate yourself about that.

INTERVIEWER: Thanks very much. My last question is: Is there anything else you would like to share about diabetes?

SARAH: No. I guess it's more of an issue with little kids who have Type I diabetes because, once again, there are so many other factors that come into play with . . . Again, if you're teaching or babysitting or something, just knowing how to treat a low, or things like that. Those things are more important with little kids because at a certain point you're old enough where, you know, it's your own responsibility, but where you're a kid I think it's, maybe a little bit, you're not entirely responsible for all of the things that are happening. That's a whole different ballgame. Not one I really have experience with. I don't have kids with diabetes. I can just imagine it's a tougher ballgame. That's probably it.

INTERVIEWER: Thank you so much for taking the time to talk with me today. I and everyone on our research team really appreciate your help. If you have any questions in the future, please feel free to contact us using the information on the paperwork we gave you earlier. Thank you again!

SARAH: Thank you.

Analyzing the Framework

Analyzing Qualitative Methodologies

Introduction

Part I of this book introduced the craft of qualitative research. Part II examines the art of it. In this chapter we focus on major qualitative research methodologies with representative excerpts from published studies.

Theoretical Premises of Qualitative Research

There are a few foundational premises to review before discussing methodologies and the logistics of research design. These are terms and understandings many qualitative researchers utilize in their thinking and inquiry processes. We keep our discussion of them brief in order to expand on methodologies—different approaches to qualitative inquiry.

Ontology and epistemology

There are two related concepts inquirers deal with when experiencing and analyzing life. **Ontology** refers to the nature of being; **epistemology** refers to ways of knowing. Researchers who focus primarily on the philosophical domains of inquiry attend to its ontological implications, such as how humans conceptualize their existence or their being in the world. One would think that reality is just that—something real and universally understood. But we interrogate ontology because we can. In other words, our minds have the capacity to not just experience life but also to wonder what it is and what it all means. And when we experience life, we come to know and understand it.

Epistemologies, like ontologies, are multiple. There is not just one way of knowing—there are many. We liken the process of coming

Learning Objectives

After reading and reviewing this chapter, researchers should be able to

1. Describe major theoretical premises of qualitative research, and

2. Identify and describe selected methodologies of qualitative research.

141

to know the world as if each person is a camera, experiencing life through different and unique lenses, filters, and angles. For example, attributes such as age, ethnicity, and gender can be seen as lenses that influence and affect how a researcher perceives such matters as workplace equity. Her disciplinary and/or methodological filters (e.g., sociological, feminist, ethnographic) shape not just what she observes but also how she takes in the experiences she observes of equitable and/or inequitable worker treatment. The angle of the researcher's positionality or standpoint (e.g., peripheral observer, critical inquirer, social justice advocate) adds yet another dimension to rendering social life observed in the workplace.

Researchers should reflect on how the multiple identities they bring to the research enterprise influence and affect how they perceive and construct one's knowledge about life—that is, how they interpret it.

Interpretation

Interpretation is the personal, subjective way people perceive and respond to social experiences. Interpretation is the signature way a researcher's unique mind constructs the meanings of action, reaction, and interaction. We believe that it is ontologically and epistemologically impossible to perceive the world in neutral, nonbiased, and objective ways. Thus, qualitative inquiry is an interpretive act. Researchers bring who they are to the project, balancing their value-laden impressions and emotional responses with the evidentiary necessities of what makes for rigorously investigated work.

As part of interpretation, qualitative researchers preface their reportage with what the reader or listener needs to know about where they're coming from. A researcher's positionality or standpoint in terms of the research agenda informs audiences about the background experiences she brought to the project, the possible connections and conflicts of interest that arose throughout the study, her personal investment or stakes in the study, and how her positioning or standpoint works to the report's advantage. Our own mentors have proclaimed, "All research is interpretive," suggesting that each individual brings a unique read or take on social life and, more important, a unique read of personal epistemological constructions and hence of the analysis of data's meanings.

The constructivist nature
of qualitative inquiry

Constructivist and constructivism refer to the cumulative processes of knowledge building within one's mind. We consider social reality subjective, meaning that each person understands the world differently because people possess a range of different experiences and perspectives. A constructivist's ontological premise is that knowledge does not exist "out there," independently of human beings. The constructivist's epistemological premise is that humans must interact with and reflect on social life in order to know and understand it.

Qualitative research is known primarily as an emergent, inductive, and evolutionary form of inquiry. A researcher's knowledge of people, field sites, and social **phenomena** accumulate as the investigation proceeds. This learn-as-you-go approach is likened to on-the-job training, in which understanding and mastery of something comes with time and from experiences. Our stance on constructivism means we have adopted a particular model or paradigm of experiencing and thus coming to know the social world.

Paradigms

A **paradigm** in qualitative inquiry is "a set of assumptions and perceptual orientations shared by members of a research community. Paradigms determine how members of research communities view both the phenomena their particular community studies and the research methods that should be employed to study those phenomena" (Donmoyer, 2008, p. 591). The unique combination of a particular ontology with particular yet related epistemologies generally forms a research paradigm. The discussion directly above proposed a constructivist paradigm for qualitative inquiry. But there are other paradigms that space does not permit us to fully address. Just a sampling of labels includes naturalist, ethnocentric, humanist, feminist, experimental, postpositivist, poststructuralist, and so on. And even then, some scholars disagree whether *paradigm* is the most accurate term to identify these philosophical approaches to social investigation.

So, is qualitative research a paradigm? According to Donmoyer's definition above, yes it is—though some within the qualitative community label it an approach, a philosophy, a methodology, a method, and so on. Such is the dilemma of a field that, to its advantage, lacks standardization. Qualitative inquiry is best explained in context. So, let's first examine its paradigmatic cousin: quantitative research.

An example of quantitative research

Quantitative research in the experimental tradition attempts either to gather data through survey research or to test a proposed **hypothesis**—a prediction of outcome—by administering a **treatment** of some kind to human subjects, then measuring and comparing their outcomes statistically to assess whether there are significant differences over the timeframe of the experiment, or between one group receiving the treatment and another group not receiving it (generally referred to as a **control group**). Variations of treatment designs exist, and data can be quantified from such qualitative sources as researcher observations, standardized interview protocols, survey responses, and tests. Many refer to this research paradigm as **positivist** (though some experimental researchers now label themselves postpositivist).

As an example, a researcher hypothesized that fourth-grade children using a more participatory, interactive, on-your-feet approach to learn vocabulary words will result in higher weekly test scores and retention than those children using an approach of traditional methods of deskwork: dictionary access and rote memorization. Over the course of nine weeks, one classroom of 30 children receives a treatment of the more active learning method, while a comparable classroom of children uses standard methods. The two groups' weekly and final test scores are plotted over time, and a statistical comparison and analysis of their mean scores reveal that the group receiving the experimental treatment did indeed achieve significantly higher scores than the group not receiving the treatment.

An example of qualitative research

Qualitative research, as described in chapters thus far, generally does not administer an experimental condition to participants. It does not rely primarily on statistics as symbols of measurement and analytic meaning, but instead depends primarily on words and images as empirical materials for reflection and analysis. Qualitative inquiry mostly examines natural social life as it is lived in the world. It examines what people say, do, feel, and create. Analyses of data can vary from straightforward descriptive accounts of human action to critical commentary on social injustices observed.

For example, imagine that in the fourth-grade classroom using traditional methods, a young girl originally from another country is selected as a case study. She, her teacher, and her parents have all consented to participate in a qualitative study of how immigrant children learn a second language. The researcher observes her as she scans through an English-language dictionary, noticing her facial expressions and the speed of her page turning and eye scan, which are much slower than her peers who speak English as their first language. The researcher observes the young girl during lunchtime, recess, and after school to perceive how she and a few classmates communicate and socially interact, and even how a few students shun her and talk about her behind her back.

The researcher interviews the instructor to discuss her pedagogical methods of teaching English as a second language, and reviews the weekly vocabulary worksheets to assess their relevance to the child's world. The researcher also meets with the child's parents and learns how their refugee status has made it difficult for the family to adapt to a new country, culture, and language. Yes, the girl's vocabulary test scores over the nine-week period are documented, but they are just a small facet of data compared to the fieldwork observations and interviews conducted with the participants. The research report profiles selected vignettes about the young girl's process of language acquisition and cultural acclimation, accompanied with a critique of the state school system's structured English immersion curriculum policies.

The purpose of the quantitative vocabulary study is to evaluate the effectiveness of a new pedagogical approach to teaching and learning. It is ontologically and epistemologically assumed that the statistical data and outcomes are both reliable and valid measures of the treatment's effects, and that the statistical results could be generalized to other fourth-grade school programs.

The purpose of the qualitative case study is to describe the process of how one middle elementary school child learns a new language, and the efficacy of the instructional methods within her sociocultural contexts. It is not presumed that this one girl's experiences over a nine-week period represent all children learning English as a second language. But the researcher makes a persuasive argument for how this case study might represent children learning a second language in comparable circumstances, and how the case speaks to state education policies for English language learners that might not be as effective as assumed. This type of knowledge can be of equal import to quantitative results when considering matters of educational policy.

A Rationale for Qualitative Research

This discussion is not intended to initiate a quantitative versus qualitative debate. We find value and utility in both paradigms (and in their blending as mixed-methods research, discussed later). Without quantitative research and its positivist and postpositivist paradigms, we would not have the advancements in science, technology, and medicine that we have today. But quantitative research methods can be misused in matters of social inquiry. If researchers wish to understand the human condition deeply, words and images rather than numbers could be more-revealing forms for collection and analysis.

We often hear and voice to ourselves the complaint that people object to being reduced to a number or statistic. When this minimizing happens, it suggests the feeling that one's identity has been lost, that one's personal significance has been devalued, and that one's individuality has been subsumed into the masses. We also proclaim the need to have voice and for others to listen attentively to what we have to say. There is affirmation of who we are when our thoughts and feelings—our stories—are revealed to a sympathetic ear. Qualitative inquiry acknowledges the importance of human expression and its revelatory insights into life. Thus, the research method's primary purpose is to provide a rich medium for examining the human condition.

Qualitative research is chosen when insight into people's personal and social lives is necessary to answer the research questions of interest. If the goal for inquiry is to learn about people's histories, experiences, motivations, opinions, perspectives, values, attitudes, beliefs, perceptions, feelings, and so on, then interviews, observations, and participants' own writings can reveal deep meanings and interpretations. Quantitative instrumentation exists for collecting and statistically measuring these same qualities of human life in a reductionist way, but numbers are not always the most appropriate means of answering the research questions of interest.

Qualitative research is also chosen when one or more of its established canon of methodologies harmonize with the research study's goals and questions. These methodologies or ways of approaching and conducting an inquiry are discussed next. We use the term *genre* synonymously and interchangeably with the term *methodology* to explain that there is not a generic approach to qualitative research, but rather an established set of different approaches, each with its unique combination of goals, methods, and outcomes.

Selected Methodologies of Qualitative Research and Analysis

In Chapter 2 we described a method as how the researcher goes about doing something. A methodology is why the researcher goes about it in a particular way. In earlier chapters we also profiled core methods for collecting data (e.g., interviews, analysis of artifacts). Virtually all of them can be used for the various **genres** or approaches to qualitative research we briefly describe below. A genre in literature refers to its form and format; examples include the short story, novel, essay, drama, poetry, and so on. Likewise, qualitative research has its own canon of genres that has evolved over the past few decades. We address only some of the most frequently used methodologies in this section and why they might be chosen for particular qualitative research projects.

Ethnography

The research methods profiled thus far have been primarily ethnographic—that is, methods for studying and documenting the culture of a group of people and how they live their everyday lives. Ethnography in its beginnings profiled the ways of cultures that were foreign to a researcher. Early and mid-20th-century ethnographies such as *Street Corner Society* (Whyte, 1993) and *Tally's Corner* (Liebow, 1967) explored local urban sites in the United States. Today's ethnographies also locate their fieldwork among microcultures such as belly-dancing groups, and document their fieldwork through the medium of film (Watkins, 2012). Some fieldwork now explores online communities. Other research projects assume critical or action-oriented perspectives with their participants—not just documenting a culture but, with the participants' consent, also jointly changing it for the better (Madison, 2012).

Rebekah Nathan (2005), a pseudonym for a university anthropologist, took a sabbatical from her tenured faculty position and enrolled as a nontraditional returning student at the pseudonymous "AnyU." *My Freshman Year: What a Professor Learned by Becoming a Student* is her firsthand, systematic account of classes, dining halls, dorm life, work ethics, peer relationships, and other aspects of higher education. Nathan employed traditional methods of data collection (participant observation, interviewing, document review) as a covert and complete participant in the setting. Her descriptions of and assertions about a university's culture are supported throughout with rich and representative quotes by students:

> The time before and after classes, when teachers were not within earshot, was instructive. It was a time for academic and social small talk, including stories about the recent weekend, the "fun" things that were done, or how tired or "wasted" the speaker was at the moment. Academic discourse was limited to a narrow sort of mutual questioning. "Did you do the reading for today?" and "Did we have anything due today?" were both common pre-class queries. Shared complaints about the way a course was going ("I can't believe he hasn't turned back either of our last two assignments") or the prospect of the upcoming class ("I hope he doesn't do that in-class writing thing again") were also heard. (p. 96)

Nathan (2005) tallied dorm talk topics among women, noting that approximately "one-third of all discussion topics reported were about boys, meeting boys, and

Figure 6.1   Rebekah Nathan (2005) studied university culture in *My Freshman Year*.

©iStockphoto.com/skynesher

sex" (p. 98). The other most frequent categories of women's dorm talk were, in descending order:

- Bodies, bodily functions, and body image

- Relationships and relationship problems

- One's childhood, personal history, and future

- TV, movies, games, and entertainment

- Alcohol and drug experiences (Nathan, 2005, p. 98).

The ethnographic method is selected as a research genre when an extended narrative about a culture is necessary for the goals of the study. The unit of study can range from a single classroom of children to an entire nation. It traditionally requires months and sometimes years of fieldwork and the systematic collection of both qualitative and quantitative data, though more contemporary ethnographies have challenged the established standards of method and created hybrid forms of research representation and presentation. For foundation readings in ethnography, see Bernard (2011); Fetterman (2010); Hammersley and Atkinson (2007); Sunstein and Chiseri-Strater (2012); and Wolcott (2005, 2008).

Case study

A **case study** focuses on a single unit—one person, one group, one organization, one event, and so on. The case merits examination for a full study because it is a unique individual or opportunity, it represents a typical instance of other comparable cases, it is one of several other cases that will be combined with or compared to others, or it serves as a stand-alone study that addresses the research questions of interest.

Marisol Clark-Ibáñez (2008) studied inner-city children labeled by their teachers as "bad." The ethnographic project included a multi-case study of two fourth-grade children: Dante, an African American boy, and Pati, a Latina. Clark-Ibáñez noticed that masculinity was compatible for "bad boys" who broke the rules in school settings. But for "bad girls" like Pati, breaking rules meant deviating from gender expectations: "Girls who get into trouble in school seem to have more to risk than do boys. The consequences of being a 'bad' girl were harsher punishment, less academic support, and less reform or social help for her problems when compared to the 'bad' boy" (p. 95). Since her study focused on the dynamics of gender inequality, it was wise for her to choose to place two contrasting case studies in context.

Clark-Ibáñez (2008) introduces her cases with physical descriptions: Dante "had a small frame, bright eyes, and closely cropped hair. . . . Because of abject poverty Dante wore the same clothes every day: blue pants and white polo shirt. . . . [Pati] was chubby and her dark bobbed hair framed her round face. Her raspy voice could easily switch from Spanish to English. . . . [She] came to school wearing skirts with hems that dragged on the floor and jackets hugely oversized" (p. 98). She then profiles Dante's classroom behaviors that defy his teacher's rules. He wanders around the classroom to chat with students, speaks out loud inappropriately and makes extraneous noises, throws his chair to the floor, and on one occasion deliberately jams a thumbtack into his finger. Pati's disruptive behaviors include yelling "I hate you!" to the teacher, angry outbursts at classmates, and physically fighting with them.

The researcher notices, however, that the consequences for the two children's disruptive actions are markedly different. Whereas the school principal finds ways to redirect Dante's energy into more-constructive forms of activity, Pati seems to have no adult allies in school. Dante receives more attention from school adults and cultivates his social capital with peers, while Pati is kept isolated and exhibits frustration and anger over her inability to learn.

Aside from participant observation, Clark-Ibáñez utilized **photo-elicitation interviews** with selected children. Participants were given disposable cameras and asked to take pictures of what was important to them. The developed photos were then used as prompts by the interviewer to ask children questions about their subject choices and their meanings. Dante's photographs included several family members, friends, residents of his apartment complex, and details about his community's property (swings, tables, trees, etc.). Pati's photographs, in contrast, reflected the isolation she experienced in school. Her photos were primarily indoor shots. Exterior shots of people and things were from a distance, whereas Dante's shots were close-ups. Pati's photo-elicitation interview with the researcher had to stop abruptly because the child broke down crying over her lack of friends and family tension with female siblings.

Clark-Ibáñez uses the two cases to discuss how teachers in inner-city schools interact differently with students of each gender, and how educators seem to know how to intervene with bad boys more than with bad girls. A case study is not intended to represent the entire population from which the participant is drawn. Pati does not reflect all fourth-grade children, but her story stimulates an analysis of how this one girl of a particular ethnic background, living in unique and difficult family circumstances, compares to and functions within the larger social settings in which she interacts. The case study provides the researcher and audience opportunities to more closely examine the human condition by focusing on an individual's life story. For more on case study research method, access Merriam (1998) and Stake (1995).

Grounded theory

Grounded theory is a systematic, methodological approach to qualitative research and analysis that constructs a theory from the ground up. It is an inductive and iterative process of data collection, coding, categorization, and analytic memo writing in order to arrive at a central or core category that helps formulate a theory to explain the phenomenon under investigation. The methodology was developed by sociologists Barney G. Glaser and Anselm L. Strauss (1967) and profiled in their germinal work, *The Discovery of Grounded Theory*.

Grounded theory relies primarily but not exclusively on separate interviews with a minimum of 10 participants to gather sufficient data to assess their variability. This variability of perspectives enables the analyst to find the properties and dimensions (i.e., the range of constituent qualities) of the phenomenon. Data are meticulously coded through processes such as In Vivo and Process Coding (see Chapter 5) to keep the analysis grounded in the participant's own language and to find key actions that drive the emergent phenomenon of interest. Composing analytic memos is an especially important part of the analytic scheme to detail the intricacies of the participants' processes and to construct how the various parts of the social phenomenon fit together.

For example, Saldaña's analysis of **secondary data** (relevant data derived from other sources and not personally collected by the primary researcher) about adolescent friendships generated the core category "discriminating." The grounded theory—a one-sentence statement with an accompanying narrative—that explains how teenagers discriminate is, "*An adolescent's inclusion and exclusion criteria for friendships are determined by the young person's ability to discriminate both positively and negatively among socially constructed peer stereotypes*" (Saldaña, 2016, p. 253;

emphasis in original). Data from young people about social dynamics with their friends and classmates suggested a developmental attunement to the stereotyped categories of cliques and types (e.g., cheerleaders, geeks, jocks, goths, and so on). But they were also able to discriminate—that is, to break through the stereotypes and acknowledge that not everyone perfectly fits a particular peer-attributed social category.

Discriminating included a dimension that ranged from accepting to excepting. The analytic memo below describes and expands on the dimensions. Related and relevant codes are capitalized and woven into the narrative to keep them integrated with the researcher's reflections:

> ACCEPTING AND EXCEPTING suggests a continuum, ranging from full admission of an individual into one's personal confidence or SOCIAL GROUP; to neutrality or indifference about the individual; through overt exclusion, rejection or avoidance of the individual. Adolescents ACCEPT others when the conditions for FRIENDSHIP are positive, including such properties as *compatibility* and *shared interests*. Adolescents EXCEPT others when the conditions for FRIENDSHIP lie on the opposite side of the spectrum. But regardless of where a teenager's choices about peers lie on the continuum, he or she is actively DISCRIMINATING. We DISCRIMINATE when we ACCEPT and we DISCRIMINATE when we EXCEPT. (Saldaña, 2016, pp. 252–253; emphasis in original)

Grounded theory is a time-intensive approach to qualitative research that requires meticulous cycles of coding and insightful analysis to derive the methodology's constituent elements of a core category, its properties and dimensions, and, of course, the grounded theory itself with an explanatory narrative of the social phenomenon at work. Thousands of published research studies in virtually every academic discipline have employed grounded theory's methods. Additional books on grounded theory can be found in the research methods literature; see Birks and Mills (2015); Bryant and Charmaz (2007); Charmaz (2014); Corbin and Strauss (2015); Gibson and Hartman (2014); and Urquhart (2013).

Phenomenology

Phenomenology, as it has evolved in qualitative inquiry, is the study of the nature and states of lived experiences. This approach distills primarily interview data to their essences and essentials to determine what something "is" or "means" to a collective body of participants. Most phenomenological inquiries are framed with research questions that begin with "What is/are . . . ?," such as "What is the nature of 'belonging,'?" "What does it mean 'to belong,'?" and "What are the lived experiences of 'belonging'?" Mark D. Vagle in his *Crafting Phenomenological Research* clarifies: "When we study something phenomenologically, we are not trying to get inside other people's minds. Rather, we are trying to contemplate and theorize the various ways things manifest and appear in and through our being in the world" (Vagle, 2014, p. 22).

As an example, Hlava and Elfers (2014) explored "The Lived Experience of Gratitude" by interviewing 51 individuals ranging in age from 18 to 80. Participants shared their stories, experiences, and understandings of the phenomenon, and the coresearchers wisely first analyzed transcripts through In Vivo Coding to remain close to people's constructions of gratitude, and then generated major categories and themes of meaning. Hlava and Elfers learned that the primary reported feature of gratitude was self–other relatedness, "an altered or enhanced feeling of connectedness. . . . Boundaries between self and other were reduced, softened, or attenuated" (p. 438). Gratitude is dynamic, meaning that it ranges in intensity from low to overwhelming, and even stimulates physical effects on one's body such as sensations in the heart and chest, warmth, and a sense of cathartic release. Emotional affects include responses such as comfort, joy, thankfulness, and a sense of feeling blessed.

Phenomenology requires an interviewer who can guide participants through carefully crafted questions about the topic of interest, because it is sometimes difficult for people to articulate clearly what something is or means to them. An open-ended question such as "What does 'home' mean to you?" can certainly generate some type of response from most interviewees, but an attentive interviewer will listen carefully to those initial responses to formulate additional prompts for participant elaboration: "You said that 'home' is a place where you feel 'comfortable.' What is it about a place that makes it 'comfortable' for you?" Also, phenomenologists are encouraged as much as possible to **bracket** or to set aside their own assumptions about the phenomenon so as not to influence the constructions by participants and the analysis of their responses. Of course, the scholarly literature related to the inquiry helps inform the study's design, but the researcher assigns priority to the experiences themselves as shared by participants for answering the primary research question.

Phenomenology can be utilized in all disciplines, and appears to have a particular affinity for qualitative researchers in sociology and psychology. It is a genre that taps into the ontological nature of the human condition and analyzes the meaningful wholes of often-elusive, taken-for-granted states of being.

Social and group experiences such as organizational change and election cycles can also be explored phenomenologically. See Brinkmann (2012); Smith, Flowers, and Larkin (2009); Vagle (2014); and Wertz et al. (2011) for insightful guidance on phenomenological studies and analysis.

Content analysis

Content analysis systematically examines primarily print and media materials' words and images for their topics, themes, concepts, and ideas through qualitative examination, often followed by quantitative analysis. The goal is to examine aspects such as frequency, type, correlation, and absence in a body of data to generate manifest readings that infer latent meanings. Content analysis colloquially "counts what counts," but only after a qualitative review of the contents.

A fascinating example of content analysis was reported by Back, Küfner, and Egloff (2010) in "The Emotional Timeline of September 11, 2001." The coauthors examined emotional words transmitted through text pagers (the technology at the time) immediately before and after the U.S. terrorist attack. The data base consisted of an Internet-accessible 6.4 million words from more than 85,000 pagers. They examined "words related to (a) sadness (e.g., *crying, grief*), (b) anxiety (e.g., *worried, fearful*), and (c) anger (e.g., *hate, annoyed*)" 2 hours before through 18 hours after the first attack (Back et al., 2010, p. 1417; emphasis in original). The most prevalent emotion immediately after the first attack was not sadness but anxiety, which lessened over time, most likely due to incoming information about the attacks. Anger strongly and steadily increased in the population, reaching a level 10 times as high than when the first attack began. Figure 6.2 shows the researchers' timeline. Read each item in the graph to grasp the details about the interrelationship between specific events and the emotions they generated. The authors concluded,

> This dynamic pattern of immediate negative emotions in response to the terrorist attacks has important implications for understanding the individual and societal consequences of September 11: On the one hand, anger might have been helpful for regaining a sense of control over the tide of events on an individual and collective level. . . . On the other hand, anger is known to predict moral outrage and a desire for vengeance, which—once aroused—seem to require an outlet. . . . This might help to explain individual acts of discrimination following the attacks, as well as societal responses such as political intolerance and confrontational policy. (Back et al., 2010, p. 1419)

Figure 6.2 The Emotional Timeline of September 11, 2001 (Back, Küfner, & Egloff, 2010).

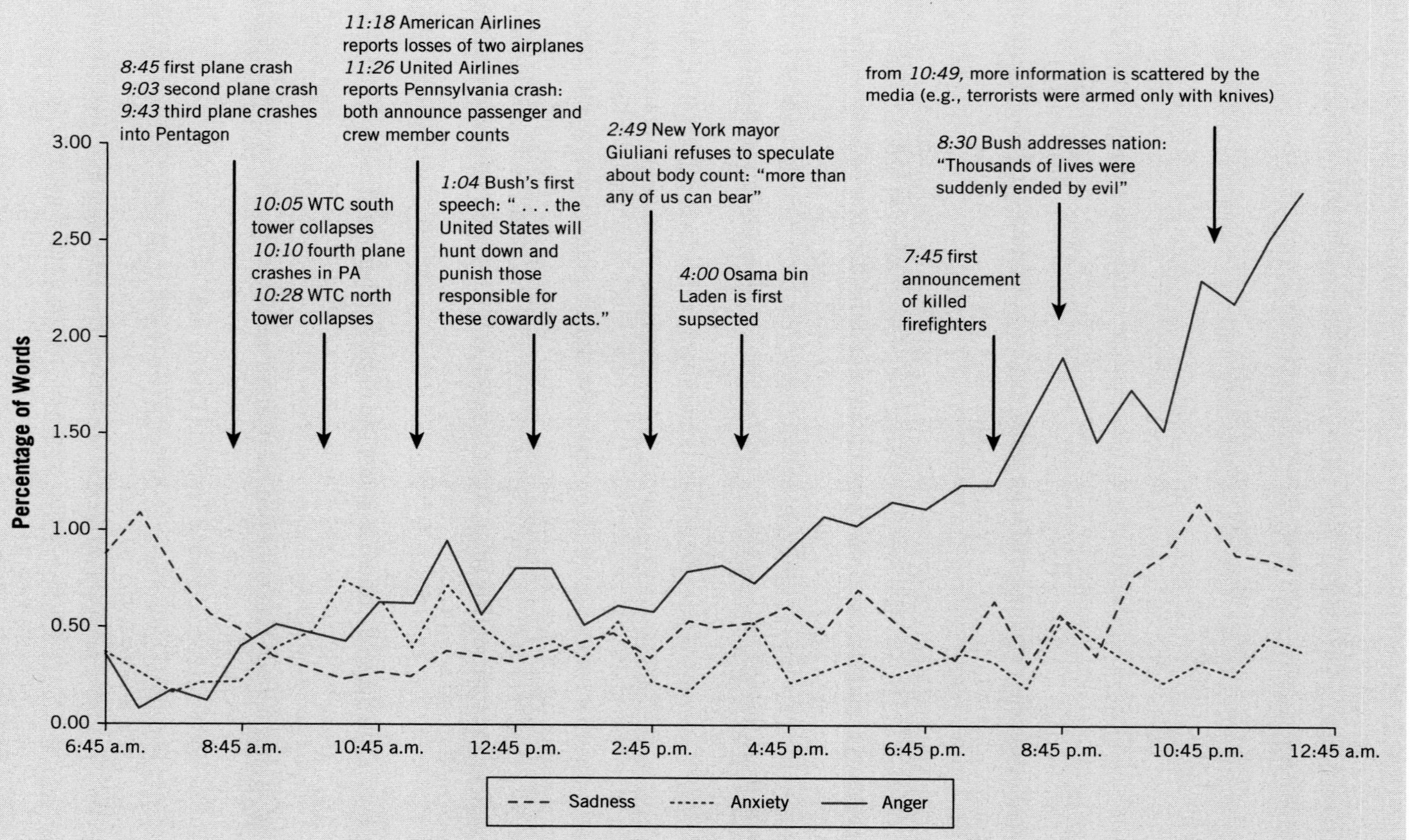

Percentage of Words

3.00
2.50
2.00
1.50
1.00
0.50
0.00

6:45 a.m. 8:45 a.m. 10:45 a.m. 12:45 p.m. 2:45 p.m. 4:45 p.m. 6:45 p.m. 8:45 p.m. 10:45 p.m. 12:45 a.m.

8:45 first plane crash
9:03 second plane crash
9:43 third plane crashes into Pentagon

11:18 American Airlines reports losses of two airplanes
11:26 United Airlines reports Pennsylvania crash: both announce passenger and crew member counts

10:05 WTC south tower collapses
10:10 fourth plane crashes in PA
10:28 WTC north tower collapses

1:04 Bush's first speech: " . . . the United States will hunt down and punish those responsible for these cowardly acts."

2:49 New York mayor Giuliani refuses to speculate about body count: "more than any of us can bear"

4:00 Osama bin Laden is first suspected

from 10:49, more information is scattered by the media (e.g., terrorists were armed only with knives)

8:30 Bush addresses nation: "Thousands of lives were suddenly ended by evil"

7:45 first announcement of killed firefighters

- - - Sadness   · · · · · Anxiety   —— Anger

Content analysis is a systematic approach to data analysis that is particularly applicable to print and media data. Quantitative content analysis traditionally requires intermediate statistical tasks, but more qualitative approaches place emphasis on coding for categories or themes. For additional readings in qualitative and quantitative content analysis, see Krippendorff and Bock (2009); Neuendorf (2017); and Schreier (2012).

Action research

Action research, also known as participatory action research, generally includes a change agenda in its fieldwork. Participants are viewed not as research subjects but as empowered collaborators working to make their local conditions better. The researcher and participants work together on a particular problem or issue to diagnose its sources, develop specific action strategies for changing the current conditions, and to assess the efficacy of their efforts. Action research is also used by many practitioners such as classroom teachers for self-reflection on their work and professional development.

Kitchen and Stevens (2008) note, "Simply stated, action research looks for answers to the question, 'how do I improve my work?'" (p. 12). To do so themselves, they conducted a meta action research project by educating preservice teachers on how to conduct action research in school settings, while Kitchen and Stevens simultaneously analyzed their own work as teacher educators. Kitchen and Stevens' primary action research question for their own reflection was, "Had we implemented an interdisciplinary action research model in such a way that we empowered PSTs [preservice teachers] professionally? Specifically, had [the PSTs] enhanced their practice and expanded their concept of what it means to be a teacher?" (pp. 14–15).

The coresearchers first examined the types of action research projects their preservice teachers created and implemented during their field experience. These projects consisted of reducing student stress and enhancing coping skill, improving girls' self-image in computer classes, increasing student engagement in history classes, and so on. The preservice teachers' final reports suggested that, for approximately two thirds of the class, "the focus and direction of the projects enhanced [their] professional development . . . by empowering them to reach out to children in significant ways; action research had enhanced their practice" (p. 20). The one third of university students who had difficultly conceptualizing and implementing action research suggested Kitchen and Stevens (2008) "respond to these challenges by providing [future] students with examples of research questions and projects written by other pre-service teachers" (p. 20).

At the end of the semester, it was time for the co-instructors as action researchers to collect student evaluation data that would inform them of their own efficacy as teacher educators. The positive testimonies provided by 75% of their students suggested, "Many of the pre-service teachers identified reflection as an important part of the process, which suggests that explicitly connecting reflection and action research can be a powerful strategy in teacher education" (Kitchen & Stevens, 2008, p. 21). But approximately 20% of the students expressed concern over the viability of the project, as in this honest response: "The action research was essentially useless. A research paper would have served us better. We do not have the experience or the time to worry about it in the practicum. I found the research part very helpful, but the action part was not" (Kitchen & Stevens, 2008, p. 21).

Kitchen and Stevens (2008) then reflected on the data they generated in addition to the students' data to formulate an action plan for future course instruction. They acknowledged the tight time frame and delays that existed getting the students' action research projects implemented. Thus, they realized that an earlier start the following year would be necessary. Though the coresearchers' unique experiences were with 32 students, they reflect further on the transferability of this project to other contexts: "When teachers learn they are capable of transforming student learning by researching their own practice, their conceptual understanding of teaching and learning changes. The connection between teacher-growth and student-growth becomes explicit" (p. 26).

Action research requires those who self-study to be deeply reflexive and honest with themselves. It often helps to have collaborators with this research genre to serve as sounding boards and reality checks for one another. For more on action research, see Coghlan and Brannick (2010); Fox, Martin, and Green (2007); Hacker (2013); and Stringer (2014).

Evaluation research

Evaluation research assigns judgments about the merit, worth, or significance of programs or policy (Rallis & Rossman, 2003, p. 492). Program evaluation is "the systematic collection of information about the activities, characteristics, and outcomes of programs to make judgments about the program, improve program effectiveness, and/or inform decisions about future programming. Policies, organizations, and personnel can also be evaluated" (Patton, 2015, p. 18). To Rallis and Rossman, evaluation data describe, compare, and predict. Description focuses on patterned observations or participant responses of attributes and details that assess quality. Comparison explores how the program measures up to a standard or ideal. Prediction provides recommendations for change, if needed, and how those changes might be implemented.

Patton (2008, p. 478) notes that four distinct processes are used to make sense of evaluation findings: analysis of the data for its patterns; interpretation of their significance, judgment of the results, and recommendations for action. "In the simplest terms, evaluations are said to answer three questions: What? So what? Now what?" (p. 5)

Santos-Guerra and Fernández-Sierra (1996) were commissioned to conduct a "Qualitative Evaluation of a Program on Self-care and Health Education for Diabetics" in a Spanish hospital. The coresearchers were invited to evaluate a medical program and a culture of practice that relies heavily on quantitative, experimental research for measures of efficacy. Santos-Guerra and Fernández-Sierra proposed to their clients that qualitative methods be used for this evaluation project—a model unfamiliar to the medical staff, but that it hesitantly accepted for the review.

The evaluation was conducted in two stages. The first stage consisted of four months of participant observation of a nurse's practice with patients, and researcher interviews with patients, their families, and doctors. Document reviews included information booklets from drug companies that were given to patients. The booklets also served as springboards for interviews with the recipients. The co-evaluators' preliminary report was critical of the program, which took the hospital staff by surprise and disappointed them. Yet this first stage of evaluation and its discussion with hospital personnel uncovered the problems observed by the outside reviewers:

> At this point an internal conflict between members of the staff was revealed. Doctors and nurses confronted each other either overtly or covertly when dealing with issues such as decision-making responsibilities, participation and evaluation of the program, and in general with internal aspects of their section. Some aspects were heavily questioned: the theoretical content of the program, functional specializations, areas of responsibility within the program management, degree of success, involvement of the doctors, benefits of the evaluating process, timetable of activities, work allocation, etc. (Santos-Guerra & Fernández-Sierra, 1996, p. 341)

With the curtain drawn back, so to say, revealing some of the hidden facets within the hospital unit, "the evaluation stimulated dialogue about the program and its value. It allowed program staff to discover and understand some of its variables and prepared the ground for improvement by a commitment to change and the next stage of exploration" (Santos-Guerra & Fernández-Sierra, 1996, p. 341).

The second stage of the evaluation lasted one year. New to this period was the addition of observations of doctors' medical sessions with patients, and self-development sessions with patients and their families. In the final report, Santos-Guerra and Fernández-Sierra (1996) offered 13 different points for the hospital staff to consider; these points included patient myths and errors about diabetes, differing patient perceptions of doctors' and nurses' roles, family members' involvement in the patients' diabetes management, and other categories such as patient training for diabetic care.

Although evaluation research utilizes many of the data collection and analytic methods profiled thus far, evaluation is considered a self-standing field of inquiry since its goals are purposely assessment driven. For resources in qualitative evaluation, access the works of Patton (2008, 2015) and Wadsworth (2011).

Autoethnography

Autoethnography is a recently developed genre of qualitative research that asks researchers to turn a reflexive gaze toward themselves. Adams, Jones, and Ellis (2015) explain that the genre is an "artistic and analytic demonstration of how we come to know, name, and interpret personal and cultural experience" (p. 1). Autoethnography is not limited to being a first-person autobiographical narrative of one's life or significant moments from it. The ethnography part of the methodology suggests that one's personal ways of living and one's ethos or value, attitude, and belief systems are critical features of the account. Autoethnography is the introspective examination of one's culture through a "culture-of-one's" experiences.

Sonny Nordmarken (2014) writes evocatively of his sex transition from female to male in "Becoming Ever More Monstrous: Feeling Transgender In-betweenness." The autoethnography traces the timeline of his testosterone treatments and other medical procedures with life story vignettes and internal monologues about his shifting identity. He explains to the reader relevant **argot** or cultural terms related to gender by defining the term *transmasculine* as "the general gender grouping I place myself within," and *cisgender* as "people whose gender identity and expression match their assigned gender" (p. 49). In this passage, Nordmarken provides an honest and revealing understanding of the tensions within himself as he interacts with the gendered, social world:

As a transgender being, my gendered shifting moves me into more betweennesses. I am *queerly between*: I occupy multiple positions at once, and different positions at different times, depending on how people read me—in regard to age and ability as well as gender. I am socially subjugated as transgender, even as I am beginning to experience in a new way what White male privilege is. And the subjugations of femaleness still shape my life. In social interactions, I still behave, perform, and position myself in the ways I have habitually done so, as someone who has been socialized female. I feel the feelings I have habitually felt as a result of being positioned as female and treated as inferior. Yet, now people often position me as male in social interactions. In many of these moments, I experience a feeling of inclusion that I have not ever felt, and in others, I feel excluded in ways I have never felt. Yet, at times, the femininity I continue to embody as a transmasculine being leads people to look at me funny. I feel new feelings particular to transness: anxiety, fear, hypervigilance. It can be dangerous to be a transsexual. It can be a lot of emotional work to navigate the cisgender world. I experience sexism, homophobia, transphobia, and White, male, able-bodied privilege. (Nordmarken, 2014, p. 38; emphasis in original)

Autoethnography, at its best, blends case study intimacy with ethnographic cultural revelation. The qualitative researcher becomes her own participant in a naturalistic study of personal life experiences. Self-inquiry can provide not only a deeper understanding of one's self: it also generates a first-person, authentic account of a way of life that informs audiences of the diversity of human nature. Yet autoethnography, if misused, can descend into an embarrassingly self-indulgent narrative of cathartic benefit for the writer but with little utility for the reader. The best stories teach us in some way, and stay in our memories for their impact and relevance to our own lives. For more on **autoethnographic** method, see Chang (2008); Jones, Adams, and Ellis (2013); Poulos (2009); and Spry (2011).

Mixed Methods

A discussion of **mixed-methods** research merits its own section because the methodology is the intentional blending of qualitative and quantitative data collection and analyses for studies that will benefit from the combined outcomes. Sometimes one type of measurement precedes the other to combine and build a stronger case. Or sometimes the first method is used and then its data are analyzed to determine how the second method's approach might be designed. Yet another approach is to **quantitize** or transform qualitative data into numeric representations for statistical analysis. Other various configurations of mixing exist, but the primary purpose is to generate a more substantive data base through different forms of inquiry in order to capitalize on each paradigm's strengths.

As an example, McCammon, Saldaña, Hines, and Omasta (2012a, 2012b) administered an online survey with 234 former students responding to the educational study, "Lifelong Impact: Adult Perceptions of Their High School Speech and/or Theatre Participation." Though many studies exist that suggest the potential benefits of the arts with adolescents in secondary school programs, virtually no research had been done on the long-term influences and affects, if any, on participants after they graduated from high school. Also, the coresearchers wanted to support the anticipated mass of qualitative respondent testimony with quantitative assessment. In other words, statistical evidence would be gathered to corroborate participants' claims, and to enable the researchers to employ several inferential tests to determine if any significant differences might exist between men and women, between those who pursued a career in theatre and those who pursued other occupational interests, between different generational cohorts, and so on.

The questions posed to participants asked for demographic and descriptive data such as gender, years of high school attendance, speech and theatre classes/extracurricular activities taken during high school, and current occupation. A series of questions asked for quantitative ratings on a **Likert scale** to key prompts, followed by an open-ended qualitative follow-up response. For example, two prompts from the 20-item survey included the following:

Quantitative

My participation in high school speech and/or theatre has affected the adult I am now.

4 = Strongly Agree, 3 = Agree, 2 = Disagree, 1 = Strongly Disagree: _____

Qualitative

In what ways do you think your participation in speech and/or theatre as a high school student has affected the adult you have become? (McCammon et al., 2012a, p. 24)

The mean rating from the 234 respondents to the above prompt was 3.82 out of 4.00, suggesting perception and consensus that affects were high. Four categories of outcome were constructed from their follow-up qualitative responses, titled

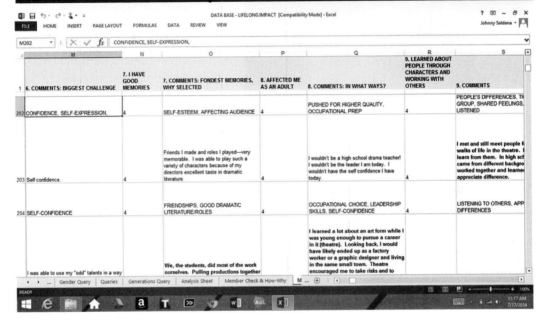

Saldaña, J. (2016).

"Lifelong Self-Confidence, Lifelong Thinking and Working, Lifelong Living and Loving, and Lifelong Legacy."

To get to these findings, each individual datum from every survey respondent was entered into its own cell in an Excel spreadsheet (see Figure 6.3). Cells were also used to enter various codes related to the narratives supplied by respondents. This data base enabled the analysts to reconfigure the matrix by gender, by high school experience, by generation, and so on, to composite and compare results. Interestingly, there were no significant quantitative or discernable qualitative differences between men and women, even though the researchers had hypothesized there would be. There were, however, selected significant statistical and qualitative differences between those who pursued speech or theatre as a profession and those who did not. In these cases, since both the quantitative results and the qualitative findings harmonized, there was **paradigmatic corroboration** or consensus between the numbers and the words. Two different and separate paradigms of measurement exhibited consistent findings and more strongly supported the researchers' claims.

Figure 6.4 The Lifelong Impact study examined the influences and affects of high school theatre and speech participation.

©iStockphoto.com/ferrantraite

One surprising outcome from the study was the subtle differences among the five decades of generations. Survey respondents aged 50 and above placed more value on extrinsic rewards and accomplishments during their high school years, whereas respondents in their 20s valued intrinsic outcomes such as friendships, personal growth, and identity development. In this case, qualitative analysis revealed what quantitative analysis could not.

Mixed-methods research is employed when the researcher determines that both qualitative and quantitative data will better inform the analysis in order to answer the research questions at hand. At its best, each paradigm not only contributes its own strengths, but also compensates for the other paradigm's information-generating deficiencies. Statistics can provide a generally acknowledged robustness to findings, whereas language offers a more human dimension and texture to the report. For additional readings in mixed methods, see Creswell and Plano Clark (2011) and Plano Clark and Ivankova (2016).

On Genres

Everything noted above about qualitative research genres and mixed-methods research has variants and exceptions, because each approach is remarkably malleable and eclectic. We have covered only a few of the wide variety of hybrid blends of qualitative inquiry practiced today. This textbook's goal is to introduce the reader to some of the most established and frequently used approaches to research. As researchers continue their professional development as scholars within particular disciplines, continuous readings of the current literature will acquaint them with several more genres available. Chapter 11 will illustrate selected styles of research presentation such as ethnodrama, narrative inquiry, and poetic inquiry, which we consider to be writing modalities (though others might consider them genres of qualitative research). As our discussion on research design and analysis continues, we will refer to particular methodologies on an as-relevant basis.

Some disciplines, including health care, seem to restrict themselves to a selected and acceptable canon of genres for publication. Other disciplines, such as communication, seem open to a range of genres, from the traditional to the arts based, in their literature. Individual research methods instructors and school faculty might espouse just a narrow band of methodologies as preferred ways of working. Other faculty and perhaps thesis and dissertation chairs might support students' forays into innovative topics, genres, and methods. Just as there are multiple ways to live a life, there are multiple ways to conduct research into life.

CLOSURE AND TRANSITION

We have provided an overview of major qualitative research methodologies. Each of these profiled studies was strategically designed beforehand. The next chapter discusses several considerations in the preparation of a qualitative research project that can draw on these methodologies.

RESOURCES FOR ANALYZING QUALITATIVE RESEARCH METHODOLOGIES

The following resources will offer you additional guidance on the major genres of qualitative inquiry:

Creswell, John W. (2013). *Qualitative Inquiry and Research Design: Choosing Among Five Approaches*, 3rd edition. Thousand Oaks, CA: Sage.

Pascale, Celine-Marie. (2011). *Cartographies of Knowledge: Exploring Qualitative Epistemologies*. Thousand Oaks, CA: Sage.

ANALYTIC EXERCISES FOR QUALITATIVE RESEARCH METHODOLOGIES

1. In a two-column worksheet, list the differences between and advantages of quantitative and qualitative research.

2. Write a reflexive essay on how you construct knowledge through experience.

3. Discuss with a peer why people have different interpretations of political candidates, political parties, and their platforms.

4. Discuss with a peer how a qualitative research study about race relations might be approached differently as an ethnography, phenomenology, case study, and autoethnography.

APPENDIX READINGS

The Appendix includes three representative qualitative research articles. Read at least two of them and compare and contrast their genres or methodologies.

Analyzing Qualitative Research Design

Introduction

Research is always about something, and is often framed as a question to answer, a topic to investigate, a mystery to solve, a case to document, new knowledge to gain, a program to evaluate, a dilemma to reconcile, or a story to tell. But before the study's fieldwork begins, there are preparatory matters that researchers must address to ensure a more informed and successful venture.

In this chapter we discuss the fundamentals of qualitative **research design**—the overall framework and provisional plan for initiating and conducting the study. Research design components are part of a formal research proposal, a written document that specifies the researcher's course of action, usually for funding applications or institutional review and approval (discussed in Chapter 8). Not everything in a research design or proposal is included in a study's final write-up (discussed in Chapter 11), but these design components are necessary preparatory matters to ensure a more successful project entry. Just as travelers should plan ahead before they take an extended long-distance trip, researchers should also plan ahead before they begin fieldwork.

Although some researchers think that anything done before collecting data is not the "real" research, the truth is that the researcher's mind actively analyzes when it considers all facets of the study, and analyzes throughout all initial design decisions and fieldwork preparations. Some tasks will be administrative and others inspiringly creative. Also, there is intricate interconnectivity among all the components discussed below. A choice made for one element triggers compatible choices for other elements. Three of Chapter 1's analytic principles are most applicable here:

Learning Objectives

After reading and reviewing this chapter, researchers should be able to

1. Identify and describe preparatory elements of research design, and

2. Explain how the components of a conceptual framework initiate research design decisions.

- Condensing large amounts of data
- Noticing patterns in textual and visual materials
- Unifying seemingly different things

Also, note that the final subtopic in this chapter, Conceptual Frameworks, is usually the first addressed in most qualitative research design discussions. We reserve it for the end because, even though a conceptual framework is one of the first items presented in a traditional qualitative report, it is usually one of the last things that crystallizes in the mind during the preparatory research design stage.

Since readers are now acquainted with the craft of collecting and initially analyzing data as well as major genres of qualitative inquiry, they can now transfer that knowledge into the principles and options described below. Here we discuss the art of qualitative research as it relates to a study's design.

Researching and Analyzing the Topic

Chapter 2 advised researchers to remain alert to what surprises, intrigues, or disturbs them in the field (Sunstein & Chiseri-Strater, 2012, p. 115). Those same three reactions can stimulate the proposed research topic. A researcher might be surprised, for example, by a news story she just happened to come across about a subject that interests her; she'd like to learn more about it. She could become intrigued by an individual who exhibits exceptional qualities in her field; she'd like to observe that person at work. Or she might be disturbed by a social injustice happening in her community that motivates her to take constructive action in some way.

The most important criterion for a topic choice is that researchers are passionate about what they wish to study. Without intrinsic motivation, researchers will believe their efforts are drudgery, which can result in lackluster work. If they have the ability to select their topic, they should choose something that excites them that they'd like to learn more about. Researchers should be cautious of simply repeating knowledge they already possess, or studying people they already know. Researchers expand their capacities when they tackle topics that have an element of the unfamiliar about them.

Focusing the study's topic

A topic crystallizes when a researcher can answer the question, "So, what's your research about?" If she can articulate her topic succinctly in one phrase within five seconds, she probably has a handle on it. As examples of topics, we list below some of our own qualitative and mixed-methods studies. Some of these were small-scale projects conducted and completed within two months; the longest one followed a participant and collected data about him over the course of 21 years. The number of participants in each study ranged from one person, to 20 children, to survey respondents from more than 1,200 high schools, as follows:

- A case study of a White, female, inner-city school teacher

- A case study of a young man from age 5 to age 26

- Bullying reduction strategies with fourth- and fifth-grade children

- Secondary school teachers' perceptions of a new state standards document

- A mixed-methods study on middle school students' values, attitudes, and beliefs

- Affluent and lower-income adolescents' perceptions of social issues

- Adults' perceptions of their high school theatre and speech experiences

- An autoethnography about an influential high school English teacher

- A survey of current theatre programs in American high schools

The world is large and life is complex. One common error beginning qualitative researchers make is conceptualizing a study with far too broad a scope. A former student admirably wanted to study "homelessness in the city." But with a Phoenix homeless population estimated at over 17,000 living over an area of 500 square miles, the lone researcher would have quite a daunting task ahead.

Deciding what to study as a first-time effort requires that a researcher focus her lens as a close-up shot rather than a panoramic view. Perhaps this student might have found it more manageable to conduct a case study of one homeless family, or an ethnography about a particular homeless shelter, or an action research project to improve a local charity's food bank program. We're not advocating that beginning researchers think small, but rather that they think realistically about what they can reasonably accomplish given the parameters of available time, resources, and accessibility to data. Condensing large amounts of data refers not just to the data corpus collected but also to the central idea for inquiry. The more time, resources, and research team members have available, the bigger the project can be.

One traditional component of many published quantitative studies is a section toward the end of reports subtitled "Limitations." This brief discussion discloses such matters as what was not addressed in the study, cautions about its findings' generalizability to broader populations, confesses any errors made during the research process, and so on. Some qualitative studies and reports do indeed have limitations, but we reconceptualize that our work also has parameters. Researchers explain to readers at the beginning, not end, of their reports, the particular facet of the social world investigated in order to establish with readers an implied contract of coverage. They define their **scope of inquiry**. Perceived boundaries, assumptions of transferability, and applications of the study's findings to other research contexts are ultimately the responsibility of the reader (Erickson, 1986).

Writing the purpose statement

A **purpose statement** formalizes the topic by addressing the what of the research and sometimes the why. Wolcott (2009) advocates that the purpose statement serves as a focusing framework for an investigation that sums up in one sentence its primary research goal. The general topic selected is now refined even further and integrated into a statement that begins, quite simply, "The purpose of this study is . . . ." This statement catalyzes other research design decisions, though what is discussed later in this chapter can be preceding steps to help refine the purpose statement.

Figure 7.1   A qualitative researcher can investigate a homeless family's experiences.

©iStockphoto.com/Steve Jacobs

Just as the topic of a research study can be overwhelming in magnitude, so too can a purpose statement. Examine this statement that is not only vague but also exceeds a lone researcher's grasp when only three to four months are available for fieldwork:

> The purpose of this study is to learn about homelessness in
> Phoenix.

There are several flaws with this statement. First, "to learn about" is a rather nebulously phrased research goal. Second, "homelessness" consists of so many constituent elements that it defies focused, short-term investigation. And third, "Phoenix" is a geographic site far too large for a single person to adequately investigate in just a few months' time. A purpose statement should include just enough specificity to identify a focused topic, its methodology, its most likely participants, and the suggested parameters of the study such as time, place, and so on. After reflection on what can reasonably be accomplished within three to four months of fieldwork, the purpose statement evolves into this manageable project:

> The purpose of this case study is to document the experiences of a
> homeless family living temporarily in a Phoenix area shelter.

Sometimes the purposes can be multiple yet closely interrelated:

> The purposes of this case study are to document the experiences
> of a homeless family living temporarily in a Phoenix-area shelter,
> and to assess the efficacy of city and county social services for the
> unhoused with this family.

Writing the rationale

Another important criterion for topic selection is its necessity. Justification for a study cannot be provided until a researcher investigates and analyzes what unpublished and published research currently exists about the topic. Research should, in some way, make an active contribution to the scholarship of a discipline and its thought and practice. Not every research study can culminate in a revolutionary, paradigm-shifting work, but every study, no matter how modest in scope, should exhibit **utility**—that is, usefulness for others. Some type of need should be met by research, including the investigator's professional development.

A narrative that is one or two paragraphs long usually accompanies the purpose statement, called the **rationale**. This consists of an overview of the professional and personal motives driving the study, brief references to key research literature, and the projected outcomes or benefits for the people involved. For example, below is the purpose statement for Saldaña's (2005b, 2010) field experiments with "Theatre of the Oppressed"—an arts-based social change modality using theatrical techniques with non-theatre participants:

> The purpose of this study is to document and assess the outcomes of a short-term action research project in Theatre of the Oppressed for bullying reduction among fourth and fifth grade children at a suburban elementary school.

After the purpose statement, the rationale explains to readers why the study is necessary and how it will productively contribute to disciplinary knowledge or social goals:

> The April 20, 1999, shooting tragedy at Columbine High School in Colorado served as a wake-up call for educators at all levels working with children and youth. Testimony by one teenage girl at a United States congressional hearing investigating violence in schools in the summer of 1999 encouraged curriculum programming and forums to provide "a place to vent anger and teach compassion." Gardner (1999) and Goleman (1995) assert that childhood and adolescence are critical windows of opportunity for such learning experiences and social development. Theatre of the Oppressed sessions I conduct with in-service elementary school teachers to help children cope with bullies and racism are well received and called "important" and "just what we're looking for" by the adult participants. Theatre of the Oppressed serves not only theatre educators but also elementary educators and the children themselves through their exploration of social issues to hopefully create a more positive school and social environment. (Saldaña, 2005b, pp. 117–118)

The rationale goes on to explain that there is little research in the published literature on Theatre of the Oppressed, particularly with children, and thus the study hopes to contribute productively to educational scholarship.

The purpose statement and rationale function both as road maps for the investigative journey; and as preliminary lenses, filters, and angles to keep the study focused as it begins. Keep in mind that qualitative inquiry is evolutionary by nature; thus, the purpose statement and rationale can change slightly or greatly as inductive learnings accumulate when data are collected and analyzed.

Analyzing the Literature

The literature review is a necessary preparatory component of all research studies. It is a survey and synthesis of previous research related to a topic to assess: its key authors and sources, what findings and theories have been developed, what lack of information or contradictory conclusions exist, and how one's own study might be informed by and build on previous work. Literature reviews also include methodological and methods literature in the field of qualitative research to determine which genre and methods might be most appropriate for data collection, data analysis, write-ups, and so forth. The literature review is not just a survey but also an analysis. It requires a researcher to first peruse massive amounts of available information and then to condense key elements as summaries, quote extracts, lists of main findings, and so on, and to find patterns or commonalities among previous studies.

Also be on the lookout for any research labeled a **metasummary**, **metasynthesis**, or **meta-ethnography**. These pieces have systematically culled and qualitatively analyzed multiple works about the same topic to find recurring themes or outcomes—a process similar to quantitative research's **meta-analysis**, which statistically validates results across comparable studies. In fact, it might be helpful to review several quantitative studies about a qualitative research topic, because those works might inform a researcher of key variables and categories which might be observed in fieldwork. Of course, reviewing both previously published qualitative and quantitative research is essential when conducting mixed-methods studies.

A network is the best metaphor for a literature review. Article A cites Articles B and C, which in turn cite each other as well as other works. Notice the same set of key authors referenced frequently, or a few articles or journal titles appearing repeatedly across different references and bibliographies. This is an important pattern to notice, and possibly signals some of the most influential research in the topic.

Initial searches

The explosion of information available in print and online makes it virtually impossible to read everything written about what a researcher plans to investigate. The strategic use of combined **keywords** to initiate an Internet or data base search about the topic is a first step. If a topic involves a particular population of participants (e.g., children, women, teachers) or a particular genre of research (e.g., grounded theory, phenomenology, etc.), including those parameters in a search narrows the items retrieved.

First, list the keywords or terms that are closely related to the topic and found within the purpose statement and rationale. Just some of the keywords that might be entered into a search engine for the Theatre of the Oppressed study discussed earlier include Theatre of the Oppressed, bullying, children, elementary school, and action research. After an initial review of the hits and a few articles, continued searches with new or revised keywords might be needed, such as Theatre for Social Change, Augusto Boal, school violence, and so on. Selected terms and concepts become canonized if not standardized within a particular discipline, yet there are also a prolific number of terms—sometimes as many as 50 or more—that generally refer to the same family of meanings.

The researcher might find several articles about the same topic in which the writers have employed different qualitative methodologies—for example, investigating the topic of bullying as a grounded theory study, a phenomenology, a case study, and so on. In addition, researchers might find that several disciplines have addressed the same topic, ranging from educational to psychological to sociological perspectives. A researcher cannot explore everything, but don't neglect intriguing material from related fields.

College/university libraries have site-specific search tools, especially for academic journal articles that tend to be cited frequently in other research reports. When we search for books about a topic, online retailer Amazon.com often presents more thorough search results than some library data bases. Unpublished theses and dissertations are lengthy reads, yet a few of them contain richly detailed literature reviews and procedures for data analysis that cannot be found in journal articles.

Organizing and managing the literature

Downloading entire articles or documents is certainly an option, but rather than storing them in one massive file, organize them into separate folders according to any emergent patterns noticed. One folder might contain materials related to theory, while another could contain articles about method. Dropbox (dropbox.com) and other cloud-storage sites can maintain voluminous downloaded materials.

It helps to keep a meticulous record of a literature review from the very beginning. Programs of choice among several qualitative researchers for this element of research design seem to be Excel and Evernote. Log all reference information about each source including the author's full name, the exact page range of a journal article or book chapter, the library call number or Internet address of the work, and a journal article's DOI (digital object identifier).

Highlighting key passages in the documents better synthesizes and extracts the salient portions for future reference. If the documents reviewed are digital, cut and paste key passages and add their sources' page numbers into individual

Excel cells. Label each passage with a prefacing code in caps to indicate its content: ABSTRACT, METHODS, FINDINGS, THEORIES, and so forth.

Consulting mentors, experts, and peers

Other researchers who have conducted studies related to the study a new researcher is undertaking, or who possess expertise in the topic, can offer valuable guidance for the new researcher's project. Most often students rely on faculty at their institutions as immediate resources. Graduate thesis or dissertation committees serve as the first go-to sources for research guidance. But student researchers should not neglect to tap into the experiences of peers at the masters and doctoral levels of study. Phone calls, Skype, e-mail, and other online communication can access specialists around the world.

Researchers should not go into a meeting before having made any preparation or preliminary research. It helps a researcher to refer to what she has learned thus far to inform the mentor of her knowledge base. By "shop-talking" about her study, she might come to some clarity about it since she has to articulate her thoughts and answer questions that bring together various thoughts swirling in her mind. After some initial conversation, a few suggested questions to ask a mentor include the following:

- What do you think are more specific research topics or questions I should consider?

- What types of studies does the field need more of?

- What's important for me to know as I go through this project?

Unifying the literature

The literature review is not just a bulky catalogue detailing everything that has been found, but also an analytic synthesis of previous knowledge. Again, the task is to condense then unify different approaches to the same topic by analyzing its patterned yet multifaceted nature. Each topic and project will cull its own unique corpus of related literature, but we provide just a few strategies for synthesizing the materials.

First, extract each study's major findings or outcomes, most often located toward the end of written reports. In the author's or researcher's own words, arrange these passages in lists and organize them thematically. In a literature review for one of our projects, we classified other studies' findings into emergent categories such as workplace skills, social development, emotional intelligence, communication skills, and so on. These clusters enabled us to learn what kinds of outcomes had already been derived, and how they might inform our own investigation into the phenomenon. Also important is to learn how the researchers got to their findings—that is, their data analytic methods.

Second, examine the studies' research design elements. Take note of the research questions their authors posed, how many participants were involved in each project, what methods of data collection were utilized, and other logistics of design discussed in this chapter. This investigation can offer ideas and resources for developing and administering the researcher's own fieldwork projects. Our own literature reviews for our studies have revealed a few poorly conducted and written pieces of research amid the mix. Thus, analyze the perceived credibility and trustworthiness of a work in addition to its contents.

Third, amalgamate the review by reflecting on and writing the answers to this question: "After reading these studies, what have I learned that will help me design and conduct my own research project?" A perceived purpose of a literature review is sometimes to prove to a teacher or supervisor that a student did indeed do her homework and has sufficient background knowledge about a particular topic. But the primary purpose of a review is to inform the researcher about the next steps to take before venturing into the field.

Expanding the literature review is an ongoing process throughout the study, even up to and including its write-up. Researchers will discover and access new works at all stages such as during fieldwork and data analysis, which will provide additional insights into the phenomena explored. Researchers should keep searching for materials as their studies continue, because they never know what serendipitous find could bring everything together.

Research Questions

Research implies the pursuit of answers, and good answers are best derived from good questions. Even the formulation of a question is an analytic act, because it requires the researcher to think through the many options available for inquiry. Development of the topic, purpose statement, rationale, methodology, and literature review might precede and stimulate a series of specific questions about the proposal. But even human puzzlement, confusion, or curiosity about a social phenomenon can set in motion an intriguing idea for a study that, in turn, generates questions that become more refined as the researcher conducts the literature review and formulates a rationale. Even during fieldwork and data analysis, new questions might emerge as the researcher reflects on the participants' and her own experiences.

Research questions can be constructed during any preliminary stage of the project, but we strongly recommend having a working set developed before data collection begins. Questions provide lenses, filters, and angles for inquiry and keep researchers on track with their endeavors.

Developing research questions

Aside from the purpose statement and rationale as frames for a study, the **central** and **related research questions** are additional guidance for inquiry. Most research questions for qualitative studies begin in one of four ways:

1. What . . . ?

2. How . . . ?

3. In what ways . . . ?

4. Why . . . ?

"What" questions get at descriptive identification of a phenomenon's elements and the nature of states and being. "How" questions get at human processes, while "in what ways" questions get at processes and categories of experience. "Why" questions address attribution (reasons for outcomes) and the processes of causation. Some qualitative researchers are leery of asking "why" questions because they believe that attribution and causation cannot be reliably documented in the data we collect. But "why" is a prompt frequently used in everyday life to inquire why things are as they are. As long as researchers present a solid case for their arguments, the answers to "why" questions address human motives, purposes, reasons, circumstances, contexts, habits, and traditions— answers to the five Rs of inquiry: routines, rituals, rules, roles, and relationships.

Think of a central research question as the center of a web that connects related research questions around it (see Figure 7.2). Also, in our figure the number of related research questions is kept to five. There is actually no standardized or required number established, but we recommend that three to a maximum of five related questions will suffice for most small-scale qualitative studies and keep the project manageable.

As you brainstorm the central and related research questions, keep in mind that you will most likely compose a series of them on a monitor screen that you will

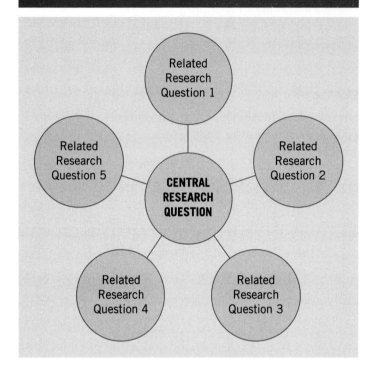

Figure 7.2 The central research question serves as a focal point that holds the related research questions.

Related Research Question 1

Related Research Question 5

CENTRAL RESEARCH QUESTION

Related Research Question 2

Related Research Question 4

Related Research Question 3

revise, combine, delete, and cut and paste into a particular order until you think you have a handle on the scope of the project. Here is the purpose statement about the study of a homeless family:

> The purposes of this case study are to document the experiences of a homeless family living temporarily in a Phoenix area shelter, and to assess the efficacy of city and county social services for the unhoused with this family.

A series of possible research questions to drive the inquiry are now composed, stimulated by the researcher's curiosity, suggested by the literature review, implied by the purpose statement, and so on. Questions are best phrased as open-ended rather than close-ended prompts (i.e., those answered "yes," "no," or "maybe"). A researcher having trouble generating initial research questions for his study should start a line with one of the four initial prompts (what, how, in what ways, why) and let his mind create possible areas for investigation. A first-draft brainstormed list of questions in no particular order follows:

- What hardships are encountered by a homeless family?
- How does a homeless family cope with everyday necessities (food, shelter, water, etc.)?
- In what ways does a shelter provide support for homeless families?
- Why do families become homeless?

- What causes homelessness?

- How do city and county social services programs provide support for homeless families?

- What is the efficacy of city and county social services for the unhoused?

- In what ways are homeless families' experiences different from those of homeless individuals?

- What schooling is provided to homeless children?

- What are the routines, rituals, and rules of homelessness?

- In what ways is homelessness a culture?

- How does a homeless family enter and leave a temporary shelter?

The next step is to reflect on the brainstormed list and revise the questions into a preliminary set of questions for the study. Again, each researcher will bring to the topic her own lenses, filters, and angles that will shape the content of each question. But for this particular case study, here is the working set that will initiate the data collection and analysis. Notice how the central research question closely aligns with the purpose statement:

- **Central Research Question**: What are the experiences and perceptions of a homeless family living temporarily in a Phoenix-area shelter?

- **Related Research Questions**
  - Why does a family become homeless?
  - How do homeless family experiences differ from those of homeless individuals?
  - What is the local culture of a homeless shelter?
  - In what ways do city and county social services programs provide support for a homeless family?

Research questions are not set in stone. They are a preliminary and provisional list of lines of inquiry for initial guidance. As new literature is reviewed and fieldwork gets underway, researchers might make discoveries about the topic or come across an intriguing opportunity to follow a different yet related path for investigation. Don't be afraid to revise questions as needed. A study is made stronger by fine-tuning questions as fieldwork proceeds.

Site Selection

Chapter 2 discussed several principles of site selection for a study. As a brief review, the researcher sets the fieldwork at a location where participant action, reaction, and interaction can be best observed as people enact their routines, rituals, rules, roles, and relationships with one another. The researcher's positionality as a peripheral, active, complete, and/or covert observer (the latter used only in special circumstances) enables her to perceive and interpret social life through various lenses, filters, and angles. When we consider a particular site for participant observation, we of course must have permission to work in closed settings that are not publicly accessible.

Site selection is a component of research design when fieldwork is necessary to provide data and thus possible answers to the research questions of interest. The purpose statement and their generated questions will suggest whether naturalistic observation is merited. The homeless study openly states that a Phoenix shelter is the primary site for learning about its culture and the way one family interacts within it. Other studies might be designed to gather people's perceptions about selected topics, and thus interviews or written surveys would be the preferred data collection methods. Yet remember that studies can be enriched when multiple methods are used to triangulate findings. It's one thing to interview a teacher once about his practice; it's another thing to read a week's lesson plans he's composed for his curriculum; and it's still another thing to observe him as he works six to seven hours a day with children in a classroom over the course of nine months.

Participant Selection

The choices made thus far for a research design also suggest the number and types of participants (if any) for a qualitative study. The genre of research in particular plays a significant role in how many and who specifically become the people observed and/or interviewed. A case study can revolve around one family, while an ethnography can focus on a small town's geographic area and general populace. Autoethnography hones in on the researcher herself as the primary participant, while a traditional content analysis of online textual and visual materials needn't rely on human participants at all.

Most beginning researchers ask, "How many people should I interview/observe?" Though many seasoned researchers often reply, "It depends," we offer, "Enough to sufficiently answer your research questions with credibility." Some methodologists prescribe a minimum number of participants ranging anywhere from 10 to 40 for selected genres such as grounded theory. Some writers of sociological survey research advise a minimum of 200 respondents to enable generalization of findings to a broader population, with 30 to 40 survey respondents sufficient for research methods course purposes (Churton & Brown, 2010, p. 225). But there are also commonsense expectations about selected genres such as phenomenology. One person's perceptions do not a trustworthy phenomenological study make, and neither do just five people's collective contributions. Ten is better, and 30 even more to provide a sufficient amount of data for a trustworthy analysis. Rich interview data from one person can make an exceptional case study, while long-term observations and periodic interviews with that same person and his relationships in various cultural milieus become the foundation for an ethnographic study.

Qualitative methodologists offer the concept of saturation as a heuristic for sensing that the researcher has learned what she can (but not necessarily all that she can) from the participants—a feeling that nothing new is being learned as more people are interviewed or observed. For example, McCammon et al.'s (2012a) mixed-methods survey analyzed the incoming data from a total of 234 respondents over several months' time. But after the first 75 of them had been coded, the same types of responses appeared in the remaining 159 returned surveys. The researchers accepted and analyzed everything they received to enhance the quantitative data base, but the qualitative corpus was saturated about one third of the way through the data collection process.

Sampling

Participant selection is not just about numbers: it's also about representative qualities. Sampling (discussed in Chapter 4) refers to the parameters and procedures used for selecting the specific people for a study. Even if the researcher decides to follow just one person as a case study, there are still numerous factors to consider before finalizing the one. Sometimes we choose participants because of a unique opportunity. An intriguing individual, group, site, or event might capture a researcher's interest for in-depth documentation and analysis. Clark-Ibáñez's (2008) case study of Pati as a "bad girl," and Back, Küfner, and Egloff's (2010) analysis of the emotional timeline of September 11, 2001, are examples of rich opportunities for qualitative study.

There are times when participant selection needs to be purposive or targeted. The research questions generated will most likely address a particular population or demographic of interest. Some studies call for a representative sample of a larger population. By collecting data from a spectrum of individuals of varying ages, ethnicities, genders, and so on, researchers cast a wider net around the diversity of human experiences and ensure an analysis with more depth and breadth. We might also make the case for the transfer of findings to larger populations. Hlava and Elfers's (2014) study on the lived experiences of gratitude interviewed 51 people ranging in age from 18 to 80. The sample consisted of 31 women and 20 men; 38 were Caucasian and 13 were people of color; their completed years of education ranged from high school to doctoral degrees. This broad sampling of participants provided a landscape of data and made a strong representative case for the authors' analysis of gratitude.

There are times when we choose readily available participants simply out of convenience, but there are a few occasions in qualitative inquiry when random sampling is appropriate. This is most often the preferred method of traditional quantitative methodology, in which every person has an equal chance to be randomly selected as a participant for a study. Qualitative random sampling might be appropriate for mixed-methods studies or for a data base that requires a broad representation for analysis and transfer of findings to the population at large.

Again, we offer that the number and types of participants studied for a research project should be just enough to sufficiently answer the research questions with credibility. When in doubt, look at the numbers of participants used in previous studies culled from the literature review, and seek the guidance of a mentor who can recommend a suitable range of people for a particular project. Remember that we are pursuing quality of data, not necessarily quantity. A researcher can interview 100 people for a grounded theory project, but if shallow questions generated shallow responses, all has been for naught. But just 10 richly detailed interviews with a strategic spectrum of participants can generate a data corpus of immense analytic value.

Data Collection Methods

The selection of a qualitative research methodology to frame an investigation greatly influences the overall research design. And the specific central and related research questions also suggest particular data collection and analytic methods to answer them. Chapters 2 through 5 introduced readers to some of the most frequently used methods of gathering qualitative data. That working knowledge now comes into play as initial decisions are made about the types and amounts of data needed.

When a study's purpose and questions focus primarily on people's experiences, perceptions, feelings, interpretations, values systems, and so on, any data gathering method can help gather those insights, but interviews will most likely be the more direct way of getting them. When a study examines processes of social interaction and the dynamics of human relationships and culture, then participant observation is a strategic choice. The documents and artifacts of the material world provide tangible evidence about their creators or owners, and allow analysts to attribute inferred meanings about their purpose or significance. A combination of two or more types of data adds value to the corpus by adding multiple dimensions to the analysis.

Specific genres of qualitative research generally prescribe a canon of methods for their data bases. Grounded theory usually, but not exclusively, relies on interview data, while traditional ethnography depends on a wide array of data forms for the documentation of a culture. Mixed methods and sometimes evaluation research include a quantitative component in addition to a qualitative data base. Phenomenological studies depend greatly on a number of interviews, while content analysis usually examines textual documents and visual and media materials. Even autoethnography is not restricted to the researcher's memories for data. Autoethnographers sometime interview friends, colleagues, and family members or examine personal artifacts for supplemental insight into one's self and cultural world.

Recall the central research question of the homeless family case study: "What are the experiences and perceptions of a homeless family living temporarily in a Phoenix-area shelter?" The question suggests that their experiences can be documented through participant observation of the family's interactions with other unhoused people and shelter staff, and interviews with family members can gather stories about their time before and during their stay at the shelter. Their perceptions could be inferred through observation of their interactions with others, but more credible data will most likely be generated through individual and family interviews and occasional informal conversations. The related research question, "In what ways do city and county social services programs provide support for a homeless family?," might be answered through a review of official print and online documents, in addition to interviews with shelter staff as well as the homeless themselves. Overall, researchers should choose the one or multiple data collection methods that will best provide answers for the central and related research questions.

Data Analysis Methods

A conundrum of research design for beginners is proposing the data analytic methods to be employed for a study. Researchers new to qualitative inquiry are not always aware of the multiple methods available. That's why we have been introducing them from the beginning of the book and we will continue to do so, yet there is still much more to learn about qualitative data analysis.

The methodology chosen, coupled with the purpose statement and research questions, suggest not only the data collection methods but also the analytic methods. For example, grounded theory prescribes coding cycles and analytic memos that help guide the researcher toward a core category and theory development. A phenomenological study most often works toward the development of themes, though how the researcher gets there varies among its methodologists. Case study research is fairly fluid in how to analyze data for eventual write-up, while newer ethnographic methods have branched into several hybrid forms, challenging the traditions of 20th-century standards and practices.

Chapters 9 and 10 will focus on qualitative analysis exclusively and discuss even more ways to engage with data. For research design purposes, propose what you believe will be best suited for your study in terms of analytic outcomes, consisting of one or more of the following:

- Major categories or concepts
- Primary themes
- Assertions
- Narratives (descriptive, explanatory, interpretive, evaluative, critical, etc.)
- Figures (tables, diagrams, matrices, models, etc.)
- Statistics
- Theory
- Arts-based forms (poetry, ethnodrama, short film, etc.)

Presentation Modes

A speculative matter of qualitative research design is proposing what the final presentation might look like. Most students in a research methods course might prepare a final paper in accordance with the instructor's requirements for format, length, and so on. Theses and dissertations are other student-related documents, yet most published research works appear as academic journal articles, both in print and online. Book chapters, monographs, and full-length books are other available formats for more established researchers. Professional association conferences are other opportunities for brief oral presentations, poster sessions, and panels to moderately sized audiences. Emergent formats at these gatherings can include poetic inquiry readings, ethnotheatrical performances, visual art installations, short videos, and other novel modalities.

Contemporary qualitative research offers exciting hybrids of representation and presentation. But be cautious of choosing novelty for its own sake or to appear trendy. The presentation format for research should be the one(s) that best represents the genre and findings of the investigation, and the one(s) that will target the most receptive readerships/audiences. If a project was grounded theory, perhaps the most appropriate formats are a standard journal article, poster presentation, and/or conference paper. Ethnographies can appear in condensed form as a journal article or chapter, yet range to a full-length book released by a commercial publisher. Autoethnographies are certainly appropriate for academic journals receptive to such works, but autoethnographies can also make an impact as performative conference presentations.

In sum, propose what the final report might look like in its first format. Chapters 11 and 12 will acquaint readers with additional presentation modes for writing, as well as oral and mediated delivery of research to various audiences.

Timeline Design

One of the most frequent frustrations we've heard from students is how much time it takes to transcribe an audio-recorded interview. After that, we hear about how long it took them to analyze a qualitative data set. Yes, one of the reasons is that they were doing these research tasks for the very first time and learning the ropes. Eventually, analysis does indeed go faster once the analyst "gets it" and establishes a personal rhythm for working with data. But we will be realistic with readers and state that, no matter what level one is at as a qualitative researcher, good research takes time—time to prepare, time to collect and analyze data, and time to write.

From our own research project experiences, we've found that approximately 15% to 20% of available time was spent on research design and preparation, 50% to 60% for fieldwork and data analysis, and 20% to 25% for the final writing stage (Saldaña, 2011b, p. 81). Keeping these rough percentages in mind, work backward from the final due date for a written report or other presentation to allocate on a calendar the provisional periods for preparation, fieldwork/analysis, and write-up. Be forewarned that time is a slippery construct, and best-guess projections can be underestimated. Plan ahead and allow a few more clock hours, days, and even weeks for the unexpected contingencies that usually arise, and the necessary time for quality data analysis and reflection. Plot an ideal calendar for all stages of the project and do your best to stick to it fiercely. If possible, put as many other responsibilities as you can on hold, and eliminate any distracting "personal drama" to provide you ample time for focused study.

Conceptual Frameworks

Up to this point, we've discussed the constituent elements of data collection, methodologies, and research design. This section discusses how they all come together into a more unified whole. A **conceptual framework** (also known as a theoretical framework by some) is, for lack of a better phrase, an intellectual game plan for the study. It's one of the most elusive elements of research design for novices, and we have deliberately placed our discussion of it toward the end of this chapter. Our reason is that everything discussed from Chapter 1 onward has been part of a conceptual framework. Now it's time to reflect on and analyze how all those different elements align with one another.

A conceptual framework is a narrative that consists primarily of the epistemological, theoretical, and methodological premises about a project (Saldaña, 2011b, p. 81). It explains to readers the researcher's assumptions about how knowledge is constructed, what major theories drive the study, and why a particular qualitative genre for the research design was selected. This trinity of concepts sets in motion all other design decisions such as research questions, participant selection, data collection and analysis methods, and so on. There is an implied unity in a conceptual framework—an investigative architecture that suggests the researcher has thought through all preliminary decisions carefully to make everything go together.

Epistemological premises refer to how the researcher perceives and experiences the social world and how she constructs personal knowledge about it. Her lenses, filters, and angles inform the reader of her positionality or standpoint. Theoretical premises offer the main ideas that serve as foundations for an inquiry. The literature review is a primary source for finding the major schools of thought about a topic. Methodological premises then present a rationale of sorts. Now that the researcher has explained who she is and what theories are important to her, she next describes why and how she's going to investigate her topic in a particular way.

Examples of conceptual frameworks

Below are excerpts from a conceptual framework for Saldaña's (1997) ethnographic study of Nancy, a White, novice, inner-city teacher working at Martinez School—a K–8 urban site with a 98% Hispanic student population. We have inserted in brackets which of the following statements are epistemological, theoretical, and methodological premises—and note that one statement meets the criteria for all three. It is not always necessary to separately discuss each premise in its own paragraph. An intermingling of them within the overall narrative illustrates and reinforces their intricate connectivity:

> [Theoretical Premises] Teacher folklore and professional literature in education are replete with examples of beginning teachers who experience "culture shock" and learn how to "survive" in inner-city schools (Lancy, 1993, pp. 168–187). Nancy's problems and perceptions as a White, first-year teacher in a predominantly Hispanic school were typical of those in similar situations reported in the research literature. . . .
>
> [Epistemological Premises] This study adopts the interpretive inquiry paradigm and methods of Erickson (1986), which state that significant participant actions, embedded in social and cultural contexts, can be observed and interpreted by the researcher who attempts to make meaning of them from the participant's point of view. [Methodological Premises] Also adopted are the methodological caveats of Stanfield (1993) and Andersen (1993), which state that multiethnic qualitative research is inherently political and emotion laden for the participants, researchers, and readers. [Epistemological Premises] Thus, emotional engagement and self-reflection by the researcher of color during all phases of the study are not considered biasing but essential qualities for social insight. . . .
>
> [Epistemological Premises] Admittedly, I develop this report with my cultural worldview—my knowledge, value, attitude, and belief systems—as an Hispanic raised in an environment not as impoverished as but somewhat similar to the Martinez School youths'. The ethnic lens I used throughout this process brought selected issues to the foreground into sharper focus for analysis. Consequently, some readers may perceive this analysis skewed and my interpretations "biased." [Theoretical Premises] But researchers such as Grant and Tate (1995) and Marín and Marín

(1991) consider my ethnic background an essential prerequisite for this particular case study. [Epistemological, Theoretical, and Methodological Premises] Andersen (1993) asserts that there can be no "color-blind stance" in qualitative work of this nature: "Minority group members have insights about and interpretations of their experiences that are likely different from those generated by White scholars" (p. 43). [Epistemological Premises] Since ethnic issues in qualitative research are, by default, emotion laden for researchers, participants, and readers, I openly proclaim my voice as a scholar of color and reject elites who would discount my worldview. (adapted from Saldaña, 1997, pp. 26–28)

With these premises in mind, the report then explains that culture is a central concept in a study of this nature, and thus ethnography was chosen as the most appropriate research genre to conduct the study. Research questions addressed educational interactions in cultural contexts, whereas data collection methods relied on traditional ethnographic practices of participant observation, interviews, document and artifact reviews, and descriptive statistics. Data analysis focused on assertion development to develop and discuss three major cultural themes.

The conceptual framework example above includes **citations** and references to sources culled during the literature review. This stage of research design, coupled with some deep analytic thinking on the researcher's part on how everything fits together, builds the framework for a study. If a new house's foundation and skeletal structure serve as analogies, consider that cement, lumber, and drywall are three necessary materials for the dwelling. If just one of those elements is substituted with a lesser alternative—such as plaster instead of cement—the house will be poorly built. The same goes for a conceptual framework and its three components of epistemological, theoretical, and methodological premises. An incompatible choice for just one of those premises makes for a shaky research foundation.

Some researchers use visual models to illustrate their conceptual frameworks. Wallace and Chhuon (2014) examined "Proximal Processes in Urban Classrooms: Engagement and Disaffection in Urban Youth of Color." Proximal processes refer to bidirectional relationships and interactions between an adolescent and a teacher that are meaningful and authentic, and that contribute toward positive youth development. The adolescent feels known by adults and has a sense of agency toward his own learning. Figure 7.3 illustrates their theoretical explanation of how proximal processes would play a role in their interviews with young people:

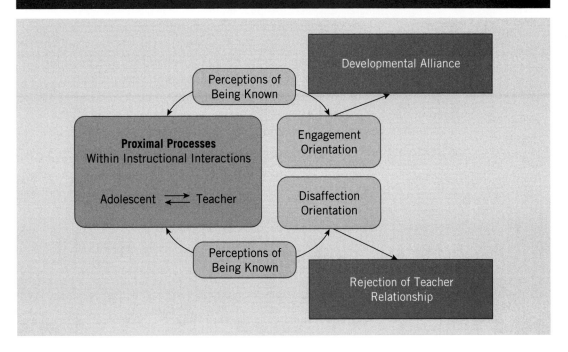

Adolescents make sense of their schooling via proximal processes experienced within instructional interactions. Examples of proximal processes constituted in instructional practice include providing feedback to students on the work they produce, structuring and implementing learning activities, and managing student behavior.

Adolescent interpretations derived from experiencing instructional interactions are hypothesized to inform short-term engagement and disaffection orientations depending upon the nature of the interaction experienced and the perceptions that are derived from the interpretations of that experience. In other words, the meaning making that results from experiencing instructional interactions informs adolescents' short-term decision to assent to learn or withhold that assent (i.e., engagement or disaffection orientation). (Wallace and Chhuon, 2014, pp. 943–944)

If you are confounded by composing a narrative of your conceptual framework, try diagramming one or more components of it. Figures can help readers and audiences quickly grasp the epistemological, theoretical, or methodological underpinnings of a study.

Again, conceptual frameworks are one of the most difficult research design elements for novice researchers to grasp. But as with many things, hands-on experience with creating them leads to better understanding. A conceptual framework is one of the first items presented in a traditional qualitative research report, but it is usually one of the last things that crystallizes in the mind during the preparatory research design stage. The core analytic skill of unifying seemingly different things is truly tested when we compose our premises for inquiry.

CLOSURE AND TRANSITION

Qualitative researchers enter an investigation with a tentative plan rather than a firmly fixed and inflexible agenda. The design choices made at the onset are provisional and one's best-informed decisions at the moment. This is not to suggest a hesitant or indecisive approach to inquiry but an open-ended one that accommodates the contingent nature of real life as it occurs in an improvisational manner. A classic saying among methodologists is that qualitative researchers should go into the field with an open mind, not an empty head.

The next chapter addresses the ethics of our work with human participants, including the proposal and presentation of research designs to Institutional Review Boards.

RESOURCES FOR ANALYZING QUALITATIVE RESEARCH DESIGN

The following resources will offer you additional guidance for methods of research design:

Marshall, Catherine, and Gretchen B. Rossman. (2016). *Designing Qualitative Research*, 6th edition. Thousand Oaks, CA: Sage.

Maxwell, Joseph A. (2013). *Qualitative Research Design: An Interactive Approach*, 3rd edition. Thousand Oaks, CA: Sage.

Ravitch, Sharon M., and Matthew Riggan. (2017). *Reason & Rigor: How Conceptual Frameworks Guide Research*, 2nd edition. Thousand Oaks, CA: Sage.

ANALYTIC EXERCISES FOR QUALITATIVE RESEARCH DESIGN

1. Review a key journal title dedicated to qualitative research in your discipline. Examine a few issues' article topics addressed in the titles and abstracts. Select an article and look for the research questions that drove the study.

2. Develop a one-sentence statement of purpose for a small-scale qualitative study you might conduct on one of the following topics: diabetes, career burnout, mathematics education, gender, or music.

3. Develop central and related research questions for a small-scale qualitative study about one of the following topics: workplace bullying, parenting an infant, teaching high school English, or living with a life-threatening disease.

4. Imagine you'll be conducting a literature review about existing research on homeless families. Search for the most appropriate academic journal titles, Internet Web sites, government and social services documents, and local resources in your area to begin the review.

5. Discuss with a peer the most appropriate sites and participants for a qualitative study about one of the following topics: dating, pets, smoking, pregnancy, or poverty.

6. Write a brief narrative about the data collection and data analysis methods you might employ for a qualitative study about social media (Facebook, Instagram, Twitter, Grindr, etc.).

7. If you were to conduct an autoethnography about some cultural aspect of your life, reflect on the specific topic and what presentation modes (oral reading, performance, print, Internet blog, video, etc.) you think would best represent your personal story.

OUTLINE FOR A QUALITATIVE RESEARCH PROPOSAL

The bullet-point outline below for a research proposal is based on this chapter's contents, but there might be course- or institution-specific guidelines for research proposals you should also follow. This is a summary overview of Chapter 7, arranged in a slightly different order. Some items might not be needed for your proposal (e.g., no field site for a content analysis), and the order of items can be rearranged as needed to create a smoother narrative:

- Title/Topic of the Study

- Researcher(s)

- Statement of Purpose

- Rationale for the Study

- Literature Review

- Conceptual Framework Narrative/Figure

- Methodology/Genre of Qualitative Research for the Study

- Central Research Question

- Related Research Questions

- Field Site Selection

- Participant Selection

- Data Collection Methods

- Data Analysis Methods

- Parameters/Potential Limitations of the Study

- Presentation Modes for the Report

- Calendar/Timeline for the Project

- References

- Appendixes (e.g., interview protocols, budget, correspondence)

- Researcher's Résumé/Curriculum Vitae (CV)

Analyzing Research Ethics

Introduction

While the philosophical study of ethics has been a central part of academia for centuries, the formal and systematic application of ethical principles to research in settings such as universities increased in earnest in the mid to late 1970s. Following the atrocities committed by the Nazi regime in the name of "research," and the unethical medical practices committed by the U.S. Public Health Service such as the "Tuskegee Study of Untreated Syphilis in the Negro Male" in which doctors deliberately withheld medical information and treatment from African American male patients in the South, the United States and countries worldwide mobilized to implement standardized research **protocols** and best ethical practices. In 1974, a few years after a whistleblower revealed details about the Tuskegee experiment, the United States passed the National Research Act, which created a commission tasked with identifying fundamental ethical guidelines that would ideally undergird the conduct of all research with human subjects. The results were published in 1979 as the **Belmont Report**, issued by the Department of Health, Education, and Welfare (DHEW), a precursor to the Department of Health and Human Services. The core tenets of this document have been incorporated into ethical guidelines by national organizations, universities, and other research institutions so broadly that it is important to highlight some of the most salient points here. We will discuss the practical implications of these findings in more detail throughout this chapter when reviewing how to prepare a study that complies with an institution's ethical guidelines. The three basic ethical principles outlined in the Belmont Report follow:

Learning Objectives

After reading and reviewing this chapter, researchers should be able to

1. Define the basic rules of research, including consent, confidentiality, comprehensive information, communication, and conflict-free research;

2. Compose and complete essential documents such as Institutional Review Board (IRB) applications and informed consent letters; and

3. Analyze complex and ambiguous ethical issues and evaluate the outcomes of possible researcher actions.

Respect for persons. This includes the conviction that people be treated as autonomous agents, along with the conviction that people with diminished autonomy (children, the mentally ill, incarcerated individuals, etc.) be entitled to protection. This also generally requires that research subjects participate in a study voluntarily and that they be given adequate information about the study to inform their decisions regarding participation.

Beneficence. This includes the classic medical tenet to "do no harm," understanding that, in many social science scenarios, harm can take forms other than physical injury. Furthermore, this principle requires that studies "maximize possible benefits and minimize possible harms" (DHEW, 1979, p. 6). Benefits to participants can be affective, such as personal insights, a sense of empowerment, and increased self-esteem (Salmons, 2016, pp. 78–79).

Justice. This principle considers who benefits from a research study and who is burdened by it, noting the need for a balance of these factors. A specific finding of the report that applies to many qualitative studies in the social sciences is, "Whenever research supported by public funds leads to the development of therapeutic devices and procedures, justice demands both that these not provide advantages only to those who can afford them and that such research should not unduly involve persons from groups unlikely to be among the beneficiaries of subsequent applications of the research" (DHEW, 1979, p. 10). Educational innovations, for example, could be considered therapeutic procedures, which thus must adhere to this principle of justice.

The Rules of Research

The principles from the Belmont Report have been widely adopted by universities. Any qualitative researcher working with human participants must adhere to selected rules, in their traditional sense. While specific guidelines at various institutions differ, there are a number of points that are nearly universal that both qualitative and quantitative researchers should be familiar with. We explore these in this section.

Consent

One of the most important legal and ethical issues researchers must face is gaining the informed consent of all participants in a research study. While there are some exceptions, which we discuss below, researchers have an obligation to clearly explain to anyone they are studying the exact nature of the study, what the researchers hope to learn, what the participants will do (and what information about the participants the researchers will obtain through various methods), and what will be done with that information. Researchers must ensure that the participants understand what has been explained to them (including taking necessary steps to ensure those not fluent in English can ask questions and have them answered in language they can comprehend). Finally, once participants understand the study, they must willingly consent to participate in it and must have the opportunity to revoke their consent at any time during the study without repercussion.

Note that minors (in the United States, usually people under the age of 18 to 21, depending on the state) cannot legally consent to participate in a study. All studies with minors as participants, including a great deal of education research, must receive consent from the participants' parents or legal guardians. In addition, it is best practice to receive **assent** (nonlegally binding agreement) from minors as well. Generally, researchers must have both participant assent and parental consent for such studies, and either the young participant or the parent/guardian is allowed to terminate the participants' involvement at any time without penalty. In some cases, K–12 schools can provide principal or school district board consent in lieu of parental/guardian consent to researchers for studies related directly to everyday classroom learning.

Confidentiality

Related to consent is the issue of **confidentiality**. Researchers should always clearly inform participants what (if any) measures will be taken to ensure their **anonymity** and the confidentiality of the information they share. Anonymity specifically means not sharing (or in some cases, never initially collecting) the identity of participants; confidentiality means protecting the data that participants share more broadly, as discussed below. In some cases, such as a hypothetical study asking U.S. senators for their views on government efficiency, disclosing the participants' identities would be a key feature of the project, and all participants would understand that the information they share would be directly attributed to them. In this case, a lack of anonymity is permissible because participants would understand from the outset that this would be the case.

In other studies, researchers make every effort to maintain confidentiality. For example, in the study of work-release prisoners described in Chapter 4, some people might reasonably want to ensure that their names were never associated with the information they shared, perhaps because they feared retribution from prison officials, did not want to publicly embarrass their families, were concerned for their reputation once released from prison, or any number of other reasons. In such cases, researchers draft informed consent documents for the participants to sign that clearly outline what the researcher will do to protect the participants' identities (anonymity) and ensure confidentiality. Such documents will usually include a clause, however, indicating that it is always possible that a participant could be identified. For example, if a participant shares a very specific story and allows the researcher to use it in a research report, it is possible that someone who is familiar with the story could determine the identity of the participant. Furthermore, there is always the small chance that security measures could be compromised. Even if all data are stored in password-protected files on a computer in a locked room, as most institutional regulations require, there is always a chance, no matter how remote, that someone will steal the computer and find a way to access the file.

One way researchers can provide participants an additional degree of anonymity is by reporting the data they share in **aggregate** form rather than through direct quotes. For example, researchers might indicate that one salient theme that emerged from interviews with numerous work-release prisoners was that many prisoners believed they had been mistreated by prison officials. While this statement does reveal that many of the participants felt this way, it is not possible to identify which specific prisoners shared this with the researchers, who would normally be barred from sharing that information with prison officials by the informed consent document. If researchers do want to share quotes, they can create **composite narratives** that bring together elements of interviews from different participants. By clearly stating that the quotes do not represent the views of one particular person, but rather have been constructed from a much larger corpus of data, a degree of confidentiality is added that does not exist when individual participants are quoted separately verbatim.

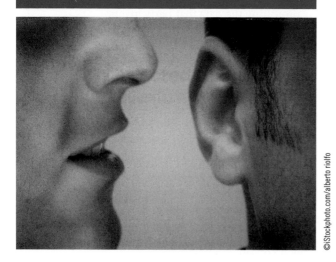

Figure 8.1   Maintaining confidentiality is an essential trait of qualitative researchers.

©iStockphoto.com/alberto riolfo

Comprehensive information

Participants, whether they are volunteers or compensated, are entitled to know as much about the study as possible in advance, as stipulated by the Belmont Report.

Among other factors, this means participants should know upfront exactly what they will be asked to do or share, when and where the research will take place, for what duration, how many other participants will be involved, what benefits and risks they might face, and what will be done with the information they provide or that is collected from them. Unless a study involves **deception**, which is usually acceptable under only the most extenuating circumstances when there is no other way to gather important information, and which will generally require extensive scrutiny by an IRB, researchers should provide all information about the study to participants at the beginning (usually on a consent form, discussed below), and be willing to answer any reasonable questions a participant might have about the study.

Communication

Participants can understand the measures of confidentiality proposed and offer their consent to participate only if they are able to understand the materials they are presented with and if they are able to speak with the researchers. In a country as diverse as the United States, it would be inappropriate to assume that all potential participants can speak and/or read any particular language, including English. It might be necessary to translate materials into other languages to ensure all targeted participants are able to enroll in a study. If a study includes children, their parents/guardians must also be able to fully understand all study materials in order to consent. Researchers should be prepared to translate consent forms into multiple languages (this might even be required by an institution for certain projects) or to have an interpreter with them when conducting a study.

In all cases, if a participant communicates to a researcher that she cannot understand a consent form or other item, the researcher should stop and resolve the issue at that moment. If she does not do so, she should not allow the participant to sign the form, but instead she should wait and obtain the assistance of someone who can help when this is possible. "Obtaining consent" from someone who does not understand what he is consenting to is not actually obtaining consent.

Conflict-free research

Researchers working for universities and other public-sector research institutions must generally always avoid conflicts of interest in their research (this is usually true in the private sector as well, though guidelines can be different). This means that a researcher should not conduct research when some factor could prevent him from reasonably and objectively fulfilling his duties to the research project. As qualitative researchers, we recognize that there is no such thing as true objectivity, given that we all come to our work from diverse standpoints, but a conflict of interest is stronger than a lack of objectivity.

For example, if a researcher studying a prison work-release program was receiving a $10,000 retainer fee from a political action committee (PAC) opposed to work-release programs, an observer might reasonably suspect that the researcher had a conflict between reporting the true results of the study (whatever they might be) and finding the program was a failure (which would please the PAC paying him $10,000). Even if the researcher was acting honorably, his findings would be suspect because of the funding he took from an invested outside party. Conflicts of interest most often occur when a researcher serves as an officer or director with any organization that could be involved in his study, or if he holds a significant financial interest in such an organization. If a researcher or member of his family has any potential financial or other gain at stake because of a study, he should recuse himself from it and not participate in any way.

Conflicts of interest can also involve holding a significant financial interest in an organization that has requested rights to tangible or intellectual property related to the study, receiving gifts from organizations related to the study, or having relationships (familial, business, academic) with individuals or organizations who have a stake in the study. It is important to note that there might be instances when a university or other organization approves a researcher working on a study despite a conflict of interest, but the researcher should always disclose potential conflicts to avoid behaving (or appearing to behave) unethically.

Institutional Review Boards

Like most rules, the rules of research we described above and those in the Belmont Report have agencies or individuals who enforce them. In the university context, this is most often the **Institutional Review Board** (IRB) (also sometimes referred to as a Human Subjects Review Board or an Ethics Committee). IRBs do not exist to arbitrarily enforce rules, but rather to protect both researchers and their institutions from liability by ensuring that all research is conducted in a legal and ethical manner. Some IRBs might approve a generally solid proposal quickly, while others might require several rounds of revisions until all of their concerns are addressed. But an IRB's ultimate purpose is always to ensure the safety and well-being of human participants. In general, researchers must have full IRB approval before beginning any work with human participants, so it is important for a researcher to approach an IRB early in the process, once the research design is completed.

What is human subjects research?

One of the first questions a researcher must consider before submitting an application to an IRB is whether her project is, in fact, human subjects research at all. Interestingly, not all research with humans is considered human subjects research, and some work that might not at first seem to be human subjects research might be, under the guidelines of an IRB. For this reason, it is generally wise for new researchers to apply to their IRB for a research determination. Answering a few brief questions will generally allow the IRB to inform a researcher whether a study is considered human subjects research and if a full application must be submitted.

For example, Omasta (2011) conducted a study exploring if and how middle school students' values, attitudes, and beliefs were affected by viewing a single theatre performance. In this case, because the purpose of the focus groups was specifically to learn about the participants themselves, his IRB determined that the study was human subjects research and an IRB-designed template had to be used to gain the young participants' assent as well as the consent of their parents/guardians. Virtually any study with minors as participants requires IRB application and review.

However, for a different project, Omasta (Omasta & Adkins, 2017) interviewed professional playwrights, directors, and other theatre professionals regarding their perspectives on writing plays for young people. In this case, because the participants being interviewed were offering their expert opinions about the topic rather than sharing information about their lives, Omasta's university's IRB determined that as long as participants were told the purpose of the project, their agreement to participate was sufficient and no formal written consent was required.

In other cases, a book or journal publisher might require a participant to sign a release that is similar to an informed consent document, even if an IRB does not require that step. For example, an IRB determined that the interviews conducted to appear in this book were not human subjects research and therefore did not require IRB review. The participants, however, were granted similar protections as if they had participated in an IRB-approved project and signed a release form generated by the publisher similar to an informed consent document.

Yet another factor an IRB considers in its determination of research of human subjects is the study's public dissemination of results. An in-house evaluation research project conducted by a university department chair that involves data collection from only her department's faculty, staff, and students might involve interviews, surveys, classroom observations, and so on. If the findings are intended solely for departmental purposes and will not be published, an IRB might waive the need for the study's approval. On the other hand, if the findings are also intended for a written report to be published in an academic journal on higher education, the IRB will most likely require a formal application from the principal investigator and all participants' consent to proceed with the evaluation study.

Review types and timelines

Most IRBs have several types of review they can employ. We will briefly discuss only four types here, as each institution has its own review process. The first type is a determination that a study is not human subjects research at all, in which case no formal application needs to be filed. Again, however, we recommend new researchers at least file for a determination rather than opting not to consult their IRB at all.

If an IRB determines a study does involve human subjects research, it can still designate the study as **exempt** from review after an application has been completed if it meets certain criteria. Specifically, these studies might include but are not limited to research normally conducted in educational settings (unless the study design would allow individual participants to be identified), studies involving the collection and analysis of public data, studies overseen by certain government agencies such as the Department of Health and Human Services, and studies involving taste and food quality. There is no guarantee that any of these studies will be found exempt, however, and there are numerous caveats that can remove a study from this category. Studies found to be exempt often do not require the completion of consent forms, but rather the distribution of **letters of information** for the participants.

The next level of review is **expedited,** in which case only selected members of an IRB review the study instead of the entire board. Studies in this category might be those that would have been exempt but did not meet all requirements, studies on human characteristics and behavior, collection of data from recordings, and a variety of medical studies subject to certain conditions. These studies will normally require informed consent paperwork and all standard requirements, but might be approved more quickly than those undergoing full review.

Studies undergoing **full review** are generally reviewed by every member of the IRB and therefore usually require several meetings of the IRB before the IRB grants approval. These are studies that do not meet the criteria for exemption or expedited review due to their complexity, multi-method research design, or sensitive research topics.

Figure 8.2   Certain populations are considered vulnerable by IRBs.

©iStockphoto.com/Christopher Futcher

The review timeline varies by institution but is rarely fast. Our experience suggests that from the date of submission it will normally take one to two months to receive approval of an exempt study, two to four months for an expedited study, and four to nine months for a study reviewed by the full board. Any of these timelines could be faster or slower depending on any given IRB, application, and even factors such as the number of other applications under review, so we encourage all researchers to submit their applications as early as possible. Also, there might be site-specific concurrent or pre- and post-application requirements for certain field settings such as hospitals, prisons, and schools that have their own research study approval procedures in addition to a university's IRB.

IRB applications

The actual IRB application a researcher must complete will differ by her institution; very few will be identical. As such, in this section we have created an application outline that amalgamates questions from several universities and presents some of the most common questions new researchers should expect to find. We then give advice on ways to respond to inquiries that will give an IRB the information it needs.

Project title Insert the full working title of a project at the time of submission application; the title itself should give reviewers a clear description and impression of the nature of a researcher's study. For example, "An Ethnographic Case Study of a Sheltered Homeless Family in the Phoenix Metropolitan Area."

Principal and other investigators The **principal investigator** is the lead researcher on a study. It is important to note that at most universities, students (including graduate students) cannot serve as principal investigators; faculty mentors must serve as the principal investigator for IRB purposes, while students are listed as either coinvestigators or student investigators, depending on a particular university's policies.

Timeline List the full range of dates you expect the study to take, from the day it is approved until all data analysis and write-ups are complete. A study does not end the last day researchers work with human participants; it ends when the analysis is complete and, in most cases, when identifiable data are deleted or destroyed (a requirement of many IRBs). We recommend you select a late end date to ensure you have enough time to complete the study, and so you will not have to file for an extension.

Proposal and scientific validity Most IRBs will request a complete copy of the research proposal. Some will ask if it has been reviewed by an internal or external source for scientific validity and for documentation of that review. If it has not been reviewed, applicants will need to perform a scientific validity check to make sure the study is sound according to the research principles of the paradigm it follows. This requirement applies generally to experimental studies rather than naturalistic studies like qualitative inquiry.

Participants Describe the participant population in detail. This requires knowing the approximate number of participants broken down by gender and age range. It might be necessary to anticipate what percentage of recruited participants are expected to complete the study; in this case, refer to similar studies in the literature or consult with experts in the field to determine what seems a reasonable percentage.

Be prepared to speak to inclusion criteria (What about these people make them ideal participants?) and exclusion criteria (What would make potential participants ineligible to participate?). In general, we recommend avoiding any exclusion criteria unless they are necessary and justifiable for a particular project. If studying a class of students, for example, excluding the male students is inadvisable unless there is a research-related reason to do so. Excluding males because the study is about female perspectives is acceptable. Excluding them because there are too many students and excluding the males would be an easy way to reach a more manageable number is not. Randomly selecting participants would be more appropriate to reduce the number invited to participate. If using recruitment materials (such as flyers or posters seeking volunteers, or texts the researcher will ask teachers to read aloud to their classes), you will likely need to compose those materials beforehand and submit them at the time of IRB application submission.

Participant incentives Be prepared to describe and justify any participant incentives offered. These incentives include anything that researchers might offer to participants as compensation for their time (e.g., money, gift cards, access to resources, products, in-kind services). Note that participant incentives are often useful but sometimes prohibited (e.g., the New York City Department of Education has historically prohibited any of its staff from receiving incentives for participating in research). Check with participants and partner organizations in advance about their own ethical guidelines related to participant incentives.

Vulnerable participants Federal law and local guidelines identify a number of populations as protected or vulnerable. These generally include minors, prisoners, senior citizens, pregnant women, people with physical or mental impairments, non-English speakers, and anyone else at risk for coercion. While many studies work with these populations, IRBs will require justification for why it is necessary to work with a vulnerable population in order to answer a research question. Certain settings such as schools, nursing homes, and hospitals might be flagged by an IRB, which will require justification for why the study takes place there. This explanation can often be simple, for example, "This study investigates a new education method being taught to second-grade students during the school day, and therefore must take place in the participants' school." While such explanations might seem obvious, it is important to include them. Remember that most reviewers will not be familiar with most disciplines other than their own and might not know common practices in other fields.

Informed consent It will be necessary to describe in detail how researchers will gain informed consent from the participants and parents/guardians if necessary. This includes providing a copy of the consent document (see Figure 8.4), indicating who will get the consent and when, and how consent documents will be made accessible to non-English speakers.

Figure 8.3 Researchers must keep all data private and secure.

©iStockphoto.com/XiXinXing

Deception In rare cases where researchers must deceive participants to some degree in order to carry out a study, a request for deception must be made to the IRB. In most cases, the IRB will grant the request only when the use of deception is absolutely necessary, when it will not have any negative impact on the participants, and when participants likely would have agreed to participate in the study even if they knew there was deception involved. When deception is used, participants must typically be debriefed (told of the deception) and given the opportunity to withdraw from the research and have any data collected from them while they were being deceived deleted. For a variety of reasons, it is therefore ideal to refrain from covert research involving deception whenever possible.

Procedures Explain in detail exactly what the participants will do as part of the study (e.g., be interviewed, be observed as they go about their daily lives), including details as to how long and how often these procedures will take place. If procedures are already being performed on the participants (e.g., if a school is trying a new education initiative that the researchers are evaluating), describe it, even though the researchers are not the ones administering the initiative. Be prepared to include copies of all surveys, interview questions, and other data collection instruments with the IRB application (again, this means they must be completed prior to applying).

The procedures section can sometimes prove problematic for qualitative researchers, especially those working with community-based or action research projects. These approaches often necessitate developing research questions once the researcher is already in the field working with participants to discover their needs, as opposed to prior to beginning the study. Researchers engaging in these types of research should consult with their IRB chairs or administrators to find ways to reconcile the IRB's desire for all questions and procedures to be determined in advance with the nature of the inquiry they are undertaking.

Risks Explain the risks to participants, recognizing that there are always risks of one kind or another involved in social research. At minimum, it is important to acknowledge that, despite the researchers' best efforts, there is always the possibility that confidentiality will be breached. Explain how the risks will be mitigated (e.g., paper documents will be stored in a locked filing cabinet in a locked room, or electronic information will be stored in a password-protected file on a password-protected computer). It is important not only to claim that these protections will be in place but also to actually follow through—for example, by always locking the door of an office where documents are stored.

Benefits As indicated in the Belmont Report, research should have benefits, ideally to the participants but at a minimum to society. Several qualitative researchers offer that a participant's opportunity for in-depth reflection on the topic of study during an interview is a tangible outcome. Research with no educational or scientific value is inherently unethical in light of its guaranteed risks. The benefits of a study should be described in detail and in such a manner that it is clear that they outweigh any potential risks.

Privacy Maintaining the privacy interests of participants is paramount in most research studies. A detailed plan for how their confidentiality will be maintained—including a discussion of how nonparticipants will be prevented from identifying actual participants, to how files will be maintained, to how data will be reported in a way that maintains anonymity—should be outlined. Explain if the participants' responses will be identifiable to the researchers themselves and, if so, how and when that identifying data will be destroyed. Again, discuss the physical security measures in place along with reporting plans such as using only aggregate data. Even when participants will not be anonymous, describe how you will protect personal data that they do not wish to have disclosed. Describe any recordings (audio, video, photographs) and discuss when they will be destroyed. Salmons (2016) advises, "You do not want your data on the cloud. Data could be accessed intentionally or unintentionally by others, and shared publicly without your permission" (p. 140).

Mandatory reporting Your IRB might ask if a study has the potential to discover illegal activities, reveal that participants or others are victims of abuse, or other conditions such as suicidal thoughts. In these cases, explain how researchers might respond to these revelations. Be sure to follow both institutional policies as well as local, state, and federal laws. This might require some researchers to determine if they are a **mandated reporter** (university employees, including student employees, often are mandated reporters under various state laws), so it is imperative to be in line with legal and ethical requirements in these areas.

Conflicts of interest Most IRB applications will ask about conflicts of interest as described above. Be sure to carefully review each question and disclose any possible conflict, keeping in mind that such conflict might not interfere with your ability to conduct the study but you must report it nevertheless.

Informed consent documents Central to ethical practice and IRB approval is the informed consent of participants, often articulated in an informed consent letter. Figure 8.4 presents a sample letter that might be used for the diabetes study described in Chapter 4. Note that because this study is being led by a graduate student, a faculty member is listed as the principal investigator, but the student researcher is included as a primary contact. All basic information about what the study hopes to learn, what the participant will do, and the potential risks and benefits are described. Most institutions have template letters for researchers to work from, but Figure 8.4 provides a basic starting point for those without a template. Though the language is severely formal, it is nonetheless a required document whose content has been carefully crafted by IRBs.

Figure 8.4 A template for an informed consent letter.

INFORMED CONSENT

Patient Perspectives of Type II Diabetes

Introduction/Purpose: Dr. Xan Escobar, a faculty member in the College of Public Health at State University, is conducting a research study to find out more about what people with Type II Diabetes think about the disease and public reactions to it. We are inviting you to participate in the study because you indicated to your doctor that you would be interested in participating in a study of this nature. There will be approximately 100 total participants in this research. Gabrielle Anderson will be serving as a student researcher on this study under Dr. Escobar's supervision.

Procedures: If you agree to be in this research study, you will first be asked to complete a survey with basic demographic and health-related questions; this survey will take approximately 15 minutes to complete. You will next be asked to participate in an individual interview with a member of the research team; this interview will take approximately 30 minutes to complete.

Risks: There is minimal risk in participating in this research. However, there is a potential risk for loss of confidentiality, but we will take steps to minimize these risks. You will be assigned a random identification number if you participate in the study, and after your interview is transcribed only this identifier (not your name) will be associated with your responses. Your name and individual responses will never be shared with anyone outside the research team.

Benefits: By better understanding how people with Type II diabetes learned about their condition and how people without the disease perceive it, we hope to create better materials for a public diabetes awareness campaign that will promote understanding of the disease and prompt those diagnosed with the disease to seek more effective treatment sooner after diagnosis.

Explanation & Offer to Answer Questions: Through this letter, the researchers have explained this research study to you. If you have other questions or research-related problems, you may reach Gabrielle Anderson at ganderson@xsu.ed (555) 555-8328 or Dr. Escobar at (555) 555-2469 or xescobar@xsu.ed.

Voluntary Nature of Participation and Right to Withdraw Without Consequence: Participation in this study is entirely voluntary. You may refuse to participate in this research without recourse. Should you withdraw from participation, you will not complete any additional surveys or interviews. Any data previously collected prior to such withdrawal will be destroyed. Withdrawing from the study will not cause any consequence or loss of benefits.

Confidentiality: Research records will be kept confidential, consistent with federal and state regulations. Only the researchers will have access to the data, which will be stored in password-protected files on password-protected computers to maintain confidentiality. To protect your privacy, personal, identifiable information will be removed from study documents and replaced with a study identifier. All identifying information will be stored separately from data and will be destroyed upon completion of data analysis.

IRB Approval Statement: The Institutional Review Board for the protection of human participants at State University has approved this research study. If you have any questions or concerns about your rights or a research-related injury and would like to contact someone other than the research team, you may contact the IRB Director at (555) 555-2325 or irb@xsu.ed to obtain information or to offer input.

Copy of Consent: You have been given two copies of this document. Please sign both copies. Keep one copy for your files and return the second to us.

Investigator Statement: "I certify that the research study has been explained to the participant through this letter, including the nature and purpose, the possible risks and benefits associated with taking part in this research study. The participant can contact the researchers with any questions about the study at (555) 555-2469."

_____	Date	_____	Date
Xan Escobar, Ph.D.		Gabrielle Anderson	
Principal Investigator		Student Researcher	
(555) 555-2469		(555) 555-8328	
xescobar@xsu.ed		ganderson@xsu.ed	

Participant Signature: By signing below, I agree to participate in this study.

_____	_____	___/___/___
Printed Name	Signature	Date

Researcher and Participant Relationships

The relationships between researchers and their participants are professional, and ethical boundaries should be maintained throughout any study. In most cases, researchers will not know their participants before a study begins, which makes it easier to establish neutral yet cordial relationships from the beginning. In rare cases, researchers will study participants they already know and have relationships with (e.g., a classroom teacher conducting an action research study with her students), but in most cases it is best if there is a degree of professional distance.

Emergent paradigms such as feminist research and community-based participatory research projects, however, advocate a more collaborative and interpersonal **rapport** between the qualitative researcher and her participants. An ethical stance considers an equitable relationship that does not exploit participants for information but genuinely cares about and learns from them. It presents the researcher as an emotionally invested human being curious about the social world, humble enough to admit her lack of knowledge, and supportive of the people she's observing and talking with. Participants are more likely to share openly and honestly about their lives with someone they believe they can trust, and trust develops not from a written informed consent letter but from mutual respect.

The researcher's positionality with her participants varies from project to project. One can't help but establish a friendship of some kind with a case study observed and interviewed over an extended period of time. Yet a series of intensive focus group interviews with different participants each round might keep the facilitator from establishing anything more than a professional role with them. Just as there are roles and relationships among the people we study, there are roles and relationships that the qualitative researcher assumes with her participants. How close or distant you choose to be with them is your own ethical decision.

Analyzing Ethical Ambiguity

As the Wizard of Oz admits when he sings about his rise to power in Broadway's *Wicked*: "There are precious few at ease with moral ambiguities, so we act as though they don't exist" (Schwartz, 2003). Unfortunately for those of this mindset, a great deal of social research involves gray areas, and situations arise in which there is no single clear-cut ethical course of action.

We present here three scenarios in which neither the law, an IRB, nor another agency can guide how researchers might respond to them. Consider first the researcher examining the life of a homeless person throughout the course of a year. The researcher would most likely witness the participant experiencing a great deal of hardship, and as they grew to know each other, might feel inclined to help the participant. He could, at one extreme, offer to assist the participant financially or medically or, on a lesser level, direct the participant to social services she might not be aware of but that could be helpful. In doing so, the researcher might very well be making a positive impact on the participant's life. At the same time, the researcher is almost certainly disrupting natural life, since the participant is likely to make different choices (or have reduced or different needs) because of the intervention. As such, the researcher cannot claim that the data he collects is representative of what he originally intended to gather.

Which option is better? We do not have an answer to that question. Each person is guided by his own personal sense of ethics in addition to those issued by IRBs and national agencies. The researcher should, however, report his intervention into the participant's life when sharing his findings in presentations and publications. Readers can then decide for themselves if the researcher's actions influenced the findings and how trustworthy they believe them to be.

Second, in Chapter 6 we shared how researchers studied text pager messages sent on September 11, 2001, including what sadly might have been the last messages ever sent by victims of the attack. The researchers clearly did not and could not have obtained consent from these thousands of individuals to use their very personal data. However, the researchers believed themselves to be justified doing so because the messages were publicly available on the Internet after they were released by WikiLeaks, an organization that publishes secret information it obtains from governments and, in this case, the witnesses and possible victims of terrorist attacks and their families.

The researchers' use of the data was legal; they personally did not steal it or post it online. Furthermore, their research resulted in knowledge that arguably advanced the public good. On the other hand, the researchers used data stolen by others, which they analyzed to compose a publication that led to citations— something of real value in academia that can result in tangible benefits such as promotions and tenure. Was it ethical to use data unethically archived from a tragedy to compose a study that ultimately benefited the researchers? We cannot say. It was important, however, that the researchers disclosed their data source so that readers could make their own judgments.

Finally, consider our hypothetical study of the prisoner in a work-release program. Suppose that during an interview the prisoner disclosed to the researcher that he was part of a drug-smuggling operation that took place by abusing certain loopholes in the work-release program. The researcher has several questions to ponder:

1. Is she ethically obligated to report this to prison authorities? Is she a mandated reporter? Did she agree to report such findings in an agreement with either the prison or her IRB? Even if not, is she ethically obligated to intervene in illegal drug trafficking?

2. Alternatively, is she ethically bound not to report this to prison authorities? Did she sign a consent form that promised the participant complete confidentiality, or that she would not disclose anything she learned unless it was directly related to topics specified in the consent agreement?

3. What is more important: stopping the drug running or completing her research, which would likely discuss the drug running in a confidential way? What other factors must she weigh?

Nothing is clear about ethically ambiguous conundrums. In cases where laws or regulations require certain actions, researchers have guidance, but in many other cases they do not. Ethics are not universal, and researchers must carefully contemplate the consequences of their actions (or lack thereof). We offer a classic adage for consideration: Not everything that is legal is ethical, and not everything that is ethical is legal.

CLOSURE AND TRANSITION

This chapter reviewed a variety of topics related to ethics, from the mandatory requirements of IRBs to the difficult decisions that researchers must make when there is no clear guidance. Qualitative researchers who work emergently and inductively have had long-standing tensions with the rigid preapproval requirements of IRBs. The debates continue as to the efficacy of these prescriptive protocols for naturalistic social inquiry.

Part I of this book discussed the multiple methods of qualitative data collection and their initial analysis, while Part II discussed their integration into matters of research design and formal preparation. Part III reviews the assemblage of all the materials from fieldwork into analytic synthesis and presentation, the culminating processes of qualitative inquiry.

RESOURCES FOR RESEARCH ETHICS

The following resources, including the official guides to ethics in the fields of education, medicine, psychology, and

sociology, offer insight into the discipline-specific perspectives on ethical standards of conduct:

American Educational Research Association (AERA). (2011). *Code of Ethics*. Washington, DC: Author. http://www.aera.net/Portals/38/docs/About_AERA/CodeOfEthics%281%29.pdf

American Medical Association (AMA). (2016). *AMA Code of Medical Ethics*. Chicago, IL: Author. http://www.ama-assn.org/ama/pub/physician-resources/medical-ethics/code-medical-ethics.page?

American Psychological Association (APA). (2010). *Ethical Principles of Psychologists and Code of Conduct*. Washington, DC: Author. http://www.apa.org/ethics/code/index.aspx

American Sociological Association (ASA). (1999). *Code of Ethics and Policies and Procedures on the ASA Committee on Professional Ethics*. Washington, DC: Author. http://www.asanet.org/images/asa/docs/pdf/CodeofEthics.pdf

U. S. Department of Health and Human Services, Office for Human Research Protections. (1979). *The Belmont Report*. Washington, DC: Author. http://www.hhs.gov/ohrp/humansubjects/guidance/belmont.html

ANALYTIC EXERCISES FOR RESEARCH ETHICS

1. Discuss whether each of the following studies would likely be considered human subjects research, and why or why not:

   a. A study of rural farmers in an area experiencing extreme recession that explores how their families are responding to economic challenges.

   b. A study of data available from the U.S. census to analyze if areas in which high numbers of people of various racial/ethnic backgrounds are more likely to receive lower median family incomes.

   c. A study that asks secondary school teachers to anonymously share lesson plans they have written in order to create a data base of plans in various subject areas.

   d. A study that asks doctors who have had patients die under their care to discuss the feelings they experienced afterward and how they responded to those feelings.

2. Locate and download a university's IRB application form for a study you are considering and answer each question.

3. Discuss with a peer the legal and ethical issues that might arise from the study with prisoners in a work-release program, including at least one specific ethical dilemma that might occur and at least two ways you might respond to it.

4. Write a letter of informed consent for a study you are considering conducting that addresses all necessary elements.

5. Watch one of the following commercial films dramatizing the dilemmas with research ethics and discuss with a peer its cautionary lessons: *Miss Evers' Boys* (Fishburne & Benedetti, 1997), *Experimenter: The Stanley Milgram Story* (Almeryda, 2015), *The Stanford Prison Experiment* (Emery, Friedman, Lauder, & Little, 2015).

Analytic Assemblage

Analytic Synthesis: Condensing, Patterning, and Unifying

Introduction

Part III of this book describes the processes researchers undertake after the assemblage of all preparatory matters, fieldwork, and data collection. Though we have encouraged readers to analyze materials in various ways from the very beginning of their studies, those initial methods have laid the foundation for more advanced and more integrated work. These final chapters illustrate the stages of synthesizing and presenting qualitative research. This chapter focuses on three specific analytic skills: condensing, patterning, and unifying. Chapter 10 addresses action, reaction, interaction, and the five Rs.

On Synthesis

Synthesis combines different things in order to form a new whole and is the primary heuristic for qualitative data analysis. Researchers review a relatively large and varied assemblage of empirical materials (field notes, interview transcripts, documents, etc.) and reflect on how they interrelate and work together. A quantitative parallel is determining the mean or average of a set of numbers. Take 20 different test scores varying in range, add each score, divide by the number of scores, and you will have calculated the mean. Twenty different scores have been synthesized into one new whole or symbol of meaning. But does qualitative data analysis have a comparable equivalent? The answer is both no and yes.

How do we average 20 different codes or 20 different interview passages or 20 different analytic memos? There is no qualitative algorithm that adds up the words and calculates their mean.

Learning Objectives

After reading and reviewing this chapter, researchers should be able to

1. Manage a data corpus throughout a research study,

2. Select appropriate qualitative data analytic methods for a research study,

3. Transform data into symbols of condensed analytic meaning, and

4. Create an analytic synthesis from a data corpus.

There are, however, methods for synthesizing the collective to arrive at a consolidated meaning. That meaning might take the symbolic form of a category, theme, concept, assertion, vignette, or it might set in motion a new line of investigation, interpretive thought, or the crystallization of a new theory.

We have introduced several analytic approaches and methods from Chapter 1 onward, in hopes that the chapters devoted exclusively to qualitative data analysis would not overwhelm readers. We have reinforced that analysis is an ongoing process throughout the research project, not a task undertaken after all the data have been collected. We remind readers again of the five critical skills qualitative researchers and analysts should possess:

1. Condensing large amounts of data;

2. Noticing patterns in textual and visual materials;

3. Unifying seemingly different things;

4. Understanding social processes of human action, reaction, and interaction; and

5. Interpreting the routines, rituals, rules, roles, and relationships of social life (the five Rs).

Under each skill is a specific set of analytic subskills to employ on an as-needed basis to make sense of and make meaning from data. We also remind readers of two very important principles:

- "Because each qualitative study is unique, the analytical approach used will be unique" (Patton, 2015, p. 522).

- "Good research is not about good methods as much as it is about good thinking" (Stake, 1995, p. 19).

We cannot offer specific prescriptions for which method(s) should be applied to particular forms of data, and we cannot guarantee that any particular method will automatically generate researcher insights. Analysts must bring to the project their own decision-making and thinking skills to apply what we offer as ways to analyze life. As for which specific method(s) are ultimately chosen for a study's analysis, we provide three general guidelines to consider:

The forms of data collected. Some data, such as interview transcripts, can be analyzed through any of the heuristics described in Chapters 9 and 10. But multiple interviews or surveys from different participants, or field notes from multiple sites, might employ methods that synthesize or aggregate data (e.g., codes, categories, themes, matrices and tabular displays).

The research methodology employed. Chapter 6 reviewed selected genres of qualitative research such as grounded theory, phenomenology, and autoethnography. Selected genres typically rely on a particular palette of analytic methods. For example, grounded theory generally relies on codes and coding, category construction, concepts, propositions, diagrammatic displays, analytic memos and, of course, theory development. Phenomenological analysis tends more toward categories, themes, and assertions, while autoethnography ventures more into found poetry, themes, or vignettes. When a particular methodological approach is selected during the research design stage, consider which analytic method(s) might best serve the study and its goals.

The study's research questions. If researchers want the best answers to their questions, they should select the method(s) that will best generate those answers. Since each study is unique, researchers should examine the nature of their research questions and what kinds of outcomes the questions suggest. "What," "in what ways," and sometimes "how" questions imply descriptive answers. "Why" and sometimes "how" questions imply explanatory answers. All of the heuristics in Chapters 9 and 10 service descriptive narratives, but selected methods such as propositions, diagrammatic displays, and theory work toward explanatory outcomes.

Condensing Large Amounts of Data

This section reviews and expands on what we've profiled thus far as ways to condense qualitative data, and offers additional methods for focusing analysis on the most salient portions of the data corpus.

Analyzing relevant text

Part of qualitative data analysis is acknowledging that—in most cases—not everything collected in the field will require intensive analysis. Auerbach and Silverstein (2003) encourage the analysis of only what is **relevant text**, that is, data that are directly related to and can help answer the research questions of interest. Sullivan (2012) refers to relevant text as rich moments from the corpus, cherry-picked portions that are exemplars of the phenomenon for closer scrutiny. Analytic memo writing transforms jottings, descriptive field notes, and OCs into richer forms of interpretation about the social scene. The examination of documents and artifacts focuses on their latent meanings of evocation such as identity, symbolism, and process. Seidman's (2013) recommendation to condense and reorganize a set of interview transcripts to one third their full length to create a profile is yet another method, while codes transform extended passages of data into rich textual symbols.

As data are collected and initially analyzed, life as it is lived in real time gets truncated to its most interesting facets—a two-hour movie of the week, rather than a 26-week season series of episodes. What is interesting, however, is a matter of emergent judgment on the analyst's part. Relevant text might be that which describes mundane routines rather than significant rituals. The interaction observed between participants in the field might not be half as interesting as the confessional narrative a participant shared during an interview.

A preparatory analytic act is not just reading but also rereading the data corpus with the research questions as a filter to determine which sections merit relevance for further analysis. Ultimately, the researcher must determine what is salient in the data corpus and what is most important and worthy of intensive analysis. We do not like to use the verb *reduce* because that implies something is diminished or lost. Instead, we offer that analysts condense data to their essences, which suggests a stronger and richer base from which to work.

Codes and coding

Chapter 1 briefly introduced codes and coding as heuristics for labeling each individual datum for purposes of pattern detection, categorizing, and unifying. Chapter 5 expanded on the method with illustrations of In Vivo, Process, Values, and Emotion Coding. Discussion in this chapter provides additional coding profiles for qualitative data analysis that might be useful for initial applications to data sets.

Remember that codes are not the only way but are instead just one way of analyzing data. They serve as prompts or triggers for reflection through analytic memo writing, but they also serve as symbolic representations for the constituent pieces of a pattern in progress. Though we discuss them separately, they can be strategically mixed and matched as needed during the first and future coding cycles. We use rich text features to help differentiate between four analytic forms:

- CODES AND THEMES ARE SET IN CAPS
- *SUBCODES ARE SET IN ITALIC CAPS*
- **Categories are set in bold**
- ***Subcategories are set in bold italic***

Descriptive coding and subcoding

Descriptive Coding summarizes in a word or short phrase—most often as a noun—the basic topic of a passage of qualitative data. It is appropriate for documenting and analyzing the material products and physical environments of ethnographic fieldwork, and the classification of general participant action and routines recorded in field notes. We recommend that this method not be used for interview transcripts because noun-based descriptive codes will not reveal very much insight into participants' minds. Nouns suggest what is being thought, but not how, why, or in what ways. Descriptive Coding will, however, lead to a well-indexed compendium of contents from multiple interviews, if needed.

As an example, below are excerpts from the visual art classroom field notes from Chapter 2. The data have been formatted into stanzas or units as a form of **precoding**. The stanzas' related codes are placed in the right-hand column. Notice that one code is used more than once and the codes are topic driven, not evaluative or interpretive. The goal is to simply create an indexical account of the fieldwork environment and the manifest action within it:

[1] Rack labels by the entry door: "Detention Forms," "Attendance Files."

    [1] MANAGEMENT

[2] On display on the south wall are laminated collages, laminated still lifes in colored pencil. [3] On the shelved counter beneath are plastic tubs with teachers' names on them to keep student class work together.

    [2] DISPLAYS
    [3] MANAGEMENT

[4] Various media supplies are moderately organized in the east wall's four gray cabinets: paper bags, paper plates, construction paper, white paper, colored paper, crayons, markers, colored pencils, scissors [child and adult sizes], etc. [5] One cabinet door's handle is broken from overuse. Another door is dented in, making it look slightly warped. . . . [6] Carol shows her class a sample mural: "Let me show you what another class did." She holds up four sheet-sized poster boards taped together for one lengthy mural that a small group developed and colored.

    [4] ART SUPPLIES

    [5] MAINTENANCE

    [6] MODELING

[7] Carol raises her hand to get the children quiet and the children raise their hands and stop talking. One child responds with a clap, but Carol says that response is for another class. [8] She continues: "The people at your table are the people in your group—you will work on a mural."

    [7] MANAGEMENT

    [8] DIRECTIONS

After data have been descriptively coded, two methods of reorganization are available. First, comparably coded data can be assembled together to explore how the topic manifests itself in the data. If we cut and paste all data coded MANAGEMENT in the excerpts above, we have the following:

MANAGEMENT

- Rack labels by the entry door: "Detention Forms," "Attendance Files."

- On the shelved counter beneath are plastic tubs with teachers' names on them to keep student class work together.

- Carol raises her hand to get the children quiet and the children raise their hands and stop talking. One child responds with a clap, but Carol says that response is for another class.

If we need more detail about this topic, or later realize that the code was too broad, we can **subcode** the data even further by adding tags to separate them into more-manageable chunks. Subcoding adds a child code to a parent code. Subcodes that share the same parent code are called siblings:

MANAGEMENT–CLASSROOM

- Rack labels by the entry door: "Detention Forms," "Attendance Files."

- On the shelved counter beneath are plastic tubs with teachers' names on them to keep student class work together.

MANAGEMENT–STUDENTS

- Carol raises her hand to get the children quiet and the children raise their hands and stop talking. One child responds with a clap, but Carol says that response is for another class.

The data collected under a parent code and its children can then be used as stimuli for analytic memo writing. For example, as more *MANAGEMENT–STUDENTS* data are pooled, the researcher–analyst might observe that the number of entries seems to appear more frequently in some classes than in others. Also, particular management actions by the teacher might elicit particular reactions from students.

A second method for analyzing the collective descriptive codes is to arrange them in outline formats to prompt an analytic memo or to organize a report's discussion about the field site and its participants. For example, one section of the outline might appear as follows:

III. MANAGEMENT

    A. CLASSROOM

        1. ADMINISTRATIVE PAPERWORK

        2. ART SUPPLIES

        3. FURNISHINGS

    B. STUDENTS

        1. FOCUSING ON TASK

            a. REGAINING ATTENTION

            b. PHYSICAL PROXIMITY

        2. DISTRIBUTION OF MATERIALS

        3. TIME PARAMETERS

        4. PERIODIC ASSESSMENT

Life does not always happen in neat outline form, but the arrangement of codes into this format helps the analyst gain an understanding of the organizational structures that contain and drive action, and the underlying patterns that might be at work in our routines, rituals, rules, roles, and relationships.

Dramaturgical coding

Dramaturgical Coding applies the basic conventions of dramatic character analysis onto naturalistic social interaction or onto a participant's stories contained in an interview. Six specific facets are examined and coded:

1. OBJ: participant–actor *objectives*, motives in the form of action verbs;

2. CON: *conflicts* or *obstacles* confronted by the participant–actor which prevent him or her from achieving his or her objectives;

3. TAC: participant–actor *tactics* or *strategies* to deal with conflicts or obstacles and to achieve his or her objectives;

4. ATT: participant–actor *attitudes* toward the setting, others, and the conflict;

5. EMO: *emotions* experienced by the participant–actor;

6. SUB: *subtexts*, the participant–actor's unspoken thoughts or impression management, usually in the form of gerunds. (Saldaña, 2016, pp. 145–146; emphasis in original)

Detailed analysis of these six interrelated facets provides the researcher multidimensional insight into some of the core drives of being human. Dramaturgical Coding is particularly relevant for case studies, ethnographies, narrative inquiry, dramatic writing, and even autoethnography for deeply introspective writers.

As an example, we return to the Type I diabetes participant and a brief excerpt from the full interview to illustrate Dramaturgical Coding. The overall objective (known as the *superobjective* in dramaturgical parlance) for this participant is OBJ: DIABETES MANAGEMENT. Note how the codes include previously discussed forms such as Descriptive, In Vivo, and Process Coding:

[I: Since you were diagnosed six years ago, are there any ways diabetes has affected the way you live your life?]

SARAH: [1] Yeah, I just have to be more aware of what I eat, is the main concern. [2] You know, the main thing you have to be worried about is [3] having a low blood sugar. [4] That's when you can have effects, and that can affect your driving, and it can affect your judgment, and that sort of thing. [5] I just have to make sure I always have a snack in my bag to ward off . . . Luckily, if you have a low blood sugar, all you have to do is eat something with carbs in it, so it's really [6] easy to treat. Those would be sort of . . . Yeah, being aware of food, and always having a snack.

[1] TAC: FOOD AWARENESS
[2] EMO: WORRY

[3] CON: LOW BLOOD SUGAR
[4] CON: PHYSICAL EFFECTS

[5] TAC: SNACK WITH CARBS AVAILABLE

[6] ATT: "EASY TO TREAT"

[I:	Have there been any other tangible tasks or physical things that are part of your life that weren't before?]	
SARAH:	[7] Yeah, again, it's mostly just I have to be aware, double check my blood sugar if I'm going to go exercise really strenuously or if I'm going on a long road trip, or something. It's just making sure I check my sugar level.	[7] TAC: "DOUBLE CHECK" BLOOD SUGAR LEVEL
[I:	How do you do that?]	
SARAH:	[8] You just stick your finger and draw some blood. And then you've got this blood sugar reader that you have to test. So, you've always got your little testers with you. [9] So, I guess you have to be a little more organized and aware, [10] which is a challenge for me as a disorganized person. [11] Again, it's a pretty manageable disease.	[8] TAC: BLOOD TESTING [9] TAC: "ORGANIZED AND AWARE" [10] CON: "DISORGANIZED" [11] ATT: "PRETTY MANAGEABLE"

Note that no SUB (subtexts) codes appear in the example above. These are usually supplemental codes based on what the interviewer infers from the participant's body language and vocal tones, which cannot always be determined from printed transcripts alone, especially when analyzed by a research team member who did not conduct the interview.

Analysis of the Dramaturgical Codes can stimulate holistic insights which are then documented in an analytic memo:

April 6, 2015

ROUTINE: DIABETES MANAGEMENT

I notice that very few EMOtion codes appear in this excerpt, balanced with straightforward ATTitudes such as "EASY TO TREAT" and "PRETTY MANAGEABLE." Sarah's been managing her diabetes for over six years now, so it's probably ingrained in her as a daily routine rather than a stigmatizing or mildly painful ritual.

Dramaturgical Codes can be examined systematically by categorizing them. For example, all the TAC: codes above could be extracted for reflection on the specific methods of diabetes management. Dramaturgical Codes can also be "chained" or "streamed" into strings of action and reaction to examine how a conflict or problem is handled:

OBJ: DIABETES MANAGEMENT → CON: LOW BLOOD SUGAR → TAC: SNACK WITH CARBS AVAILABLE → ATT: "EASY TO TREAT"

Dramaturgical Coding is an interpretive approach to analyzing life as performance. It asks the researcher to serve as an audience member of the participants as actors in a social drama. For more on this paradigm, see Goffman (1959).

Versus coding

Versus Coding is best applied to data in which conflicts between and among participants are overtly evident or covertly implied. The codes label in binary or dichotomous terms two opposing stances in an X VS. Y format, such as FAITH VS. SCIENCE, and "OUR WAY" VS. STANDARD OPERATING PROCEDURES. Versus Coding is appropriate for critical inquiry, evaluation research, action research, and studies that collect data with an unanticipated amount of microaggressions or conflict-laden perspectives. This method hones in on how people associate within the five Rs, particularly with rules, roles, and relationships.

As an example, below is an excerpt from the movie theatre employee discussing some of the more problematic issues with his former job. As with other coding methods, note that some of the choices are In Vivo Codes:

[I: Are there any other thoughts on customer service in retail that you would share in anecdotes, or just thoughts that you might have on the subject of customer service from the perspective of an employee?]

COLIN: From that of an employee's, specifically of a movie theatre. It was hard, particularly towards the end. [1] What disgruntled me as an employee the most was the fact that we were selling and trying . . . not to take advantage of guests, but getting money from them and charging really expensive—the business side—but also trying to be accommodating and the face of customer service. [2] You might gripe

    [1] PROFIT VS. CUSTOMER SERVICE

    [2] GRIPING VS. "FACADE"

about a guest, but as soon as a guest is there we put on this facade that things are good. It just seems kind of two faced and kind of cheesy. [3] I understand why it happens, but it's just unfortunate that that has to be the case, that [4] we have to play two fronts, that of a business making money and ripping people off, and then also making sure they are happy and that they are coming back for more.

[3] UNDERSTANDING VS. "UNFORUNATE"

[4] PROFIT VS. CUSTOMER SATISFACTION

[I: Any thoughts on what you would do? If you could make any changes that you wanted, how might you approach that?]

COLIN: [5] Just be a little bit more forthright. I think just some of the backwardness behind the scenes isn't really appropriate, and I think it's . . . Not many people know about it unless they've done customer service, and so I think being forthright about it is something that the public wants, in fact.

[5] "FORTHRIGHT" VS. "BEHIND THE SCENES"

For initial analysis, Versus Codes can be categorized into three general classifications of what's "at stake":

1. The Stakeholders

2. The Issues at Stake

3. Stakeholder Perspectives

Or, the array of Versus Codes can be clustered into what the researcher believes are the most appropriate categories for a study-specific analysis. Using the short data excerpt above, the five codes could be arranged into two categories—with labels borrowed from Colin's own words in the interview transcript, and one of them retaining the **X vs. Y** format:

Category: Profit vs. Customer Accommodation
CODES:
PROFIT VS. CUSTOMER SERVICE
PROFIT VS. CUSTOMER SATISFACTION

Category: Two-Faced Employees

CODES:

GRIPING VS. "FACADE"

UNDERSTANDING VS. "UNFORTUNATE"

"FORTHRIGHT" VS. "BEHIND THE SCENES"

As more data are collected from other employees about their on-the-job tensions, additional categories of conflict might emerge. Analytic memos focused on rules, roles, and relationships can reflect on the sources of conflict and whether they can be reconciled.

For more methods of coding qualitative data, see Saldaña's (2016) *The Coding Manual for Qualitative Researchers*. Remember that coding is not the only way but instead is just one way of analyzing qualitative data. We next present other approaches to the analysis of written materials.

Found poetry

Poetic inquiry (Prendergast, Leggo, & Sameshima, 2009) utilizes the conventions of literary poetry to construct an evocative representation of fieldwork or the researcher's reflections about self or others. It is a modality that attempts to capture the essence and essentials of an inquiry through carefully selected words and their strategic formatting in print. Analysis of interview transcripts and other participant-generated materials might benefit from this as a stand-alone method, or it can serve as a backstage, for-the-researcher's-eyes-only exploration of the corpus before a more traditional write-up is composed.

As an example of research-based **found poetry** or poetic material found within the data corpus, we extracted key In Vivo Codes from the analysis of Colin's interview transcript (discussed in the next section) to compose an impressionistic mosaic (Mears, 2009) of his perceptions. Notice how the use of italics and ellipses enhances the disillusionment expressed by the participant about his movie theatre job:

Facade

(facade)

Clean movies theatres for everyone!

(because of policy)

Clean! Fast! Easy! Fun!

(customer service first)

> Cordial,

>> accommodating,

>>> first to apologize . . . .

(two faced:)

> *the business side*

>> *conflicted*

>>> *trying to be polite . . . .*

(behind the scenes:)

> *cheesy*

>> *wasn't consistent*

>>> *ripping people off . . . .*

>>>> *discouraged*

>>>> *disgruntled*

>>>>> *we didn't care . . . .*

(this is garbage)

Sometimes technical approaches to qualitative data analysis can stymie and fatigue the researcher. Found poetry exercises one's creative capacities and can reveal unique insights about the phenomenon through its representational and aesthetic power. We will discuss this analytic heuristic more in Chapter 11.

Patterning Textual and Visual Materials

After or concurrent with data condensation, pattern construction is a second necessary analytic skill for qualitative researchers. Recall the *Three for All!* game explained in Chapter 1. Players have to identify what three different things have in common, such as butter, ice, and candle (they all melt). That gaming process is comparable to category construction and thematic development. An array of codes or themes are grouped according to comparability of some kind. The label applied to that patterned assemblage is its category name, primary theme, or theoretical construct.

Categories

A **category** in qualitative analysis is a label in the form of a word or short phrase applied to a grouped pattern of comparable codes and coded data. A category also condenses the collective symbolic meanings of codes even further into a new symbolic representation according to their pattern. It both groups and sometimes hierarchically organizes the array of things it represents.

We use the analogy that each room in a house is like a category in which relevant patterns of human action occur. A kitchen is for cooking, food storage, and dish washing; a bedroom is for sleeping and personal intimacy; a bathroom is for showering, grooming, and hygiene; and so on. Categories, then, both label and symbolically represent a collected group of comparable things that constitute an action pattern of some kind.

Categories, when appropriate to the analysis, are condensed chunks of meaning about the phenomenon. When researchers work inductively with a study, there are usually no predetermined categories to hunt for, unless several different studies from the literature review have identified the same types of categories, suggesting a pattern of some kind. Any codes and categories formulated before fieldwork and analysis are referred to as **a priori** codes and categories.

As an example of category construction, the movie theatre employee's interview transcript was first In Vivo Coded, and the 64 resulting codes are listed below in alphabetical order—an initial organizational tactic that can be accomplished quite easily through a data-sort function with Word or Excel. **Eyeballing** or analytically browsing the list several times can make one aware of repeating ideas (several codes appear more than once) and possible clusters for potential categories. Our analytic filter for the coding and subsequent categorization processes is the phenomenon or experience of employee/customer relations:

"ACCIDENT"

"ACCOMODATING"

"ACCOMODATING"

"APOLOGETIC"

"APOLOGIZED"

"BACKWARDNESS"

"BECAUSE OF POLICY"

"BECAUSE OF POLICY"

"BEHIND THE SCENES"

"BIG FUSS"

"BIG FUSS"

"CHEESY"

"CLEAN MOVIE THEATRES FOR EVERYONE"

"CLEAN, FAST, EASY, FUN"

"CLEANLINESS"

"COMPLACENT"

"CONCISE AND CLEAR"

"CONFLICTED"

"CONFLICTING"

"CONFLICTING"

"CORDIALLY"

"CUSTOMER SERVICE FIRST"

"CUSTOMER SERVICE FIRST"

"DISCOURAGED"

"DISCOURAGED"

"DISGRUNTLED"

"DISGRUNTLED"

"DON'T CARE"

"EXCUSE"

"EXTREMELY CORDIAL"

"FACADE"

"FIRST TO APOLOGIZE"

"FORTHRIGHT"

"GRIPE"

"HAD ISSUES WITH"

"IMPOLITE"

"IT WAS HARD"

"JUST NOT CARING"

"KEEP THE POLICIES"

"KIND OF WEIRD"

"LOUD NOISES"

"MORE FORTHRIGHT"

"MORE ON THE BUSINESS SIDE"

"MY OWN VALUES AND PRACTICES"

"NEVER BLAME"

"OFFICIAL POLICY"

"ONLY ABOUT FORTY PERCENT"

"PUSHED"

"PUSHED US"

"RIPPING PEOPLE OFF"

"STIGMA"

"THE BUSINESS SIDE"

"THIS IS GARBAGE"

"TRAINED"

"TRIED HARD"

"TRUE IN WORD"

"TRY TO BE CORDIAL"

"TRYING TO BE POLITE"

"TWO FACED"

"UNFORTUNATE"

"UNFORTUNATELY"

"VERY ADAMANT"

"WASN'T CONSISTENT"

"WE DIDN'T CARE"

Next comes the task of categorizing codes through cut-and-paste functions into groups that "look alike" and "feel alike" according to what the analyst interprets they might have in common (Lincoln & Guba, 1985, p. 347). Each category—divided further into subcategories if the data merit them—is then assigned a label that best symbolizes the collection. The category label can consist of a word or phrase from the codes, or a new word or phrase that represents the group. Two different people undertaking this task will most likely generate two completely different category sets and labels. What we list below is our own organizational interpretation, based on a first impression read of how the negative descriptors outnumbered the positive descriptors two to one. We also observed that smaller subcategories were possible after the major categories had been created. The order of the categories and subcategories was also rearranged several times until we believed there was a logical sense of storyline or flow to them, based on the contexts of the participant's interview content. Now the focus is on the bolded categories and subcategories:

Category 1: Impression Management

Subcategory: Onscreen Policy

CODES:

"BECAUSE OF POLICY"

"BECAUSE OF POLICY"

"CLEAN MOVIE THEATRES FOR EVERYONE"

"CLEAN, FAST, EASY, FUN"

"CLEANLINESS"

"CUSTOMER SERVICE FIRST"

"CUSTOMER SERVICE FIRST"

"KEEP THE POLICIES"

"OFFICIAL POLICY"

Subcategory: Behind the Facade

CODES:

"BACKWARDNESS"

"BEHIND THE SCENES"

"FACADE"

"MORE ON THE BUSINESS SIDE"

"RIPPING PEOPLE OFF"

"THE BUSINESS SIDE"

Category 2: Positive Interactions

Subcategory: Cordiality

CODES:

"ACCOMODATING"

"ACCOMODATING"

"CONCISE AND CLEAR"

"CORDIALLY"

"EXTREMELY CORDIAL"

"TRY TO BE CORDIAL"

"TRYING TO BE POLITE"

Subcategory: "Apologetic"

CODES:

"APOLOGETIC"

"APOLOGIZED"

"FIRST TO APOLOGIZE"

"NEVER BLAME"

Subcategory: Integrity

CODES:

"FORTHRIGHT"

"MORE FORTHRIGHT"

"MY OWN VALUES AND
PRACTICES"

"TRAINED"

"TRIED HARD"

"TRUE IN WORD"

"VERY ADAMANT"

Category 3: Negative Interactions

Subcategory: Inconsistency

CODES:

"ONLY ABOUT FORTY
PERCENT"

"TWO FACED"

"WASN'T CONSISTENT"

Subcategory: "This is Garbage"

CODES:

"ACCIDENT"

"BIG FUSS"

"BIG FUSS"

"CHEESY"

"GRIPE"

"HAD ISSUES WITH"

"IMPOLITE"

"KIND OF WEIRD"

"LOUD NOISES"

"PUSHED"

"PUSHED US"

"STIGMA"

"THIS IS GARBAGE"

Subcategory: Defeatism

CODES:

"COMPLACENT"

"CONFLICTED"

"CONFLICTING"

"CONFLICTING"

"DISCOURAGED"

"DISCOURAGED"

"DISGRUNTLED"

"DISGRUNTLED"

"DON'T CARE"

"EXCUSE"

"IT WAS HARD"

"JUST NOT CARING"

"UNFORTUNATE"

"UNFORTUNATELY"

"WE DIDN'T CARE"

The categories and subcategories initiate reflection through an analytic memo, or even the framework for the narrative write-up itself.

Coding does not always have to precede category construction, because there are other ways to formulate categories. But with just three major units to explore (**Impression Management**, **Positive Interactions**, **Negative Interactions**), the mind can now more easily grasp the essential qualities of the phenomenon of interest—employee–customer relations—especially when reflecting on how the three categories interrelate. Separate categories are not always isolated topics or bins—they should connect or unify in some way, thus generating further mental exercises in hierarchy, propositions, causation, and so on as the data and study suggest.

There is no standardized number of final categories that should result from qualitative analysis. Methodologists vary in their recommendations for a final number ranging from three to seven. Other studies, due to the magnitude of their data or the complexity of their research questions, might compose up to thirty or more categories. But remember that there can even be categories of categories, suggesting that condensation can continue further for richer synthesis.

Themes

A **theme** is an extended phrase or sentence that identifies and functions as a way to categorize a set of data into a topic that emerges from a pattern of ideas. The topics generate extended narratives that elaborate on the statements and describe or explain their constituent elements. Themes can derive from initial analytic work with codes and categories, or they can be independently constructed from a holistic review of the data corpus for patterns of reoccurring ideas. To clarify with an example, CORDIALLY is a code; CORDIALITY IS AN EMPLOYEE FACADE is a theme.

Themes extrapolate from the data their main ideas, and are not just topical content. It helps if analysts frame their lenses, filters, and angles with the proper question. If they go looking for themes with, "What are the participants talking about?" they'll more than likely develop nothing more than a topical index, which will not move them toward thematic analysis. Instead, they should go "looking for trouble" by asking of the data,

- What worries or concerns are the participants expressing?

- What unresolved issues are the participants raising?

- What do the participants find intriguing, surprising, or disturbing? (Sunstein & Chiseri-Strater, 2012, p. 115)

- What types of tensions, problems, or conflicts are the participants experiencing?

- What kinds of trouble are the participants in?

These evocative prompts could generate more evocative ideas for thematic structures (Saldaña, 2015, pp. 34–35).

Below are three excerpts from the interview with the female diabetic, Sarah. The themes placed alongside her interview text each begin with DM, an abbreviation for DIABETES MANAGEMENT, the focus of this particular analysis. "DM IS _____" indicates specific actions taken by the participant that are observable; "DM MEANS _____" refers to more general or conceptual ideas about diabetes management. Bigger-picture ideas will emerge after the themes have been categorized or themed even further in this section:

[I: First, in your own words, how would you describe diabetes to someone who had no experience with it and limited knowledge of the condition?]

SARAH: [1] So, Type I diabetes is when your pancreas no longer makes insulin, and you need insulin to open up your cells to allow sugar to be processed by your cells. So if you don't have insulin, your cells can't process sugar, and basically you kind of end up where you don't have any energy, and it affects your brain, and that sort of a thing. So you have to take insulin. They have synthetic insulin you can take, so you sort of have to operate as your own pancreas to administer insulin to yourself, to process food and to get energy . . .

[1] DM IS KNOWING HOW THE DISEASE AFFECTS YOUR BODY

[I:	How do you recall feeling and reacting when you were first diagnosed with diabetes? What questions did you have?]	
SARAH:	[2] I was . . . First I was relieved because it explained a lot of the . . . unusual sort of feelings I had been having. The usual symptoms, you know?	[2] DM MEANS UNDERSTANDING YOUR SYMPTOMS
[I:	What were some of those feelings or symptoms?]	
SARAH:	I was losing a ton of weight, I was going to the bathroom all the time, I was constantly thirsty. . . . I had all the classic symptoms, and I was really tired. So, all of a sudden, all of that made sense. And yeah, it was a little bit of a learning curve. I had a lot to learn. But it was also—So yeah. It was unexpected, but not devastating, or anything like that . . .	
[I:	How do you learn to do some of the things, like counting carbohydrates?]	
SARAH:	[3] So, there's all kind of books that you can get that give you the carb counts of basic foods, fast foods, those sorts of things. Then you just get really good at reading labels. Luckily, there's labels on pretty much everything. And then, after a couple of months, you pretty much . . . I've discovered most people eat the same things most of the time. When you're not eating the same things, you can always look it up, and there's all kinds of apps on phones now, and stuff. So it's pretty easy to look things up and develop a sort of working knowledge of how many carbs there are and stuff. It takes time. It's doable.	[3] DM IS CARB KNOWLEDGE

Below is the complete set of themes the analyst constructed from Sarah's full interview, listed in the order they appear in the transcript. Note that some begin with "DM IS" (observable action) and others with "DM MEANS" (conceptual action):

DM IS KNOWING HOW THE DISEASE AFFECTS YOUR BODY

DM MEANS UNDERSTANDING YOUR SYMPTOMS

DM MEANS VIGILANCE

DM IS CARB KNOWLEDGE

DM IS EATING A HEALTHY DIET

DM IS EXERCISING REGULARLY

DM IS SEEKING RELIABLE INFORMATION

DM IS CLEARING MISCONCEPTIONS

DM MEANS TAKING RESPONSIBILITY

DM MEANS PREPARATION

DM MEANS ORGANIZATION

DM MEANS AWARENESS

As with codes and categories, themes can be initially analyzed by arraying them into an outline format according to commonality and, if feasible, **hierarchy** to suggest importance. One possible reconfiguration of the themes is as follows and note that, in this particular case, there is one overarching theme the analyst deemed central. For diabetes management (DM),

I. **DM MEANS TAKING RESPONSIBILITY**

    A. DM MEANS AWARENESS

        1. DM MEANS UNDERSTANDING YOUR SYMPTOMS

           a. DM IS KNOWING HOW THE DISEASE AFFECTS YOUR BODY

        2. DM IS SEEKING RELIABLE INFORMATION

           a. DM IS CLEARING MISCONCEPTIONS

        3. DM IS EATING A HEALTHY DIET

           a. DM IS CARB KNOWLEDGE

    B. DM MEANS ORGANIZATION

        1. DM IS REGULAR BLOOD TESTING

        2. DM IS EXERCISING REGULARLY

    C. DM MEANS VIGILANCE

        1. DM MEANS PREPARATION

An organizational array such as this now prompts an analytic memo on its suggested meanings or an outline for the written narrative.

Just as codes are categorized for further analysis, themes can get categorized into **theoretical constructs** (Auerbach & Silverstein, 2003) or phrases that serve as category-like, abstract summations of a set of related themes. Since one of the goals of themeing the data is to get to ideas, not topics, theoretical constructs better ensure an analytic leap into bigger-picture meanings. The same themes are utilized, yet their organization into clusters is not hierarchical but categorical. If appropriate, a word or phrase from the supporting themes can serve as a theoretical construct:

Theoretical Construct 1: DM as Physical Caretaking

Supporting Themes:

DM IS KNOWING HOW THE DISEASE AFFECTS YOUR BODY

DM IS EATING A HEALTHY DIET

DM IS CARB KNOWLEDGE

DM IS EXERCISING REGULARLY

DM MEANS UNDERSTANDING YOUR SYMPTOMS

Theoretical Construct 2: DM as Mental Vigilance

Supporting Themes:

DM MEANS VIGILANCE

DM MEANS AWARENESS

DM MEANS TAKING RESPONSIBILITY

DM MEANS PREPARATION

DM MEANS ORGANIZATION

DM IS SEEKING RELIABLE INFORMATION

DM IS CLEARING MISCONCEPTIONS

As with all initial work, an analytic memo expands on the two main ideas— diabetes management as physical caretaking of oneself, and as mental vigilance for long-term health maintenance.

Thematic statements can get analysts into the conceptual scheme of things by looking beyond case-specific data and working toward broader meanings for general populations and applications. If the highly condensed format of codes is too essentialist for personal ways of thinking, or if categorization is an artificial approach to organizing topics, themes might be a more narrative-friendly way of exploring the ideas inherent in data. Themes are particularly helpful if a research study's methodology is phenomenological, content analytic, or ethnographic.

Unifying Seemingly Different Things

The condensing and patterning of data need one more stage: unification. Unifying condenses and patterns the data even further by exploring how the constituent elements of the analysis interrelate in some way. Sometimes unity might be realized through the development of an overarching concept. It might also occur through a proposition of outcome. Matrices and tabular displays are ways of visualizing the analytic work to explore their intersections and possible connections. Mixed-methods studies attempt to unify both qualitative and quantitative data.

Be aware that qualitative data are sometimes if not often variable, particularly when multiple perspectives from multiple participants have been collected through interviews or surveys, creating a three-dimensional landscape rather than linear continuum of data. The challenge then is to include contradictory data **outliers** or extreme cases that vary from the typical or majority of responses as part of the pattern in progress. Sometimes that means acknowledging that variation is the pattern itself. At other times it's finding ways to unify the variation through a higher-level category, theme, theoretical construct, or concept.

Concepts

A **concept** is a word or short phrase that symbolically represents a suggested meaning broader than a single item or action—a bigger picture idea beyond the tangible and apparent. Analysts conceptualize in order to transcend the local and particular of what is studied to find possible applicability and transferability to other settings and contexts. We also conceptualize to discover possible latent meanings and deeper significance embedded in our everyday lives.

A concept is something that literally cannot be touched; thus, it suggests an idea rather than an object. For example, a smartphone is something one can hold, but its higher-level or bigger-picture meanings are the concepts of communication or technology. The so-called touch test is a heuristic to transcend the reality of what we can experience with our senses to develop an entity with more magnitude. A school building can be touched, but not the concept of education. A person can run her fingers across a cashmere coat, but cannot touch luxury or, depending on her values system, arrogant entitlement. And people can internally feel immersed in a strong emotional bond that literally affects their heart and respiration rates, but they cannot physically touch their personal feelings of love. Note that these concepts are nouns.

Concepts also refer to observable actions—processes—and their bigger picture or broader meanings. For example, one can see someone deposit money into a savings account, earn a college degree, marry a partner, and purchase a home, but the overall concept is building a future. Dressing in a swimsuit and sunglasses, drinking a cocktail, and lounging in a deck chair on a cruise ship are observable actions, but the broader concepts for this scene are pampering one's self, escaping from reality, or living the good life. Note that these concept phrases begin with gerunds—"-ing" words—to describe broader processes at work.

A concept is somewhat comparable to a category's function. It is a label for an assemblage of patterned comparability. But whereas a category could consist of observable actions or things perceived (e.g., applying for governmental assistance, going to sleep hungry, living in a home in disrepair, receiving minimum-wage paychecks), a concept—like poverty—is broader in scope and intangible in sensory terms. Concepts are ideas that unify and embody related realities. They are constructed from the researcher's ability to reflect deeply on the data and to transcend into broader patterns of meaning.

Concepts become essential building blocks for theory development (discussed in Chapter 10). Once the concepts are labeled and defined to represent broader phenomena, they can be integrated or interrelated into statements that suggest general applicability. For example, in the set of field notes about the elementary school visual art class profiled in Chapter 2, three observations were pooled to form the code **qua** (in the role of) concept, management:

- Rack labels by the entry door: "Detention Forms," "Attendance Files."

- On the shelved counter beneath are plastic tubs with teachers' names on them to keep student class work together.

- Carol raises her hand to get the children quiet and the children raise their hands and stop talking. One child responds with a clap, but Carol says that response is for another class.

Other concepts suggested by these observations are procedures and organization. If a researcher wishes to analyze these observations as processual concepts in gerund form, they might be rephrased as managing the classroom or organizing daily routines. Assuming enough observations have been made to verify selected patterns, concepts can be combined to formulate statements such as an assertion, proposition, theme, or theory. The following are examples of assertions:

- Teacher organization is key to successful classroom management.

- Organized classroom routines alone do not ensure a productive learning environment.

Concepts, like categories, are symbols or metaphors of patterned data. They unify various human actions into a broader domain. They can serve as stand alone outcomes for a research study with an accompanying narrative to unpack its meanings (e.g., emotional intelligence, possible selves, coping), or serve as building blocks for a more complex analysis.

Propositions

A **proposition** is a predictive statement, usually with two primary elements, that "proposes" a conditional event, such as

- A → B
- If → then
- When → then
- Because → that's why
- Since → and so

Propositions are usually not formally written with such phrases, but the intent should be clear. Explanation or **causation** is purposely embedded in or suggested by the proposition, such as these:

- Where there's smoke, there's fire.
- To ensure student preparation for classes, the teacher administered an occasional "pop quiz."

- Nominees who do not win a competitive award will tend to bond with each other out of shared defeat or common loss.

- Worker performance and productivity will increase when observers are present. (This is known as the Hawthorne Effect.)

Propositions meet several analytic goals for qualitative inquiry. First, they unify or connect an action and reaction to compose an interaction or interrelationship between two or more phenomena. Second, they assert—this is, they make a research-based truth claim about the conditions of social life. Third, they explain or attribute causation to actions and reactions, describing how, why, or what kinds of certain actions happen. And fourth, they often predict possible actions or outcomes, which are necessary elements for theory development.

Propositions establish evidence-based reasons and rationale for what, how, in what ways, or why certain **outcomes** happen when certain **antecedent conditions** exist and certain **mediating variables** intervene (see Figure 9.1). As a simple illustration drawn from one of the examples above, we offer this propositional argument:

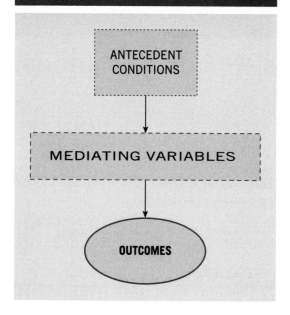

Figure 9.1 The relationship between antecedent conditions, mediating variables, and outcomes.

ANTECEDENT CONDITIONS

MEDIATING VARIABLES

OUTCOMES

- *Proposition:* To ensure student preparation for classes, the teacher administered an occasional pop quiz.

- *Antecedent Conditions:* Possible little to no student preparation for classes, exhibited by a lack of discussion over the day's assigned readings, some absenteeism.

- *Mediating Variables:* Pop quizzes that affect the students' final course grades, students' concern for good grades.

- *Outcomes:* Better prepared students for class, enhanced discussion, less absenteeism.

Propositions put forth logical arguments in short storylines that are then fleshed out through extended narratives. But some propositions might not always transfer to other settings, contexts, and times. Therefore, provisional language is often woven into these types of statements: might, likely to, possible that, often, to better guarantee, and so on.

The best propositions are pattern derived and pattern driven. When an analyst observes certain antecedent conditions, mediating variables, and consequential outcomes happening frequently, that provides more substantive evidence for propositional claims. Summarizing the patterns of **influences and affects** (our qualitative paradigm for the positivist cause and effect) provides a little bit of order to what can sometimes be perceived as random or chaotic in social life. Not all predictions are foolproof, however, so we must couch our claims with provisional language when necessary.

Matrices and tabular displays

A **matrix** (see Figure 9.2) is an intersection of lists, set up as rows and columns, comparable to the layout of a Microsoft Excel spreadsheet. It is a table or tabular display that summarizes and arranges data from a larger corpus by such factors as time, site, case, variable, and so on, for easy, unified, at-a-glance viewing. The display permits the analyst's mind to better grasp the condensed essentials of fieldwork through its organized format. It prompts analytic reflection through eyeballing or simply looking repeatedly at the cells and keeping one's mind open to what ideas they trigger through comparison and contrast.

Qualitative analysis generally inserts words and phrases rather than numbers in matrix cells, though a few descriptive statistics can certainly be included if necessary for the analytic task. Cell contents can consist of verbatim quotes from participants or In Vivo Codes, summaries of the larger data base, concepts or themes developed by the researcher, and any other information necessary for analytic reflection. Matrices are particularly useful for comparing things side by side such as different participants, time frames, and categories. Cut-and-paste functions of text editing software enable the researcher to change the order and layout of rows, columns, and individual cells to explore if a new arrangement might prompt a discovery about something unique about the data in terms of a pattern, category, concept, or theme.

Figure 9.2, a table originally drawn with Microsoft Word software, is a matrix constructed from online survey data collected for a "Lifelong Impact" study of adults recalling their high school theatre and speech experiences

Figure 9.2 A matrix of "lifelong impact" across high school graduates from the 1950s to 2000s.

COHORT/ Survey Item	1950s–1970s HS GRADUATES	1980s HS GRADUATES	1990s HS GRADUATES	2000s HS GRADUATES
Perceptions of Teachers	"Enthusiastic" and "motivating" ————→ "Challenging," "encouraging," "inspiring" ———		"Supportive" in "safe spaces"; "experienced" and "demanding" ———→ ———————————→	
Personal Challenges Faced	"Shyness," "lack of confidence," search for "identity" ———	Explorations of "self" ———————————→	A need to "belong" and "fit in"	"Fear"
Fondest Memories	Extrinsic rewards ————————————→ Connections with audience ——→ "Camaraderie" "Friendships" and "fun"	"Feeling part of something bigger" ——— "Community," "family," "teamwork" ———	Connections with self, characters portrayed, peers ——→ Independent production projects ——→	Intrinsic rewards ———————→ ———————→ ———————→
Affects on Adulthood	Work ethics ("confidence," "leadership skills," "public speaking skills," presentation of self) ———	Benefits to self, Increased social consciousness ———	"Outgoing" ————	"Maturity," stronger "identity" ———————→

(McCammon & Saldaña, 2011; McCammon et al., 2012a). This information symbolizes the corpus of more than 1,400 cells of raw survey data. The four main rows represent the analyst's summaries of 234 participants' collective responses to four major survey prompts:

- **Perceptions of Teachers** ("I had a good high school speech and/or theatre teacher(s)"/"Describe briefly why you selected your response")

- **Personal Challenges Faced** ("Looking back, what do you think was the biggest challenge you overcame/faced in high school speech and theatre?")

- **Fondest Memories** ("What are a few of your fondest memories of your speech and/or theatre participation? Why did you select those moments?")

- **Affects on Adulthood** ("In what ways do you think your participation in speech and/or theatre as a high school student has affected the adult you have become?")

The four main columns group together participants who graduated from high school in a particular decade. (Those who graduated in the 1950s through 1970s were grouped together due to the smaller number of survey respondents from those periods.) Each cell thus represents an intersection between a specific survey prompt's collective response by graduation or generational cohort. If a particular pattern was observed across two or more cohorts, an arrow is used to indicate its presence across the decades.

The purpose of this matrix arrangement was to explore and determine whether participants from different age ranges held different memories and perceptions of their high school experiences. Each cell includes a representative summary of the data base—sometimes with the participants' own words (e.g., "enthusiastic," "motivating") and sometimes with the analyst's interpretive summaries of the data (e.g., extrinsic rewards, increased social consciousness). Repeatedly eyeballing the matrix both horizontally and vertically stimulates the analyst to consider some emergent ideas about the data which can be noted through simple bullet pointing and analytic memoing. For example, in the **Fondest Memories** row, a shift from "Extrinsic rewards" to "Intrinsic rewards" occurs in the 2000s HS GRADUATES column. Vertical eyeballing of the 2000s column also reveals that related summaries such as connections with and benefits to self, and a stronger sense of identity appear with intrinsic rewards. These intersections or informal correlations trigger analytic reflection on why these items cluster together among more-recent high school graduates and not from the older generations. The research team speculated,

> Older generations who graduated from the 1950s–1970s may have placed more value on the tangible products and publicly announced merit from high school speech and theatre participation (awards, trophies, etc. as symbols of "winning") since this is *concrete evidence* of significant accomplishment in one's lifetime—milestones accorded more value from middle-aged and elder adults. . . . Young adults in their twenties, developmentally still in ripe searches for evolving personal identities, may have placed more value on intrinsic accomplishments (peer status, affirmation, etc.) of speech and theatre participation because of their immediate impact on and relevance to the current search for and evolution of one's self. (McCammon & Saldaña, 2011, pp. 87–88; emphasis in original)

Studies in qualitative content analysis, mixed methods, comparative case studies, longitudinal qualitative research, and research genres with multiple participant groups can utilize matrices and tabular displays as a way of synthesizing and unifying the corpus for analytic reflection. For a more comprehensive discussion on matrix displays, see Miles et al. (2014).

Mixed methods

Mixed methods, discussed as a research genre in Chapter 6, is the intentional blending of qualitative and quantitative data collection and analyses for studies that will benefit from their combined outcomes—that is, their unification. Below, we offer just two principles of this genre to consider for analytic synthesis.

First, mixed-methods studies can compare their quantitative and qualitative findings to assess whether there is paradigmatic corroboration—this is, consensus or harmony between the numbers and the words. For example, in the "Lifelong Impact" study just profiled, the research team compared men's and women's survey results. We anticipated significant differences of some kind based on our previous readings in gender studies and our attunement to developmental differences between boys and girls in educational research. But when we ran a statistical test between men's and women's numeric ratings to survey prompts, there were no statistically significant differences. And when we qualitatively compared and analyzed each gender's written survey responses, there were also no overt differences of note between their codes or categories. In this case the statistical and qualitative data analyses harmonized with each other. If there had been different or even contradictory results observed between the two forms of data collected and separately analyzed, some type of analytic reconciliation would have been in order.

Second, an analytic synthesis might be initiated when the quantitative results inform or help guide the forthcoming qualitative inquiry (or vice versa). Saldaña and Otero (1990) administered an age-appropriate **semantic differential** test to fifth grade youths to assess their so-called theatrical sensibility, or audience receptiveness to live performance. The semantic differential is a standardized quantitative survey instrument that asks participants to mark in one of seven spaces an affective rating somewhere between a series of bipolar adjectives in response to a prompt such as,

MY ATTITUDE TOWARD WATCHING [title of play production]:

good ___:___:___:___:___:___:___ bad

ugly ___:___:___:___:___:___:___ beautiful

valuable ___:___:___:___:___:___:___ worthless

Briefly, there were strong significant differences ($p < .001$, loosely meaning a 1 in 1,000 chance that the results were due to something other than the treatment) between treatment group children with six years of classroom drama and theatre viewing experiences, and a control group that had none. These quantitative survey results informed the next year's qualitative final exit interviews with the treatment group (Saldaña, 1995). Since the research team had found rigorous statistical evidence to support the development of children's theatrical sensibility, interview questions were then designed to further assess young people's relationship with the art form:

- "What do you like most [then, least] about theatre?"
- "What do you think your relationship with theatre might be in the future?"
- "Is theatre necessary? Do we have to have it?"

A loosely standardized nomenclature for the design of mixed-methods studies has been developed (Creswell, 2015). For the "Lifelong Impact" study, the simultaneous or convergent quantitative and qualitative survey would be labeled: QUAN + QUAL. The sequential semantic differential and final exit interview design for the theatrical sensibility study, with the quantitative results playing a lesser role among seven years of qualitative data, would be labeled: quan → QUAL.

We have profiled just two of several approaches to the design and synthesis of mixed-methods data. For more on this methodology, see Bryman (2006); Creswell and Plano-Clark (2011); Morgan (2014); and Tashakkori and Teddlie (2010).

CLOSURE AND TRANSITION

The first part of analytic synthesis explored the condensing, patterning, and unifying of a qualitative data base. The next chapter examines analyzing the social processes of action, reaction, interaction, the five Rs, and their continued synthesis into theory. Resources and Sample Data for Analytic Synthesis are included in the next chapter.

ANALYTIC EXERCISES FOR ANALYTIC SYNTHESIS

1. Take a 15-minute field note observation of natural social life and apply Descriptive Coding to the data. Then, organize the codes into outline form.

2. Take an interview transcript of 15 minutes' real-time duration and create a found poetry piece from the data.

3. Take an interview transcript of 30–45 minutes' real-time duration and analyze the data through thematic statements. Explore the outlining of themes or development of theoretical constructs.

4. Take an interview transcript of 15 minutes' real-time duration and apply In Vivo Coding to the data. Then, categorize the In Vivo Codes with category or concept labels.

CHAPTER 10

Analytic Synthesis: Understanding, Interpreting, and Theorizing

Introduction

This chapter continues the discussion of analytic synthesis by focusing on the social processes of action, reaction, interaction, and the five Rs through three heuristics: understanding, interpreting, and theorizing. The previous chapter's analytic methods were mostly systematic in their methods of data management. These methods venture into more creative and highdeep levels of reflection.

Understanding Social Processes of Human Action, Reaction, and Interaction

A **plot** is the overall structure of a story. A **storyline** consists of the units of action contained within the plot. These heuristics for synthesizing qualitative data examine the "plot points"—the processes—of the participants' journeys through brief and extended narrative constructions: assertions, vignettes, and diagrammatic displays.

Assertions

Frederick Erickson (1986) outlined interpretive methods for qualitative field research. The heuristics are based on the development of assertions—declarative statements of summative synthesis about the researcher's fieldwork observations, supported with or instantiated by evidence from the data corpus. If any **disconfirming evidence** or discrepant cases appear that negate the validity of the assertion, the statement is revised to accommodate the data.

Learning Objectives

After reading and reviewing this chapter, researchers should be able to

1. Manage a data corpus throughout a research study,

2. Select appropriate qualitative data analytic methods for a research study,

3. Transform data into symbols of condensed analytic meaning, and

4. Create an analytic synthesis from a data corpus.

As a simple example, someone might assert, "Anyone who smokes cigarettes gets lung cancer." But we can think of exceptions to or disconfirming evidence for that assertion, based on our knowledge of people who have smoked for decades and are cancer free. Thus, the assertion is modified to read, "Most people who smoke cigarettes will get lung cancer." But even then, an individual cannot possibly observe "most people" who smoke and predict their future health status. There are also individuals who have contracted lung cancer from causes other than smoking. After reviewing the literature and interviewing health-care professionals, the assertion is revised once more to accommodate the evidence to read, "People who smoke cigarettes are at much higher risk than nonsmokers for developing various cancers."

Erickson (1986) promotes analytic induction or constructivist exploration of and inferences about the data, based on a careful examination of the corpus and an accumulated knowledge base with each reading. The goal is not to look for proof to support assertions, but rather to look for plausibility of inference-laden observations about the local and particular social world under investigation, and their possible implications for broader generalizations. Assertions can range from factual description ("Many classroom teachers regularly work with children who are homeless"), to researcher impressions ("The teachers seemed helpless and frustrated by the lack of school resources for homeless youths"), to claims of transference ("The growing number of homeless youths in this country suggests a dysfunctional society indifferent to some segments of the current generation's most basic needs"). **Low-level inferences** address and summarize what is happening within the particulars of the case or field site—the "micro," such as an individual classroom. **High-level inferences** extend beyond the particulars to speculate on what they mean in the more general social scheme of things—the "meso" or "macro," such as schooling in general or national education policy. High-level inference extends beyond the case yet derives from it to posit a **synoptic** generalization (a view of the whole) about the data's suggested meanings.

Figure 10.1 illustrates that the central argument or all-encompassing interpretive claim about the researcher's fieldwork is labeled the **key assertion**. This statement derives from, is supported by, and is linked to its related assertions, which are in turn further supported by their constituent **subassertions**. Though you could be reading the model from the top down, the subassertions and assertions provide the **evidentiary warrant** or data foundation on which the key assertion is built. The key assertion and assertions should also interrelate with each other through **key linkages** or statements of connection (Erickson, 1986).

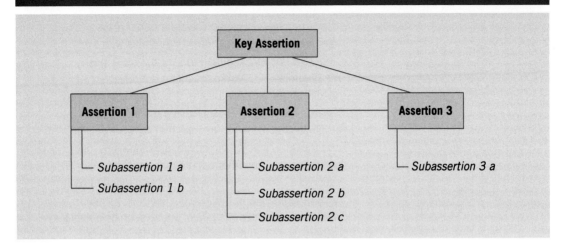

Figure 10.1   The key assertion derives from assertions and subassertions.

Key Assertion

Assertion 1   **Assertion 2**   **Assertion 3**

— *Subassertion 1 a*   — *Subassertion 2 a*   — *Subassertion 3 a*

— *Subassertion 1 b*   — *Subassertion 2 b*

                            — *Subassertion 2 c*

Source: Based on Erickson, F. (1986). Qualitative methods in research on teaching. In M. C. Wittrock (Ed.), *Handbook of research on teaching* (3rd ed., pp. 119–161). New York, NY: Macmillan.

Coding or themeing the data beforehand is not always necessary to develop assertions, though those methods might help an analyst become more intimately familiar with each datum. Erickson instead advises multiple readings of the data to gain holistic and intuitive awareness of their contents as the analyst's mind formulates and the researcher documents interpretive summaries of participant perceptions and interaction. As with themes, the statements are arranged in outline format according to their evolving status as assertions and their constituent subassertions, and revised as needed when any disconfirming evidence merits it. The report can use assertions as topic sentences for the narrative, accompanied with illustrative vignettes (discussed next) to support them. This narrative approach to condensing a data corpus keeps the analyst grounded in the particulars of the data while transcending them to suggest more general applications.

We demonstrate assertion development by comparing and pooling selected data from the movie theatre employee (Colin) and retail clothing sales employee (Monique). Our research goal is to examine employees' job experiences with customer relations. As we review the data, we notice from the two the emotional labor involved with their minimum wage jobs (Ehrenreich, 2001; Hochschild, 2003). As you read the two interview excerpts below, consider their emergent patterns—that is, what they have in common—and how you might phrase those patterns into single sentences:

COLIN: They [managers] pushed us very much that we needed to sell large popcorn, large drinks with every single transaction, but then they said, "Don't push merchandise." . . . From that of an employee's, specifically of a movie theatre, it was hard, particularly towards the end. What disgruntled me as an employee the most was the fact that we were selling and trying . . . not to take advantage of guests—but getting money from them and charging really expensive—the business side—but also trying to be accommodating and the face of customer service. You might gripe about a guest, but as soon as a guest is there we put on this facade that things are good. It just seems kind of two faced and kind of cheesy. I understand why it happens, but it's just unfortunate that that has to be the case, that we have to play two fronts, that of a business making money and ripping people off, and then also making sure they are happy and that they are coming back for more.

MONIQUE: It was kind of like a fine line between just letting the customer roam around the store and pick out things they want, and almost being like the employees that work on commission, where you like push them to buy everything. . . . . I always think that everyone should have a job where they're either in retail customer service, or food customer service because there's always like that one customer who is just a jerk. "Give me everything I want. Give it to me now." And you're like, "I am bound by these rules. Also, I've been on my feet for six hours. I'm tired. You're tired. Leave me alone. Don't be a jerk to me." But you, as the customer service person, still have to like plaster on that smile and be really nice and everything like that. I feel like people would be nicer if they had to work customer service jobs, in general.

Assertion development utilizes holistic, summative interpretations of the data. Loosely, the method relies on asking, "After reading and reflecting on the data, what are your evidence-based impressions that summarize what's going on?" First, we noticed that both employees were told to push sales, even though they held mixed feelings about that job responsibility (discussed further in other portions of their interviews). This led us to develop the following assertion:

> Sales staff must reconcile conflicts with their personal values system as they covertly manipulate customers in order to push additional merchandise purchases.

Next, we were struck by two comparable phrases the employees used to negatively describe their required interactions with customers/guests: "put on this facade" (Colin) and "plaster on that smile" (Monique), along with related stories in the interviews. This led us to develop the assertion:

> Despite personal feelings, sales staff must assume a positive facade with difficult customers.

And finally, a more general assertion composed about these two employees' perceptions is

> Sales staff sacrifice their own emotional well-being to accommodate customer service needs.

We have condensed 332 words from interview excerpts into three single-sentence assertions. They might seem like obvious, commonsense statements, but they are solidly rooted in the data. Other researchers might interpret different things about the employees' experiences or might have worded our three assertions differently. As long as researchers have evidence to support their claims, they can make the case for their interpretive summations.

But what about discrepant data and their integration as an assertion? Each participant was asked the following question in separate interviews:

> INTERVIEWER: In your opinion, did your employer's official policies on customer service align with their actual practice in customer service? Both in terms of what they expected of you, and also in terms of what you saw your supervisors do?

Colin, the movie theatre employee, responded as follows:

> COLIN: Probably, for the most part, no. I think, for the most part, we were true in word, but when it

came to application, I'd guess only about forty
percent of the employees or managers actually
took that part of the policy ["clean, fast, easy,
fun"] serious.

But Monique, the retail clothing sales clerk, responded differently:

MONIQUE: Oh yeah, definitely. They [managers] were very
            good at practicing what they preach.

We cannot assert that "Supervisors do not adhere to official customer service
policies" because Monique's datum disconfirms that assertion. A range of
perspectives such as this must now generate an assertion that accommodates the
differences:

Supervisors, in the presence of employees, vary in their modeling
of customer service policies.

All of the assertions thus far have been low level—meaning, site- and case-specific
inferences. Transcending to a high-level inference requires that we build on our
existing assertions to suggest an interpretive meaning at the meso or macro level.
The three low-level assertions about the employees' experiences follow:

1. Sales staff must reconcile conflicts with their personal values
   system as they covertly manipulate customers in order to
   push additional merchandise purchases.

2. Despite personal feelings, sales staff must assume a positive
   facade with difficult customers.

3. Sales staff sacrifice their own emotional well-being to
   accommodate customer service needs.

As with themes, our analytic goal is to synthesize these assertions into one, while
rising above the employee-specific cases. Again, remain grounded in the data
as evidence for a claim, but extend beyond the particular to get to the general.
Below we offer what might be considered a key assertion, based on the data
excerpts above in addition to the entire sets of interviews with the movie theatre
employee and retail clothing sales clerk:

Salespersonship consists of personal devaluation through covert
manipulation of and emotional subservience to consumers.

This key assertion might be revised as more data are collected from additional salespeople, supplying both confirming and disconfirming evidence to instantiate the claim.

Vignettes

Erickson (1986) advocates the development of **vignettes** as not just a presentational form in reports but also as a method for analyzing moments of significant interaction processes among participants. The literary genre of the short story is perhaps most comparable to how narratives about participants are composed. The qualitative researcher embellishes on yet remains strongly grounded in the empirical materials to render an evocative account of social life. The purpose is to stimulate within readers a vivid and engaging experience with the participants and their actions, reactions, and interactions. It also calls on the researcher's creative energies to write with flair.

Vignettes emerge from what we observe participants say and do during fieldwork, what they share during interviews, and what our imaginative reconstructions as "omniscient" researchers create about their points of view. Like self-standing monologues for the stage, vignettes are portraits in miniature. As an example, below is a researcher-composed story based on the retail clothing sales clerk's interview of navigating store policy with a difficult customer that supports the key assertion, "Salespersonship consists of personal devaluation through covert manipulation of and emotional subservience to consumers":

> Monique had been working on her feet for six hours straight. It was almost closing time as she mindlessly folded T-shirts that thoughtless customers earlier had picked up and thrown down haphazardly into a messy pile. The front door to the clothing store swung open as ten minutes remained to her shift. Monique felt a surge of dread when she saw it was one of their regular customers whom she nicknamed "Creepy Flirty Guy." He always seemed to visit the store right before closing when the manager was locked away in his office closing the books for the night. Creepy Flirty Guy continuously asked for discounts on regularly priced merchandise. It was not that Monique minded the requests, but she did mind his cheerfully insistent and inappropriately flirtatious way of doing so.

> The man found a T-shirt he liked and held it in front of his torso to check its size, then walked briskly toward Monique with the garment. She knew what was coming—his persistent negotiating ritual—so she plastered on a smile as he approached. Creepy Flirty

Guy told her he wanted to purchase the shirt and, as usual, grinned and said as if it was most certainly going to happen, "Give me a discount." Monique shook her head, smiled apologetically to mask her discomfort and said, "I can't." Creepy Flirty Guy grinned and cloyingly retorted, "Oh, you can do it for me."

Monique, as she had been trained, plastered on a bigger smile and countered, "We have sales that change all the time, multiple times throughout the week. If you buy something now and it goes on sale later, you can come in and we'll give you the difference." Creepy Flirty Guy took one step toward her and almost bellowed as he smiled back, "Give me a discount!"

Monique stared at him directly in the eye for a moment with a mix of firmness and pleading, then spoke softly, "Look. If I give you a discount I will be fired. I will lose my job." Creepy Flirty Guy stared back at her in silence, then smiled in his usual leering way and replied, "Oh, I was just teasing with you, darling." He dropped the T-shirt on the counter and left the store with a laugh. Monique stood motionless for a bit, swallowed her discomfort, then retrieved the large push broom to sweep the dirty floors.

Selected vignettes can appear throughout a final report as part of the evidentiary warrant, as an opening illustration to raise the curtains on the research study, or solely as for-the-researcher's-eyes-only summaries to parse the data corpus into more meaningful moments for continued analytic reflection. As representations of participant action, reaction, and interaction, vignettes provide readers vivid, prosaic, "video clips" of social life to better understand the phenomenon investigated.

Diagrammatic displays

A visual method for understanding and conveying process is through diagrammatic display. A **diagram** is an active, illustrated representation of the participants' experiences or the phenomenon under investigation. It is visual storytelling of the key factors at work in the data and the depiction of participant action, reaction, and interaction. A diagram is a model of how life works—the researcher's interpretation of people and their intrapersonal and interpersonal social dynamics.

Figure 10.2 is an example of a diagram. Its contents will be explained later, but for now let's examine its structure or plot. Bins or enclosed shapes generally include major categories, concepts, or the action plot points of the research story that move it forward. There is no standardized meaning to the shapes themselves, but we prefer to use rectangles and squares for distinct phases and

Figure 10.2 A model in progress of HIV test anxiety.

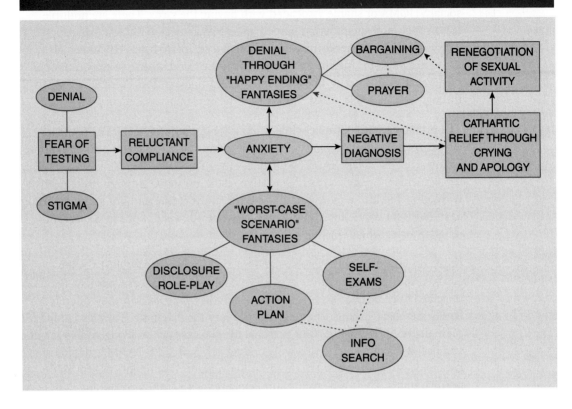

stages of action, and ovals and circles for participant states that are more internal, or as simple contrast to boxed action.

Lines illustrate the connections or relationships between bins. Solid lines generally suggest a direct connection like a category to a subcategory, while dashed lines suggest a more tenuous connection or interrelationship. Arrows suggest the direct flows of action from one bin or plot point to another. One-way arrows are linear paths of action through time, while bidirectional arrows suggest cyclical or reverberative interaction. If necessary, we will change the thickness of a bin or line for visual emphasis, and even explore creative applications such as different fonts and rich text formatting, if appropriate.

Figure 10.2 is to be read from left to right. This model of HIV test anxiety from one of Saldaña's unpublished pilot studies in the late 1990s illustrates the process of gay men reluctantly undergoing an HIV test, waiting for at least three days (the average turnaround time during that period), yet receiving negative results. The storyline begins with a participant's FEAR OF TESTING rooted in two primary causes: fearful DENIAL that one has HIV, and the social STIGMA or shame associated with having the virus. There are multiple factors that motivate different participants to actually take the test (e.g., upon a physician's recommendation, learning that a sex partner has HIV, unusual physical symptoms, needing a "clear conscience," and so on), so they cannot all be graphed at this point. But eventually the participant does consent to the test through RELUCTANT COMPLIANCE for health status awareness.

The primary emotional state while waiting for test results is ANXIETY, and participants experience two vacillating states during this stage of personal intra-action. The first is DENIAL THROUGH "HAPPY ENDING" FANTASIES in which the participant imagines an HIV-negative result, bolstered through BARGAINING with oneself to lead a more cautious sex life in the future and, for many, resorting to PRAYER for divine intervention and good health, even if one is not devoutly religious or a regular worship service attendee.

At the negative end of the experience is mentally enacting "WORST-CASE SCENARIO" FANTASIES in case of HIV-positive results. Several participants imagine DISCLOSURE ROLE-PLAY in which they prepare how they will tell family members, friends, and/or partners about the diagnosis. They also prepare a preliminary ACTION PLAN for personal life choices such as living arrangements and health maintenance. Some will conduct physical SELF-EXAMS, an almost paranoid search for skin blemishes or other markers that might confirm HIV-positive status. These actions are supplemented with a primarily online INFO SEARCH for medical information and stories of those living with HIV.

Eventually, test results are received, and if a NEGATIVE DIAGNOSIS is given by a health professional, many participants share two actions that follow: CATHARTIC RELIEF THROUGH CRYING AND APOLOGY to the doctor or clinician for the reaction. This "dodging a bullet" or "lucky" outcome motivates several participants to reflect on a personal RENEGOTIATION OF SEXUAL ACTIVITY in the future—for example: less-frequent sexual encounters or abstinence, safe sex practices, and so on.

Also notice the dashed arrows between CATHARTIC RELIEF THROUGH CRYING AND APOLOGY and DENIAL THROUGH "HAPPY ENDING" FANTASIES; and between RENEGOTIATION OF SEXUAL ACTIVITY and BARGAINING. Though these connections are not part of the primary linear process through time, the references hark back to previous states in which the "happy ending" is indeed achieved, and the participant now tries to meet the conditions he "bargained" with himself through different and safer sexual behaviors.

Diagrams truncate a research narrative into its essentials for at-a-glance review, and Figure 10.2 serves as a graphic outline of the experience of taking and waiting days for HIV test results that end up negative. The diagram represents a work in progress—a model based on preliminary interviews with a few adult gay men, and can be revised as more data are collected and new patterns and categories are detected. As of 2016, results of some HIV tests can be provided the same day. It would be interesting to determine if these same iterative thought patterns occur within a truncated time frame, or if this model parallels waiting for test results about other severe diseases. Thus, figures such as these are not just finished products but also are analytic tools for mapping the evolving processes of human action, reaction, and interaction.

Miles et al.'s (2014) advice to "think display" can assist with concurrent coding, categorizing, and analytic memo writing efforts. Dey (1993) notes, "[When] we are dealing with complex and voluminous data, diagrams can help us disentangle the threads of our analysis and present results in a coherent and intelligible form" (p. 192). Friese (2014) adds that diagrams in the form of networks display not only our analytic categories, but also the answers to our research questions. For a more comprehensive discussion on diagrams with numerous examples, see Evergreen (2014); Knowlton and Phillips (2013); Miles et al. (2014); and Wheeldon and Åhlberg (2012). Also explore the vivid compendium, "A Periodic Table of Visualization Methods," for an online overview of representing data in various visual forms: http://www.visual-literacy.org/periodic_table/periodic_table.html.

Interpreting the Routines, Rituals, Rules, Roles, and Relationships of Social Life

Any of the heuristics discussed thus far for synthesizing qualitative data will help reach an understanding of the five Rs. But here we focus on two methods that require deep holistic reflection on the researcher's part to weave all the constituent elements of analysis together: writing analytic meta-memos and developing theory.

Analytic meta-memos

Chapters 2 through 5 reviewed analytic memos as reflective forms of analysis. These researcher-crafted monologic narratives are think pieces that articulate mental processing of the data that have been collected. But now is the time to synthesize the empirical materials and to think about how everything comes together, fits together, and works together.

Meta-memos integrate previously written reflections into a new whole. Deliberate weaving of two or more analytic memo topics (see Chapter 2) stimulates thinking about the data's connections, interrelationships, and the bigger picture. Some examples of weaving (with an emphasis on the five Rs) might include the following:

- How routines pattern a participant's daily life

- How a participant's rituals suggest particular themes of living

- How rules constrain or enable a participant's actions, reactions, and interactions

- How a participant's roles validate or counter extant theories

- How a participant's relationships generate processual concepts

Part of thinking analytically is cognitively framing oneself to write with the express purpose of synthesizing two or more elements, rather than just waiting for serendipitous connections to happen on their own. Thus, spend some reflective writing time weaving together A with B and possibly with C. But make certain that the connections are plausible, based on the evidence at hand. An example of an analytic memo on the weight-loss workbook discussed in Chapter 3 reads as follows:

March 19, 2016

WEAVING: SELF AND PROCESS WITH WEIGHT

One obvious connection to make is that daily exercise routines/rituals lead to the theme of leading/living a healthy life. Another obvious connection is how the rules of dieting constrain the actions of what you can and cannot eat. One more is that the role of "health nut" supports the theory that a good diet with exercise most often leads to a long life. But I'll never forget that former student of mine who was fit and strong and full of life—then died of cancer in his mid-30s. So much for *that* theory . . .

An interesting relationship, though, is with one's self. What processes are inherent in self-image and self-concept? *Liking self* and *feeling good* come to mind. I remember when I was once at my physical best in terms of weight and muscularity, I was *taking chances, showing off, pushing limits*. "When you look good, you feel good" is a proposition that certainly holds up. But that, too, is disrupted by anorexics and their self-image issues. Perhaps it's not a matter of "looking good" but *liking good*. It's liking how you look. It's positive *reaction* to one's self. *Liking good* should be a daily routine—consisting of processes such as *legitimizing your appearance* and *absolving shame*. The problem is, nutritionists and physicians don't want you to tell yourself that if you're overweight or out of shape. But I'll affirm that *when you like good, you feel good*.

Theorizing

Throughout this book we've emphasized particular attention to the five Rs of social life. Through such observation and the formulation of interaction patterns, we've been laying the foundation for condensing data even further into a rich summative statement—a theory.

Four properties of a theory

A **theory**, in traditional social science research, is a generalizable statement with four properties and an accompanying explanatory narrative. A theory, most often,

- Predicts and controls action through an if–then logic;

- Accounts for variation in the empirical observations;

- Explains how and/or why something happens by stating its cause(s); and

- Provides insights and guidance for improving social life. (Gibson & Brown, 2009, p. 11; Saldaña, 2015, pp. 145–147; Tavory & Timmermans, 2014, pp. 66–67)

A theory summarizes the totality of the research experiences into one or more sentences about social life that holds transferable applications to other settings, contexts, populations, and possibly time periods. It is, for lack of a better phrase, a "big truth" based on observations of repeated patterns of specific actions, reactions, and interactions. It's a formidable charge for just one sentence to possess all four properties listed above. Many solid theories overtly contain just two of them while the other two are implied. That's why an accompanying narrative is necessary to unpack and describe the condensed meanings of a rich theory.

One example is the following statement by sociologist Joel M. Charon discussing the question, "Why is there misery in the world?" Charon explains that one reason—that is, a theory—is that

> Inequality is largely the cause of crime in society. (Charon, 2013, p. 158)

Since a theory needs an accompanying narrative to explain its condensed meaning, Charon offers before and after the statement:

> [Some people] see no reason to follow laws that seem to work against them in the competitive order, laws made by those who most benefit from that order. Stealing, prostitution, selling illegal drugs, and violent crime become attractive options. Some overcome poverty through crime; the vast majority do not. Those who do not [overcome poverty] remain poor, increasingly victimized by the welfare, court, medical, and prison systems that attempt to exercise control over their lives to ensure that they are not threats to the rest of society. Over time their misery worsens. . . .

> Almost everything in society teaches us that being more successful materially is what makes life worthwhile, causing some people to see crime as the easiest way to achieve that success. Street crime, drug dealing, price fixing, and bank robbery are all consequences of a society that emphasizes material success. And such crime has important consequences for all of us; we are all victims, because crime brings disorder to society, as well as fear and distrust to our everyday existence. (Charon, 2013, pp. 157–158)

Let's examine how the statement "Inequality is largely the cause of crime in society" meets the four properties of a theory. First, a theory predicts and controls action through an if–then logic. Charon predicts that if inequality exists, then crime will emerge. The control portion of the theory is suggested: if we want to decrease or control the rate of crime, then we need to decrease inequality.

The second property of a theory accounts for variation in the empirical observations. This property is suggested by the statement because we infer that in settings where there is less social inequality, there should be less crime—and that its opposite should also hold true: more inequality equals more crime. The statement also meets the property of variation because it includes conditional language that suggests it is contingent and not absolute. By including the term *largely* instead of terms such as *absolutely* or *the only* cause, Charon acknowledges that the theory does not take into account other possible causes of crime such as deviance.

The third property explains how and/or why something happens by stating its cause(s). This is overtly stated in the theory: the cause of crime is largely inequality.

And the fourth property provides insights and guidance for improving social life. This is suggested: if we as a society wish to make our world safer by reducing crime, then we need to take measures to reduce if not eliminate inequality among its citizens. Handwerker (2015) corroborates this with his theory qua [in the role of] proposition: "Because equals rarely violate behavior norms in significant ways, equalities produce stability in social relations" (p. 96)

Elements of a theory

A theory contains at least two primary elements, most often phrased as concepts. Let's review the example theory, "Inequality is largely the cause of crime in society." Inequality is a broad concept that applies not only to lower classes or people of color but also to those "at all levels of society because of the widespread inequality and the passion of people to improve their rank. It exists because the rich try to stay rich or get richer" (Charon, 2013, p. 158). This concept applies to stockbrokers, doctors, and politicians, though—if these individuals were to be prosecuted for committing a crime—inequalities might result in lesser punishments for those from some races, ethnicities, and social classes than for others.

Crime is the second concept included in the theory. Remember that a concept consists of constituent elements—thus, crime consists of actions such as robbing, shoplifting, forging, and so on. And crime is a concept because it cannot be touched (recall the touch test in Chapter 9); but its constituent elements such as counterfeit money, stolen property, and weapons can be handled. This particular theory also contains a third concept, society—a broad collective rather than a narrow population, thus making the theory applicable or generalizable across different settings and possibly across different time periods. As other examples of related theories, consider the statistics-based model that "violent crime rates vary dramatically by specific neighborhoods" (Handwerker, 2015, p. 63); and the famous yet contested broken windows theory (actually, a propositional piece of "folk wisdom" as it was originally labeled) of Kelling and Wilson (1982): "Serious street crime flourishes in areas in which disorderly behavior goes unchecked" (n.p.).

Theory links the interrelationship between at least two concepts because of the if–then logic and causal condition properties of a theory. Chirkov (2016) astutely observes, "Concepts for a theory are as firewood for a campfire" (p. 157). But theory does not always have to be concept based, as long as it has broad applicability beyond site-specific contexts. Practitioners develop theories based on their own accumulated knowledge and formulated patterns while working with others. For example, most school teachers know that

> Children tend to be less focused on classroom work the day before an extended holiday break.

Counselors who work with sex offenders and their victims have learned that teaching young people about "stranger danger" is only one facet of prevention, because

> The vast majority of victims of sexual abuse know or are acquainted with their perpetrators.

Neither of the two theories above is concept based, but rather both are practitioner based and just as legitimate as formal theories. Review the four properties of a theory and reflect on how the two statements above meet the criteria.

In sum, a theory claims that, given a particular set of circumstances and conditions, something specific will most likely happen or also holds true. Theories are insightful predictions and commentaries about social life that help us understand the world, plan ahead, and potentially make our lives better. Dey (2007) posits that the criteria for a well-developed theory are its "elegance, precision, coherence, and clarity" (p. 186).

Constructing theory: Life learnings

"What did you learn?" is sometimes a trite question posed by others after a grueling experience. But if answered sincerely and with careful thought, we might unknowingly generate something akin to a **proverb**. This is comparable to the final moral from an Aesop Fable, or a theme (in the literary fiction sense) suggested by a character's outcome. This life-learning holds reflections of experience transferable to comparable future situations, which is one of theory's main purposes. Perhaps one of the most famous "What did you learn?" responses comes from Dorothy at the end of the classic film *The Wizard of Oz*:

> If I ever go looking for my heart's desire again, I won't look any further than my own back yard—because if it isn't there, I never really lost it to begin with. . . . There's no place like home. (LeRoy & Fleming, 1939)

"There's no place like home" is a famous folk saying and song lyric that suggests universality, and there are other well-known home proverbs: "Home is where the heart is," "Home is where you hang your hat," and "You can never go home again." Proverbs meet one key property of a theory: they provide insights and guidance for improving social life. But unlike well-written theories, these proverbs are flawed because they do not account for variation or explicate causation. In other words, disconfirming evidence for them can be found through empirical observations and experiences. For some people, a former home is not "where the heart is" but where bad memories of a troubled childhood reside.

Constructing a theory is the researcher's response to the question, "What did you learn?" What we offer might be something learned about the participants, what the participants themselves learned about their circumstances, or what the researcher learned from analyzing and reflecting on the data. Proverbs are not theories in the social science sense, but they are similar to theories and a way of understanding how to construct them. Feel free to borrow from the canon of existing proverbs as a starting point for theory construction (e.g., "You're never too old to learn") as foundations for transformation into first draft theoretical statements—for example, "Continuous relevant professional development experiences throughout a career accelerate expertise."

Constructing theory: An analytic review

Some researchers and methodologists place great stock in theory development as an essential outcome of qualitative inquiry. As for us, we would rather read a well-formulated set of assertions about the local and particular contexts of a site and its participants than a weakly constructed and ambiguous theory with little utility or transfer. Nevertheless, we offer below a recap of this chapter and how its analytic heuristics serve the construction of theory. We use the topic of *home* as an example.

Madden (2010), from an anthropological perspective, offers that the concept of home is not universal but actually quite subjective, based on varying geographical, social, emotional, and cultural components of individuals (pp. 45–46). It's quite reasonable to assume that home is subjective because some people are raised and live in comfortable and secure home environments, but others are not. Madden offers several phenomenological descriptors to describe home (e.g., home is "birth," "habitual," "permanent," and so on), yet the overall construct he develops is that home is "familiar."

Constructing a theory of home (or any research topic) means that a researcher should now review the literature on the subject from multiple disciplines, collect other people's perceptions and experiences as data, reflect on and analyze the empirical materials, and develop a statement with an accompanying narrative that meets the four properties of a theory described earlier. There's no magic algorithm to get there—theory construction comes from a lot of synthesis and good thinking. But the researcher gets to that stage through one or more of the analytic heuristics discussed in Chapters 9 and 10, which we now recap.

Condensing Large Amounts of Data

Analyzing relevant text. Theories are elegant. Condense the data corpus to those portions that focus exclusively on the emerging topic of the theory. Look for unique moments in the corpus (e.g., a specific fieldwork observation on a particular day, a rich passage from an interview transcript) that seem to best embody and represent the experience or phenomenon (e.g., a participant speaking about why he never wants to return to his hometown, field notes about a rural home that appears to be and feels "lived in").

Codes and coding. Codes are text-based symbols of meaning. They condense longer portions of data into rich essences. Since theory includes concepts, select code words and phrases that are more conceptually based (e.g., HOME AS "SANCTUARY," ENTRAPMENT, SUBURBAN STEREOTYPE) to extend beyond the descriptive. Codes serve as prompts or triggers for continued reflection through analytic memos or category development.

Found poetry. The heuristic of careful word selection from the data and arraying them in unique formats extend thinking toward creative representations of a phenomenon that might not be possible through inductive analytic processes. The exercise is just one way of stimulating interrelationship or connection-making—a strategy that assists with a theory's core properties— for example,

> Home
>
>   is not where the heart is
>
> but where memories reside
>
> each room an adventure story
>
>   (with secret places to hide)

Patterning in Textual and Visual Materials

Categories. Patterns observed in the data are solidified when they're labeled as categories. A qualitative theory of social life relies on consistent patterns of human action for its credibility. Thus, categories are building blocks for the components of theoretical statements. Researchers utilizing the genre of grounded theory will hopefully construct a central/core category that becomes the stimulus for articulating a theory. Just some of the possible categories for a theory of home might include **Childhood Memories**, **Alienation**, or **Family Ties**.

Themes. From a phenomenological perspective, themes capture the essence and essentials of an experience. Themes serve theory by stating manifest and latent meanings through theoretical constructs—a level of abstraction that can be incorporated into theoretical statements. Madden (2010) puts forth several constructs when he proposes that **Home Is Birth**, **Home Is Ambivalence**, and **Home Is Permanent**.

Unifying Seemingly Different Things

Concepts. Concepts are the heart of theory. They enable the researcher to transcend from the particular to the general. If initial analytic work generates codes or categories that do not pass the touch test, rephrase them as gerunds or abstract ideas to stimulate big picture ideas. For example, a Descriptive Code like CHILDHOOD BEDROOM could be transformed into a Process Code such as BECOMING A TWEEN. A group of In Vivo Codes such as "WISH I COULD GO BACK," "GOOD TIMES," and "GREAT MEMORIES" can combine together to form the conceptual category **Nostalgia**.

Propositions. The if–then property of a theory rests on a series of reliable propositions that hold true across cases. Propositions are predictive statements, comparable to theory, that link at least two actions through a conditional premise. Propositions are pilot tests of sorts for the construction of theory because they are subject to confirmation from the empirical evidence. Assembling propositions in progress for further analysis enables connection-making between different yet related elements, as in these observations from a study about people and their homes:

- When asked to define their home, most participants first specify a particular city or town.

- If childhood homes were abusive, participants tend to speak somewhat angrily about their memories.

- Virtually all participants initially look off in the distance when they describe childhood memories from home.

Matrices and tabular displays. These formats enable an analyst to see the landscape of data and its ranges at a glance. Theory accounts for variation, so data should be arrayed to help the researcher grasp the dynamics of the phenomenon under investigation. Since home is perceived differently by individuals, comparing opposing perspectives in a matrix exhibits variation and stimulates thinking on why that variation might exist. Figure 10.3 utilizes Madden's (2010) eight categories of home and how two participants' data provide contrasting views.

Figure 10.3 Eight categories of "home" and two participants' contrasting responses.

PARTICIPANT/Concept	GENE	JERRY
Home Is Familiar	Returns to hometown 2–3 times a year and observes little change in the area.	Has not returned to hometown in decades so is unaware of its growth.
Home Is Parochial	Considers suburban hometown connected to larger metropolitan area.	Considers hometown centered around its local university.
Home Is Discrete	Specifically located in suburban Pennsylvania.	Specifically located in a metropolitan New Mexico city.
Home Is Habitual	Maintains some aspects of small town culture as an adult living in a metropolitan area.	Maintains both familial and regional cultural traditions of birthplace.
Home Is Permanent	Parents still living in hometown; siblings living in state.	Parents deceased; siblings still living in hometown.
Home Is Birth	Grew up in hometown; oldest child with two younger sisters; "a kind of rocky but typical childhood, I guess."	Grew up in hometown; "My parents were great, but because I was the youngest I didn't get along too well with my older sister and brothers."
Home Is Death	No immediate family deaths yet.	Family members (parents, two siblings) buried in cemetery nearby childhood home. Jerry wishes to be cremated.
Home Is Ambivalence	Continuous visits to childhood home (holidays, summer breaks, special occasions, etc.); "It's where I grew up."	Has not returned to childhood home for over 20+ years; "There's nothing for me there."

Mixed methods. Both qualitative and quantitative data are collected, when appropriate, to support and help answer the research questions of interest. Their synthesis generates outcomes that mutually inform, collectively corroborate, or reveal contradictory findings for reflection and reconciliation. A theory of home might employ statistical data on demographics, population density and mobility, real estate values, cost-of-living indexes, crime rates, climate and weather patterns, and so on, coupled with qualitative inquiry about participants' short- and long-term residencies, geographic identity, perceptions of quality of life, phenomenological experiences of place or belonging, and other emotional facets of their personal and social home lives.

Understanding Social Processes of Human Action, Reaction, and Interaction

Assertions. Main and key assertions and high-level inferences progress toward the generalizable for theory construction. Assuming the assertions have been confirmed from the evidentiary warrant, the particular of field observations can be reasonably extrapolated to the conceptual of theory. A few examples related to home might include these:

- Assertion: Home is most often referred to as a specific place and space.

- Low-Level Inference: Home is more easily described through concrete references.

- High-Level Inference: Home is a geographic referent.

Vignettes. A theory needs an accompanying narrative to unpack its condensed meanings and explain its underlying principles. An illustrative vignette, derived from the data, supplements a theory's abstraction with a more concrete life story. The vignette is not just an example but also an exemplar—an ideal model of how the theory works. Assuming that a theory of home has been developed utilizing memory, below is an example of how a particular vignette might represent the concept at work:

> The day after their mother's funeral, almost eight years after their father's burial, the three surviving adult children returned to the home where they grew up—a structure long abandoned and empty, its front and back yards covered in dried grass and drier weeds. Jacob (the eldest), Susan, and Jerry were now on their own, with no parents to help them out of financial binds, no mother to fret and nag them about their mistakes, and no more Sunday

dinners together around the large oak table. They didn't feel abandoned but instead felt alive in their aloneness.

They entered the house (unlocked for some reason) with anticipation, the memories of their childhoods rushing in as they stepped over the threshold. The rooms seemed small—too small to house what was back then a larger family of seven. Jerry told his older brother and sister as they walked through the living room, "When I was little, this is where I used to pretend that I was a mouse and actually hide cheese under the furniture! Mom caught me doing it one day and was so mad." Jacob looked at his old bedroom and silently thought of the advice his father gave him on the day of his wedding. Susan, the only daughter in the family, stood in the old kitchen with its abandoned appliances from the 1960s and asked, "How did she do it? How did mom feed us all? Look at the size of this place." The three siblings huddled together in the family room and disagreed over where the Christmas tree usually stood. Jerry remembered, "Mom and dad accidentally left the price tags on the presents one year, so that's how I learned there was no Santa Claus."

Each room evoked different memories. Each room held a chapter of their early histories. With both parents now gone, the three surviving adults were children once again. The return visit home was not so

Figure 10.4 Four variables of "home" and their components.

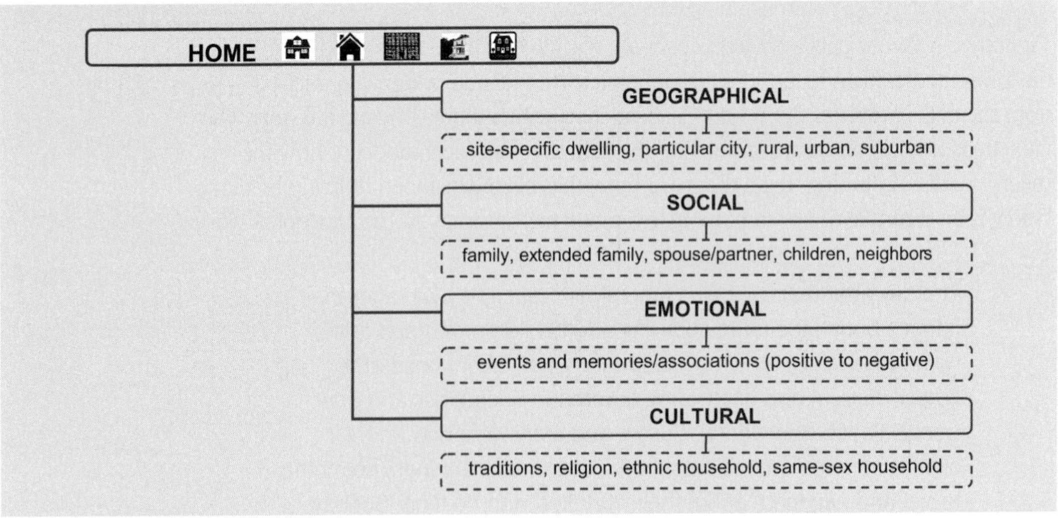

HOME

GEOGRAPHICAL
site-specific dwelling, particular city, rural, urban, suburban

SOCIAL
family, extended family, spouse/partner, children, neighbors

EMOTIONAL
events and memories/associations (positive to negative)

CULTURAL
traditions, religion, ethnic household, same-sex household

much a need for closure as it was a need to remember who they once were. It was a need to remember who their deceased parents were. It was a need to remember what being a family meant to them.

Diagrammatic displays. Some theories and their accompanying narratives can be intricately complex. A diagram can help the researcher and reader grasp the embedded story of a theory by illustrating its process or essential elements. When we model the components with graphic software, we can rearrange the bins and arrows until a visual representation "clicks." Yet even just a simple graphic representation of concepts emphasizes the ideas in progress or at work. For example, Figure 10.4 illustrates Madden's (2010) four variables of home and some examples of their connotations.

Interpreting the Routines, Rituals, Rules, Roles, and Relationships of Social Life

Analytic meta-memos. Analytic meta-memos can serve as first and revised drafts of theories in progress. They are personal sites of conversation that help synthesize all the observations made thus far about the phenomenon. Meta-memos bring together different facets of the research study for reflection on how everything fits together. Remember that good research is not about good methods as much as it is about good thinking. So, if we deliberately write with the goal of trying to blend things to construct a theory, we cognitively frame ourselves better for the task. Following is an example of an analytic meta-memo:

March 18, 2016

AN EMERGENT THEORY: HOME AS BELONGING

Belonging seems to be connected to home: most participants remember fondly selected aspects of what they define as home. But a few mentioned that home is not a place where they belong, and is instead a place they feel alienated from—a participant calls a particular city he visits frequently his "home," even though he's never actually lived there. But, as he said, "I feel as if I belong there—even when I'm not there."

Home as belonging is the closest and tightest theoretical construct I can develop at this time. It refers to actual physical belonging and emotional connection. Belonging implies ownership, something deeply held by some of the participants about their homes ("Home is a place I can call my own"). The "longing to be" of "be-longing" is also part of a strong nostalgia theme among many participants. Memories—both good and bad—are uniquely owned, deeply personal, and they serve as connections between a person and home as that person conceives it. Belonging suggests an intimate role in a close relationship, even with oneself.

It might take one or more of these heuristics to work toward a theory, but it is the ultimate exercise in data analytic synthesis. Also, we have addressed only conventional social science theory construction and encourage readers to explore other forms such as critical theory and feminist theory. For more on theory and theory development in qualitative research, see Abbott (2004); Alvesson and Kärreman (2011); Jackson and Mazzei (2012); and Tavory and Timmermans (2014).

CAQDAS

CAQDAS is an acronym for Computer Assisted Qualitative Data Analysis Software. These programs maintain a data corpus and enable a researcher to apply codes, memos, comments, and other addenda to specific portions of the files. Several commercial CAQDAS packages include analytic and display features that can bring comparably coded data together, illustrate through diagrams the interrelationships between codes and categories, and perform statistical operations with qualitative data such as frequencies and correlations. The software does not actually code data for the user; that task is still the responsibility of the researcher. The software efficiently stores, organizes, manages, and reconfigures data to enable human analytic reflection.

Following is a list of several major CAQDAS programs to explore for textual and visual materials, whose Web sites provide online tutorials or demonstration software/manual downloads of their most current versions:

- AnSWR: www.cdc.gov/hiv/library/software/answr/index.html
- AQUAD: www.aquad.de/en
- ATLAS.ti: www.atlasti.com
- CAT: http://cat.texifter.com/
- Dedoose: www.dedoose.com
- DiscoverText: www.discovertext.com
- HyperRESEARCH: www.researchware.com
- INTERACT®: www.mangold-international.com
- MAXQDA: www.maxqda.com
- NVivo: www.qsrinternational.com

- QDA Miner: www.provalisresearch.com
- Qualrus: www.qualrus.com
- Quirkos: www.quirkos.com
- Transana: www.transana.org
- V-Note: www.v-note.org
- Weft QDA: www.pressure.to/qda/
- WordStat: www.provalisresearch.com

Figure 10.5 displays a screenshot from Quirkos Software, a program that can simultaneously show both textual and visual representations of coded data. The size of each circular bin in the left pane grows according to its code or subcode frequency. Researchers can reconfigure the bins according to emergent interrelationships as coding proceeds. Figure 10.6 displays a screenshot from Dedoose Software, an intuitive CAQDAS program that is especially appropriate for mixed-methods studies, as it manages and transforms for analytic review both qualitative and quantitative data. Its multiple windows provide simultaneous varying configurations of the data base. And Figure 10.7 shows a screenshot

Figure 10.5   A screenshot from Quirkos Software (courtesy of Daniel Turner, Quirkos Software, www.quirkos.com).

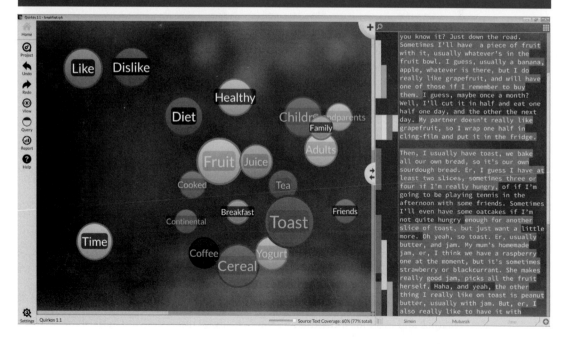

Figure 10.6 A screenshot from Dedoose Software (courtesy of Eli Lieber, SocioCultural Research Consultants LLC/Dedoose, www.dedoose.com).

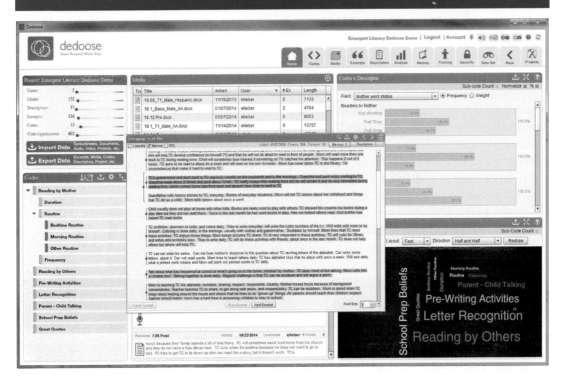

from INTERACT®, illustrating its comprehensive video analysis features. The software, designed for qualitative and quantitative data analysis, enables researchers to synchronize and evaluate videos, audio, physiology, and live observations in one single program.

Selected CAQDAS programs come in both PC and Mac versions with a selected few available for iPad, iPhone, Android, and other hardware. Programs such as AnSWR, AQUAD, and Weft QDA are available free of charge. The "Resources for Analytic Synthesis" at the end of this chapter includes a few book titles with extensive coverage about digital analytic software and tools. Several CAQDAS companies have also uploaded multiple short films about their products and features on YouTube (search for the clips by product name).

We cannot prescribe which software program is best for particular qualitative studies and even for individual researchers. Sometimes nothing more than

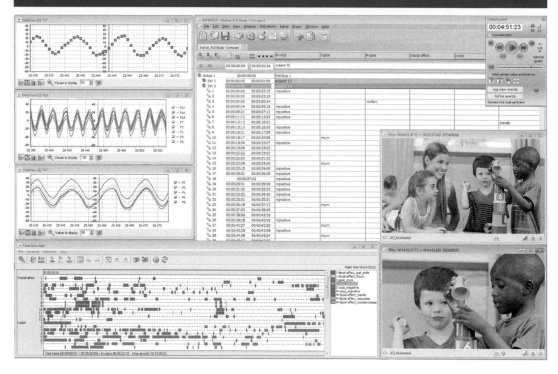

Microsoft Word or Excel will suffice for small-scale studies. Researchers are the best judges of the software needs for their data, their available financial resources, and their personal preferences for user friendliness, so they should explore several of the programs available to them on their own to make an informed decision.

On Credibility and Trustworthiness

Lincoln and Guba (1985) reconceptualized the standards for assessing the rigor and truth value or **trustworthiness** of naturalistic inquiry. To them, positivist terms and concepts from the quantitative paradigm such as *reliability* and *validity* are inapplicable to qualitative research studies and the nature of their data. Instead, they proposed four perspectives that address the soundness of text- and visual-based analyses from fieldwork: credibility, transferability, dependability, and confirmability. In this section, we focus primarily on the first perspective and refer readers to the original source for a more extensive discussion of the underlying principles of naturalistic inquiry.

Credibility refers to the audience's belief that the way a researcher conducted the study and the analytic processes and outcomes of the work have generated findings that make sense and persuade readers that an effective or trustworthy job was done. Most of this trustworthiness comes from a strong qualitative work ethic and the way the report documents the measures taken to better guarantee a rigorous effort. Credibility is achieved by convincing readers that the researcher not only did her homework but worked very hard on it, as well. This accountability comes from straightforwardly self-reporting the research journey—warts and all.

There are several ways to achieve and establish trustworthiness through credibility. First, ensure that the initial research design was carefully conceived and implemented. The literature review should demonstrate a careful search of preexisting materials and key authors cited. The conceptual framework includes a thoughtful and well-integrated set of epistemological, theoretical, and methodological premises. Overall, the preliminary decisions made and the way they were realized should demonstrate a researcher who was competent and well-prepared.

Second, data collection methods chosen and the data themselves should harmonize with elements such as the research questions composed, and genre or methodology selected. A prolonged amount of time has been spent in the field for participant observation, and/or a sufficient number, types, and variety of participants have been interviewed to generate a substantive body of data. The researcher has conducted herself in an ethical manner throughout the endeavor, and carefully documented the data collection procedures in the report (e.g., "Forty clock hours of fieldwork were spent for participant observation, resulting in over 200 pages of field notes. The five key participants were each interviewed twice and they reviewed the transcripts for accuracy and any necessary clarification."). If anything went wrong, the researcher has confessed it rather than try to cover it up.

Third, data analyses should permit the reader to informally audit the work. In other words, the researcher has presented just enough information to enable an outsider to learn how the analyst got to certain categories, themes, theories, and so on. Some research projects with multiple team members collaboratively code data to ensure the consistency and thus accuracy of analysis. The methods employed have been sufficiently described and interview excerpts, sample field notes, tables, diagrams, and so on, provide essential evidence for any assertions. If you've conducted a rigorous analysis in the first place and reflected deeply on the meanings of your data, you're more than halfway there.

Finally, the written report or other form of presentation must be professional. The researcher attends to the craft as well as the art of writing. Ideas are clear, the tone is humble and unpretentious, and the report presents both believable and hopefully insightful perceptions about social life. Wolcott (2009) muses that researchers might not be able to convince others that they got it absolutely right, but at least they can demonstrate that they didn't get it completely wrong, either. The research study excerpts and writing principles in Chapter 11 will illustrate more about credibility and trustworthiness.

CLOSURE AND TRANSITION

Based on our own teaching experience, we believe data analysis is one of the most difficult stages for novices to qualitative inquiry. We hope we have made the process easier to grasp and execute. We profiled traditional and rather conventional methods for synthesizing data, but we did so to acquaint novices with the established canon of approaches available. Figure 10.8 summarizes the primary analytic methods we discussed in Chapters 9 and 10.

Other methods exist for more-sophisticated approaches to inquiry, and we encourage readers to explore those intermediate and advanced ways after gaining experience with these analytic fundamentals (see Clarke et al., 2015; Koro-Ljungberg, 2016).

The next chapter discusses different ways to write about a study's findings and basic principles of effective research composition.

Figure 10.8   A summary of analytic methods profiled in Chapters 9 and 10.

ANALYTIC PRINCIPLES	ANALYTIC METHODS	DESCRIPTIONS AND ANALYTIC APPLICATIONS
Condensing Large Amounts of Data	Jottings, Analytic Memos	Jottings provide brief notes of descriptive action from fieldwork for expansion into more detailed field notes; analytic memos serve as narratives that summarize the researcher's reflections about data, or that focus on particular moments from fieldwork; meta-memos synthesize selected analytic memos
	Analyzing Relevant Text	Selects only those portions from the data corpus directly related to the research questions of interest for analysis; condenses data into exemplars of the phenomenon studied

(Continued)

Figure 10.8 (Continued)

ANALYTIC PRINCIPLES	ANALYTIC METHODS	DESCRIPTIONS AND ANALYTIC APPLICATIONS
Condensing Large Amounts of Data	Codes and Coding	Words or short phrases that symbolically assign a summative, salient, essence-capturing, and/or evocative attribute for a portion of language-based or visual data; condenses large amounts of data into more manageable units for analysis
	In Vivo Coding	Uses verbatim words from participant interview data as codes; keeps the analysis grounded in the participant's perspective and honors the participant's voice
	Process Coding	Uses gerunds ("-ing" words) and gerund phrases as codes; identifies participant action, reaction, and interaction in realistic or conceptual forms
	Values Coding	Identifies a participant's values, attitudes, and beliefs; explores cultural values, identity, intrapersonal and interpersonal participant experiences and actions
	Emotion Coding	Labels the emotional states experienced or recalled by the participant, or inferred by the researcher about the participant; explores the intrapersonal and interpersonal, especially in matters of social relationships, reasoning, decision-making, judgment, and risk-taking
	Descriptive Coding	Summarizes in a word or short phrase the basic topic of a passage of data; documents and analyzes the material products and physical environments of ethnographic fieldwork, and the classification of general participant action and routines recorded in field notes
	Subcoding	Tags added after primary codes to separate them into more detailed units for classification and analysis
	Dramaturgical Coding	Applies the basic conventions of dramatic character analysis onto naturalistic social interaction or onto a participant's stories contained in an interview; extracts core motives and internal drives

ANALYTIC PRINCIPLES	ANALYTIC METHODS	DESCRIPTIONS AND ANALYTIC APPLICATIONS
Condensing Large Amounts of Data	*Versus Coding*	Labels in binary or dichotomous terms two opposing stances; appropriate for critical inquiry, evaluation research, action research, and data containing microaggressions or conflict-laden perspectives
	Found Poetry	Utilizes the conventions of literary poetry to construct an evocative representation of fieldwork or the researcher's reflections about self or others; captures the essence and essentials of an inquiry through carefully selected words and their strategic formatting in print
Noticing Patterns in Textual and Visual Materials	Analytic Memos, Meta-Memos	Serves as narratives that expand and expound on the researcher's observations of patterns in fieldwork and data; meta-memos synthesize selected analytic memos to formulate patterns
	Categories	Labels in the form of words or short phrases applied to grouped patterns of comparable codes and coded data; condenses the collective symbolic meanings of codes into new symbolic representations according to pattern and sometimes hierarchy
	Themes and Theoretical Constructs	Extended phrases or sentences that identify and function as ways to categorize a set of data into a topic that emerges from a pattern of ideas; theoretical constructs serve as category-like, abstract summations of a set of related themes
Unifying Seemingly Different Things	Analytic Memos, Meta-Memos	Serves as narratives that expand and expound on the researcher's reflections about interrelationships in data; meta-memos synthesize selected analytic memos to unify the corpus
	Concepts	Words or short phrases that symbolically represent a suggested meaning broader than a single item or action; a bigger picture idea beyond the tangible and apparent that unifies and embodies related realities

(Continued)

Figure 10.8 (Continued)

ANALYTIC PRINCIPLES	ANALYTIC METHODS	DESCRIPTIONS AND ANALYTIC APPLICATIONS
Unifying Seemingly Different Things	Propositions	A predictive statement, usually with two primary elements, that "proposes" a conditional event; explanation or causation is purposely embedded into or suggested by the proposition
	Matrices and Tabular Displays	An intersection of lists, set up as rows and columns; a table or tabular display that summarizes and arranges data from a larger corpus by factors such as time, site, case, variable, etc., for unified, "at a glance" viewing
	Mixed Methods	Intentional blending of qualitative and quantitative data collection and analyses for studies that will benefit from the combined outcomes
Understanding Social Processes of Human Action, Reaction, and Interaction	Analytic Memos, Meta-Memos	Serves as narratives that expand and expound on the researcher's reflections about social action in fieldwork and data; meta-memos synthesize selected analytic memos to formulate broader understandings of social life
	Assertions	Declarative statements of summative synthesis about the researcher's fieldwork observations, supported with or instantiated by evidence from the data corpus; inference-laden observations about the local and particular social world under investigation, and their possible implications for broader generalizations
	Vignettes	Research-based accounts of fieldwork in the form of brief literary narratives; stimulates within readers a vivid and engaging experience with the participants and their actions, reactions, and interactions
	Diagrammatic Displays	Active, illustrated representations of the participants' experiences or the phenomenon under investigation; visual storytelling of the key factors at work in the data and the depiction of participant action, reaction, and interaction

ANALYTIC PRINCIPLES	ANALYTIC METHODS	DESCRIPTIONS AND ANALYTIC APPLICATIONS
Interpreting the Routines, Rituals, Rules, Roles, and Relationships of Social Life	Analytic Memos, Meta-Memos	Serves as narratives that expand and expound on the researcher's reflections on the "5 Rs" in fieldwork and data; meta-memos synthesize selected analytic memos to formulate broader interpretations of social life (connections, interrelationships, the bigger picture)
	Theory	A generalizable statement with four properties and an accompanying explanatory narrative; the properties: predict and control action through an if-then logic; account for variation in the empirical observations; explain how and/or why something happens by stating its cause(s); and provide insights and guidance for improving social life; summarizes the totality of the research experiences into one or more sentences about social life that holds transferable applications to other settings, contexts, populations, and possibly time periods

RESOURCES FOR ANALYTIC SYNTHESIS

The following resources will offer you additional guidance for methods of analytic synthesis:

Qualitative data analysis

Bazeley, Pat. (2013). *Qualitative Data Analysis: Practical Strategies.* London: Sage.

Gibbs, Graham R. (2007). *Analysing Qualitative Data.* London: Sage.

Miles, Matthew B., A. Michael Huberman, and Johnny Saldaña. (2014). *Qualitative Data Analysis: A Methods Sourcebook*, 3rd edition. Thousand Oaks, CA: Sage.

Saldaña, Johnny. (2016) *The Coding Manual for Qualitative Researchers*, 3rd edition. London: Sage.

Schreier, Margrit. (2012). *Qualitative Content Analysis in Practice.* London: Sage.

Wertz, Frederick J., Kathy Charmaz, Linda M. McMullen, Ruthellen Josselson, Rosemarie Anderson, and Emalinda McSpadden. (2011). *Five Ways of Doing Qualitative Analysis.* New York: Guilford Press.

Technology for qualitative data analysis

Bazeley, Pat, and Kristi Jackson. (2013). *Qualitative Data Analysis With NVivo*, 2nd edition. London: Sage.

Friese, Susanne. (2014). *Qualitative Data Analysis With ATLAS.ti*, 2nd edition. London: Sage.

Silver, Christina, and Ann Lewins. (2014). *Using Software in Qualitative Research: A Step-by-Step Guide*, 2nd edition. London: Sage.

ANALYTIC EXERCISES FOR ANALYTIC SYNTHESIS

1. Take a 15- to 20-minute field note observation of natural social life and compose a series of assertions from the data. Organize them into subassertions and main assertions and, if possible, compose a key assertion.

2. Find a moment or self-standing story from a set of field notes or an interview transcript and compose a vignette about the participant's experiences.

3. Access three Web sites for CAQDAS software and explore the products.

Download any available trial software from one of the commercial companies and explore the product with a sample of your own data.

4. Read the transcript excerpt below several times, formulate a research question of interest, and conduct an analysis using one or more of the methods described in Chapters 9 and 10. (The complete transcript can be downloaded from the book's companion Web site at study.sagepub.com/saldanaomasta.)

SAMPLE DATA FOR ANALYTIC SYNTHESIS

Below is an excerpt from an interview with Monique, a college-aged retail clothing sales clerk. The interview concerns her three years of work experience at a national chain's store that caters "mostly towards young teenagers, more specifically girls, but there was a men's line there," as she put it.

INTERVIEWER: In your opinion, did your employer's official policies on customer service align with their actual practice in customer service in general? Both in terms of what they expected of you, and also in terms of what you saw your supervisors do?

MONIQUE: Oh yeah. Definitely. They were very good at practicing what they preach.

INTERVIEWER: Can you give me any specific examples of times you saw that happen?

MONIQUE: It was always very much a . . . I mean, there's a lot of the idea of "save the sale." If people want to come in and return things you can always go, "Oh yeah. Definitely. We'll return it, no problem, but you know you could always use that to exchange. We have some really great sales going on. What can I do to help you find something that works better?" type of a thing. Does that answer the question?

INTERVIEWER: So, in actuality, if somebody—I think you called it "push the sale"—you did see if somebody came back, people would try to do that.

MONIQUE: Yeah. It was always definitely you wanted to save the loss because, I mean, at the end of the day you wanted to have more actual sales than returns. So it was definitely a try to turn it around and try to get them to just exchange something—like if it was the wrong size—or buy something completely different with the refund that they got . . .

INTERVIEWER: Did your employer have any other policies relating to other matters that conflicted with the customer service policies and your ability to give good customer service? Were there any policies that ever impacted your ability to give your customers the best experience?

MONIQUE: No, not really. I mean, it was always more stressful during the holiday rush just because there would be so many people in the store, but no, I don't remember anything contradicting itself.

INTERVIEWER: Was there ever a situation in which you specifically could not provide a customer with what you would describe as good service or were not able to meet a request of theirs either due to a policy or other situation?

MONIQUE: Yeah. It was only because they wanted a specific item—I don't remember if it was a shirt or a pair of jeans, or whatever—but we didn't have the size, so we were calling all of the other stores in our area, like to see if they had any sizes, and there was like one store that did have it, but for this particular customer I think it would have been like an hour and a half drive, one way, to get it. And they were like, "Oh, can you ship it to . . . Can you do store-to-store shipping?" and we were like, "No, we don't really do that because we don't have a system currently set up so that we could tell this is for a specific customer and this is for the rest of your stock." Like I said, I don't remember it escalating super high or being terrified or whatever.

INTERVIEWER: What was their reaction?

MONIQUE: They still came back. And we told them they could try looking online to see if anyone has it, but you'll have to pay shipping and handling. They were upset about that because can't we just ship it to the store. No, we still don't have a system currently that we can do that. I think they ended up just returning it, and they were like fine. But they came in the next week and were still, like, shopping.

INTERVIEWER: And you were being truthful that you could not ship it store to store?

MONIQUE: Yeah. That was a true thing.

INTERVIEWER: So even if a manager got involved, they could not have been able to do that?

MONIQUE: Yeah. I think the only way that you would have been able to do that was if it was a personal item. You didn't use company money, like whatever. I personally just mailed you a package, and I paid for shipping out of my own pocket type of thing.

INTERVIEWER: Do you remember, by any chance, if there was a supervisor who saw that situation? How they responded? Did they comment at all on the way it was handled?

MONIQUE: I mean, that happened multiple times. Like, there were multiple really similar situations to that, and there were times where the supervisor was there. The first couple of times the supervisor was there because I didn't know what to do, so I was asking for help. But by the time I left, it was like, "Fine, if you're going to be screaming at me the whole time, yes I'll call my manager and they'll tell you the exact same thing." But usually . . .

INTERVIEWER: And is that what happened in each instance? The manager did tell them the same thing?

MONIQUE: Yeah. It was the exact same thing. There's really nothing we can do. It's not that we don't like you. There's nothing we can do.

INTERVIEWER: How did the managers ever comment to you on how you handled the situation? Anything between you that you remember?

MONIQUE: The only time that I only would get comments, that I remember anyway, was when it was a particularly difficult customer who would try to push, you know, "Give me a discount on the sale. Make it happen. Make it work," and they'd be like, "Good job on sticking to policy. There's nothing we can do. They were being a jerk."

INTERVIEWER: So generally a positive reinforcement for following policies. In general—just in terms of your own approach—how did you approach customer service at your own job? What was kind of your own philosophy, informed by the store's policies and your own beliefs? What was kind of your take on providing customer service?

MONIQUE: Always leave people better than you found them. No matter if they're in a great mood, still make them better than you found them.

INTERVIEWER: Do you have . . . Do you remember any specific examples of a time that might have happened?

MONIQUE: Sorry, it's been a while.

INTERVIEWER: It's kind of far back.

MONIQUE: Kind of far back. There was one, like, Back-to-School season where I could tell—it was like a mother and her daughter . . . and the daughter wanted a specific outfit, but the mom didn't think it was appropriate for her, so I had to see how to appease—I think that's the right word—how to appease both of them. So I, like, try to . . . . The daughter really wanted that specific outfit. Really wanted it. The mother was like, "That's not appropriate for school. I'm not buying that." I had to, thinking both don't lose the sale and don't make them both angry at me, it was a lot of, "Well, if you paired this bottom with this top and this top with this bottom, it's a little better." And they were things they had already been looking at, so it wasn't even like "buy more stuff." They had already been looking at it so, I mean, they were already frustrated at the point I got involved. Like, they were really frustrated with each other, and then they left in a pretty good mood.

CHAPTER 11

Analytic Write-Ups

Introduction

Like genres, qualitative research reportage can be presented in a variety of ways. This chapter focuses on the written **styles** of presentation. We illustrate several tale types for ethnographic reports proposed by John Van Maanen (2011), and three forms of transforming qualitative data advocated by Harry F. Wolcott (1994, 2009). Qualitative research writing ranges from traditional forms and formats to more arts-based modalities such as poetry and drama. The style(s) chosen depends on several factors such as the conceptual framework and requirements by supervisors (e.g., dissertation chairs, journal editors). But it also comes down to selecting a writing style(s) that will most credibly, vividly, and persuasively report the research journey and make the case for its findings.

Qualitative inquiry consists of a variety of writing and dissemination modalities, so the field is not lacking in creative ways to share research. But researchers must also consider their potential readerships/audiences and their expectations. Consider their available time and particular needs, which in turn shape a presentation's length, summary of findings, and stylistic approach. We offer several excerpts from final published reports as examples of effective qualitative writing. The appendix includes three full-length journal articles that exhibit a range of research genres and styles.

Stylistic Approaches to Research Writing

We begin with a survey of writing samples from selected works to acquaint readers with options for their own composition. Some

Learning Objectives

After reading and reviewing this chapter, researchers should be able to

1. List and describe various writing styles available for qualitative research reportage,

2. Identify selected techniques of effective qualitative research writing, and

3. Compose original qualitative research writing that follows recommended guidelines for quality work.

styles are generally more appropriate for selected methodologies. Most published studies in grounded theory, content analysis, and mixed methods exhibit a combination of analytic and formal writing, and descriptive and realistic writing. Autoethnographies tend to incorporate primarily the confessional and impressionistic styles, while case study reports can be remarkably malleable and employ virtually any of the writing styles profiled below. There's no standard that suggests specific methodologies must use only certain styles for reportage. Some writers have used poetic forms to convey the meanings of lived experiences for phenomenology, while others from a range of disciplines have used dramatic writing as a presentation modality for topics from education to health care. We advocate that if students want to become good writers of research, they should read a lot of it to know how others approach the craft and art of documenting their analyses of social life.

Analytic and formal

Analytic and formal writing is the most predominant style in scholarship and the form that exemplifies what a majority of academics consider rigorous investigation and solid research. Wolcott (1994) identifies this style as scientific in character. It is sound technical writing that illustrates how key factors interrelate and presents the patterned regularities of data through a sense of ordered management. Van Maanen (2011) notes that the formal tale emphasizes theory generated from logical analyses, though he cautions that such writing can make the researcher's work appear dry and stilted.

Nevertheless, there are times when analytic findings are best presented in formal discourse, particularly within scientifically oriented social sciences such as psychology and sociology, health care, and selected subfields of educational research. Certain academic journal editors sometimes require that submissions adopt this writing style for review and publication. It is a traditional, entrenched approach to research presentation, yet—if presented well—can legitimize the investigator's work.

In a *Journal of Adolescent Research* article, "A Qualitative Exploration of Adolescents' Commitment to Athletics and the Arts," Fredricks (2002) and her five coauthors' goal was to gain "an understanding of the factors that influence adolescents' commitments to extracurricular activities over time" (p. 68). Forty-one teenagers participated in the study. In the "Interview Procedure" section of the report, the coauthors outline their methods in straightforward language and a listing of topics:

> We chose to use a semistructured in-depth interview to prompt discussion about adolescents' involvement in their activity

from childhood to adolescence. The interview questions were organized around the following areas: (a) general changes in the adolescent's life over the past 3 to 4 years; (b) the adolescent's general hopes and plans for the future; (c) the adolescent's history of involvement and accomplishment in the activity; (d) hopes and concerns about the activity; (e) the impact of the activity on other aspects of life, such as school, peers, and the family; (f) the role of significant others such as family members, coaches or teachers, and peers on his/her involvement; and (g) hopes and plans for involvement in the future. . . . Each interview was audiotaped and lasted from 1 to 1 1/2 hours. (Fredricks et al., 2002, pp. 73–74)

The coauthors organize their results through both main headings and subheadings by the researchers' categories (e.g., "Psychological Factors," "Weighing the Benefits and Costs") and the young people's In Vivo Coded subcategories (e.g., "Because My Friends Are There," "What's in It for Me?"). In the "Discussion/Implications" section, the coauthors conclude with a review of the evidence that supports their recommendations:

Finally, our findings highlight the many positive aspects of participation in extracurricular activities. Our interviews indicate that participation can provide multiple benefits, including enjoyment, recognition, increased confidence, and social support. . . . Unfortunately, participation in high school extracurricular activities is often viewed as nonessential and is one of the first items to be cut during fiscal constraints. Educators should reevaluate these assumptions because of the potential benefits and importance of participation in the high school experience of many adolescents. (Fredricks et al., 2002, p. 92)

Figure 11.1 Adolescents benefit from extracurricular activities in athletics and the arts.

©iStockphoto.com/Christopher Futcher

Some beginning researchers mistakenly believe they have to "write smart" by using complex vocabulary and sterile prose to be taken seriously and to demonstrate their scholarly prowess. Formal and analytic writing succeeds when it is clear and unpretentious.

Descriptive and realistic

A stylistic cousin of writing analytically and formally is **descriptive and realistic writing**. Description is straightforward reportage of what the investigator saw and heard. It is factual storytelling of the participants' daily lives and critical incidents, yet needn't outline a bulky account of excessive details (Wolcott, 1994). This realist tale (Van Maanen, 2011) usually adopts a third-person perspective with neutral and objective writing in the past or present tense. The researcher keeps his own subjective commentary and interpretations out of it (for the moment) to paint a vivid picture of reality for the reader. Virtually all genres of qualitative research include descriptive and realistic writing in their reports.

As an example, Miller, Creswell, and Olander (1998) explored the writing of their fieldwork in three different ways for their *Qualitative Inquiry* article, "Writing and Retelling Multiple Ethnographic Tales of a Soup Kitchen for the Homeless." In this excerpt, the coauthors provide visual elements of the setting through concrete imagery and through what we call **significant trivia**—rich, telling details:

> The Soup Kitchen, run by a Catholic church, provides dinner 7 days a week and lunch on weekends. Daily Refuge rents the kitchen on weekdays to serve free lunches. St. Tabor's dining area is one modest sized room, about 45 by 30 feet. Guests sit around three rows of tables (2 by 24 feet each) covered with green, plastic, flannel-backed tablecloths with tiny paw prints. When not in use, chairs line one of the walls of the room. The dining area is modern and clean, with sparse accessories—a couple of trash cans, a small cross hanging on the wall, a bulletin board advertising services available to the homeless, and a few community service awards. A long serving counter divides the dining area from the kitchen—a modern, clean cooking area with a stove; commercial size oven; microwave; stainless steel, locked refrigerator; dishwasher; and mops and buckets for clean-up. (Miller et al., 1998, p. 474)

Participant action, reaction, and interaction can also be written descriptively and realistically. Below is a vignette based on an observation of a homeless man's interactions with a staff member at the soup kitchen. Again, note its factual reporting tone for a realist tale:

> Michael was tall, bearded, with medium long, dark matted hair twisted in every direction, greasy hands and a dirty face. While mopping the floor he began talking about a trip he took to Turkey after he graduated from college in the early seventies. Michael described a man in Turkey, "part of the FBI or CIA," who wanted him to loan him "a million dollars," and related how "pissed off" the agent was that Michael had refused. As he rolled the mop and bucket to the dining area, Michael continued and referenced the government and the Pentagon. Rich [the facilities manager with rehab training], who overheard the conversation, asked, "Are you sure all those things are accurate?" Michael nodded confidently. "I just wondered," said Rich, "You are kind of getting 'out there' with your talk about the CIA and FBI—kind of loose, almost delusional," and asked, "Are you supposed to be on medication?" Michael looked Rich squarely in the eye and replied, "No, are you?" (Miller et al., 1998, p. 478)

Wolcott (1994) asserts that description is the foundation on which analysis rests. Data must be systematically collected and richly articulated before they can be put through analytic methods and the next level of writing: interpretation (discussed later). Ethnographic field notes utilize descriptive and realistic writing, and those empirical materials provide substantive passages for inclusion in a final report.

Confessional

The **confessional tale** (Van Maanen, 2011) is the researcher's first-person account of the subjective experiences she encountered throughout the project. This style departs from the supposed objectivity of analytic, formal, descriptive, and realistic writing to admit to readers the researcher's own emotions, vulnerabilities, uncertainties, fieldwork problems, ethical dilemmas, and data collection or analytic blunders. It is a reflexive, prosaic self-portrait of sorts that reveals the investigator's inner thoughts. Virtually no research project is conducted perfectly; thus, the confessional tale also serves as a cautionary tale for readers to consider before venturing into comparable projects.

Connolly and Reilly (2007) openly portray their vulnerabilities in their article, "Emergent Issues When Researching Trauma: A Confessional Tale," in *Qualitative Inquiry*. Connolly, as lead author, researches the effects on neighbors following a gruesome series of murders in 2001 in a suburban community. The murderer, due to financial pressures and bankruptcy, killed his wife, three sons, father-in-law, and a business associate, then set his house on fire before taking his own life. Connolly interviewed neighborhood residents and city officials about the tragic incident with a focus on the trauma they experienced in the aftermath. Connolly was trained in more traditional research methods, and the fieldwork demands with this sensitive issue generated mixed feelings within her:

> In the research that I conducted with the . . . neighborhood residents, I became aware that in asking others to open up about their personal experience of trauma as a result of the mass murders and suicide, I found myself in roles that conflicted with what I understood to be appropriate for even a qualitative researcher. Seeing the home where the murders occurred, hearing the stories of the residents who shared conversations "over the fence" with the . . . family, and seeing the memorial set up for the boys by their friends has had an impact on me as the researcher. Michael, one of the neighbor kids who grew up adjacent to the [murderer's sons] described the close relationships he'd had his whole life with the youngest . . . boy, Justin. He was describing how the two of them used to run back and forth between each other's homes:
>
> *There was a wooden board that fell off the fence, and there's like . . . on our driveways, two cement curves and we put the board across it and we didn't go down the driveway or nothin' to get to each other's houses. . . . We'd just run across the board or jump across. We didn't go like . . . up and down the street, we didn't know that path . . . like down the driveway, up the driveway . . . we'd just run across the board. Across the board. That's it, you know? (Michael, April 13, 2004).*
>
> I found this account gripping, for a reason that still somewhat perplexes me. I reflected on the childhood patterns that I had developed with my friends in the neighborhood in which I grew up. I reflected on my son squeezing through the bushes that bordered our property line to get to his friend's house faster. The depth of childhood friendships, the play that we develop as neighbor kids, the innocence that is part of childhood, the familiarity that results from growing up day by day as neighbors, adjacent to each other—this all seemed to be captured in Michael's story about his friend. (Connolly & Reilly, 2007, pp. 525–526)

The coresearchers share reflections about the moral dilemmas of reciprocity they faced in their roles as interviewers and analysts, and the stressful compassion fatigue they experienced after hearing neighbors' heart-wrenching stories. "Emergent Issues When Researching Trauma" is a poignant confessional tale about the researcher's issues rather than the participants' (that report is published elsewhere). Connolly and Reilly (2007) offer a rare glimpse into the vulnerabilities that accompany such work, and share their personal learnings with qualitative colleagues.

Confessional writing should be used selectively. Readers do not need to be informed of every problem encountered in the field. But if there is noteworthy advice to pass along, share it honestly. As the saying goes, "When in doubt, tell the truth."

Impressionist

Impressionist tales (Van Maanen, 2011) recount the memorable, striking, and vibrant. It is first-person writing that helps the reader relive the researcher's fieldwork and/or personal experiences that are exceptional rather than typical. The literary elements of fictional writing—imagery, metaphor, characterization—can be incorporated into these tales. They present facets of self or culture that arrest an audience with their vivid portrayals of action.

Autoethnography is, by default, both confessional and impressionist. Fox (2014) presents a candid account in his *Qualitative Inquiry* article, "Are Those Germs in Your Pocket, or Am I Just Crazy to See You? An Autoethnographic Consideration of Obsessive–Compulsive Disorder." Fox alternates between "Being here" (present writing and reflection) and "Being there" (memories of past experiences) to provide an unabashed insider's view of his thinking patterns:

> **Being there. August 24, 2012.** I sit in front of my computer and author an explanation of autoethnography, focusing on why the method is a good fit for a qualitative investigation of the psychiatric-industrial complex. Fingers dance across the keyboard as I write. . . .
>
> "Bing, bong," the doorbell screeches. I stop typing and collect a cardboard box from a UPS driver. Panic grips me the minute I shut the front door and lock my deadbolt. The doorbell's scream echoes in my head, getting louder with each repetition. I try to start writing again. My fingers clumsily crash down on the keyboard: A-u-t-o-e-t-h-n-o-g-r-a-p-h-y—

BING! BONG! Tune it out, Fox. Keep typing: i-s a-n i-d-e-a-l m-a-t-c-h f-o-r—

BIIIIING! BOOOONG! It's just a panic attack. Type: i-n-v-e-s-t-i-g-a-t-i-o-n-s o-f m-e-n-t-a-l i-l-l-n-e-s-s—

BIIIIIING! BOOOOONG! What is wrong with me? Sweat shimmers over my paling skin. My stomach feels like it is crawling up my esophagus. My heartbeat provides a percussion beat to the "Bing! Bong!" horror tune playing in my head. I feel as if my child psychologist's evaluation of my sixth-grade self was a foretelling. I fear that I am—***BIIIIIING! BOOOOONG!***—coming unravelled. Each ring of the bell signals all that I might lose. Bing! Madness wants to devour the tenure I was just awarded. Sweat drenches my hair. Blood rushes away from my fingertips, causing them to tingle. Bong! After years of being single (and hating it), I finally have an amazing boyfriend. Mental illness wants to ravage our relationship. My arms shake and eyes spit tears to the wooden floor. My dog Bella cocks her head to the right and looks at me with wide, brown, concerned eyes. Bing! Bong! I will lose everything! BING BONG! I am going crazy! BinG! BOng! BING! BONG!

Being here. August 24, 2012, marked the first day of a long, treacherous, mental, and emotional breakdown. I had struggled with intrusive thoughts sporadically throughout adulthood. I spent the last 20 years worrying that my morbid thoughts were a sign of something more serious, like schizophrenia. The August 24th panic attack seemed to prove my greatest fear. By the end of the week, a man named Dr. Schmidt diagnosed me with obsessive-compulsive disorder (OCD). (Fox 2014, pp. 966–967; emphasis in original)

Fox discusses both individual and group counseling sessions, his internal dialogical struggle between emotion and logic, and his reconciliation with OCD through his own research about the disorder and personal writing as a form of therapy.

Impressionist writing is not limited to being autoethnographic or to case studies. An ethnography can reveal a particularly riveting moment of fieldwork; a grounded theory report can accentuate an intriguing interview excerpt. Impressionist writing is about something that made an impression on the researcher and hopefully makes an impression on the reader.

Interpretive

Wolcott (1994) explains that interpretation is not a style of writing but a level of insightful understanding. Interpretation addresses the questions, "What does it all mean?" and "What is to be made of it all?" (p. 12). This is not to suggest the development of theory, though that can certainly be one outcome. **Interpretive writing** is transcendence—extending "beyond the boundaries of a particular case to find broader application or meaning" (Wolcott, 1994, p. 256).

Good interpretation is built on data that have been meticulously described and rigorously analyzed. Those experiences provide the researcher deep knowledge of the empirical materials, enabling thoughtful reflection on their transfer to big-picture ideas. Thus, interpretation in qualitative reports generally appears in the final section under headings such as "Discussion," "Implications," or "Conclusion."

Wierzbicka (2012), in her *Emotion Review* journal article, poses an intriguing question: "Is Pain a Human Universal?: A Cross-Linguistic and Cross-Cultural Perspective on Pain." Wierzbicka analyzes through "natural semantic metalanguage" and "universal semantic primes" how concepts such as *think, body, one, live, die, big, touch,* and others are cross-cultural/universal. But surprisingly, the concept of *pain* is not. Pain—in English—can refer to both the physical and psychological, a dual purpose not shared by several other languages. The Australian Aboriginal language Yankunytjatjara has no exact counterpart to the word *pain*. Instead, the word *pika* refers to a part of the body that hurts or feels bad. English words such as *suffering, ache, sore,* and so on muddy the precision of diagnosing pain for medical practitioners. *Hurt* is perhaps a more universal concept than *pain,* according to Wierzbicka.

It takes time to build good interpretation in a report, so it is difficult to provide a self-standing passage that clearly exemplifies the writing style. Excerpts below from the "Concluding Remarks" section of Wierzbicka's (2012) study meet several criteria for interpretation. First, that section summarizes the major findings from her analysis. Second, it offers recommendations for professional practitioners. Third, it makes readers aware of things they might not have known before. And fourth, it addresses what is considered universal while simultaneously dispelling misconceptions of universality:

> Everywhere in the world, people often feel something bad.
> Everywhere in the world, things happen to parts of people's bodies
> because of which these people feel something bad in these parts
> of their bodies. Everywhere in the world, people can often feel

something so bad in their bodies that they think something like this: "something bad is happening to me, I don't want this."

Perhaps it is important for all people to be able to tell others that "something hurts"—to elicit their sympathy and to appeal for help. But to do that, one doesn't need the concept of "pain" as we know it from English. The knowledge that the concept of "it hurts" may well be universal whereas the concept of "pain" is not, should discourage medical practitioners from insisting that patients should try to describe the quality of their experience in terms of adjectives and participles ("pulsing," "flickering," "quivering," "dull," "drilling," "beating," etc.) and to allow the patients to tell them, in their own words, where it hurts and how it hurts. . . .

Not all languages have a word corresponding exactly to the English word *pain*, and that other languages may offer somewhat different perspectives on the range of phenomena associated in English with the words *pain*, *hurt*, *ache*, and *sore*. In that sense, "pain" is not a conceptual universal, even though all people feel, at times, what in English can be thought of as "pain." (Wierzbicka, 2012, pp. 315–316; adapted; emphasis in original)

After the audience has read the core portion of a report, the writer offers thoughts on how the readers themselves can make meaning of the study and consider the larger or broader issues at stake. Kozinets (2015) wisely offers, "Interpretation uses not just the brain for thinking, but the gut for understanding" (p. 204).

Critical and advocacy

Critical inquiry examines inequality and injustices through sound investigation of social conditions. An openly political and moral agenda drives the research to uncover and document evidence of social ills and to critique their origins and effects on human life. By raising awareness of problematic issues, researchers take the first step advocating for productive solutions and emancipatory action. **Critical and advocacy writing** is not a knee-jerk, emotion-laden diatribe or rant, but instead is a thoughtful inquiry that surveys the manifest and latent meanings of people's discourse and the actions, reactions, and interactions that result in power imbalances.

In *Critical Sociology*, Bloch (2014) analyzes online racist posts in "'Anyone Can Be an Illegal': Color-Blind Ideology and Maintaining Latino/Citizen Borders." Bloch scrutinizes the Web site and online discussion forum of the Americans for Legal Immigration (ALIPAC), identified as a nativist extreme organization by the Southern Poverty Law Center. Bloch first reviews the literature on White national identity and immigration issues, specifically with Mexicans, in addition to relevant concepts and theories related to racism, nationalism, and culture. She then outlines the history and influence of ALIPAC and presents statistical evidence of their Web traffic. Notice how her assertions are supported with posts, related research literature, and causal analyses:

> Consistent with the dominant color-blind ideology, being racist threatens the legitimacy of both the group and individuals. This is a problematic identity dilemma since group members reinforce racist ideology, some more explicitly than others. For example, in one instance, a forum participant posted discussions from a perceived pro-immigrant organization. The members referred to this as a Chicano forum. This post prompted an example of a more explicitly racist statement. EX_OC writes, "They resort to that because (a) their level of sanity is limited and (b) the macho rapist/tough guy image makes up for their pigmy stature and mental midget failure of Mexico to achieve what America has." In this statement, EX_OC is connecting the physical makeup of Chicanos (pigmy stature) with mental abilities, "mental midget failure". In response, No2illegals posts, "Wow. . . . I couldn't have said it any better. . . . Awesome!" and wilro writes, "It's amazing how childish the chicken forum—ooops, I mean chicano forum is. Only small minds like theirs can produce something so moronic." The quotes above attach negative attributes with genetic characteristics and liken Mexicans to animals. However, comments that are so blatantly racist, referring to physical features, are rare. They are also inconsistent with today's color-blind ideology. Less explicit statements that reinforce racist ideology are much more common.

> Consistent with today's color-blind ideology, group members maintain that they are not racially motivated. There were 67 posts across 25 threads where forum participants explicitly state that they, or nativists in general, are not racist. Diminishing the importance of race as an explanation for inequality is one form of color-blind racist discourse (Bonilla-Silva, 2002). Bonilla-Silva (2002: 62) notes that white students interject "anything but race" phrases into their stories to stress that their color-blind story is truly devoid of racial explanations. This is a central tactic used by the ALIPAC forum members to attempt to neutralize any part of their

explanations regarding immigration that have racial messages in them. For members of ALIPAC the specific "anything but race" strategy is to rely on rhetoric of legality. When nativists rely on "the law" as the moral measuring stick, the discourse suggests some level of rational decision making because it relies on seemingly immutable laws. (Bloch, 2014, pp. 54–55)

Critical writing works best when it is akin to investigative journalism. The report grounds itself in facts as supportive evidence for the revelation of social ills and recommendations for social change. Nevertheless, the writer makes no apologies for her values-laden perspective and the goal of righting the wrongs.

Literary narrative

Literary narrative writing, also known as narrative inquiry, is a short story form of research reportage. It is a kind of creative nonfiction that uses the power of storytelling to recount the participants' perceptions, experiences, and their psychology through imaginative data (Leavy, 2015). Also known as the literary tale (Van Maanen, 2011), narrative writing employs evocative prose with literary elements such as local color, symbolism, and an omniscient point of view. Some consider narrative inquiry a methodology as well as a writing style, but we classify it as an approach to documenting research.

Figure 11.2   Finley and Finley (1999) developed poignant narratives about homeless youths.

©iStockphoto.com/AvailableLight

As an example, Susan Finley and her son Macklin Finley (1999) reported their lived experiences and ethnographic research with homeless youths in pre-Katrina New Orleans in *Qualitative Inquiry*'s "Sp'ange: A Research Story." "Sp'ange," a contraction of "spare change," is a term used by what Finley and Finley found New Orleans residents called "street rats" to solicit money from passersby. Macklin lived the life of a street poet in the city and befriended the unhoused, mostly runaway youths. His mother, a critical ethnographer with a strong sense of social consciousness, visited her son in New Orleans and came to know his cadre of friends. They collaborated on several writing projects about the homeless youths; one such project is this narrative about a streetwise young man named Roach. His language is rather coarse but authentic:

"Spare change?"

"I ask, but Mr. Blue-suit-on-his-way-to-work-business-maaan never even looks my way," Roach grumbles to himself, glaring down at the sidewalk. "Asshole! All these suit-assholes who're up in the morning, they got money in their pockets. Actin' like he don't see me. You see me, motherfucker!"

Another suit approaches and he repeats the refrain, "Spare change?" It's a cold winter morning in New Orleans and bitter winds slap chapped hands where money doesn't fall. For the better part of 5 years now he's been homeless, moving back and forth across the country, riding trains, hitching with truckers, squatting in abandoned buildings in temporary homes with other travelers. He's in New Orleans now to avoid winter cold in northern climes, but warmth has a way of avoiding him. Cold and wet followed him this time from New York and hang on him like bedclothes.

His dawn walk takes him along the lower Quarter's down-river boundary on Esplanade. Here, historic mansions follow years of neglect with facelifts to greet new lives as bed and breakfast spots or to promise new, upscale restaurants.

"This city's always cold for mornin'." He repeats the local expression, liking the way it sounds, "No matter how hot the day, cold for mornin'." He mutters half to himself, half aloud, "Every square Dad and Arab between here and there gonna look me up down, hate me, throw me away with their eyes." He pulls the collar of his army jacket up high around his neck and braces his shoulders to the enemy cold. "All I gotta do is walk through it."

"Spa' change?"

"Spa' change?" Passers-by, pass by. Roach walks past a newly opened leather bar, the cold wind feeding his anger at being ignored, denied. "The Marigny is fulla shit; all these gay-yuppie assholes."

He trips over his torn pant leg and bends down to tuck the loose material into the laces of his boot, keeps walking, complaining in his head. (Finley & Finley, 1999, p. 320)

Narrative inquiry provides the opportunity to break away from rigid academic discourse and to exercise one's creativity as a writer of human experiences.

Collaborative and polyvocal

The **jointly told tale** (Van Maanen, 2011) brings the researcher and participants together as coauthors of an account. At times, labels indicate which author has written each section; other times, a dialogic exchange of ideas occurs between the writers. Some pieces juxtapose two or more separate sets of writing side by side to offer parallel commentary or perspectives. A recent writing innovation is **duoethnography**, in which two (or more) researchers exchange ideas, usually through e-mail, which cumulatively builds into a full-length report. Duoethnographers respond to each other's ideas about a central topic, exchanging stories from personal experience, and citing the professional literature, as needed (Sawyer & Norris, 2013). Regardless of form or format, **collaborative and polyvocal writing** assumes a democratic process among participants to provide voice and agency to the researched.

One example is Jane Speedy (2011) and her group therapy clients co-participating in their evocative article, "'All Googled Out on Suicide': Making Collective Biographies Out of Silent Fragments with 'The Unassuming Geeks.'" Speedy is a therapist working with young men considered at risk for suicide. Aside from talk, creative writing became one of the treatment modalities for her clients who labeled themselves "The Unassuming Geeks." Unfortunately, one of the men left the group, moved to another country, and eventually took his own life. Jane and the remaining young men gathered after the news to mourn and reflect on the loss. The collaborative *Qualitative Inquiry* article that documents their experiences alternates between Speedy's texts and the men's individual and collective voices as a theatrical "Geek [Greek] chorus":

> We came back together about 6 months after he died. We met in the pub to chat. Then we went back to Jane's office to write and now we are meeting again to try and generate something from that writing. But we've been caught out once already by believing what we wrote, or rather, by not paying attention to what we didn't write, to what was left out.

> *Jane says:* I don't remember the chat in the pub. I remember sitting in silence for about half an hour.

> *Jane says:* And I don't remember going up the hill to write. I remember, going back up the hill to my office and just sitting in silence.

The Geeks' chorus: And then you said "I wonder what was going on for us in all that silence?" And then we all started to write, without talking, which we'd never done before. And then we read out what we'd written. Nobody commented at all, we just read it out:

Man in Orange writes: Remembering.

Remembering him.

I was remembering his wildlife passions

especially for birds—for sea birds

Gulls, cormorants, razorbills, shearwaters

Guillemots, curlews, sand pipers and arctic terns

and then I remember thinking—shit—

I bet the others are thinking really profound stuff

and here I am dribbling on about curlews and

cormorants. . . .

But all I could really remember

was some kind of longwinded dirty joke about seabird

cities,

it was all about high-rise cities on Scottish cliffs and it

ended with the punch line:

"Crested shag"

I never really got that joke.

I'm even not sure there was one.

The whole point was that we were about nineteen.

Nineteen-year-old British geeky boys are hardwired

to laugh awkwardly

every time somebody says "shag."

So we all did.

He'd say "crested shag" and we'd all fall apart.

Ornithological stand-up. Undervalued really.

Man in Purple writes:

When we got to the pub, I was relieved to hear that his mum and sister weren't coming because I didn't know what to say to them. I didn't know what to say to anyone actually, but then nobody did and the silence, I thought was quite companionable. (pp. 136–137)

Collaborative writing is one of the least-employed forms in qualitative inquiry. It asks the researcher to relinquish authority as lead author and to coordinate a polyvocal composition and shared contribution to the literature.

Dramatic

The use of dramatic or theatrical writing as research representation goes by many names such as performance ethnography, nonfiction playwriting, verbatim theatre, and ethnodrama (Saldaña 2005a, 2011a). A play script dramatizes the participants' and/or researchers' experiences into monologic or dialogic forms. Theatrical elements such as scenery, lighting, costumes, and sound are utilized to enhance the aesthetics of the research story.

Foster (2002) dramatized the marital discord and separation from her husband in her autoethnodramatic one-act play, "Storm Tracking: Scenes of Marital Disintegration." The *Qualitative Inquiry* text intersperses "Deborah" lecturing to her interpersonal communication class about relationship dynamics, with scenes of arguments between Deborah and her husband, "Brett." The play is punctuated with occasional weather reports about an impending storm. Notice how the italicized stage directions in the following scene, which is Scene 2, suggest a stylized rather than realistic presentation of the stark confrontation between the spouses:

WEATHER ANNOUNCER: Well, just like I predicted, Tropical Storm Fred has moved west and seems to be gathering some intensity out there in the Gulf. He's churning up some waves (*ocean sounds for the following scene can begin at this point*) but isn't doing anything definitive yet. Looks like we have to wait and see if Fred is ready to come ashore.

DEBORAH: (*to audience*). Brett went to see a therapist last night. We walk in the

dark as Brett speaks and I listen.
Like waves through the flow of Brett's
words, phrases pound me, one after
another.

Both Brett and Deborah stand side by side and deliver the following lines to the audience until Deborah addresses Brett directly after his speech.

BRETT: I told her how we met doing the graduate school thing, and how we got married primarily for convenience—

DEBORAH: (*to audience*). The first wave knocks me to the sand.

BRETT: I told her how every month or so I would bring up something about your weight to try to motivate you to do more stuff, and how I know that hurts you a lot—

DEBORAH: (*to audience*). And again.

BRETT: I told her that you always knew you wanted me, but I just tended to take the path of least resistance, so I never really decided if I wanted you or not—

DEBORAH: (*to audience*). I try to struggle to my feet.

BRETT: We talked about the time we were dating long distance and I broke up with you. I couldn't see the point of a long-distance relationship. I told her I wasn't unfaithful, but I let myself get emotionally attached to someone else. I got back together with you because it was Christmastime, and it didn't seem right to break up with you then. She said it sounds like I didn't think it through enough—

DEBORAH: (*to audience*). The waves break over my head.

BRETT: She asked me if I would put a hundred dollars down right now on whether I would stay or go. I said, "Listening to this conversation, I'd bet that I would go." She asked me if my love for you had grown since we got married and I said, "Yes," and she seemed to stop and think. She said, "That's one sign of a strong relationship—it grows."

DEBORAH: (*to audience*). At this point, we stop at a water fountain. I drink the tepid water, tasting rust. (*Brett and Deborah turn to each other. Ocean sounds stop abruptly*). Brett, do you think for one minute that I would be standing here right now if you hadn't convinced me time and time again that you desperately wanted to be with me? (Foster, 2002, pp. 808–809)

Figure 11.3 Hanauer (2015) poetically represents a U.S. soldier's experiences in the second Iraq war.

©iStockphoto.com/Bryan Myhr

Whether live or video recorded, **dramatic writing** makes its best impact when a well-scripted text is well performed.

Poetic

Poetic inquiry is a methodology to some, but we profile it here as a distinctive approach to writing research. **Poetic writing** utilizes the conventions of the literary genre to evocatively represent and present data. The words can originate from participant interview transcripts or other written texts (adapted into found poetry), or the work can be originally composed by the researcher as fieldwork representation or autoethnographic expression. The elegant, carefully selected content and form of poetry can generate emotional and aesthetic response from readers and listeners. In a way, poetry achieves the same goal of phenomenology—to capture the essence and essentials of the meanings of lived experiences.

Hanauer (2015) interviewed a U.S. soldier about his experiences in the military in 2003. In his *Qualitative Inquiry* article, "Being in the Second

Iraq War: A Poetic Ethnography," Hanauer explains his process of adapting the interview transcripts:

> The poetic technique of lining was used to create the poetic text. The core principle for this rearrangement consisted of using line endings, line beginnings, and line length to provide emphasis and reflection on specific aspects of the participant's descriptions and explanations. The initial process of analysis directed the choices made as to what to emphasize and at which points to make the reader reflect on particular aspects of the soldier's experience. All the words used in the poem are the direct words of the participant but were arranged poetically by the researcher. (Hanauer, 2015, p. 85)

Hanauer's participant reviewed the poetic draft, offered recommendations for revision, and expressed gratitude that his story was being told. The example below is one of the more riveting excerpts from the poetic suite:

XVI. The Lady Who Blew Herself Up

I think about the first lady

    who blew herself up.

I was right there.

    I was sitting there.

Watching the guard,

    and the one guy's

    on the road with the other trucks

    on the road blocking it.

    So when people come,

    stop and get down,

    Check 'em out.

    Let 'em go or not.

Pregnant lady.

    Stops the car.

All black.

    Face, you can see.

I don't remember if she was with someone or not.

I don't remember.

I just remember her walking up to the man.

Soldiers.

Cause they're like "stop stop stop stop stop.

Don't move, don't move!"

She keeps coming towards them.

You know she's pregnant.

She just stands up

and they're confused,

like I guess it's a pregnant woman

and the next thing you know,

big fireball.

And I just stared at it for a second (pp. 102–103)

Poetic inquiry has a small but dedicated following of exceptional researcher artists. Not all scholars are receptive to the writing style, considering it unscientific or too literary in character. But an openness to the power of the form can generate a deep understanding of the human condition.

Other writing and presentation styles

Other forms have been published and posted online that are intriguing to explore. The written screenplay permits the reader to envision the fieldwork in her mind as a film as the writer describes camera action, settings, and onscreen dialogue (Berbary 2011, 2012; Park, 2009). Video and film themselves are presentation modes of research that have surged in number over the past decade. As examples, qualitative researcher Kip Jones interviewed gay elders in England reflecting on rural life in the 1950s, and codeveloped a fictional yet fact-based film based on their composite stories, *Rufus Stone* (http://vimeo.com/109360805). Sport scholar David Carless and colleague Kitrina Douglas created *The Long Run*, a research-based short film of a man's experiences with medication and running to cope with his enduring mental illness (https://www.youtube.com/watch?v=v-fprKKUGKo). Dedicated Web sites for ethnographic projects include not only fieldwork videos but also researcher and participant blogs, links to related sites, and opportunities for visitor interaction (Collins & Durington, 2015).

Photovoice combines original participant photography with accompanying texts written by the participant. Participants take photos of what is considered important or significant in their world. Reflective writings in prose or poetry are stimulated by the images and exhibited for viewers in a studio, gallery, or Web site. Some present audio or video recordings alongside the photographs. Of course, participants and the researcher can also express their lived experiences through other art forms such as collage, sketches and renderings, sculpture, and others.

Figure 11.4 Dance utilizes the body as an expressive instrument of lived experiences.

©iStockphoto.com/PeopleImages

Dance utilizes the body as an expressive instrument of lived experiences, using movement to convey what cannot be communicated through oral language. The art form can be presented as a choreographed representation of the researcher's findings, or as a participatory forum with research participants to explore an issue through embodied inquiry. For examples of dance, view John Bohannon's intriguing TED Talk on the power of dance to explain and understand complex concepts: http://www.ted.com/talks/john_bohannon_dance_vs_powerpoint_a_modest_proposal.html. And view choreographer Bill T. Jones' dance workshops as a therapeutic modality for the ill, a form of autoethnographic catharsis and healing: http://www.pbs.org/moyers/journal/archives/billtjones_stillhere_flash.html.

Finally, see Knowles and Cole (2008) and Leavy (2015) for more on intriguing arts-based approaches to qualitative research.

On Writing About the Major Elements of a Study

Now that an overview of qualitative writing and presentation styles has been presented, we examine some of the mechanics of reporting that document researchers' and participants' experiences. It is impractical if not impossible to offer detailed methods of writing for every combination of genre and style we've discussed thus far. In addition, there are no established standards for qualitative research reports and it is not our goal to propose any. For the remainder of this chapter, we focus on a few key principles when writing about selected elements of a qualitative study.

Writing is prewriting

The preliminary documentation of a project during the research design stage, in addition to field notes, analytic memos, interview transcripts, qualitative data analytic work, and other elements of the study, have served as substantive **prewriting** efforts for the final report. As the study progresses, devote some analytic memo writing time to reflect on the evolving shape and possible outline of the final document or presentation. For master's theses and doctoral dissertations, students should create a file with all required formatting in place (title page and front matter, margins, line spacing, headers, page numbering, font size, appendix and reference headings, etc.) even before fieldwork takes place. As the study continues and students generate ideas, entries are written or cut and pasted from other working files into the formatted document, albeit in rough draft form. The rationale for this tactic is that it frames the student and cumulatively realizes the goal for the final product. Make the draft look like a thesis/dissertation, and it will start feeling like a thesis/dissertation.

We also advise a simple but tried-and-true formula for final document development: Write a minimum of one full page a day, and in a year a writer will have a book (or thesis, dissertation, etc.). There's no need to write the draft in its chronological reading order (e.g., Chapter 1 completed before Chapter 2 is begun). Write whatever can be written at any time. If a researcher is stuck on how to synthesize the literature review, she can write about the data collection and analytic methods instead. When fatigued with a particularly lengthy chapter, writers can spend some time editing what's already been written, proofreading references, or drawing any necessary tables or figures. Since writing is thinking, researchers sometimes find that their work on a particular section of the report helps consolidate ideas about another portion yet to be written.

The research design as a preliminary report outline

The initial and evolved research design, as well as any necessary application required for an IRB review, serve as source material for the written report's **front matter**.

The beginning sections of analytic and formal tales generally consist of such elements as the following:

- Title
- Abstract
- Keywords
- Introduction
- Statement of Purpose
- Rationale for the Study
- Conceptual Framework
- Literature Review
- Central and Related Research Questions
- Methods
  - Site Selection
  - Participant Selection
  - Data Collection
  - Data Analysis

Following these preliminaries are general headings showcasing the analysis such as these:

- Findings, Results, etc.
- Discussion, Interpretations, etc.
- Implications, Future Research, Summary, Conclusion, Closure, etc. (Creswell, 2016, p. 232)

Some styles of qualitative writing such as literary narrative, dramatic, and poetic, and some research genres such as autoethnography, do not generally follow the traditional outline just listed. Analytic and formal tale plotting might be better suited to genres such as grounded theory, ethnography, mixed methods, and phenomenology, when readers expect such conventions.

Some writers have balanced their more creative, arts-based representations with explanatory front-loading or follow-up narratives that discuss the more conventional research elements, such as Hanauer's (2015) poetic ethnography of the soldier, or Finley and Finley's (1999) literary narrative about homeless youths. Other arts-based pieces, however, have muddied the stylistic waters by citing or footnoting the academic literature throughout the poetry, short story, or dramatic script itself, thus weakening the potential aesthetic power of their evocative writing. We find nothing wrong with several different writing styles within a single report, but we strongly recommend that writers keep them separated within the document.

Something to say

As researchers compose field notes and analytic memos or document their analyses as assertions or vignettes, they might realize that the action of writing helps (if not forces) them to formulate their thinking and to formalize it through language. We facetiously offer, "Writing is a lot easier and goes much faster when you have something to say." But don't discount messy, stream of consciousness, first-draft composition as a way to consolidate what's going through the mind.

Belcher (2009) reinforces that an **argument**—that is, something to say—is necessary for a good journal article. And something to say will most likely not emerge until data have been carefully analyzed. Another anecdotal piece of research reporting advice is, "What's the news?" In other words, what are the major headlines or the quick read summary that give readers the knowledge gained or insights made from analytic work? Saldaña jokes in his research methods courses that students should eventually end up with the "big kahuna" paragraph—a five- to seven-sentence narrative that reveals not what was done, but what was discovered.

Sometimes the magnitude of writing the entire report overshadows the necessity of highlighting for readers the gist of what was learned. Writing about the study itself is certainly one way to get there, but the task will be a lot easier and go much faster when efforts begin by composing a "big kahuna" paragraph and considering its best placement in the final report.

Below is one example of how an article summarizes the study's major findings and interprets their meanings for broader application. Eastman (2012) in "Rebel Manhood: The Hegemonic Masculinity of the Southern Rock Music Revival" in the *Journal of Contemporary Ethnography*, studied 27 underground rock bands, interviewed 44 men, content analyzed 1,063 of the bands' song lyrics, and gathered other forms of data at concerts and on band Web sites. His study of this subcultural group profiles three major categories of their ethos (values system). The first paragraph in the final discussion recaps the major headlines of his analysis. The second paragraph addresses the famous "So what?" question of inquiry criteria—that is, How does this study provide transferable meanings?

Economically disenfranchised men find themselves in a precarious situation as cultural expectations pressure all males to adhere to hegemonic masculine ideals, yet marginalized men lack the resources and authority most men use to signify manhood. In this study, I reveal how rebel men compensate for their marginal class status by using a variety of identity work strategies to signify hegemonic masculine selves. Rebel men highlight their hegemonic masculine independence by rejecting the responsibilities of being students, workers, husbands, and fathers. Rebels also symbolically empower their masculine selves by protesting those in positions of authority, including bosses, teachers, politicians, judges and law enforcement officers. Rebels further claim hegemonic power by exploiting women's labor and bodies. Additionally, rebel men empower their hegemonic masculine selves and protest middle-class conventions using compensatory manhood acts including drinking, taking drugs, and fighting. . . .

Given the widespread notoriety of rebel manhood, many in the United States stereotype Southern men as backwards and deviant because of the ways rebels protest middle-class conventions and use compensatory manhood acts to signify hegemonic masculine ideals. However, when I contextualize the Southern identity into hegemonic masculine ideals, I reveal that rebel men simply use alternative identity work strategies to signify the same ideal tenets of manhood shared by most men across all social classes and regions. Perhaps Americans contrarily consider the South (especially as expressed in music) unique and deviant, yet somehow also central to the U.S. cultural landscape partially because Southern men exemplify identity work strategies that help disempowered males all across the country signify the hegemonic masculine ideals shared by all men. (Eastman, 2012, pp. 212, 214)

The evidentiary warrant

The evidentiary warrant (Erickson, 1986) refers to the presentation of data that supports assertions. Though a backstage analysis most certainly needs this record to ensure a researcher has done his homework, an interpretive claim in a report might be all that's needed to persuade readers about an analytic finding. Not every assertion in a report needs data like a participant quote or fieldwork observation passage to back it up. But there are times throughout the account when an occasional datum provides evidence or truth value for summative statements. This enhances the credibility and trustworthiness of the analysis.

As an example from Eastman's (2012) "Rebel Manhood" article, the researcher discusses how the musicians he studied protested education and rejected cultural capital. Below, he weaves data from song lyrics and excerpts from interview transcripts, and cites the scholarly literature twice, to provide an evidentiary warrant for his summative assertions:

> In the one lyrical mention of schooling in the data, Bob Wayne sings "you won't catch me in no college classroom," a phrase that substantively and grammatically highlights how Southern rockers reject educational cultural capital. Like other marginal men who substantiate claims to hegemonic masculinity by defining education as "nerdy" (Morris, 2008), many rebel men draw on their lack of schooling to signify their manhood, such as when one informant boasts of his "barely eighth-grade education." Similar to others of the working-class who define college as a waste of time and money (Gorman, 2000), the four Southern rock musicians with bachelor's degrees denigrated their educational achievements. One claimed his religious studies degree was "worthless," and then protested authority by describing college as "learning pompous professors' opinions." Another comments, "I graduated from college with an art degree, which is good if you like to paint houses," before adding how in college he only "learned how to smoke a lot of dope and drink a lot of beer." (Eastman, 2012, p. 196)

An entire report needn't consist of data-rich paragraphs like the one above, but it illustrates how to represent participants and the literature as testimony for an analysis. We encourage researchers to use verbatim quoting of a participant as occasional evidentiary support, with intact passages no longer than half a page in length (unless extended excerpts are provocative or absolutely necessary as an evidentiary warrant). The choice to include a participant's words over the researcher's is determined by whether the quote could evoke a strong emotional response in readers, if the story is a compelling vignette, or if the participant says what needs to be said better than the researcher can articulate it.

Point of view

Traditional research reports have employed the third person **point of view** (the researcher, the investigative team) instead of the first person (I, we). Qualitative research reports have generally adopted the first person voice to personalize the author and to connect more with readers. In fact, researchers might feel better connected with their own work when they have the freedom to use the pronoun *I*. Not all publishing houses and professional journals have adopted this perspective, and some still require use of the third person. But some genres such as autoethnography and styles such as confessional writing require no other point of view but the first person. We encourage students to use the first person in research reports whenever possible and permitted. It does not lessen one's credibility as a researcher, and it creates a relationship with readers.

Write easy, not hard

A classic saying goes, "Things can be complex without being complicated." The best qualitative writing is not simple but, instead, is accessible. By this we mean that the best research report is one that expresses its ideas in clear, straightforward language. Certainly, researchers should use rich words when needed to articulate intricate thinking, but they ought not "write smart" just to try to prove their intellect. We have read reports by students who believed they needed to reproduce the complicated sentence structures with sometimes convoluted vocabulary used by some published authors to document their own research. Not only did it make for difficult reading, but it also actually reduced—rather than increased—our trust in the writer's abilities. One example of such writing is this passage:

> The preteens appeared to have rejected the notion of autonomous planning activity, preferring instead teacher intervention and supervision of their classroom efforts in order to generate exemplary group work.

Here's a clearer way of expressing the same idea:

> The children preferred direct teacher guidance over small group independence to increase the quality of their class work.

Students are sometimes subject to a classroom teacher's, dissertation supervisor's, or journal editor's preferences for an acceptable writing style, but should give elegance a chance when possible. In fact, researchers should read aloud what they themselves have written. If they feel comfortable speaking the text, that's usually a good sign that they have developed a smooth and natural narrative. If, however, they feel awkward, if not foolish, they should revise the work until it's easy to speak out loud.

Figure 11.5   Create and work in ideal conditions for research writing.

©iStockphoto.com/pixdeluxe

On citations and references

One of the most common (if not most frustrating) problems we see most often in our students' work is a sloppy set of citations and **references**, information about an accessed print or media source for the research report. Sometimes a citation in the text will not appear in the references. Or, the year in a citation (e.g., "Smith, 2008") does not match the reference's year (e.g., "Smith, A. [2009]."). We also see missing journal volume and issue numbers, and missing page ranges in article and book chapter references. Occasionally there will be a mix of APA and MLA manual styles, and even different font styles and sizes from cut-and-pasted work. Sometimes references are not even listed in alphabetical order by the authors' last names. These errors diminish researcher credibility because they show inattention to detail. If we can't trust a researcher with the details of references, how can we trust him with the details of the research? Researchers should proofread citations and references carefully, going through them with a fine-tooth comb. If writers discipline themselves to make a complete and correctly formatted reference entry immediately after they have inserted a citation in a report's draft, they'll save a lot of proofreading and editing time later. There are several online commercial programs available (e.g., easybib.com) that assist researchers with proper citation formatting.

On titles, abstracts, and searches

The title of a work, its abstract, and keywords should be carefully considered. In this era of digital search engines, a published piece is more likely to be accessed by other researchers if its search terms correspond with its primary front matter. Reflect on the keywords and phrases that summarize the major contents of the article and integrate them into the title, abstract, and list of keywords (such lists are not used by all journals).

The title is a symbolic summary of the research story—a headline that tells readers what to expect. This is most often the first thing a reader will see, so it needs to be descriptive and, if possible, evocative to capture interest in proceeding further into the abstract and article itself. Just a sampling of a few qualitative research article titles that exhibit useful descriptive features such as discipline, topic, participants, site, method, targeted readership, and so on, follow:

- "Young People Negotiating the Stigma around Their Depression"

- "Characteristics of Lifelong Physically Active Older Adults"

- "Nursing Home Stakeholder Views of Resident Involvement in Medical Care Decisions"

- "*Salir adelante* (Perseverance): Lessons from the Mexican Immigrant Experience"

- "American Indian Perceptions of Educational Achievement in Predominantly White Culture: Implications for Marriage, Couple, and Family Counselors"

- "'And all of a sudden my life was gone': A Biographical Analysis of Highly Engaged Adult Gamers"

- "Learning to Deliver Care in a Medical Home: A Qualitative Analysis of Residents' Reflections on Practice"

- "Maintaining and Losing Control During Internet Gambling: A Qualitative Study of Gamblers' Experiences"

Virtually no one will read a piece during a literature review stage if it does not appear on a search results page. Personal preferences for titles must consider its potential readers. Catchy titles might indeed capture someone's interest if she stumbles across it, but will it appear as a retrieved item out of millions of published article links compiled in a data base?

Write the abstract of a work with just as much care as the title. Include essential information about the research topic, purpose, questions, methodology, and participants, and explicitly state the study's major findings—a formidable charge since different journals will set word limits on abstracts with 150 words as an approximate average. As one example, the 128-word abstract of "A Qualitative Exploration of Adolescents' Commitment to Athletics and the Arts" by Fredricks et al. (2002) is included below. Note how it succinctly summarizes the research design of the study and that almost half of the text is devoted to stating the analytic outcomes:

This study sought to enhance, through qualitative methods, an understanding of the factors that influence adolescents' commitments to extracurricular activities over time. We obtained semistructured interview data from 41 adolescents who had been highly involved in athletics or the arts since middle childhood. We examined their interpretations of the factors that supported or hindered their continued involvement in these activities over the years. Thematic analysis of the interviews revealed that psychological factors, perceptions of the context, and emerging identity all played a role in decisions to remain involved or quit. Perceived competence and peer relationships emerged as important psychological factors, whereas perceptions of challenge and costs and benefits were important contextual influences. We discuss implications of the findings for the implementation of extracurricular programs that support adolescent development. (Fredricks et al., 2002, p. 68)

As the researcher does with the title, she needs to ensure that the abstract includes descriptive language that might be accessed through a keyword search. In the example above, some of the major keywords include *qualitative, extracurricular, adolescents, athletics, arts, interview, thematic analysis,* and *psychological.* In sum, researchers should write study titles and abstracts to help potential readers locate targeted research among millions of works available in print and online. Two sample journal article titles, abstracts, and related keywords appear at the end of this chapter.

Journal Article Submission and Publication

There's no better way to learn about writing qualitatively than by reading exemplary works from prestigious peer-reviewed academic journals. There's no one "right" way to write a qualitative research report, but some journal titles do dedicate themselves to particular disciplines, methodologies, and/or styles (e.g., *Qualitative Health Research, Journal of Mixed Methods Research, Narrative Inquiry*), while others are quite open to publishing a variety of works (e.g., *Qualitative Inquiry, International Review of Qualitative Research, Cultural Studies ↔ Critical Methodologies*).

If students submit research papers to peer-reviewed journals, they should first determine if the journal's mission or focus is right for the work. Survey its most recently published articles to get a sense of its contents and styles. Carefully follow submission guidelines to the letter, attending to such matters as maximum length, preferred manual of style, and formatting requirements. It's general protocol to submit a work to only one journal at a time. The vast majority of journal publishers today utilize an online submission system that makes the process remarkably expedient.

Don't waste the reviewers' and editor's time with a first draft or substandard manuscript. Provide the highest-quality paper possible for (hopefully) constructive feedback. We have found reviewers' comments and recommendations for revision of our own articles to be most often helpful, sometimes unrealistic, and a few times unprofessionally destructive. Good peer reviewers take time to offer thoughtful responses to a researcher's piece. Some editors will encourage an author to revise and resubmit a manuscript if it holds promise. If an article is rejected, researchers should not be dissuaded from revising (not just resubmitting) and considering a different journal. Article publication is necessary for an academic's professional advancement, but its most important contribution is to inform a journal's subscribers and outside readers about the insights into life the researcher has made.

CLOSURE AND TRANSITION _____

Qualitative research reports that have made an impact on us were those that demonstrated both analytic prowess and writing finesse in addition to the original ideas their authors developed. A well-written piece can look effortless, but it most likely came from months (and sometimes years) of careful thought and continuous revision. Writing is indeed hard work; but when researchers have something to say, it gets easier. That's why we've emphasized analysis throughout this book from Chapter 1 onward. If the qualitative data collection and analysis have been successful efforts, the writing will bear fruit.

The next chapter focuses on the summative presentation of research to live audiences in classes and at professional gatherings such as conferences.

RESOURCES FOR ANALYTIC WRITE-UPS

The following resources offer you additional guidance for writing qualitative reports:

Allen, Mitchell. (2016). *Essentials of Publishing Qualitative Research*. Walnut Creek, CA: Left Coast Press.

Goodall, H. L., Jr. (2008). *Writing Qualitative Inquiry: Self, Stories, and Academic Life*. Walnut Creek, CA: Left Coast Press.

Prendergast, Monica, Carl Leggo, and Pauline Sameshima (Eds.). (2009). *Poetic Inquiry: Vibrant Voices in the Social Sciences*. Rotterdam: Sense Publishers.

Saldaña, Johnny. (2011). *Ethnotheatre: Research From Page to Stage*. Walnut Creek, CA: Left Coast Press.

Van Maanen, John. (2011). *Tales of the Field*, 2nd edition. Chicago: University of Chicago Press.

Wolcott, Harry F. (2009). *Writing Up Qualitative Research*, 3rd edition. Thousand Oaks, CA: Sage.

Woods, Peter. (2006). *Successful Writing for Qualitative Researchers*, 2nd edition. London: Routledge.

ANALYTIC EXERCISES FOR WRITE-UPS

1. Access and read some of the full-length articles cited in the "Stylistic Approaches to Research Writing" section of this chapter.

2. From a data corpus, select a moment of social life and write about the same event using three different styles of qualitative research writing.

3. Select a self-standing portion from a full interview transcript and transform the participant's experiences/story into a found poetry piece.

4. Select a field note excerpt with two or more participants interacting. Dramatize the excerpt into play script form with italicized stage directions, or as a short screenplay scene with suggested camera angles and action.

5. Access three of the full-length journal articles cited in this chapter. On a separate text editing page, list each article's headings and subheadings in the order they appear. Examine the outlines to reflect on the organization of the pieces.

6. Access one of your discipline's major qualitative research journals. Study its guidelines for manuscript submission.

SAMPLE ABSTRACTS FOR ANALYSIS

The following two journal article titles, abstracts, and related keywords reflect different qualitative research genres, analytic approaches, and styles. Review each one to assess the writers' approaches to inquiry, and infer what the full article might be like. Access the complete article for one of them and compare the abstract with the full manuscript.

"From Facebook to Cell Calls: Layers of Electronic Intimacy in College Students' Interpersonal Relationships" by Chia-chen Yang, B. Bradford Brown, and Michael T. Braun (2013), *New Media & Society*

Abstract

Communication technologies are widely used to manage interpersonal relationships, but little is known about which media are most useful at different stages of relationship development, and how the pattern of usage may be influenced by contextual factors or users' gender. Drawing on theories of relationship development, this study examined usage patterns among 34 college students participating in six geographically stratified focus group interviews. Analyses revealed a sequence of media use tied to stages of relationship development—from Facebook in early stages to instant messaging and then cell phones as a relationship progressed. Judgments about the efficacy and appropriateness of using a medium were based on how well its salient features matched prominent goals or addressed major concerns of a relationship at the given stage. International students added two technologies to the sequence to accommodate time differentials and distance from communication partners. Males were less explicit about the sequence, except when referring to cross-sex relationships.

Keywords: adolescence, cell phone, communication norms, gender differences, instant messaging, international students, media selection, relationship development, social media, social networking site (Yang, Brown, and Braun, 2013, p. 5)

ᑕᑌᑏᑐ

"Sensegiving and Sensebreaking via Emotion Cycles and Emotional Buffering: How Collective Communication Creates Order in the Courtroom" by Jennifer A. Scarduzio and Sarah J. Tracy (2015), *Management Communication Quarterly*

Abstract

Municipal courtroom employees face a variety of positive and negative emotional interactions, especially when defendants are encountering the criminal justice system for the first time. Based on qualitative data from participant observation and informal and formal interviews, this study analyzes how emotion cycles between judges and bailiffs help provide sensegiving and sensebreaking cues to defendants and observers in the courtroom. The heart of the analysis explores the routines and previous enacted environments of the courtroom, and the emotional buffering role of bailiffs—who we call intermediary actors—and names three types of emotion cycles: (a) the positive complementary emotion cycle, (b) the negative compensatory emotion cycle, and (c) the negative complementary emotion cycle. Theoretical implications include extensions of emotion cycle research through the use of participant observation data, the role of emotional buffering among three or more actors, and the impact of sensegiving and sensebreaking cues on organizational visitors.

Keywords: emotional buffers, emotion cycles, sensegiving, sensebreaking (Scarduzio & Tracy, 2015, p. 331)

Analytic Presentations

Introduction

After completing the data collection, analysis, and write-up stages of their studies, researchers are ready to share their results with the scholarly community. Ultimately, it is up to researchers to decide what they want to present in the final version of their work. Most strong research projects eventually take the form of a published journal article, but before publication many are presented at academic conferences. Conference presentations both allow researchers to share their work (and increase their reputations as scholars) and to get feedback (both positive and constructive) from other attendees. It is wise to listen to all feedback, take notes on it, and later reflect on what is and is not useful for future publication opportunities.

All conferences are unique, so in this chapter we focus only on the most common types of presentations at conferences. We begin with **paper presentations**, perhaps the most frequent type, in which researchers share their findings verbally. We next discuss **poster presentations**, in which researchers prepare large displays other conference attendees can view. Student theses and dissertations, completed or in progress, provide substantive material for these types of scholarly endeavors.

Slightly less common are the types of presentations that we do not discuss in depth here but that researchers might want to be familiar with are **roundtables**, in which groups of researchers sit around large tables, briefly discuss their work, then engage together in conversation

Learning Objectives

After reading and reviewing this chapter, researchers should be able to

1. Compare and contrast a variety of conference session formats, their protocols, and how each functions;

2. Create compelling graphics and media (charts, images, slideshows, etc.) to accompany conference presentations; and

3. Understand basic principles of professionalism and networking at academic conferences and comparable events.

about the aspects of their studies that overlap. Similarly, **working sessions** bring together groups of scholars who have already read each other's papers before arriving at the conference, and spend their session discussing the papers individually and/or collectively. The goal of such sessions is usually for researchers to help each other move their work forward toward publication by giving extensive feedback.

Before turning to specific forms, there are a few matters that apply to virtually all presentations. The majority of conferences held by leading research associations announce a **conference theme** when they release their call for submissions, and encourage submissions to address the theme. This can cause problems for researchers because the theme is often announced less than a year from the conference itself, and many qualitative studies cannot go from initial conceptualization to readiness for presentation in such a short amount of time, so it might appear that some conferences fail to give researchers adequate time to design, conduct, and finalize a full study. In some cases, this is true, but in others, the theme is not nearly as important as it might seem. If the theme of a small symposium is "Longitudinal Effects of Homelessness in Southwestern U.S. Cities," then indeed submissions do need to be longitudinal in nature and must address homelessness in that specific geographic area. Far more common, though, are general themes such as "Toward Justice: Culture, Language, and Heritage in Education Research and Praxis" (the American Educational Research Association [AERA] 2015 theme), or "Traversing the Rockies: Local to Global Theatre and Education" (American Alliance for Theatre & Education 2014 theme). These themes are broad, and researchers could likely find a way to connect almost any research project to these themes. While some organizations will consider how well a session meets a theme, many give it little or no weight in the actual decision-making process.

Finally, the goal of almost every presentation is the same, regardless of its format: researchers should hook the attention of the audience and present their most salient analytic findings. It will never be possible to share everything. Presentations are limited by time and/or physical space, so they must identify what they want to convey at this time, knowing that there will be other opportunities to present different aspects of their work in the future. Ideally, researchers will project confidence in their methods and analysis, raise questions audience members will want to discuss, and foster an environment where other scholars want to know more about the researchers and their work.

Paper Presentations

In paper presentation sessions, the room is normally set up theatre-style with rows of chairs facing tables and/or a podium and/or screens for projection at the front. Typically, three to four panelists will present their work, each having 15–20 minutes to do so. Often a question and answer (Q&A) period will be held at the end of the session when audience members can pose questions to panelists. In most cases, panelists are presenting work that is (at least loosely) connected by a theme for the session.

Roles of participants

In addition to the panelists themselves, many paper presentation panels include a session chair, a discussant and, hopefully, audience members. The **session chair** is responsible for all logistics of the session. She is responsible for ensuring that the session begins and ends on time and for introducing the panelists and discussant. In addition, the chair keeps track of time during the session, usually signaling speakers when their time is almost up and, if necessary, interrupting them to end their talk if they have gone over their time limit. If there is no discussant, the chair will usually moderate the Q&A portion of the session. Chairs sometime have a vested interest in the session (they might have proposed the session, or they might even be one of the panelists); other times they are simply picked from a pool of volunteers willing to serve as chairs.

A **discussant** is responsible for leading a feedback session at the end of a paper presentation panel. The discussant is almost always required to have read all of the papers in advance, and should come prepared with a series of comments for each presenter and/or questions for the panelists. In some cases, a high-profile discussant will be the only person to speak, which allows her to share her expertise with everyone present. Other discussants might choose to speak very little, preferring to ask the panelists and/or audience members about the studies in order to probe deeper into the topics discussed. The AERA has detailed descriptions of the roles of chairs and discussants at their conferences; see the resources section at the end of this chapter for details.

Protocols and etiquette

Perhaps the most important rule for oral paper presentations is to remain within one's allocated time limit. Sessions rarely budget extra time into their schedule, so if a researcher goes even one to two minutes over his 15-minute presentation, he is effectively reducing the next panelist to having only 13 or 14 minutes. Normally a session chair will indicate when time is almost up, but ultimately it is the presenter's responsibility to stay on time. We cannot overstate the importance of this. Running over and essentially stealing time from others is considered extremely unprofessional.

The researcher should arrive at her presentation venue at least 15 minutes in advance, especially if the researcher is using technology for a slideshow. To avoid the loss of time that occurs when four different panelists individually try to connect their laptops to a projector, then disconnect it so the next can begin, it is best for all panelists to load each slideshow on a single laptop. If that is not possible, having panelists put their slideshows on flash drives so they can still use just one device will save time and keep the session flowing.

Researchers should stay visibly engaged with each of the other panelists' papers. They should take notes on areas that are of interest to them, or that they might want to discuss later. Even if a researcher thinks there is no personal relevance with another speaker's work, it is critical to stay focused and appear engaged— even if solely for the sake of professional courtesy. Usually, however, other panelists will say intriguing or related things. When this happens, researchers should ask their co-panelists questions during the Q&A (or after the session, depending on what time permits). It is appropriate to talk with other panelists at the end of the session about their work and to exchange contact information to continue the dialogue established during the session itself.

When a researcher's own time to speak comes, he should try to touch on all of the key points from his study without going into excessive detail. Listeners who want to hear all of the evidence or more fully contextualize an argument can contact the researcher later. Elegant simplicity is best in the presentation itself. It is not possible to discuss everything from a study in just 15 minutes, so craft a clear, coherent, concise narrative. Many presenters spend far too much time on the study's front matter such as the conceptual framework, literature review, methods of data collection, and so on, leaving little time for what is perhaps the most important part of the presentation and what audiences really want to hear: the analytic findings.

We suggest speaking in a positive, upbeat tone when presenting, unless it would be inappropriate given the topic. Audience members will probably have attended several sessions by the time an afternoon rolls around (and might be tired in the morning if they were up late the night before), so it is best to remember that speaking at a conference is a form of performance. Researchers must play the role of an energetic and engaging presenter. Standing to present is preferred over sitting behind a table, along with frequent eye contact with listeners. In most forums, the use of humor and direct address to audience members is entirely appropriate. Finding ways to be interactive is essential, whether simply asking audience members to raise their hands if they agree with a certain statement, or asking them to discuss something briefly with a partner and then share what they found.

Slides can supplement a presentation by providing a visual guide to accompany the spoken word. As discussed in the next section, slides can contain key quotes audience members might want to record, as well as graphs and charts, photographs, diagrams, and other illustrations. It is appropriate to have a blank or nearly blank screen during times when no images are necessary, as opposed to projecting old slides about material that has already been addressed. Also, some researchers will bring paper copies of their slides to distribute to the audience in addition to or instead of having a projected presentation. We discourage this, because most of these copies will end up in a recycling bin. If a researcher wants audience members to be able to access the slides later, we suggest reducing waste by posting them online or distributing business card–sized handouts with contact information to those who are interested.

Slide design

One primary purpose of a slideshow is to convey the headlines and gist of the study. If a journal article was transformed into slideshow format, the slides would likely be based on the main headings and subheadings of the article. Interspersed with these headings would be quotes, diagrams, and other data that help illustrate the ideas under discussion.

Numerous software programs can help researchers create high-quality slideshows, including Microsoft PowerPoint, Prezi, or Apple's Pages. Each program offers slightly different features; we encourage researchers to explore a variety of programs to determine which one best suits their presentation and ways of working. Most examples in this chapter were created using PowerPoint.

One of the first things to select in most programs is a template that sets the look for the entire slideshow. Nearly all programs come preloaded with numerous templates. Some universities and other organizations have institutional templates they prefer (or possibly require) researchers to use when they present to help with branding. Similarly, if research was funded by a particular organization, it might require that its logo appear on all slides. Researchers should check with their institution's research office and ask if there is an official template. If not, we suggest selecting one that is subdued but aesthetically pleasing and engaging. For example, consider the two cover slides in Figures 12.1 and 12.2 (located on the inside back cover of this book), which serve as potential covers for the study on a work-release program for prisoners we have discussed throughout the book.

Both slides contain exactly the same information and both include a university logo, but they have very different qualitative connotations. Figure 12.1, with its shades of blue and white, suggests feelings of tranquility and innocence. The gradient background implies changes over time and space. The sharp diagonal lines suggest a sense of excitement or urgency. Figure 12.2, on the other hand, definitely grabs attention. But rather than tranquility, the fusion of vibrant colors suggests chaos, and the heavy presence of red, orange, and yellow evokes agitation. Like the lines in 12.1, the color scheme in 12.2 suggests a sense of urgency. Figure 12.2 also evokes an artsy feeling; the colors seem to have been created by a paintbrush.

Given all this, we would suggest that there is no right or wrong template; but the images certainly possess different meanings. Both will gain attention; 12.1 comes across as more polished and calm, whereas 12.2 projects a frenetic sense of energy. Of course, the color schema for Figure 12.1 should be grounded in the study's findings—presently it suggests tranquility and innocence, which would be appropriate if the study found the program to be a success, but might not be the best choice if the program was a chaotic failure. The point is that slide design—including color, font, readability, and aesthetics—matters because visuals carry certain meanings. Picking any template because it happens to look nice is not wise.

Researchers can use connotation to their advantage when designing charts and graphs. Consider the pie charts in Figures 12.3 and 12.4 (located on the inside back cover of this book) and determine which seems more appropriate.

Figure 12.3 relies on colors and layouts that connote certain meanings, at least within contemporary North American culture. First, it groups together varying levels of agreement with the same color. Green usually means "go" and agreement, and the darker shade indicates more intensity for "strongly" agreeing. Red implies "stop" and disagreement, again in different shades. Gray represents indecisiveness or in-betweenness (i.e., a gray area). Furthermore, Figure 12.3 begins with agreement on the left, then moves counterclockwise to disagreement on the right. Thus, colors, tints, shades, and arrangement all serve to help make Figure 12.3 more effective. Figure 12.4 uses the opposite layout than one might expect and a random color scheme. Figure 12.4 is not "wrong," but is less effective than 12.3.

Types of slides

Most slideshow programs can generate a wide variety of slide types. We have already demonstrated cover slides in Figures 12.1 and 12.2. These slides are typically displayed before a session starts as people enter the room. They should clearly display the title of the presentation, the name of the authors and, in most cases, the institutions with which the authors are affiliated. Institutional or sponsor logos are sometimes included as well. These slides should be clean and clear with little distraction.

Content slides convey single figures, such as the charts in Figures 12.3 and 12.4. These slides should contain a caption that identifies what that slide is about along with the actual figure, picture, or quote. Comparison slides are similar but are used to present two figures, lists, or other data.

Figure 12.5, for example, shows the results of a hypothetical study on public knowledge of diabetes. The slide allows the author to clearly lay out what she learned was common knowledge among the population and what, by contrast, was not well known. An advantage to most slideshow software is that the presenter can control what elements of each slide appear, in what order, and at

Figure 12.5 A PowerPoint text comparison slide.

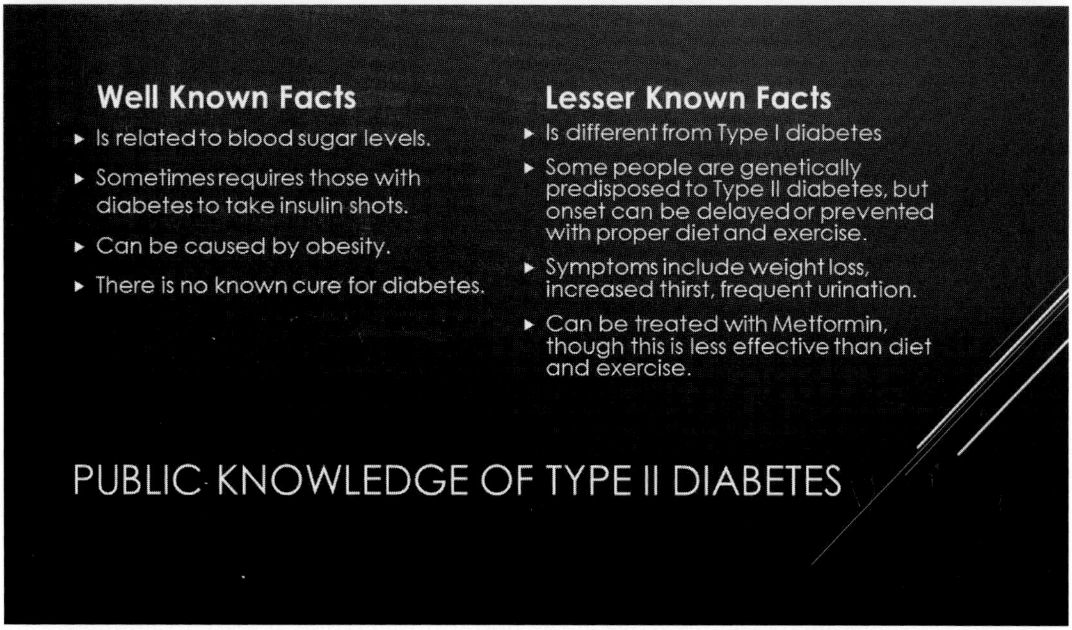

Well Known Facts
- Is related to blood sugar levels.
- Sometimes requires those with diabetes to take insulin shots.
- Can be caused by obesity.
- There is no known cure for diabetes.

Lesser Known Facts
- Is different from Type I diabetes
- Some people are genetically predisposed to Type II diabetes, but onset can be delayed or prevented with proper diet and exercise.
- Symptoms include weight loss, increased thirst, frequent urination.
- Can be treated with Metformin, though this is less effective than diet and exercise.

PUBLIC KNOWLEDGE OF TYPE II DIABETES

what time. In this case, for example, the slide could begin with only the caption and two headings, and then each bullet point could be revealed individually as the presenter worked her way through the demonstration using the animation feature built into many programs.

While a wide range of slide types are available, a degree of minimalism can be highly effective when creating an overall presentation. Limiting the total number of slides by including only those that are necessary and reducing unnecessary text on each slide can be beneficial. The researcher will be speaking about the slides, so it is not necessary to have everything visually displayed; avoid reading slides verbatim and instead use them to support the overall presentation.

There are also some instances when paper presentations must be given without the use of technology. In these cases, it is more important than ever for researchers to commit as much of the presentation as possible to memory so they can make eye contact with the audience during their presentation and demonstrate engagement while staying on topic and avoiding tangents. We recommend printing the entire presentation (either in outline form or the full text) in an easily readable font size and rehearsing it several times before the event so the researcher needs to refer to the script only a few times throughout the presentation. Distribute to audience members any necessary handouts with materials (data samples, figures, etc.) for reference.

Poster Presentations

After paper presentations, perhaps the second-most common type of conference session is a poster presentation. As the name implies, researchers at these sessions create and display large posters that summarize their research. Poster sessions can be dynamic and interactive or dull and forgettable, based not just on the posters themselves but also on how the researchers engage with others during the session.

In most cases, poster sessions take place in ballrooms or other large spaces where dozens of presenters share their work simultaneously. Researchers are usually assigned a spot in which to hang their posters; the size of the poster is generally prescribed by conference organizers in advance to ensure uniformity and to make certain everyone has enough space. A common poster size is four feet by six feet, though researchers should always adhere to the rules of the conference they attend.

Presenters should arrive at the poster presentation at least 15 minutes in advance of the session to set up their display unless the conference dictates otherwise, and should plan to remain at their station throughout the entire event and perhaps up to 15 minutes after it officially concludes. Posters should be set up precisely where indicated, and the area around them should be kept clean (researchers should avoid having bags, coats, or other miscellaneous objects in their space in order to have a clean showroom).

While many attendees will peruse the posters silently, we strongly encourage presenters to proactively engage with viewers. It is appropriate for a researcher to ask someone who has stopped to examine her poster if he has any questions about it, and to give a brief description of all elements of the poster such as the major findings of the research. She should also be prepared to answer detailed questions, because some audience members might be conversant in the topic and want to engage in an extended conversation about the study. In this way poster sessions present excellent opportunities for networking. Know that not all audience members will be comfortable directing questions to presenters, so presenters should take the initiative to begin conversations, when appropriate, and have plenty of summary handouts to distribute and business cards ready to exchange.

The AERA provides detailed requirements for presenters at its conferences. We quote portions of these guidelines here since they effectively cover the most salient points:

> A sign containing the paper title and the authors' name and affiliations should appear at the top of the poster. . . . Figures and tables should be kept as simple as possible. . . . A brief large type heading of no more than one or two lines should be provided above each illustration, with more detailed information added in smaller type beneath the illustration.

> A copy of your abstract . . . should be placed in the upper left portion of the poster, with a conclusion in the lower right hand corner. Although there is considerable room for flexibility, it is often useful to have panels indicating the aims of the research, [and] the methods and subjects involved. . . .

> When working on the arrangement of your display on the poster, be aware that it is preferable to align materials in columns rather than rows. (AERA, 2016, n.p.)

For more information and to view sample posters, visit the AERA Web site listed in the resources section at the end of this chapter.

Dramatic/Staged Readings

As discussed in Chapter 11, data from qualitative studies can be written up in a number of arts-based forms such as drama and poetry. Various conferences and venues are becoming more open to these types of presentations, though researchers should always check with conference organizers to be sure their approach is appropriate. When arts-based presentations are of high quality, this can lead to exciting work that draws in audiences and presents data in an evocative manner. Below we share some brief advice for presenting dramatic/staged readings.

Well-written scripts consist both of the text that is spoken as well as stage directions written in italics. We recommend that the group of performers/ presenters first rehearse the reading exactly as written (e.g., standing up and sitting down when the stage directions say to do so, directing lines either at the audience or at other performers as indicated). After this read-through, assess what went well and what didn't, and make adjustments as necessary. If possible, ask a third party to watch the reading rehearsal and then share her thoughts; this allows researchers to learn how their work is coming across to audience members, which can be difficult to ascertain from inside the action.

Figure 12.6 shows the ending of a staged reading written by this book's authors and their collaborators that considered how adult participants' lives were influenced by their high school theatre and speech experiences. As indicated, the performers are seated for their first lines, then stand as they describe the positive contributions of theatre, become more emphatic toward the end through italicized words, and ultimately all stand looking at just one character/researcher for the final moment. The original script did not include all of the elements, such as the final moment; these elements were worked out in rehearsal. As such, it is wise to plan for at least three to five rehearsals with the entire cast of researchers who will be reading/performing.

Figure 12.6 A scene from a research-based reader's theatre script.

SCENE 7	
ALL:	Closure
MATT:	Call Center Manager, Class of 2004: "I can sum up theatre's impact on my life as making me a leader, refining my work ethic, and creating lifelong friendships. So many of the friends I still talk to, including my best friend, I met through high school theatre. The bonds of friendship built in theatre – through the hard work and emotional discoveries – cannot be found in other activities."

Figure 12.6 (Continued)

ANGIE: History and Business Management Major, Class of 2003: "I appreciated the limitless possibilities I had with theatre, and although I never pursued it further with my education, I loved doing the work and being a part of an ensemble. It's unforgettable."

LAURA: Data analysis suggests that quality high school speech and theatre programming develops in most young people during adolescence and through adulthood – regardless of future occupation – such things as:

MATT: *(stands)* increased self-confidence;

ANGIE: *(stands)* collaborative teamwork, problem-solving, and leadership skills;

JOHNNY: *(stands)* public speaking, communication skills, and presentations of self;

LAURA: *(stands)* pragmatic work ethics such as goal setting, time management, and meeting deadlines;

MATT: heightened historic, cultural, and social awareness;

ANGIE: empathy and emotional intelligence;

JOHNNY: identity, values systems, and a sense of personal significance;

LAURA: lifelong friendships;

MATT: and artistic living and patronage.

JOHNNY: Overall, theatre and speech experiences, according to survey respondent testimony:

LAURA: empower one to *think and function improvisationally* in dynamic and ever-changing contexts;

MATT: deepen and accelerate development of an individual's *emotional and social intelligences*;

ANGIE: and expand one's verbal and nonverbal *communicative dexterity* in various presentational modes.

*(**LAURA**, **ANGIE**, and **MATT** look at **JOHNNY** for the final testimony)*

JOHNNY: Internet Strategy Consultant, Class of 1999: "I have a measure of confidence and composure that would not exist were it not for speech. I wouldn't have the same set of job skills and abilities. I wouldn't have had the same influences that created my political ideologies and many of my individual beliefs. I believe that my participation in speech and theatre in high school has influenced who I am as an adult more than any other single influence in my entire life."

Source: McCammon et al. (2012b); www.informaworld.com.

Presenting Data Effectively

In this section we discuss how to create compelling, appropriate, and informative images that can be used in slideshows for a paper presentation, included on posters, or otherwise be shared at a conference session. As discussed in Chapters 2–5, a variety of empirical materials can serve qualitative and mixed-methods studies. In this section we avoid demonstrating primarily quantitative data representations such as scatterplots and histograms. Instead, we offer advice on some less common but highly effective visuals.

Ground plans

One of the first types of data discussed in Chapter 2 was a ground plan of an elementary school visual art classroom (see Figure 2.5). While the hand-drawn plan could be helpful to a researcher as she analyzed it alongside other data, it does not have the polished look she would want if she decided to share it in a slide for a presentation. Fortunately, there are numerous digital tools she can use to develop a more professional look, and many of these are free. Easy-to-learn software products such as SketchUp (sketchup.com) or Room Arranger (roomarranger.com) are fairly intuitive, and many researchers would be able to start using them without formal training.

Figure 12.7 replicates the original hand-drawn ground plan from a bird's-eye view, while Figure 12.8 is a three-dimensional view of the classroom. There are advantages to both approaches. For example, although the two-dimensional image makes it easier to view the relative distance between furnishings, the three-dimensional view shows the walls and gives viewers greater insight into what the teacher included in her room.

Word clouds

One method for examining the frequency with which certain key terms appear in qualitative data is to create a word cloud. These images depict words, often in a scattered array, that appear in the data corpus and indicate the regularity of their appearance by size. Terms that appear often are larger, while words mentioned only a few times are smaller. Word clouds offer a fast way to give audiences a holistic view of key terms in a study, and can be particularly effective in poster sessions or other times when researchers have little time to draw the attention of audience members. The word cloud in Figure 12.9 draws on data from a study that Omasta and Brandley (2016) conducted in which they asked high school

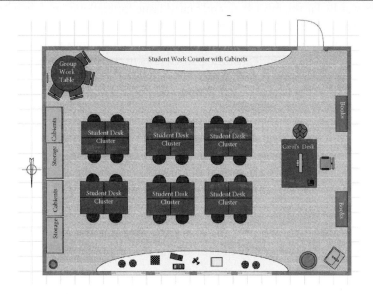

Figure 12.7 A Room Arranger 2D bird's-eye ground plan view of a classroom.

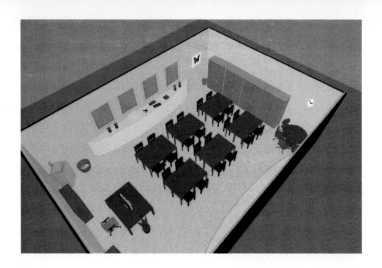

Figure 12.8 A Room Arranger 3D ground plan view of a classroom.

students what social issues they thought should be addressed in secondary school theatre programs.

Bullying was by far the most frequently cited issue for exploration, followed by topics such as sexual identity, prejudice/discrimination, and acceptance/diversity. Without reading a lengthy paper or even consulting a graph, it becomes evident in just a few seconds that the participants in the study seemed to believe theatre needed to address issues of equity and power. A number of free word cloud applications such as Wordle (wordle.net), TagCrowd (tagcrowd.com), and WordItOut (worditout.com) are available online.

It is important to use word clouds (or any visual tool) only when appropriate. For example, in this study the word cloud represented views raised by many people, but if a word cloud were created based on a single interview transcript it might misrepresent what was important. For example, a participant might have used a highly significant word only once, but the word and its conceptual magnitude would be lost in the word cloud array. Researchers should always select their tools carefully for both gathering and representing data.

Photos and videos

When selecting photographs, we recommend researchers limit themselves to only those that are necessary to advance the research narrative. Too many

Figure 12.9 A word cloud of term frequencies.

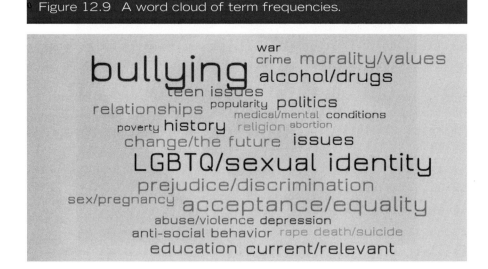

photos can distract audience members, whose attention will constantly be drawn away from the speaker and to the projection screen every time an image changes. We recommend a simple approach, with the image made as large as possible (so people farthest from the screen can see it) with a clear, summative caption. Figure 12.10 presents a sample slide from a case study about a man living without a home, illustrating the dog who followed him in outdoor environments.

Many slideshow programs such as PowerPoint also allow researchers to embed video into a presentation, and we recommend the same guidelines here: include only what is necessary and keep the display simple. We also recommend that videos be limited to the shortest length possible; if 5 minutes of a 15-minute presentation are spent watching a video, the researcher has only 10 minutes left for description, analysis, and other important presentation components.

Diagrams/models

Software such as Microsoft Word, PowerPoint, and Cmap (cmap.ihmc.us/) can be used to create basic yet professional looking diagrams for presentation and publication. CAQDAS software (see Chapter 10) can

Figure 12.10   A PowerPoint photograph slide.

JOHN'S DOG, CHESTER

create more-sophisticated models, particularly when the number of categories and interaction patterns are intricately complex. Figure 12.11, drawn with NVivo software (qsrinternational.com), illustrates the numerous interactions between and among qualitative factors that contribute to lifelong confidence from participation in high school speech and theatre experiences (McCammon et al., 2012a, p. 14). Selected CAQDAS programs can even generate proposed models and other visual data arrays for the researcher, based on the coding and descriptive information entered.

We believe there is nothing wrong with old-school methods such as paper and pencil for initial sketches of diagrams. In some cases, they can even be developed faster than computer modeling, and can serve as preliminary drafts before the final, finished renderings composed with software. Miles et al. (2014) advise that qualitative researchers *think display*, meaning to transform

Figure 12.11 A diagram of interacting factors, drawn with NVivo software.

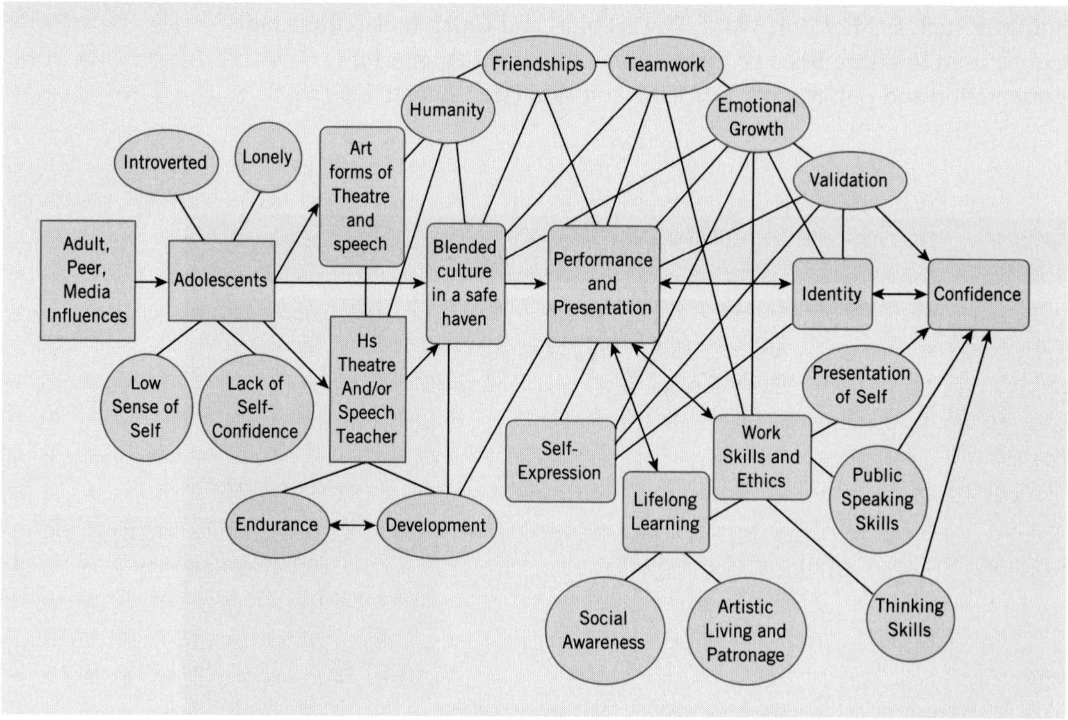

Source: McCammon et al. (2012a); www.informaworld.com.

the analysis into not just words, but also active images that illustrate the dynamics of social action investigated in a study. Such displays inform the analyst and communicate with audience members and readers the salient findings in an at-a-glance format.

Professional Networking

Researchers have several goals at professional conferences aside from presenting their own work. Scholars will often attend numerous sessions that other researchers present to stay up to date on the most current thinking in their field, and might visit an exhibition hall to review newly published work. Keen researchers always network during all activity at conferences. At its core, **networking** is simply developing relationships with fellow scholars, publishers, and others in the field. These relationships can result in future collaborations, professional opportunities, or even just colleagues to run ideas by.

Many professional conferences have systems in place for matching junior scholars to more established researchers, and include an option to sign up for this on their registration forms. Business meetings for researchers in certain areas are common and a great place to meet others interested in similar topics. Most organizations also have special interest groups for students, which are excellent for lateral networking (peers often have just as much to offer in the long run as senior scholars). Even when these opportunities are not available, such as at smaller conferences, taking a few moments to ask to speak to someone whose work is intriguing or related is usually a good idea, as is attending various social events such as receptions. It is in informal settings that a great deal of progress is made in academia.

We highly recommend ordering or self-printing business cards if you do not have them so you can swap contact information easily. Even in the 21st century, cards present a more polished image than a handwritten note or exchange of information logged in a smartphone. Researchers should also be careful what information they share. While most consider it acceptable to connect with new scholarly contacts on professional sites such as LinkedIn (linkedin.com) or ResearchGate (researchgate.net), the same is not true for socially driven sites such as Facebook. Overall, scholars should take every opportunity they can to build relationships both at conferences and beyond, staying in touch so that they can help each other in the future.

CLOSURE AND TRANSITION

This chapter reviewed several types of presentations, how to create and display images effectively, and professional networking at conferences. In essence, we discussed the routines, rituals, rules, roles, and relationships of researchers at conference gatherings. The next and final chapter brings closure to this book and proposes how to live an analytic life.

RESOURCES FOR PRESENTING QUALITATIVE RESEARCH

The following resources offer insights into specific strategies for designing and presenting data for the social sciences:

American Educational Research Association (AERA). (2016). *Presenter and Participant Information.* http://www.aera.net/EventsMeetings/AnnualMeeting/PresenterandParticipantInformation/tabid/16170/Default.aspx

Becker, Lucinda. (2014). *Presenting Your Research: Conferences, Symposiums, Poster Presentations and Beyond.* London: Sage.

Browner, Warren S. (2012). *Publishing & Presenting Clinical Research.* Philadelphia, PA: Lippincott Williams & Wilkins.

Evergreen, Stephanie D. H. (2014). *Presenting Data Effectively: Communicating Your Findings for Maximum Impact.* Thousand Oaks, CA: Sage.

Reynolds, Farr. (2011). *Presentation Zen: Simple Ideas on Presentation Design and Delivery,* 2nd edition. Berkeley, CA: New Riders.

Thody, Angela. (2006). *Writing & Presenting Research.* London: Sage.

ANALYTIC EXERCISES FOR PRESENTATIONS

1. Identify qualitative research studies (published or in progress) and identify what type of conference format (e.g., poster session, paper session, dramatic/staged reading) would be most effective for sharing the studies' findings. Explain your reasoning.

2. Draw by hand a ground plan of a space in which you might conduct participant observation. Next, use a software program to create a polished version of the ground plan that would be suitable for a presentation.

3. Quantify descriptive data from an existing or new mixed-methods study. Create a figure (e.g., chart, graphic) that cogently, concisely, and engagingly displays the data.

4. Locate online any professional/academic associations and their upcoming conferences related to your discipline or field of study. Review their procedures for paper/poster submissions. As opportunities permit, consider proposing a single-authored presentation as a student scholar, or as a copresenter with peers or a faculty mentor.

Introduction

We have presented in Chapters 1 through 12 an introduction to qualitative research methods that we hope has informed and guided readers. We emphasized analysis as a through-line because it is one of the most elusive components of qualitative inquiry for newcomers to the subject. Hopefully students have gained some knowledge along the way about practical approaches not just to collecting but also to analyzing data in their myriad forms.

Like all things, including life, there's still much to learn about qualitative research. This chapter provides additional information about resources for professional development. We also encourage students to seek guidance from academic specialists in their disciplines on materials and associations related to their fields of study.

Learning More About Qualitative Research

There are so many publications, associations, and online resources available for qualitative researchers that it is virtually impossible to stay informed of them all. We offer below just a very few of these groups and their Internet addresses to provide a starting point for exploration.

Key book and journal publishers

Several major academic and textbook publishers carry a line of qualitative research methods titles in various formats and several book-length works of anthropological, educational, and

Learning Objectives

After reading and reviewing this chapter, researchers should be able to

1. Survey selected resources for qualitative researchers, and

2. Devise a professional development trajectory as a qualitative researcher.

sociological studies. All of the publishers can be accessed online, and many of them exhibit at national and international conferences. We recommend subscribing to their mailing lists to stay informed of new and forthcoming titles, discounts, and catalogs. Just a few publishing houses (with their U.S. Internet addresses) to explore are:

- SAGE Publishing: sagepub.com
- AltaMira Press: rowman.com/Altamira
- Guilford Press: guilford.com
- Left Coast Press and Routledge: routledge.com
- Oxford University Press: oup.com

Several of these houses along with others publish a series of journals dedicated to qualitative research within multiple disciplines. Access their sites and enter the word *qualitative* as a keyword for a search to access relevant titles. Many journals will e-mail subscribers the table of contents of their latest issues as they become available online or in print. Researchers can also customize their alerts by entering keywords or requesting notices of when a particular article gets cited in another future work. College/university libraries will most likely hold institutional subscriptions to many of the key journals in qualitative inquiry. A few publishing houses we recommend follow:

- SAGE Journals: online.sagepub.com
- Elsevier: elsevier.com/journals/title/a
- Emerald Group Publishing: emeraldgrouppublishing.com/journals
- Springer: springer.com/gp/products/journals
- Taylor & Francis: tandf.co.uk/journals
- Wiley Online Library: onlinelibrary.wiley.com

Key Internet resources

Several qualitative research resources are available exclusively online. They offer services ranging from information to discussion forums, as well as links to other related sites. Google Scholar (scholar.google.com) is just one of several sites that connects researchers to a wealth of academic materials, and YouTube (youtube.com) provides instructional videos on many qualitative topics. Just a sample listing of sites includes the following:

- SAGE Publishing: methodspace.com, sageresearchmethods.com, socialsciencespace.com

- Forum: Qualitative Social Research: qualitative-research.net/index.php/fqs

- Online QDA: onlineqda.hud.ac.uk

- Text Analysis Info: textanalysis.info

- The Weekly Qualitative Report: tqr.nova.edu

Subscriptions to electronic newsletters and LISTSERVs® will inform its members of topics ranging from calls for papers to job opportunities.

Key organizations and conferences

Disciplinary professional associations (e.g., American Educational Research Association, British Psychological Society, American Anthropological Association) sponsor regular conferences, **webinars**, and professional development workshops with special interest group presentations in qualitative research. Attendance at these events provides networking opportunities with colleagues as well as forums to present one's own research. Just a few organizations with a focus on qualitative inquiry include:

- International Congress of Qualitative Inquiry at the University of Illinois, Champaign-Urbana: icqi.org

- Centre for Qualitative Research at Bournemouth University's School of Health and Social Care, UK: research.bournemouth.ac.uk/centre/centre-for-qualitative-research

- International Institute of Qualitative Methodology at the University of Alberta, Edmonton: iiqm.ualberta.ca

- The Qualitative Report of Nova Southeastern University: nsuworks.nova.edu/tqrc/

Selected universities in the United States offer graduate programs and certificates focusing on interdisciplinary qualitative research methods through online, hybrid, and on-campus courses:

- The University of Georgia: https://coe.uga.edu/academics/non-degree/certificates/qualitative-research

- Nova Southeastern University: tqr.nova.edu/graduate-certificate/
- Kansas State University: coe.k-state.edu/academics/graduate/certificates/qualitative-research.html

Many colleges/universities and professional associations offer travel grants, awards, and other forms of support for students and emerging scholars. Application to these opportunities might result in funding or honors, and might also familiarize an association's membership with a researcher and her work.

On Professional Development

The average lifetime is simply not long enough to learn everything there is to know about qualitative research. We hope that students' academic and professional experiences permit them to read from the voluminous amounts of material available. We also hope that time and resources permit attendance at professional gatherings of like-minded scholars to learn firsthand from colleagues' presentations. Qualitative researchers are a culture unto themselves where they can find good friends and energizing communities of interest.

We caution, however, that researchers not become too enamored with just one genre of qualitative inquiry at the beginning of their careers. It is the purpose of the inquiry and its related research questions that suggest which methodology is most suitable, and not just one's knowledge of or comfort level with a particular approach. We believe it is worthwhile to remain malleable and eclectic and, as opportunities permit, to conduct various kinds of research studies with various kinds of research methodologies to learn about as many of them as possible.

Analysis as a Lens, Filter, and Angle on Life

Both coauthors have grown tremendously as researchers from what we humbly propose as our strong work ethic. We read a lot and we write a lot. As artists we think deeply about life and try to understand its purpose, significance, and meaning. We facetiously refer to ourselves as "research geeks," using method as a way to analyze the messy mysteries of being human. Sometimes we get the answers, sometimes we don't; but we keep trying nevertheless.

We hate unanswered questions and we hate unresolved problems. Our lenses, filters, and angles on life seem always attuned to figuring out how and why things are as they are, and what can be done to make things better. We remain vigilant to how people act, react, and interact in their roles and relationships as they experience their daily routines and rituals, framed within socialized rules. Among the overwhelming details of life, we look for patterns and unity to understand what it all means. Sometimes we get it right, sometimes we get it wrong, but we never stop trying.

It's not our place to tell readers how to lead their lives, but it is our responsibility to tell students to live their lives with insatiable curiosity. Everyone should analyze lives thoroughly—their own and others—not with clinical detachment, but with emotional investment. Be afraid and brave, angry and joyous, anxious and calm, confused and at peace. Like life, answers through qualitative research emerge from hard work, deep reflection, sometimes a bit of luck, and always through interaction with a variety of people.

CLOSURE

No single textbook about qualitative inquiry can possibly cover everything necessary for a beginning researcher to know. Nevertheless, we hope that this book has provided a strong foundation for a scholar's current and future growth in multiple disciplines. We are still walking on our own journeys and learning more about the world each day. We hope that readers, too, will make personal insights, discoveries, and revelations about themselves and their fellow human beings as life is analyzed in its intricate complexity.

RESOURCES FOR LEADING AN ANALYTIC LIFE

The following resources will offer you additional guidance for qualitative research in various disciplines:

Chirkov, Varlery. (2016). *Fundamentals of Research on Culture and Psychology: Theory and Methods.* New York: Routledge.

Denzin, Norman K., and Yvonna S. Lincoln, eds. (2011). *The SAGE Handbook of Qualitative Research,* 4th edition. Thousand Oaks, CA: Sage.

Given, Lisa M., ed. (2008). *The SAGE Encyclopedia of Qualitative Research Methods.* Thousand Oaks, CA: Sage.

Leavy, Patricia, ed. (2014). *The Oxford Handbook of Qualitative Research.* New York: Oxford University Press.

ANALYTIC EXERCISES
FOR LEADING AN ANALYTIC LIFE

1. Access the Web page of a book publisher of qualitative research methods titles. Browse through its catalog and create a personal wish list of future purchases.

2. Access the Web pages for a general journal title for qualitative research methods and a journal title dedicated to your discipline of study. Subscribe to their alerts for information about forthcoming issues.

3. Access the Web page of a professional association dedicated to qualitative research. Review its contents with a focus on its forthcoming gathering and procedures for submitting a proposal for a paper, session, poster, and so on.

4. Brainstorm a list of possible research topics, questions, problems, issues, and so on, that you would like to investigate in the future.

5. In your own words, define "qualitative research," "analyzing," and "life."

APPENDIX

Three Representative Articles in Qualitative Research

Introduction

We include as an Appendix three articles from SAGE Publications journals that illustrate a variety of qualitative research methodologies and analytic approaches to data. These articles are also available from the book's companion Web site: study.sagepub.com/saldanaomasta.

First, Michael V. Angrosino's classic case study, "On the Bus With Vonnie Lee: Explorations in Life History and Metaphor," was published in 1994 by the *Journal of Contemporary Ethnography*. The study focuses on a developmentally disabled young man's upbringing, integration into the work force, and his curious love for city bus transportation. Some of the terminology of the time (e.g., "mental retardation") seems outdated and politically incorrect decades later, but Angrosino's masterful and elegant writing demonstrates how the individual case study can be profiled through poignant vignettes and revealing excerpts from participant observation field notes and interview transcripts. His analysis in the "Discussion" section ventures deeply into interpretive writing by examining case study method and how the life of one person can be generalized to broader contexts.

The second article is "Nightmares, Demons, and Slaves: Exploring the Painful Metaphors of Workplace Bullying," coauthored by Sarah J. Tracy, Pamela Lutgen-Sandvik, and Jess K. Alberts. This intriguing 2006 *Management Communication Quarterly* article first explains the constituent elements of bullying and their long-term emotional effects on its victims. The researchers conducted interviews and focus groups to solicit participant stories, and applied a unique metaphor analysis to extract insightful meanings of how victims conceptualized themselves, their bullies, and their experiences. This piece tends to resonate powerfully among its readers who most likely have their own painful memories of being bullied in one form or another throughout their lives.

The third article showcases Quaylan Allen's "'They Think Minority Means Lesser Than': Black Middle-Class Sons and Fathers Resisting Microaggressions in the School," a 2012 *Urban Education* piece. Allen incorporates critical race theory "to examine how the daily and sometimes subtle experiences of racism adversely affect the schooling opportunities for Black middle-class men." Interviews, participant observation, documents, and other data collection methods were employed to rigorously analyze his participants' experiences. He presents a strong evidentiary warrant to demonstrate how teacher and peer assumptions of intelligence and deviance, and differential treatment, can negatively affect Black youth's identity and educational achievement. This is a richly designed and analyzed piece of scholarship that examines the intricate interrelationships among race, class, gender, and age in the context of schooling.

Of course, three articles represent just a very small fraction of the qualitative research literature and its range of methodologies and writing styles. We would include many more if space permitted us. Refer to some of the articles we profile in Chapters 6 and 11 for additional readings from a broad spectrum of disciplines.

On the Bus With Vonnie Lee:
Explorations in Life History and Metaphor

MICHAEL V. ANGROSINO

This article discusses the use of life history as a method of ethnographic research among stigmatized, unempowered people. The author describes and analyzes the process of eliciting the life history of a man with mental retardation. To combine life history interviewing with the detailed observation of behavior in a naturalistic setting is typical of the ethnographic tradition; interviews with people from marginalized social groups (particularly those who are considered mentally "disabled") are, however, often decontextualized and conducted in quasi-clinical settings that emphasize the retrospective reconstruction of the life. By treating a person with mental retardation as a contextualized participant in a world outside the clinical setting and by eliciting the life narrative in the course of following that person as he attempts to make sense of life outside the institution, it is possible to clarify the dynamic in the formation of a metaphor of personal identity. This technique might not be appropriate for all persons with mental disability, but when it *can* be used, it helps to demonstrate the proposition that mental retardation is not a monolithic condition whose victims are distinguished by arbitrary gradations of standardized test scores. Rather, it is only one of many factors that figure into a person's strategy for coping with the world.

A LIFE IN PROCESS

VONNIE LEE

Vonnie Lee Hargrett celebrated his 29th birthday while I was writing this article in the summer of 1993 in the Florida city to which his parents had migrated from a rural part of the state. The family was, in Vonnie Lee's own words, "poor White trash—real crackers." His father was mostly absent, supposedly shuttling around Florida, Georgia, and Alabama seeking work; if he ever did work ("Not like I even once believed he did," Vonnie Lee told me) he never sent any money home, and he disappeared for good ("real good," Vonnie Lee smirked) about 8 years ago. His mother is an alcoholic who has, over the course of the years, taken up with countless men, most of whom were physically abusive to everyone in the family. Several of them were apparently encouraged in their sexual abuse of Vonnie Lee's two sisters; at least two of them also sexually abused Vonnie Lee.

JOURNAL OF CONTEMPORARY ETHNOGRAPHY, Vol. 23, No. 1, April 1994, 14–28

The children were sent to school on a come-and-go basis as the mother moved from place to place around town with her different boyfriends. All three children developed serious learning deficits, although only Vonnie Lee seems to have been tagged by a counselor as mentally retarded. He was never in one school long enough to benefit from any special education programs, however, and he stopped going to school altogether by the time he was 12 years old.

During his teen years he lived mostly on the streets in the company of an older man, Lucian, who made a living by "loaning" Vonnie Lee to other men on the street. Vonnie Lee often says, "Lucian, he's like the only real father I ever had—whatever he had he shared with me. I'd-a done anything for him. *Anything."*

Lucian was found one morning beaten to death in an empty lot. Vonnie Lee, who had been with one of Lucian's clients that night, discovered the body upon his return to their campsite. The police found him, sobbing and gesturing wildly over the body, and took him into custody. He was held briefly on suspicion of murder, but there was no hard evidence linking him to the crime and he was never charged. His disorderly behavior, however, was sufficient to have him "Baker Acted" (involuntarily committed for psychiatric observation under the provisions of the Florida Mental Health Act). He spent the next few years in and out of psychiatric facilities, developing the remarkable—and, to any number of clinicians, the thoroughly frustrating—capacity to turn into the most level-headed, socially appropriate, even intelligent young gentleman after just a short time in treatment. He would be released, make his way back to the streets, survive quite well for a time, then "break up" (a term he explicitly and consistently prefers to "break down") and be carted off to jail or the hospital.

Vonnie Lee was finally remanded to Opportunity House (OH), an agency designed for the habilitation of adults with the dual diagnosis of mental retardation and psychiatric disorder; most of them also have criminal records. There he made sustained academic, social, and vocational progress, and in June 1992 he was deemed ready for "supervised independent living."

One of the key steps in preparing OH clients for independent living is to teach them to use the public transportation system. I had been a member of OH's Board of Directors since 1982 (a position I was asked to fill as a result of my long-term research involvement with the program) and had also been a frequent volunteer classroom tutor. I was, however, never directly involved with the "social skills habilitation" aspect of the program until I was asked to fill in for an ailing staff member who was supposed to show Vonnie Lee the bus route from his new apartment to the warehouse where he was to begin working. I was not entirely pleased with the prospect: Our city, despite its substantial size and pretensions to urban greatness, has a notoriously inadequate bus system, and I knew that even the relatively simple trip from Vonnie Lee's apartment to his work site involved several transfers and could mean long, hot waits at unshaded bus stops.

VONNIE LEE AND ME

I first met Vonnie Lee shortly after his arrival at OH in 1990. The teacher asked me to help him with his reading assignment: a paragraph about some children taking a walk with their dog. (The fact that reading materials for adults with limited reading ability are almost always about children or about topics that would typically engage the imaginations of children is a subtle but nonetheless painful insult that merits at least a parenthetical complaint here.) Vonnie Lee did not have any particular difficulty reading all the words, but he was having trouble with comprehension. After reading the paragraph, he was unable to answer questions requiring recall and synthesis of information. He seemed more depressed than angry over his failure, and so I said, "Let's put the book away for a minute. Why don't you tell me about a time you remember when *you* took a walk." My intention was to allow him to refocus on the elements constituting a simple narrative in his own words instead of on the specific details about the unfamiliar Tom, Sally, and Spot. Instead, he just said, with inexpressible and totally unexpected sadness, "Yeah. Take a walk. Story of my life." I little realized the full import of his remark but did make a mental note to see if he would at some later time be amenable to telling me the "story of my life" along with the other OH clients among whom I was conducting life history research.

We eventually got around to taping some conversations that would lead to the production of his autobiography, but I was frankly stumped. The problem was not that his discourse was jumbled; in fact, it proceeded in the most nearly linear, chronological sequence of any of the stories I worked on at OH. The problem was that even after numerous sessions I could form no clear sense of who or what Vonnie Lee Hargrett thought he was. Was Vonnie Lee perhaps a person whose mental disorder was—despite his surface demeanor of reasonable intelligence and even a sense of humor—so profound that he couldn't be fitted into my emergent analytical scheme?

Like my other OH life history collaborators, Vonnie Lee worked in an anecdotal style of narrative. That is, rather than say, for example, "I was born in this city. I lived with my mother and father. I remember the house we lived in," he would say, "When I was a real little kid. Yeah. Let me tell you about that." And he would go on to relate an encapsulated anecdote that was meant to represent his life as a "real little kid." Then he would go on and say, "So then I got a little older. Yeah. Here's what it was." And he would launch into another encapsulated story. My problem, though, was that in Vonnie Lee's case the stories were almost devoid of characters, except in marginal scene-setting roles, and of plot, even of the most attenuated type. For example:

> So Hank [one of his mother's boyfriends] says, "Let's you and me go see Ronnie" [a dealer in stolen auto parts for whom Hank sometimes worked]. So we're on the bus. It starts over there next to the Mall and it cuts across and then it stops on the corner where it's that hospital. It stopped there a good, long while, you know. Then it goes on down 22nd Street. Past the Majik Mart. Past that gas station with the big, yellow thing out front . . .

And on and on the story would go, except that it was essentially a description of the bus route. Vonnie Lee seemed to have a photographic memory of every convenience store, gas station, apartment complex, newspaper machine, and frontyard basketball hoop along the way. But in the process he completely lost the point (or what I assumed was the point). There was no word about his reaction to all these sights nor any mention of what Hank was doing. Indeed, they never got to Ronnie's place—the anecdote ended when they got off the bus in front of a Salvation Army thrift shop, apparently several blocks from their destination. When I asked him what happened when they got there, he shrugged and said, "Oh, nothing." I sensed that he wasn't trying to cover anything up (he had already made it perfectly clear that Hank was a thief), and I felt certain that he wasn't just goofing around. He truly believed that the point of the story was the bus ride, not the destination. Vonnie Lee was cooperative in responding to direct questions aimed, on my part, at identifying key players in his life and the events that linked them together. But on his own initiative, he was inclined only to offer what he seemed to feel were these deeply revelatory bus itineraries.

BUS TRIP

On the day I picked up Vonnie Lee at OH to show him the bus routes, we drove first to his new apartment complex. I parked my car and we walked up to the corner bus stop. Vonnie Lee was visibly excited, more animated and seemingly more happy than I had ever seen him. It was a crushingly hot Florida summer day and thunderstorms threatened, but he seemed so elated that my own spirits were lifted. "I bet you're really excited about having your own place," I ventured (violating the first rule of life history interviewing by putting words into the mouth of an informant). "Nah," he replied, "I like the streets to live on—but they won't let me or else I go back to lockup." Nothing daunted, I went on, "But it must be great to have a real job." "In that old dump? Hell no!" he retorted. So what *was* he so happy about? It dawned on me that the bus itself was the object of his joy, as I watched him bounce into the vehicle when it finally lumbered to a stop. The symbol of the city's bus line is a large red heart, and Vonnie Lee made a dash for a seat directly under a poster bearing that logo; from time to time during the ride, he would reach up and touch it lovingly.

Vonnie Lee seemed to be very familiar with the route we were taking. "Yeah, I walked it about 13 million times," he said with contempt. But now as we sat on the nearly empty bus he kept swiveling from one side to the other calling out local landmarks with great glee. At one point, we passed an elderly lady laboriously dragging several large plastic supermarket bags across the street. "I know her type," he sneered. "Uses up every last damn dime she got and she can't ride the bus back home. Drags her ass around like some goddam retard."

We reached the junction where we needed to transfer. "Oh, *here's* where I do it!" Vonnie Lee shouted ecstatically. "I *love* this street, but I never get a chance to come here no more!" The street in question is one of the city's shabbiest, lined with unpleasant-looking bars, secondhand clothing stores, and unkempt, garagelike structures from which used furniture, carpeting "seconds," rebuilt appliances, and sundry "recyclables" are delivered. The place where Vonnie Lee was to work was on a street like this one but which required a further transfer to reach; he was, I had to admit, quite right in characterizing such a place as an "old dump," but his mood betrayed not the slightest hint of regret.

We waited for a very long time at the transfer stop. Two heavily made up young women were lolling in front of one of the bars but were making no real attempt to secure business—they seemed stunned by the heat and shook their heads wearily at the spectacle of Vonnie Lee jumping up and down to catch a glimpse of the approaching bus. When it came at last, it was more crowded than the first had been, and Vonnie Lee's face clouded briefly when he saw that the favored seat under the heart was already taken. He resigned himself to a less desirable place but kept turning his head toward the heart as if to reassure himself, even as he resumed his practice of announcing every building on the street. He was less familiar with this street than with the first, and his litany seemed to be serving the purpose of fixing the sights in his own mind as well as of enlightening me.

Vonnie Lee seemed sorry to get off when we reached our stop, but he brightened immediately when he saw the street down which our third and final lap would take us. It was a street very much like the second, although it led off to a part of town he hardly knew at all; the thrill of the new gave him added zest. It began to rain while we waited and waited for the third bus, and we found only modest shelter in the boarded-up doorway of what had once been a storefront church. Vonnie Lee's spirits didn't sag in the least, even when the bus arrived, packed full of damp and irritable riders. He managed to find a standing spot near enough the heart logo and immediately set about his recitation of the sights. Some of the people nearby looked a little annoyed, but no one said anything. The crowd was as thoroughly depressed and defeated as Vonnie Lee was giddy.

It bears mentioning that the city's buses are *very* slow. Not only do they run infrequently but once they do arrive they appear to obey an unstated mandate to stop at *every* marked stop, whether or not anyone wants to get on or off. As a result, the trip from the apartment to the warehouse, which might have taken at most 20 minutes by car, ended up consuming an hour and a half by bus. The other anomaly in the bus system that I had ample time to observe that day (and I had lived in the city for nearly two decades at that time without ever having ridden a city bus) was that all the riders (including my own wet and bedraggled self) looked like stereotyped versions of either very poor or mentally/physically disabled people. I came to realize that no bus route connected one "nice" part of town with another; all of them took off into and covered most of their distance within "bad" sections. (Since my trip with Vonnie Lee, the transit authority has added several routes connecting upscale residential neighborhoods with the downtown business and government districts, but they are all "express" runs that zoom right through the intervening "bad" spots.) It was clear that the bus system had been primarily designed for domestic workers going to and from the posh homes and business offices and for blue-collar workers traveling from low-rent districts to downscale factory zones. In many big cities, going to work by bus is a perfectly appropriate thing for even the most affluent of business people to do. But in our city, the bus is the very embodiment of stigma—the slow, inconvenient transport of the poor, the powerless, and the socially marginal.

When we reached our stop, literally in front of the plumbing supply warehouse where Vonnie Lee was to work, it began pouring again. We dashed inside where Vonnie Lee's supervisor, Mr. Washington, was very gracious in showing us around and then allowing us to wait out the storm. The warehouse was cramped and dingy, but it seemed to be doing a brisk business ("People are going to need toilets, even during a recession," Mr. Washington noted), and the supervisor and most of the other workmen showed a genuine interest in Vonnie Lee's welfare. (Several other OH clients had been employed there over the years; the owner of the business had a mentally retarded brother who died young, and he looked upon his employment program as a way of honoring his memory.) "I love it!" Vonnie Lee shouted as one of the other men took him through the back door to show him a tiny commissary where they could buy soft drinks and snacks.

"It's the bus he loves—coming here on the bus," Mr. Washington said to me when we were alone. I admitted that Vonnie Lee did seem to have had an unaccountably good time on the ride. "Yeah. I've seen it before. Ask him about it, why don't you?"

The return ride was a replay of the first; Vonnie Lee had already memorized all the new landmarks. "Why do you like the bus so much?" I asked at last—the question that had been obvious all day but had seemed too silly and irrational to bring up. And, as he always did when I put a direct question to him, he gave me a straightforward answer. He repeated his answer on tape later on, telling me,

> Like I always said, we was dirt-poor at home. Mama never had no car or nothing. Most of them guys was even more worthlesser than Daddy. Why that woman has a thing for big losers I'll never know! Now every once in a while one of 'em took me on the bus. And poor old Lucian—he didn't like to get on the bus because he said everybody looked at him funny but still we did it now and again just to show we *could*. I mean—it's only the lowdownest who can't *never* do it.

> Jeez! I'd walk a street and say, "If I was a bigshot, I'd be on the bus right now!" The bad thing—a man just can't ride one end of the street to another like he was some retard with no place to go. A man gotta go *somewheres* and I never knew how to get *anywheres* like from one to the other one. I nearly peed my pants when they told me I could learn—they never thought I could before now. I got kinda scared when they told me Ralph couldn't take me and you was gonna do it—I thought, "Hey, he don't really

work at OH. Maybe he don't know how and he'll screw me up." But then I figured you'd figure it out and then you'd show me.

THE MEANING OF THE BUS

It all became clear to me. The bus—to the "nice" people the symbol of poverty, the despised underside of the glittery urban lifestyle touted by the city's boosters—was for Vonnie Lee a potent symbol of empowerment. Coming from a family that was *too poor even to take the bus* was a humiliation that had scarred his young life. He spent his years grimly walking, walking, learning the details of the streets and yet yearning for the time when he could be chauffeured high above those streets in the style to which he felt himself entitled. For Vonnie Lee, the payoff for all his hard work in overcoming both his background and his numerous "break up" reversals was neither the apartment nor the job but the fact that he was finally deemed worthy to learn how to ride the bus between the two. So many of the OH clients with whom I spoke longed to see themselves in positions of power, and their dreams of driving fancy cars, while unrealistic, were at least recognizable ambitions. I had completely missed Vonnie Lee's ideal—because he saw escape and empowerment in the bus (something to which *anyone,* even a person with mental retardation, could reasonably aspire), I had ignored the fact that it *was* a dream for him and that it gave shape and meaning to his life.

I finally say why, when telling his life story without specific prompts, he did so in the form of bus routes. For Vonnie Lee, those rare rides were the stuff of which his dreams were made—they embodied his values, his aspirations, and even his self-image. My other informants' stories led me to conclude that they had developed stable self-images that survived all the vicissitudes of their lives. Vonnie Lee's self-image, on the other hand, was bound up not in who he was but in who he wanted to be: a man on a bus, going somewhere. Since his earlier rides had been dry runs, as it were, they didn't add up to a consistent pattern, and he went along as someone else's adjunct (and the someone else was, at best, only a temporarily significant other)—he never felt that they represented any sort of defined closure. As a result, he did not feel impelled to "finish" those stories, as the real finish—the point at which he was ready to believe himself to be someone—was in the future.

Mr. Washington had indeed seen a number of his charges who liked to ride the bus because it was so liberatingly different from the heavily supervised minivan that shuttled the OH clients around prior to their graduation. But Vonnie Lee's fixation on the bus went even further than the supervisor could have imagined. When we finally got back to OH, I took a careful look around Vonnie Lee's room as I helped him pack up some of his belongings. Taped to his mirror was an outline drawing of a heart; it had been cleanly scissored out of a coloring book about seasons and holidays that one of his "lower functioning" roommates was using in class. Vonnie Lee had carefully colored the big valentine with a neon-red marker. Before that day, I would have assumed that he was, like some of my other informants, pretending to have received at least one passionate proposal of marriage on Valentine's Day. But now I knew immediately that it was not a valentine at all but the closest thing he could find to the bus company logo.

DISCUSSION

Vonnie Lee's autobiography, and the story of my interaction with him, is part of a long-term research project whose methodology and conceptual framework were described in some detail in earlier writings (Angrosino 1989, 1992; Angrosino and Zagnoli 1992). That project was designed to demonstrate three points: that individual identity is conceptualized and communicated as much through the form as through the content of autobiographical material (Crocker 1977; Hankiss 1981; Howarth 1980; Olney 1972), that autobiographies are best interpreted as extended metaphors of self (Fitzgerald 1993; Norton 1989), and that even persons with conditions that interfere with their ability to construct conventionally coherent narratives nevertheless sustain self-images (Zetlin and Turner 1984) and can communicate those images to others of the same culture by using culturally recognizable metaphorical forms.

In earlier analyses based on this research, I relied essentially on literary theory as applied to autobiography to define "metaphor." In accordance with that view, I was less concerned with specific, expressive metaphors ("The house I grew up in was a toilet") than with the way in which an entire life was reconstructed in the narration around a master concept of self. The informants profiled in the other studies had adopted clearly defined social roles (the "blame attributer," the "tactical dependent," the "denier," the "passer") and told their stories in ways that marshaled rhetorical devices ("antithesis," "compensation," "allusion," "anecdote," "oratory," "dialogue") to buttress the presentation of that role. In so doing, the role became a dominating metaphor of the stigmatization experienced by the informants.

Although this perspective on metaphor was a useful framework for analyzing the stories of some informants who, in their various ways, perceived a continuity between their early experiences and their current lives, it was inadequate in Vonnie Lee's case. Although reasonably articulate about his past, Vonnie Lee is a person who adamantly refuses to live in the past; his orientation is so thoroughly toward the future that he resists characterizing himself in terms of what he has always been. Far from operating on the assumption that he is a product of his past (even if only in reaction to it), Vonnie Lee sees his life as beginning only when he makes a definitive break with that past. For Vonnie Lee, the past is not even prologue—it is, to all intents and purposes, irrelevant as a predictor of his future.

The dominating metaphor of Vonnie Lee's life, then, emerges not out of retrospective narrative but out of the actions he is currently taking to remake himself into his desired new image. For this reason, it is important not to limit the dialogue of discovery to retrospective interviews conducted in a time and place of their own. Rather, it is crucial to conduct what amounts to a personalized ethnography of this informant—to catch him in the act of self-creation, as it were. He does not use metaphor to symbolize the asserted continuities of his broken life as do the other informants; his metaphorical image is created in the actions that define his trajectory of "becoming."

For an ethnographer who works in an applied field (such as the formulation of policy for and the delivery of services to people with a defined disorder, such as mental retardation), this research demonstrates the benefits of the in-depth autobiographical interview methodology for establishing the human dimensions of mentally disordered persons, who are all too frequently described in terms of deviations from standardized norms. Vonnie Lee's story goes one step further: It demonstrates the desirability of contextualizing the autobiographical interview within the ongoing life experience of the subject rather than treating it as a retrospective review.

Such contextualization is, to be sure, an article of faith among anthropological ethnographers and is widely accepted by other social scientists working in the ethnographic tradition. It is, however, a conclusion that has rarely been applied to studies of "deviant," "stigmatized," or "marginalized" people.

There is a great deal of published material based on the life histories of people with mental retardation, but, as Whittemore, Langness, and Koegel (1986) point out in their critical survey of that literature, those materials are almost entirely lacking in any sense of an insider's perspective. Much of it is more focused on the experiences of caregivers, the assumption being that the person with retardation is unable to speak coherently on his or her own behalf. It is true that retarded people in clinical settings are interviewed with an eye to telling their life stories, but such accounts (which are rarely published) presuppose a clinically defined disorder and focus on the psychodynamics of the illness; the whole person is subsumed into the "disorder," and the interview itself is part of the process of correction and therapy.

My work is more closely allied with the tradition pioneered at the University of California (Los Angeles) by Edgerton and his colleagues in the "sociobehavioral" group, who have made it a practice to study the lives of their subjects in their entirety. "Because these lives change in response to various environmental demands, just as they develop in reaction to maturational changes, we emphasize process" (Edgerton 1984, 1–2) rather than retrospection; moreover, they do so by providing detailed descriptions of the communities where the subjects live so as to situate the life histories outside the strictly clinical milieu. Nevertheless, even this approach begins with the acceptance of clinically defined disorder, such that the contextualized life history serves mainly to illuminate the process of "adjustment" to a presumed mainstream norm.

My encounter with Vonnie Lee taught me that his worldview was not a failed approximation of how a "normal" person would cope, nor was it, when taken on its own terms, intrinsically disordered. His fixation on the bus is only "disordered" or an "attempt at adjustment" if we assume that the rest of us are not without our own idées fixes regarding the world and our place in it. Were we to suffer the misfortune of being labeled "retarded," would all of our ideas, attitudes, and practices stand up to scrutiny as being unimpeachably "normal"? Once we start looking for evidence of "disorder," then "disorder" is almost certainly what we find. If anything, Vonnie Lee's logic is more clearly worked out, and better integrated than that of more sophisticated people—his "retardation" may, indeed, lie in the way he has purified his obsession down to its basics, rather than veiling it in varieties of symbolic discourse as "normal" people do. Interviewing him in a way that arose out of a normal activity did not merely "contextualize" his disorder—it removed the emphasis on disorder altogether. Like a conventional anthropologist conducting participant observation in a community other than his or her own, I only began to make progress when I stopped thinking that there was something "exotic" in Vonnie Lee's approach to the world and started asking him simply what things meant to him. This insight might not come as a surprise to theoreticians who work in the autobiographical genre, or to anthropologically oriented ethnographers in general, but it is certainly a different point of view from that typically seen among professional service providers in the mental health/mental retardation field.

It is certainly true that Vonnie Lee's is only one story. I have been asked by several people who have read drafts of this article, "But is he typical of retarded people in his ability to concentrate and integrate his life experiences?" The honest answer is that I don't know. But in a larger sense, to ask the question is to assume that "mental retardation" is a defined, bounded category fixed within the parameters of clinical, statistical norms. Vonnie Lee is "retarded" in the sense that he has been so labeled and has been dealt with by "the system" as a retarded person for much of his life. And yet he copes with the world around him in a way that, while out of the statistical "norm," is not entirely dysfunctional—as long as we stop trying to see his experiences as illustrations of disorder. Mental retardation is a broad and heterogeneous category; I do not doubt that many persons so diagnosed would have great difficulty in expressing as coherent a worldview as Vonnie Lee's. This kind of methodology would almost certainly not work with all people so diagnosed.

What this fragment of a research project demonstrates is that for at least some people with mental retardation it is possible to do what anthropological ethnographers have long done: get away from asking retrospective questions that only emphasize the "exoticism" of the subject and, instead, allow questions to flow naturally out of observations of the subjects in their ordinary round of activities. That method has long been a way to see cultural differences as variations in human responses to certain common problems; here it is a way of seeing that a person like Vonnie Lee might be extreme in some of his responses but is still part of the same continuum of experience. Perhaps in his specialness and individual quirkiness, Vonnie Lee *is* typical after all—not of "mentally retarded persons" but of human beings who learn how to use elements of the common culture to serve their individual purposes.

REFERENCES

Angrosino, M. V. 1989. *Documents of interaction: Biography, autobiography, and life history in social science perspective.* Gainesville: University of Florida Press.

——. 1992. Metaphors of stigma: How deinstitutionalized mentally retarded adults see themselves. *Journal of Contemporary Ethnography 21*:171–99.

Angrosino, M. V., and L. J. Zagnoli. 1992. Gender constructs and social identity: Implications for community-based care of retarded adults. In *Gender constructs and social issues,* edited by T. Whitehead and B. Reid, 40–69. Urbana: University of Illinois Press.

Crocker, J. C. 1977. The social functions of rhetorical form. In *The social uses of metaphor,* edited by D. J. Sapir and J. C. Crocker, 33–66. Philadelphia: University of Pennsylvania Press.

Edgerton, R. B. 1984. Introduction. In *Lives in process: Mildly retarded adults in a large city,* edited by R. B. Edgerton. Washington, DC: American Association on Mental Deficiency.

Fitzgerald, T. K. 1993. Limitations of metaphor in the culture-communication dialogue. Paper presented at the annual meeting of the Southern Anthropological Society, Savannah, GA, 25 March.

Hankiss, A. 1981. Ontologies of the self: On the mythological rearranging of one's life history. In *Biography and society: The life history approach in the social sciences,* edited by D. Bertaux, 203–10. Beverly Hills, CA: Sage.

Howarth, W. L. 1980. Some principles of autobiography. In *Autobiography: Essays theoretical and critical,* edited by J. Olney, 86–114. Princeton, NJ: Princeton University Press.

Norton, C. S. 1989. *Life metaphors: Stories of ordinary survival.* Carbondale: Southern Illinois University Press.

Olney, J. 1972. *Metaphors of self: The meaning of autobiography.* Princeton, NJ: Princeton University Press.

Whittemore, R. D., L. L. Langness, and P. Koegel. 1986. The life history approach to mental retardation. In *Culture and retardation,* edited by L. L. Langness and H. G. Levine, 1–18. Dordrecht: D. Reidel.

Zetlin, A. G., and J. L. Turner. 1984. Self-perspectives on being handicapped: Stigma and adjustment. In *Lives in process: Mildly retarded adults in a large city,* edited by R. B. Edgerton, 93–120. Washington, DC: American Association on Mental Deficiency.

MICHAEL V. ANGROSINO is Professor of Anthropology at the University of South Florida. He received the Ph.D. from the University of North Carolina at Chapel Hill. His research interests include public policy and program development for persons with mental disabilities and the use of qualitative ethnographic methods in the study of "deviant" or marginalized populations. He is author of *Documents of Interaction: Autobiography, Biography, and Life History in Social Science Perspective* (University Press of Florida) and serves as editor of *Human Organization,* the journal of the Society for Applied Anthropology.

Discussion Topics and Activities for "On the Bus With Vonnie Lee"

1. Evaluate the effectiveness of the data forms (e.g., participant observation vignettes, interview transcript excerpts, artifacts, etc.) employed by Angrosino to create the portrait of Vonnie Lee Hargrett.

2. Discuss how Angrosino represents himself as a co-participant in this case study report.

3. Discuss how a qualitative researcher can make a persuasive argument for the individual case's story as a representative study of a larger population.

Nightmares, Demons, and Slaves: Exploring the Painful Metaphors of Workplace Bullying

Sarah J. Tracy
Arizona State University, Tempe

Pamela Lutgen-Sandvik
University of New Mexico, Albuquerque

Jess K. Alberts
Arizona State University, Tempe

Management Communication Quarterly

Volume 20, Number 2

November 2006, 148–185

© 2006 SAGE Publications 10.1177/0893318906291980

http://mcq.sagepub.com

hosted at http://online.sagepub.com

Although considerable research has linked workplace bullying with psychosocial and physical costs, the stories and conceptualizations of mistreatment by those targeted are largely untold. This study uses metaphor analysis to articulate and explore the emotional pain of workplace bullying and, in doing so, helps to translate its devastation and encourage change. Based on qualitative data gathered from focus groups, narrative interviews, and target drawings, the analysis describes how bullying can feel like a battle, water torture, nightmare, or noxious substance. Abused workers frame bullies as narcissistic dictators, two-faced actors, and devil figures. Employees targeted with workplace bullying liken themselves to vulnerable children, slaves, prisoners, animals, and heartbroken lovers. These metaphors highlight and delimit possibilities for agency and action. Furthermore, they may serve as diagnostic cues, providing shorthand necessary for early intervention.

Keywords: *workplace bullying; emotion; metaphor analysis; work feelings; harassment*

> So many people have told me, "Oh, just let it go. Just let it go." What's interesting is people really don't understand or comprehend the depths of the bully's evilness until it's done to them. Then they're shocked. I had people come up to me at work and say, "Bob, we thought that it was just a personality conflict between you and so-and-so but now we understand." And it's very hard for somebody looking from the outside in to try to resolve the situation or totally understand it.
>
> Bob, city engineer[1]

When abused workers try to describe the pain they suffer at the hands of workplace bullies, listeners are often dubious. Even when we, as researchers who study the phenomenon, talk to professionals, journalists, and other scholars about the issue, people often say things such as "This is the real world, not school, and these people should just toughen up," and "Are you sure they're not just problem employees?" or "Is it really *that bad?*" As illustrated in the opening quote, employees who are targeted admit that bullying can sound unbelievable. Indeed, Amy, an employee in the sports fishing industry, explained that the bullying at her office was so strange that when new people applied for jobs, "I withheld the truth because the truth seemed surreal. . . . To tell anybody the truth in 15 minutes—they would look at me and say, 'She's just a disgruntled employee. It can't be.'" However, bullying should not be disregarded as a childish problem or simply a manifestation of overly sensitive workers. From 25% to 30% of U.S. employees are bullied and emotionally abused sometime during their work histories—10% at any given time (Keashly & Neuman, 2005; Lutgen-Sandvik, Tracy, & Alberts, 2005). If 1 in 10 workers currently suffer at the hands of workplace bullies, then bullying is a pervasive problem and not just the rare experience of a few "thin-skinned" employees.

Increasingly, organizations are beginning to recognize and analyze the distinct costs associated with stress, burnout, and depression at work. Research on health and wellness in organizations establishes that workplace stress has significant deleterious effects, resulting in poor mental and physical health and increased employee use of sick days, workers' compensation claims, and decreased productivity (Farrell & Geist-Martin, 2005). Furthermore, workplace stress is connected to psychological strain (Cooper, Dewe, & O'Driscoll, 2001; Tattersall & Farmer, 1995) and to social health, described as "the quality of an individual's network of professional and personal relationships" (Farrell & Geist-Martin, 2005, p. 549). Workplace bullying is linked to a host of physical, psychological, organizational, and social costs. Negative effects include psychosomatic illness (Djurkovic, McCormack, & Casimir, 2004), increased medical expenses (Bassman, 1992), and reduced productivity (Hoel, Einarsen, & Cooper, 2003). Better understanding employees' emotions about workplace bullying is an important part of attending to its negative effects on personal and organizational wellness.

In this study, we analyze abused workers' naturally occurring metaphors to better explicate the costs and feelings associated with workplace bullying in a U.S. worker cohort. Metaphors compare unlike things (e.g., workplace bullying) to better understood or known entities (e.g., war, nightmares; Lakoff & Johnson, 1980) and provide verbal images of emotional experiences (Morgan, 2003). This compact, vivid shorthand (Ortony, 1975) has the power to translate the meaning and feeling of abuse to a range of American stakeholders (scholars, laypeople, managers, policy makers) who are familiar with sexual harassment and discrimination but largely unacquainted with adult bullying.

The majority of bullying research is internationally situated, survey based, and authored by management or psychology scholars (Einarsen, Hoel, Zapf, & Cooper, 2003a; Hoel et al., 2003; Zapf, Einarsen, Hoel, & Vartia, 2003). However, scholars in the United States have begun entering the dialogue from the fields of organizational communication (Alberts, Lutgen-Sandvik, & Tracy, 2005; Lutgen-Sandvik, 2003; Lutgen-Sandvik et al., 2005; Meares, Oetzel, Derkacs, & Ginossar, 2004), law (Yamada, 2000, 2005), management (Keashly & Neuman, 2005; Neuman, 2004), and psychology (Keashly, 1998, 2001; Namie, 2003). This body of work convincingly links the consequences of bullying to serious harm for targeted workers, nontargeted coworkers, and organizations (Bassman, 1992; Einarsen & Mikkelsen, 2003; Hirigoyen, 1998; Leymann, 1990; Vartia, 1996; Yamada, 2000).

Identifying the material effects of adult bullying is an important step in persuading organizational policy makers to pay attention to the phenomenon. However, little research qualitatively develops the emotional aspects of bullying or answers questions such as "What does it feel like to be bullied?" and "Is it really that bad?" Answering such questions is both theoretically and practically vital. Practically speaking, even the strongest argument based on measurable costs of bullying is not likely to move people to action without an engagement of emotion (Aristotle, 1954; Cialdini, 1984; Planalp, 1993). Understanding what bullying feels like, therefore, is necessary for motivating change (Weiss & Cropanzano, 1996). Furthermore, employee emotion serves an important signal function (Freud, 1926; Hochschild, 1983); the emotion of fear signals danger, which in turn leads to action (e.g., a fearful person is likely to be moved to take safety precautions). Emotion can serve as a warning sign that organizational interaction is askew. Thus, uncovering and publicizing the emotional pain of bullying may be a precursor for organizational intervention, change, and prevention.

Our study expands current knowledge about workplace bullying by exploring, from a communicative and interpretive perspective, the emotional experiences of those targeted with abuse. Although popular books include anecdotes describing devastating bullying experiences (e.g., Adams & Crawford, 1992; Davenport, Schwartz, & Elliott, 2002; Field, 1996; Namie & Namie, 2000a; Randall, 2001), abused workers' emotional stories are essentially missing in most academic research. This is, in part, due to traditional writing styles and scientific rationalities that typically "write out" emotion (Fineman, 1996; Tracy, 2004); however, an appreciation of abused workers' subjective experiences is integral to understanding how and why bullying is so costly to individuals and organizations. The article opens with a review of the definitions, characteristics, and costs of workplace bullying. We then discuss our grounded analysis of focus groups, interviews, and participant drawings and describe how metaphor analysis emerged as an appropriate avenue through which to make sense of the data. The heart of the article details the metaphors used by targets to conceive of and frame bullying, abusers, and themselves. The article concludes with practical and theoretical implications, limitations, and future directions for research.

WORKPLACE BULLYING: TERMINOLOGY, CHARACTERISTICS, AND COSTS

The range of terms used in U.S. research to describe persistent abuse at work is difficult to differentiate, even for academics (see Keashly & Jagatic, 2003). Common names include workplace bullying (Einarsen, Hoel, Zapf, & Cooper, 2003b), mobbing (Leymann, 1990), emotional abuse (Lutgen-Sandvik, 2003), social undermining (Duffy, Ganster, & Pagon, 2002), generalized workplace abuse (Richman, Rospenda, Flaherty, & Freels, 2001), work harassment (Björkqvist, Osterman, & Hjelt-Back, 1994; Brodsky, 1976), and workplace mistreatment (Meares et al., 2004). Although abuse at work can certainly be gendered (Lee, 2002) or raced (Schneider, Hitlan, & Radhakrishnan, 2000), workplace bullying, by definition, is not explicitly connected to demographic markers such as sex or ethnicity.

Although the term *workplace bullying* is similar to a wide array of behavior, subsumed under a number of labels, we use *workplace bullying* for several reasons. First, the label *workplace bullying* appears to be more practical and accessible to the working public than academically framed terms. As researchers, we were overwhelmed with the media interest and participant response to our research.[2] Second, abused workers identify with the term. As researchers noted in a study of women's bullying experiences, "naming experiences as *bullying* [italics added] was important. . . . [I]dentifying an external problem may have enabled them to maintain or recover a sense of their own value and competence" (S. E. Lewis & Orford, 2005, p. 40). Indeed, the term highlights the perpetrator's role in aggression (the bully). Relatedly, we often refer to abused workers as "targets." As one of our participants said, "I saw myself as a victim of verbal abuse. When [a friend] said, 'You're not a victim, you're a target' . . . talk about self-esteem! Suddenly, there was this change of 'Dadgonit, I'm a target.'" In short, the terms *bullying* and *target* appear to be useful to the broader public and help affected workers name and make sense of their experiences in preferred ways. In using these terms, we follow the lead of international researchers who are aiming toward a common language (Einarsen et al., 2003a).

So what does workplace bullying look like? Adult bullying at work is perpetrated through a variety of tactics or negative acts that can be verbal, nonverbal, and physical (Baron & Neuman, 1998; Einarsen et al., 2003b). In contrast to workplace incivility, which is defined as "low intensity deviant . . . behaviors [that] are characteristically rude and discourteous, displaying a lack of regard for others" (Andersson & Pearson, 1999, p. 457), workplace bullying is escalated and can include screaming, cursing, spreading vicious rumors, destroying the target's property or work product, excessive criticism, and sometimes hitting, slapping, and shoving (Zapf et al., 2003). Bullying is not limited to active communication but is also perpetrated through passive, nonacts of social ostracism (Williams & Sommer, 1997) that harm or stigmatize through the "silent treatment," exclusion from meetings and gatherings, or ignoring of requests (Rayner, Hoel, & Cooper, 2002). Most often, workplace bullying is a combination of tactics in which numerous types of hostile communication and behavior are used.

Bullying is characterized by several features: repetition, duration, escalation, power disparity, and attributed intent (Lutgen-Sandvik, 2005). Adult bullying at work involves situations in which employees are subjected to repeated, persistent negative acts that are intimidating, malicious, and stigmatizing (Einarsen et al., 2003b; Rayner & Hoel, 1997). It is also enduring, lasting over an extended period of time (e.g., 6 months; Einarsen, 1999). Therefore, if someone experiences one hostile interaction—regardless of how disturbing—this does not equate to bullying. The persistent character of bullying at work is also linked to escalated aggression; the intensity of hostility and toxic effects increase when bullying is left unchecked (Harlos & Pinder, 2000; Leymann, 1996; Zapf & Gross, 2001). Power disparity is another hallmark feature of bullying; power can be position based or emerge from informal sources (e.g., charisma, social networks, communication skills). Targeted workers usually report being unable to stop the abuse once it has become an established mode of interaction (Leymann, 1990; Rayner et al., 2002). Furthermore, attributed intent is central to workers' judgment that they have been bullied (Adams & Crawford, 1992; Keashly, 1998; Rayner et al., 2002); bullied workers typically perceive abuse as intentional efforts to harm, control, or drive them from the workplace (Lutgen-Sandvik, 2005).

Understanding bullying at work is crucial considering its devastation to individuals' physical and psychological health and to organizational productivity. Bullying terrorizes, humiliates, dehumanizes, and isolates those targeted and is linked to serious health risks for bullied workers (Leymann, 1990; Leymann & Gustafsson, 1996). Repeated abuse can result in emotional responses such as helplessness, anger, despair, and shock (Janus Bulman, 1992) and health problems such as musculoskeletal complaints (Einarsen, Raknes, & Mattheisen, 1994), sleep problems, chronic fatigue, and loss of strength (Brodsky, 1976). Adult bullying at work also has a measurable negative impact on organizations. Direct costs include increased disability and workers' compensation claims, increased medical costs (Bassman, 1992), and risk of wrongful discharge (Yamada, 2000) or constructive discharge lawsuits (Matusewitch, 1996). Indirect costs include low-quality work, reduced productivity, high staff turnover, increased absenteeism, and deteriorated customer relationships and public image (Hoel et al., 2003; Keashly & Neuman, 2005). These costs should not be surprising; heightened emotional states—especially those that are negatively valenced—draw attention and energy away from and can interfere with task completion (Weiss & Cropanzano, 1996).

The existing research links bullying to organizational costs and professional diagnoses of harm and, in doing so, substantiates abused workers' stories through rational, expert verification of problematic effects. However, just as much research about emotion in organizations is nonemotional (Tracy, 2004), most research that pinpoints the costs of bullying glosses over the emotional pain of abuse. Several factors contribute to this. First, collecting and analyzing victim narratives can be emotionally exhausting and time intensive. Furthermore, abused people often have trouble telling their stories and making sense of what has happened in the form of efficient narratives. Relatedly, ideological discourses discourage stories of victimization and weakness (Deetz, 1992). Similar to victims of domestic violence (Ferraro, 1996) and sexual harassment (Clair, 1993), individuals often blame themselves for being targeted and have trouble creating coherent story lines that persuasively and succinctly convey their situation.

Nevertheless, quantifying abused workers' emotional experiences using rational yardsticks of prevalence, antecedents, and effects provides only part of the picture regarding their pain and the effect of bullying on organizations. In this study, we turn our attention to what bullying feels like. Examining targets' emotional experiences illuminates what occurs between the onset of bullying and the measurement of costs associated with it. Such an approach examines how targeted persons make sense of being badgered and humiliated at work and why they react the way they do. We entered the study with the following research question:

Research Question: What does workplace bullying feel like?

METHOD

The data for this study were drawn from 10 in-depth interviews and two focus groups with 9 and 8 participants, respectively. Participants self-identified as targets and were determined by the authors through pre–data collection consultations to fit the characteristics of bullied workers.

Participants

We recruited participants through a series of media releases and a link on the Workplace Bullying and Trauma Institute Web site (www.bullyinginstitute.org). The overall sample is similar to other studies examining bullying in professional worker cohorts (D. Lewis, 1999; Salin, 2001), and sex, ethnicity, and age were similar across the focus groups and interviews. Of the 27 participants, 17 were women and 10 were men. The ethnic diversity was similarly homogeneous to past studies of workplace bullying (Einarsen & Raknes, 1997; Hoel & Cooper, 2001; Rayner & Cooper, 1997; Zapf, Knorz, & Kulla, 1996), with 24 participants being White, 2 Hispanic, and 1 who described herself as White and African American. Participants' mean age at the time of bullying was 45.3 years (range of 26 to 72). Together, the participants reported the following industries as the site of abuse: education (7), services and sales (7), local and state government (6), professional and technical fields (3), mental and medical health (2), construction (1), and recreation (1).

The primary demographic dissimilarity between the focus group and interview participants was that only 4 focus group participants were being bullied in their current job, whereas 13 reported bullying in a past job. For those interviewed, however, half (5) were still working in the abusive context. This difference is most likely because, although we could promise confidentiality for interviewees, we advised potential focus group participants that we could not promise confidentiality on behalf of other group participants. Employees bullied in their current jobs may have felt more comfortable in a one-on-one interview than in a group interview. Despite this difference, we found that the emotional pain reported and metaphorical language used across the two samples were remarkably similar. Although more focus group members were removed from the abusive working situation, research suggests that decades after experiencing abuse at work, people still vividly recall the painful, oftentimes shattering and life-changing, experience (Leymann & Gustafsson, 1996; Rayner et al., 2002; M. J. Scott & Stradling, 2001).

Data Collection Procedures

Focus groups are well poised to explore the emotional experience of bullying for several reasons. First, the power of focus groups is similar to that of therapy groups; a synergy occurs when participants hear others' verbalized experiences that, in turn, stimulate memories, ideas, and experiences in themselves. This is known as the *group effect* (Carey, 1994) in which participants engage in "a kind of 'chaining' or 'cascading' effect; talk links to, or tumbles out of, the topics and expressions preceding it" (Lindlof & Taylor, 2002, p. 182). Second, bullied workers discover a common language to describe similar experiences and use a form of "native language" unique to the experience. This is especially relevant for issues that blame the victim (e.g., domestic violence, sexual assault, workplace bullying) and topics that are in a state of linguistic "denotative hesitancy" (Clair, 1993), in which there has yet to be developed an agreed-on language to describe the experience. Third, focus groups provide an opportunity for disclosure among similar others in a setting where abused workers are validated, have voice, and learn they are not alone. Given participants' lack of voice in the bullying situation, their feelings of isolation, and their missing stories from current research, we believed focus groups to be not only an efficacious but also an ethical venue for collecting data.

Focus groups, which were facilitated by the first two authors and conducted in a university focus group room, lasted from 10 a.m. to about 2:15 p.m., included two breaks and lunch (equaling about 30 minutes that were not part of the data analyzed), and were videotaped and audiotaped for later transcription. Following Lawler's (2002) suggestion, we attempted to "set in place the conditions in which people are likely to produce narratives" (p. 253) by providing an informal environment with food and conversation. An interview guide structured the focus groups and included questions such as "When did you first know something was wrong?" "What did a single bullying situation look like?" and "How has this affected you, the organization, and your family?"

We also employed creative drawing—an approach that can be restorative for people experiencing trauma or pain (Liebermann, 1991). Creative drawing evokes emotions and provides an outlet for expressing complex and subtle information that is difficult to verbalize (Meyer, 1991). Zuboff (1988), for instance, asked employees to draw pictures indicating how they felt about a new organizational technology and argued that the drawings helped staff to identify and discuss emotions that were difficult to define. Similarly, in a study of emotions and organizational change, Vince and Broussine (1996) used drawings to "act as a catalyst for members of teams to 'say the unsaid' both on an emotional / psychological and on a political level" (p. 9). Finally, drawing analysis methods fit into collaborative, action research, allowing the researcher to work with the participants rather than on them (Reason, 1994; Sarri & Sarri, 1992). During the creative drawing exercise, we asked participants to visualize a bullying episode, particularly how they felt during the experience. Participants then drew pictures that expressed these feelings—a scene, a face, an abstract object or design—and wrote 5 to 10 words or phrases they felt described the drawing. Participants then presented drawings to the group.

In addition to the focus groups, we conducted 10 in-depth interviews. Doing so helped to ensure that we heard from participants who might have been reticent about focus group participation.

Furthermore, during the focus groups, despite efforts to direct abused workers' conversation toward specific topics—bullying incidents, coworker responses, emotional reactions—participants wanted to historically contextualize their experiences. The interviews provided a space where participants could narrate their experiences in an uninterrupted manner "from the beginning."

The second author conducted the interviews, each of which lasted 1 to 3 hours (56 to 180 minutes) and together equaled 27.5 hours. The interviews were loosely structured, allowing the stories to spontaneously unfold (Mischler, 1986). They began with a "grand tour" question (Spradley, 1979) such as "Why don't you begin by telling me where you work, what kind work you do, and when you started noticing that things weren't quite right." Interviewees needed little prompting and proceeded to narrate their experiences in a mostly chronological manner. Interview probes asked about coworker and supervisor reactions, how abuse affected work tasks, and specific instances of general claims.

The focus groups were professionally transcribed, resulting in 103 pages of single-spaced typewritten data. Transcripts included interactive discussions and the creative-drawing dialogue. Interviews were transcribed by the second author and resulted in 201 single-spaced typed pages. A research team member reviewed the recordings and occasionally corrected transcripts for accuracy.

Grounded Metaphor Analysis

During the early stages of analysis, we found that we had much difficulty trying to sum up the intense emotional pain experienced by bullied workers into short vignettes. Even when we edited and attempted to connect participants' stories coherently, most were much too long to report in a journal-length article. This perhaps should not have been surprising, given that victims of tragedy and sexual harassment often face difficulty in neatly emplotting their narratives (Ferraro, 1996). Thus, we were challenged with how to feasibly attend to our research question, stay true to the data, and do so in an efficient manner. Throughout these early readings, we found that participants often spoke metaphorically. Therefore, we turned to the literature to explore the appropriateness of metaphor analysis.

In short, we found that metaphor analysis would provide a promising avenue for understanding the ways abused employees frame and make sense of the complex, confusing feelings associated with abuse at work. Metaphors provide people with a way to "express aspects both of themselves and of situations about which they may not be consciously aware, nor be able to express analytically and/or literally" (Marshak, 1996, p. 156). As such, metaphor analysis is especially worthwhile when used to examine topics, such as adult bullying, that are in a state of "denotative hesitancy" (Clair, 1993). Metaphors that emerge in everyday talk provide a vivid "way of thinking and seeing" (G. Morgan, 1997) and serve as "linguistic steering devices that guide both thinking and actions" (Kirby & Harter, 2003, p. 33). For instance, understanding conflict metaphors (e.g., war or impotence; Buzzanell & Burrell, 1997) says much about how people frame and react to conflict. Metaphors do not just rhetorically "dress up" speech but fundamentally guide how people experience their world (Deetz, 1984).

The current metaphor literature, coupled with the emotional tenor and length and complexity of participant stories, suggested the appropriateness of metaphor analysis to explore and understand the intense feelings associated with adult bullying. Using a grounded approach, we re-entered the data analysis with the revised guiding research question:

> *Revised Research Question:* What types of metaphorical language do participants use to describe the emotional experience of bullying?

We examined the data and created several descriptive analysis matrices (Miles & Huberman, 1994) summarizing metaphorical themes in both the words and drawings of participants. We subsequently used NVivo qualitative data analysis software to reduce and unitize the data. In this advanced analysis stage, we identified and isolated metaphorical data related to bullying from the rest of the transcribed data. This resulted in 37 pages of single-spaced metaphor data (or about 15% of the interview and focus group data). We found that metaphors about the feelings of workplace bullying emerged as being grouped around metaphors that described the bullying process, the bully, and abused workers. Using open coding and the constant comparative method (Charmaz, 2001; Glaser & Strauss, 1967), we ultimately analyzed the unitized data line by line with the guiding statements of "bullying feels like . . . , the bully feels like . . . , and being a target of bullying feels like . . . ."

We then looked for patterns among coded metaphors, how they were embedded within participants' stories and drawings, and how they logically and semantically cohered. Some metaphors presented a continuum (e.g., bullying as "game" was similar to but less intense than bullying as "war"), whereas others were topically connected (e.g., feeling like a "child," a "slave," or "chattel" all expressed diminished humanity or agency). During multiple meetings, the research team discussed metaphorical meanings and constructed core metaphor categories that best characterized the feelings of adult bullying.

WHAT BULLYING FEELS LIKE: METAPHORS OF BULLYING, BULLIES, AND TARGETED WORKERS

With several exceptions, including comments such as "I was fearful, vulnerable, isolated" and "This is emotional shit," participants used few explicit emotional terms to describe bullying.

Table 1	What Does Workplace Bullying Feel Like? Central Metaphorical Themes

Category	Themes and Examples
Bullying process as	Game or battle: Bullies "play dirty" and "make their own rules."
	Nightmare: "It's the Matrix. We live in two different worlds."
	Water torture: It is a "hammering away," "drum beat," or "pressure screw."
	Noxious substance: "It just kind of drips on down, just festers." (He would) "feed us a whole line of garbage."
The bully as	Narcissistic dictator or royalty: "You literally have a Hitler running around down there."
	Two-faced actor: Bullies put on "a good show for the boss," or they would "be real sweet one time one day, and the next day . . . very evil, conniving."
	Evil or demon: Bullies were "evil," "devils," "witches," "demons," and "Jekyll and Hyde."
The target as	Slave or animal: "You're a personal servant to the owner and his will;" "He considers you his property."
	Prisoner: "I feel like I'm doing time." "I felt like I had a prison record."
	Child: "I felt like a little girl." (It) is like having an abusive father."
	Heartbroken lover: "My heart was broken." (I felt) "sad, confused, exposed, unworthy and broken hearted."

However, their emotions were vividly apparent in their metaphorical language and creative drawings. In the following, and as summarized in Table 1, we discuss the metaphors targeted employees used to characterize their feelings about the bullying process, the bully, and being a target.

Metaphors of the Bullying Process

As illustrated in the following discussion, participants likened the bullying process to a game or battle, nightmare, water torture, and managing a noxious substance (e.g., "being fed garbage").

Game or battle. More than any other metaphor, narratives and drawings characterized bullying as a contest or battle. This metaphor continuum ranged from playing a game to outright war, including killing and death. On the less destructive end of the spectrum, those targeted described feeling as though bullying was a matching of wits with an opponent who played unfairly. Participants spoke in terms of bullying as strategic attack, defense, and a set of shifting rules saying, for instance, that bullying was "playing a game," "playing their game," and "I had no rights . . . and they played on that." Dale, who worked in a security business, said the bully was "up to his old tricks." These metaphors of play and game suggest a less-than-serious issue and something that all members ostensibly should also be able to negotiate. However, as illustrated below, targets viewed the rules of the game as unfair and playing the game as dangerous and threatening.

Targeted workers characterized the contest as fixed or unfairly weighted in the bully's favor. They said bullies created the rules, changed them without notice or input and, as an aircraft mechanic named Ben explained, did so "behind closed doors." Dolly, a dental office administrative assistant, noted that bullies "make their own rules." Stephanie, a callcenter employee, said that the only way the bully would win was "to play dirty," whereas Jack, the director of an online university program, said that bullying "really has to do with making up the rules as you go along." Sadly, this metaphor of a game that is difficult to win extended to targets' seeking external help through the courts. Going to court was a gamble and "a crap shoot." Furthermore, in this "game," abused workers could see themselves as the prey of the hunt; Dale explained, "everybody's fair game" for bullying. Hunting, of course, can result in significant and even lethal injury.

Indeed, participant narratives were saturated with metaphors of beating, physical abuse, and death. Wendy, a religious educator, said, "I have been maimed. . . . I've been character assassinated." Others expressed feeling "beaten," "abused," "ripped," "broken," "scarred," and "eviscerated." The battle metaphor is perhaps most complexly illustrated in a drawing by Stephanie (Figure 1). Stephanie's picture depicts a professional wrestling match in which she is a champion wrestler fighting her manager—the "heel" or "bad guy who pulls tricks." Her manager and the company's vice president are shown holding her down and taking jabs at her face. She portrays a disloyal employee as a small dog biting at her leg and the human resources (HR) manager as a blindfolded referee. As such, Stephanie depicts HR as "in on the game" and in fact prolonging the abuse by appearing to intervene but actually turning a blind eye to the situation. She also includes two signs: one that reads, "Will her posse come to help?" and another that says, "Kill." These signs reflect Stephanie's feeling that coworkers refused to come to her aid and actually turned on her when it became clear that she was losing the fight.

When bullying is viewed as a fight in which the target can be "killed," "destroyed," and "annihilated," it becomes clear why abused employees characterized their defensive discursive and nondiscursive behavior in fighting terms such as "I'm gonna stick to my guns." Whereas the bully's actions were viewed as deceitful and underhanded, many targeted employees framed fighting back as a "righteous battle" and "standing up for what's right." Diane, a children's hospital nurse, said she stayed because "I have a mission that I want to make this right. This is wrong."

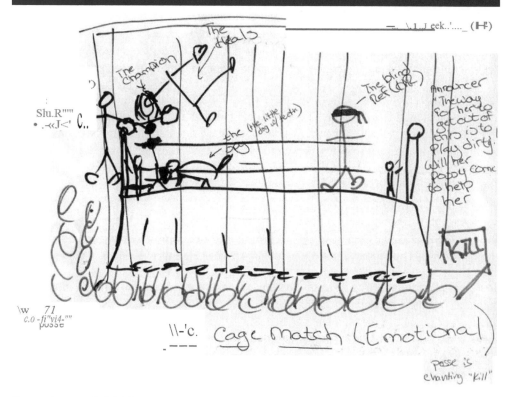

Source: Tracy et al. (2006).

In standing up for their rights, abused workers also report feelings of anger, extreme injustice, and wanting revenge. However, targets' efforts to fight back often fail and reinforce the unfairly matched competition. Abby, a postsecondary school librarian, told us,

> The other librarian . . . [quit], but I was gonna stay and fight it out. I said, "This isn't right," so, I went to the new dean and the new HR person. . . . Not only weren't they helpful, the HR person . . . helped to sabotage me. I eventually lost my job. I had been there 6 years.

Laura, a state employee, said, "You get so exhausted with the fight . . . it's not worth the time or the energy to go on [to] . . . make the wrong a right." Indeed, some targets became so exhausted and overwhelmed with the fight that they viewed bullying as an uncontrollable nightmare.

Nightmare. Similar to a nightmare from which one cannot awake, many participants described how their work worlds did not make sense. There was a feeling of instability and "crazy making"—targets of abuse felt as though something "real" would happen in the organization (e.g., their supplies would disappear, they would be excluded from a crucial meeting, or the bully would scream and rage)—and the bully would deny its occurrence. Lydia, an electrical sales accountant, said that it was so difficult for others to believe her that she almost did not believe herself: "It's so crazy I don't know if I can tell you all these details. . . . I almost thought I was going crazy. I taped one conversation just to show my husband I wasn't making it up." Similarly, Terry, employed in an education training firm, exclaimed,

> She literally made me feel like I was *going crazy!* She would tell you to do things. She would tell you that she didn't say what she just said. She would write me notes. She would tell me one thing, then she would tell me something else, then she would question what I was doing.

By likening bullying to a waking nightmare, we can begin to understand the complete lack of control targeted workers feel they have in changing the situation. Indeed, Wendy said that she finally was only able to make sense of the experience by equating it to the movie "The Matrix," in which the main character lived in a dream world that was distinct from the real world where his oppressors lived. In comparing her experience to the hero of "The Matrix," she explained,

> It [the movie] was like an epiphany. . . . It's the Matrix. We live in two different worlds. Two different understandings. Two different world views. For the most part, that helped, but again, you've seen my vulnerability. I need to watch the movie again. The Matrix has really helped me to understand. I'm not nuts. He doesn't think he's nuts. We're just in two different worlds.

For Wendy, framing the bullying process as part of a different alien world appeared to make her feel better about her inability to change the situation. However, many abused workers felt trapped in a torturous experience from which they could not escape.

Water torture. Many participants had difficulty picking out one incident, on its own, that was egregious or ultimately typified their bullying experience. Rather, they described it as "hammering away," a "drum beat," being "under the gun," and "Chinese water torture"—a means of driving a prisoner mad through the practice of dripping water, little by little, on the captive's forehead. (The actual practice is traced to 16th-century Italy; Innes, 1998). As such, bullying often feels like a never-ending process that gradually intimidates and wears down the target. These metaphors underscore the nature of bullying; it usually consists of numerous, seemingly nonserious negative acts that comprise a relentless pattern (Keashly & Neuman, 2005). Moreover, the wearing-down process often accounts for the emergence of power disparity between actors (Einarsen et al., 2003b; Keashly & Nowell, 2003; Leymann, 1996).

On the milder end of the spectrum, respondents likened bullying to being picked on, saying, "Anything they could find to pick on, they would write it up;" "It's like . . . kids decide to pick on so and so;" and "do I set myself up to get picked on?" The word "picking" refers to tearing off bit by bit, such as one might do meat from a bone. This metaphor illustrates how and why bullying is so difficult to identify, especially in its early stages (Adams & Crawford, 1992). The metaphor also summons feelings of childhood and vulnerability. Skyler, a sales consultant, described his picture by saying, "Like I tried to draw myself bigger like the Hulk. I think it's all. . . . It dates back to high school. My last name is Bird so everybody is like 'Big Bird' whatever, picking on me."

This juvenile "picking on" then became code for describing grown-up, relentless abuse. Bullied participants explained, "He would always come by my desk and hound me and hound me" and "It's stuff that chips away and chips away." Kristie, in a state department of labor, described the relentless nature of the attack as "gouging me about another project . . . she was just really gouging me, gouging me, gouging me." Many comments, such as these, indicate the linguistic form of "reduplication" in which individuals repeat certain words or phrases (e.g., hound me and hound me). As Lakoff and Johnson (1980) argue, "more of form stands for more of content" (p. 127). Therefore, it is not by happenstance that bullied persons use repetitive phrases to describe bullying. The existence of reduplication indicates that targets view bullying as chronic and relentless.

For some abused workers, repetition was akin to torture. Greg, a police officer, suggested that bullying was like "pulling the wings off a fly." Brad, in a nonprofit substance abuse treatment center, described the constant criticism as "Chinese water torture." This suggests that each act of bullying could be as harmless as a drop of water dripped on the forehead but added together, it was enough to drive him insane. Targets described ongoing pressure, like a "pressure screw" and slowly ticking "time bomb." It is difficult to believe that workers in these environments were producing at their highest level and finding satisfaction at their jobs. Most likely, they were merely surviving.

A sense of inescapability marked abused workers' stories. Stephanie disturbingly portrayed how she felt when experiencing the repeated infliction of pain, inability to escape, and resulting numbness:

You're with a serial rapist. You know, you're clinching your teeth. So I just sat there and I took it and then when we were done, I just got up, because . . . I was just in a zone somewhere. I just kind of numbed myself so I wouldn't react to them.

Similar to a victim of torture, Stephanie felt as though her best defense was tuning out, which appears to be a common response to workplace bullying that helps the target to manage in the short term. Elizabeth, a school teacher, described being "just like a zombie." However, becoming numb in the long term may serve as a barrier to overcoming workplace bullying, an issue to which we return in the implications.

The "water torture" metaphor speaks to the difficulty targeted workers (or researchers) have in succinctly answering the question "What is bullying?" Brad explained how he kept notes and said, "When I look over some of the stuff, I'd say to myself, 'that in and of itself isn't that big of a deal.' It's when you start putting all the stuff together that you start saying, 'okay that was kind of crazy.'" Single horrific events are rare; rather, bullying is often perpetrated through many small discursive and nondiscursive acts.

Noxious substance. Last, abused employees characterized bullying as a rotten, corrupt substance they were forced to "suck up" at work and "get out" to heal and move forward. This metaphor is orientational and ontological (Lakoff & Johnson, 1980) as it describes bullying as a material, toxic matter that makes its way into or out of the person. As such, the noxious material metaphor highlights how targets feel that bullying can suffocate, smother, foul, or obstruct them. Comments include "Here I have been through 2 years of this shit"; "[The bully] would sit there and feed us a whole line of garbage"; and "It just kind of drips on down, just festers." These images present bullying as a form of excrement that rots with time.

Participant language characterizes bullying as a harmful substance that is forced into them against their will. They spoke of having to "take it," a metaphor that has sexually violent undertones. Participants said, "It's just force feeding, and that's a form of abuse"; "He was being the aggressor, and I'm just kind of sucking it all up like a sponge until finally I can't take it anymore" and "You don't want to dare to let them see you cry, so you're just sitting there holding everything in and you're shaking inside." Holding in the toxicity of workplace bullying, however, did not come without a price. Being fed "shit" and "garbage," understandably not only leaves, as Dale noted, "an awfully bad taste in my mouth," but can lead to myriad emotional and physical illnesses as well (Brodsky, 1976; Djurkovic et al., 2004; Einarsen & Mikkelsen, 2003). A mining equipment operator named Tim compared bullying to a malignancy, suggesting that "organizations should cut [bullies] right out and just get rid of them . . . because some cancers are incurable."

Abused workers describe coping with bullying as a noxious substance by "getting it out." Some reported taking years to heal from and "get over" their bullying experience. However, targets often feel constrained from letting it out until they are outside organizational boundaries; this unfortunately does little to break the escalation of bullying. Participants also spoke of trying to "let it out" through venting with family members. This process can amplify the negative effects of bullying by bringing the "shit" and "trash" to other areas of life. When abused workers can only "empty the garbage" of workplace bullying when they go home, it can and does negatively affect family life (Davenport et al., 2002; Wyatt & Hare, 1997). It was only those who had left the bullying workplace that spoke of trying to "close the door on" and "get over" bullying. Although leaving the organization does not necessarily lead to instant happiness (Alberts et al., 2005), in the long run, exit is often the most efficacious path back to emotional and physical health (Namie & Namie, 2000b; Rayner et al., 2002).

As illustrated, our analysis suggests that bullying can feel like a fight or battle, a nightmare, water torture, and a noxious substance. These metaphors serve to sum up conceptualizations of bullying as an active process apart from specific actors. Nevertheless, they also begin to hint at the most common metaphors used to describe bullies.

Metaphors of the Bully

The three central metaphors that emerged for describing the bully were "narcissistic dictator or royalty" "two-faced actor," and "evil or demon." Together, these represent a continuum that included viewing bullies as selfcentered crowned heads, duplicitous actors, and outright devil figures.

Narcissistic dictators or royalty. First, abused workers discussed bullies in terms of privileged crowned heads. They said, for instance, that bullies "lord" over meetings like "knights at the roundtable" and use meetings for "public floggings." Jack drew a picture in which the bully was wearing a crown and giving the thumbs down sign to a small, confused-looking man confined in a straight jacket (Jack). These images suggest that targeted workers perceive bullies as thinking of themselves as better, greater, and more important than others. Those targeted felt undeniably trapped and threatened by bullies who were compared to evil dictators; Ted said, "You literally have a Hitler running around down there who's a mile away from the management who can't see it." As with the Hitler metaphor, it becomes clear that an additional dynamic were bullies' duplicitous performances.

Two-faced actors. Targets felt frustrated in their attempts to report bullying because the perpetrators were skilled performers, who were excellent at "acting" nice when doing so would advantage them or impress organizational superiors. Lynn, a senior accountant for a defense contractor, said, "She could be real sweet one time one day and the next day . . . she was very evil, conniving," whereas others explained that bullies could put on a "good show" for the bosses. For example, Diane described the bully as a manager who screamed at people so close that "her spit would hit you in the face." However, in a meeting with doctors, the bully was "kissing the floor . . . and kissing the guy's [doctor's] feet. . . . It's like the Emperor has no clothes." Marilyn, a corporate IT manager, drew the bully as "Superman," because, when the bosses were around, he would come in with his cape on "to save the day." These metaphors vividly illustrate the sentiment that abused workers view their oppressors as powerful (if fake), and as such, feel frustrated trying to convince others of their plight or successfully defend themselves.

Evil demons. Identifying bullies as evil demons corresponds to the nightmare metaphors used to describe bullying. Participants described perpetrators as "evil," "devils," "witches," and "demons." Bob, the city engineer, even referred to the bully's children as "the devil's spawn; they are just evil, evil children." Marla, a sales administrator for an industrial corporation, drew pictures of the bully with demon horns. Cheryl, a university secretary, drew a devil with a pitchfork and explained, "It felt like the devil was sticking the fork into me." During a particularly volatile incident, a male bully reportedly "threw his chair back and his whole face contorted, his body was contorted. It was like he was going through this epileptic seizure of some sort." Marla recounted an experience when the bully's "eyeballs looked like they were going to bulge out. His face contorted, and he starts screaming at the top of his lungs. . . . I mean he even flung the chair back, and he was like a demon." Characters framed as being from the "dark" side provide clues to targets' difficulty explaining and understanding bully behavior. Wendy likened the bully to a Jekyll and Hyde character who was extremely unpredictable and against whom she had little defense.

Characterizing bullies as deluded narcissists, possessed of evil spirits, and cunning actors suggests that targeted persons frame bullies and their behavior as surreal, shocking, bizarre, and inexplicable. Metaphors of the bully portray aggressors who feel superior to others, possess dark powers, and convincingly shape-shift into whatever façade is necessary given the audience. Such mythic characters are impossible for mere mortals to engage with and emerge triumphant.

Metaphors of Targets

Last, we explored the feelings of being a target of workplace bullying. Our analysis found that abused workers feel like slaves and animals, prisoners, children, and heartbroken lovers.

Slaves or animals. At the more extreme end of the dehumanized spectrum, abused workers invoked feeling as though they were "a piece of property," "slaves," and "chattel." Participants explained that "He treats you just like slaves"; "She acts like she owns me";

"You're a personal servant to the owner and his will"; and "He considers you his property 24 hours a day, seven days a week." Similarly, participants invoked feeling objectified and degraded as insects, animals, and beasts of burden. As noted, Greg characterized bullying as "pulling the wings off of flies." Lynn explained that the bullying, "kept on and on and I felt like dirt; I felt like a dog." Bob said he felt like "a caged animal" and Dale indicated that the bully "treats us like his personal chattel." As such, Dale was referring to a common American meaning of chattel—a type of slavery defined as the absolute legal ownership of a person (O'Rourke, 2004).

Targets also used mixed animal metaphors describing themselves in relation to the bully. In doing so, they characterized the bullying situation as dehumanizing. Wendy suggested that targeted workers were like llamas that had to protect each other from the wolves. Amy and her coworkers labeled an unfortunately mild-mannered newcomer as the bully's future "chew toy." These comments paint bullies as ruthless animals and targets as defenseless prey in one-down situations—whether as the bully's entertainment (chew toy) or quarry. As such, these metaphors accentuate feelings of vulnerability and degradation.

Prisoner. Many participants reported feeling as though they were imprisoned in their jobs and cut off from important networks with friends and family. Abby explained, "I felt disconnected; disconnected from my job, disconnected from my life," whereas Laura summed it up, saying, "I've been blackballed." Respondents invoked the metaphor of "doing time" to describe feeling trapped. Captive metaphors included "I feel like I'm doing time for the next 3 months," "I felt like I had a prison record," and "I was so tied to my job." Indeed, bullying could result in the horror of feeling forever isolated and ensnared. Abused workers said they felt "alone," "black," "empty," and "suffocated." Stephanie explained, "I had a lot of people who supported me, but when things started happening, all of a sudden, they backed away and denied everything."

Isolation can serve as a punishment and further complicate targets' efforts at collective resistance (Lutgen-Sandvik, 2005); however, isolation is also paradoxical. It oppresses targeted workers by disconnecting them from others but simultaneously may shield them from continued abuse. Bob's statement encompasses this paradox: "It's a trap. A caged animal trapped-type feeling. Because a lot of times you just want to hide." Indeed, targets repeatedly discussed how they would often purposefully isolate themselves to try to avoid negative attention. They spoke of trying "to fly under the radar" and "not to fly too close to the sun." This desire to hide is also vividly illustrated in the next metaphor.

Child. Numerous respondents indicated that they felt treated like a child. Several described feeling "scolded," "shrinking," and "small" when bullied. Terry likened her bullying boss to a "baby-sitter." Lynn drew a picture in which she was much smaller than the bully and explained, "I felt like a little girl and [the bully] was up higher, she was working on a stepladder. She was shouting down, 'Now, be sure to do this.'" Being treated like a child reflects the bully's dismissal of targets' adult status and, for some targets, brought back painful childhood memories. Lothar, a flight technician, explained,

> When I was kid, my old man was a little hard on me. This guy reminds me so much of my old man, it starts dragging up crap from when I was a kid, and I'm sitting there going, "I've got to feel like 10 years old again."

In response, the abused workers felt righteous anger, as illustrated in Bob's comment, "I'm a 40-year-old man, you don't scold a 40-year-old man. It's just ridiculous!"

Some participants expressed feeling like the unpopular kid at school, being targeted by numbers of "nameless" tormentors and trying to avoid bullying "like when you're a kid on the schoolyard." Abby, trying to hold back her embarrassment, said, "It sounds totally silly but the two people involved would whisper. It sounds like junior high school." Feeling this way led to mistrust and humiliation. Bob said he felt as though someone taped a "kick me" sign to his back.

Others said they felt like a child in an abusive family, saying, "I thought this woman was going to hurt me. The way I felt at the time—it was very—it pushed me into a role of being a child." The following comment from Amy vividly captures this sentiment:

> Working for Hal is like having an abusive father and all the children—when they're dressed up on Sunday afternoon and guests come visiting to the house—everything is wonderful and perfect, and we have this deep dark secret about the abusive father that nobody will tell about.

Like children in abusive families, bullied workers felt depressed and sad, explaining that they cried, experienced extreme dread, and at times screamed and wailed when they considered their situations. They also felt ambivalent emotions; they were angry about being treated as an incompetent and shameful that they allowed bullies to push them into a child role. Furthermore they felt confused—wondering what they had done to bring bullying on themselves. As with abused children, many admitted to a fleeting sense of relief when someone else was targeted. However, relief was coupled with guilt, both for feeling the relief and failing to defend an abused colleague. Some characterized the inevitability of being targeted and thus the pointlessness of intervening on another's behalf. Dale frankly noted that when someone was bullied, "It was just your turn in the barrel." However, most still felt as if they were somehow to blame and that they should have done something different to prevent the abuse. Some targeted workers expressed worry about whether they were bullied because they failed to speak up for themselves soon enough; other abused workers stated concern about whether they were too quick to respond to the abuse and therefore were at fault for further aggravating the bully.

Heartbroken lover. Last, a number of our female participants described feeling betrayed and brokenhearted by their experience. The loss of a job they loved was paramount in their stories. Terry poignantly described how much she loved her work before the bully drove her from the job:

> What bothered me the most out of all of this, I loved my job. I could not wait to get to work in the morning, and I hated to go home at night. I loved every day; I loved every minute. It was so enjoyable for me. I liked what I did; it made me feel good; it made me want to get up in the morning. That's really hard to find, and I just keep looking at it, and I keep thinking *why? Why* did that happen? *Why? Why* did it have to happen? Why was someone so deceitful that she wanted this to come down? I mean, I did nothing but make her look good, so why?

Terry's description is similar to how one might discuss a lost love affair and echoes the vital importance of work both to identity and social relations (Buzzanell & Turner, 2003). Other women noted similar sentiments about their work, stating, "I loved that job," "I loved those people I worked with," "I actually loved the job and everybody else there," "I loved the company; I loved the work," "I enjoyed the people in that company. I enjoyed my job. I loved it." It is not surprising, then that they also connected bullying with broken hearts and betrayal.

Three pictures, each drawn by women, prominently featured their damaged "hearts." Wendy actually ripped her paper, showing the heart torn apart and explained, "My heart was broken." Laura drew three figures, each progressively more upset and confused, the last with a large "X" scrawled through the red heart. She described her feelings as "sad, confused, exposed, unworthy and broken-hearted." Similarly, Mandy, a school media specialist, drew a series of stick figures, each one smaller than the last, but each with a bigger, blue heart. She said, "I'm a small person with a heavy heart." The heart has long been thought to be the center of emotion. Our heart "skips a beat" when we are excited and in love, and we get a pang in our heart or feel heartbroken when we're sad. This imagery illustrates how abused workers feel the weight, scarring, and betrayal of abuse, and the loss of a beloved job, to their very core.

DISCUSSION

In sum, participants compared bullying to a game or battle, a nightmare, water torture, and a noxious substance. Bullies were framed as narcissistic dictators or royalty, two-faced actors, and evil demons. Targeted workers likened themselves to abused children, slaves, animals, prisoners, and heartbroken lovers. As such, through an analysis of the metaphors used to describe the bullying process, the bully and the target of abuse, the article provides qualitative evidence that helps to answer the questions "What does bullying feel like?" Providing an answer to this question is theoretically and practically significant.

Theoretical Implications

Metaphorical language provides linguistic shorthand to describe long, difficult-to-articulate, and devastatingly painful feelings associated with workplace bullying. This is an important step for better explicating a phenomenon such as workplace bullying that is in a state of denotative hesitancy (Clair, 1993). Knowing these stories is integral because, as Lawler (2002) notes, "it is through such stories that we make sense of the world, of our relationship to that world, and of the relationship between ourselves and other selves" (p. 249). Understanding what the bullying process feels like serves to contextualize, enrich, and augment the current survey-based research that statistically links bullying and negative outcomes (Djurkovic et al., 2004; Einarsen & Mikkelsen, 2003; Leymann & Gustafsson, 1996). In highlighting abused workers' metaphors about bullying, this analysis also uncovers the frames within which targets place themselves, providing insight not only into individuals' communicative construction of their experience but also into their cognitive processes (Fraser, 1993; Hart, 2003). These interpretations play a role in future interaction and point out the range of difficulties targeted workers encounter when trying to name, describe, and manage their situation. In short, the metaphors analyzed graphically suggest why bullying feels so devastating and why targets believe there is little they can do to change their situation. Although these consequences were largely teased out within the previous section, here we review the implications of several metaphors in detail.

First, let us consider the implications of viewing oneself as a child. Children who are abused day after day, by a parent or by mobs of other students, are likely to try to isolate themselves, try to be invisible, and if visible, be ingratiating. Doing so might decrease the abuse, but it is also likely to serve as a stumbling block if targets want to increase their status in organizational settings. Certainly, fleeing a bully may assist small children from being hit. However, if a person consistently escapes interactions with a workplace bully, then the target may decrease his or her own options for organizational advancement. In short, the child metaphor fleshes out a sense of powerlessness in alleviating the maltreatment. Targeted workers can try to be good, try to fit in, but most often avoid abuse by escaping the situation.

Likewise, a tortured prisoner has limited options for changing or feeling better within the circumstances. Someone who is tortured or imprisoned can try to black out or become numb, both of which participants said they felt. This lack of focus, although it may ease the torture, is likely to have problematic ramifications in the workplace. Becoming emotionally numb effectively prevents an important way of knowing the world (Freud, 1926; Weiss & Cropanzano, 1996).

If bullying is viewed as a nightmare, complete with uncontrollable plot lines and perpetrators from the dark side, efforts to control the situation are usually perceived as fruitless. Those who view themselves in a nightmare are likely frightened and, as identified through a number of metaphors, feel as though they have little control over the circumstances or actions of their evil oppressor(s). As such, they may try to focus on the very small parts of the situation that they can control. Or they may become withdrawn and disengaged, feeling as though there is nothing that can be done. Again, this may help the abused worker (having the nightmare) feel better, but ultimately, the most efficacious way to change the situation is probably to wake up and escape the scene.

The most common metaphor, that bullying feels like a game or battle, is perhaps the most liberating, because a fighter has some control over the outcome of a battle. Soldiers can psyche themselves up to fight hard, do more damage to the bully or enemy than the bully does to them, feign an injury to save themselves from further pain, and at least "go down swinging." Targets often report that the decision to fight back is a turning point at which they begin to feel better (Namie & Namie, 2000a). However, the outcome of fighting back can lead to retribution, and targeted persons can quickly become so damaged that they are no longer good to anyone. Indeed, although many participants talked about fighting back, none said he or she won the fight. Furthermore, the more employees are abused, the more they resist, both constructively and destructively (Tepper, Duffy, & Shaw, 2001). This has foreboding implications. As Waldron (2000) suggests from hundreds of interviews with abused employees, "the resulting desire for revenge and the potential for physical violence . . . is alarming" (p. 79). And of course, in a workplace setting, a subordinate "fighter" is also akin to "problem employee" or "troublemaker" (p. 79).

When we consider these and the other metaphors through which targets frame their experience, it helps flesh out why scholars and practitioners suggest that once workplace bullying has become an entrenched pattern of negative interaction, it can be difficult or impossible to disrupt (Rayner et al., 2002; Zapf & Gross, 2001). A target's best recourse may be quitting the job and moving on. Metaphors also explain why employees feel such significant pain and despair. They feel suffocated by a toxic substance that is difficult to manage, powerless to control nightmarish evil-doers, and "crazy" because of two-faced performances. At the same time, they fear being trapped and feel lonely, isolated, desperate, and broken hearted about their disconnection from important others at work.

Focusing on the subjective experiences of bullied workers spotlights the way targets, themselves, struggle to make sense of their abuse. This is in contrast to the rather large body of bullying literature that has focused on delineating academic definitions over what counts as workplace bullying, aggression, or discrimination (Cowie, Naylor, Rivers, Smith, & Pereira, 2002). As reviewed earlier, the range of terms used to describe workplace injustice is dizzying and difficult to differentiate (see Keashly & Jagatic, 2003). Targeted persons' metaphorical images of bullying notably shift the focus from how researchers label workplace abuse to how those targeted perceive and make sense of abuse and its impacts. We believe the latter to be a fundamentally crucial issue for attention.

In addition, the analysis extends research on the role metaphoric analyses can play in examining employees' experiences at work, especially bullying. Past organizational research has been critiqued for its neglect of analyzing spontaneous emergent metaphors in organizational talk (Grant & Oswick, 1996b)—although communication scholars offer some important exceptions (e.g., Koch & Deetz, 1981; J. M. Morgan, 2003; Smith & Tuner, 1995). Indeed, previous work analyzing bullying targets' metaphors is limited because of a "forced metaphor" approach. Sheenan, Barker, and McCarthy (2004) relied on a method that specifically asked targets to describe their bullying experiences in metaphorical terms. Despite expecting rich metaphorical data, Sheenan et al. found that their respondents were unclear about what metaphors actually were and that their data produced "less valuable information with respect to metaphors than was expected" (p. 30).

In contrast to instructing participants to respond in metaphorical language or to ranking a priori metaphors (Grant & Oswick, 1996b), the current analysis was idiographic and inductive and found a wealth of organically occurring metaphors. As such, the research aligned with some findings from Sheenan et al.'s (2004) forced metaphor approach; their participants also described the bully as insincere and two-faced, characterized their own feelings as trapped and vulnerable, and described the organization as blind to the bullying situation. However, our study provides many more examples of these feelings and additionally uncovered a number of other complex and less obvious metaphors for the bully process (e.g., bullying as noxious substance), some of which grouped together as a range (e.g., from "picking on" to "torture"). As such, this analysis suggests that an inductive approach is especially worthwhile for making sense of messy interactive processes, such as bullying, that have no definite "face." Such an analysis serves to name and make tangible a process that can be invisible.

Practical Applications

Our analysis suggests that abused workers could profit from identifying and reflecting on the metaphors they use to frame the bullying experience. The mere recognition and identification of metaphors in use allows individuals to better understand how they are framing and thus limiting and constraining their viewpoint on a situation (Marshak, 1996). At the same time, metaphors also can have a "generative quality" (Schön, 1993); they create new meaning and, as such, can be liberating—allowing individuals to learn and see the world anew (Grant & Oswick, 1996a). Our grounded analysis uncovered outlying metaphors for making sense of bullying that are more hopeful than the primary ones explored here. For instance, Laura explained that when she thought about leaving, her colleagues said, "No, be our Rosa Parks, please stay here. Things are gonna be better." This metaphor, of target as survivor or hero figure, was not as common in our data. However, it suggests the possibility that targeted workers could choose to frame themselves in different ways—perhaps as survivors of a shipwreck, revolutionaries, war veterans, or "the resistance." Each of these metaphors, albeit in different ways, highlights more promising ways for framing and perhaps transforming the bullying experience.

In differentiation from the self-help thrust of most popular press books about workplace bullying,[3] our study aims to underscore the emotional experiences of targets so that managers, colleagues, and other laypeople can "feel their pain." As such, various stakeholders may be more inclined to believe abused workers' stories and perhaps be moved to prevention and intervention. Studies that engage emotion are fundamental to motivating ethical change (Aristotle, 1954; Cialdini, 1984). Understanding the emotional pain of workplace bullying can serve as a warning device for managers and potential bullies alike, identifying the onset of problematic interaction and providing a window for early intervention.

As reviewed, adult bullying results in significant employee and organizational costs. One of the key ways to avoid such costs is early intervention before the bullying escalates into an established pattern (Rayner et al., 2002). Unfortunately, as it stands, most workplace bullying interventions are reactive if existent at all. For instance, European health professionals have founded specialized clinics to treat the injuries resulting from bullying at work (Crawford, 2001; Zapf et al., 2003). Although such clinics may be ameliorative, workplace wellness research suggests organizational social health may be most dependent on employees' perceptions of camaraderie and communication with peers, supervisors, and family (Farrell & Geist Martin, 2005)—all issues that must be proactively maintained and protected through everyday practices.

Of course, a difficulty in early intervention is that most subordinate voice—resistance and complaint in particular—occurs in hidden transcripts away from the view of powerholders (J. C. Scott, 1990). Explicit stories of pain and victimization are particularly likely to happen behind closed doors (Deetz, 1992). Metaphors, though, are more subtle. And because metaphors express issues about which individuals may not be consciously aware (Marshak, 1996), metaphorical language is likely to seep into both the public and private talk of employees. In our ongoing informal participation with bullied employees, we find their talk to be peppered with many of the metaphors noted herein. Although our picture-drawing exercise was designed specifically to get at the emotional pain of workplace bullying, the nondirective questions in our research, such as "tell us about your bullying experience" are not unlike those that might be posed by HR professionals, colleagues, or family and friends. Employee emotion expressed metaphorically can provide a signal to managers for the need of organizational involvement and change. An audience member who listened to a presentation of this research, for instance, was able to identify her own bullying behavior in light of these metaphors because she remembered how her target looked and behaved like a "frightened child" in their interactions.

Understanding targets' metaphors can also assist organizational policy makers and human relations professionals specifically to identify links between negative social interaction at work and the powerful effects such behavior can have on individuals. These metaphors not only graphically detail the pain that abused workers endure but also point to two specific types of workplace stress and illness as identified by Farrell and Geist Martin (2005). Namely, these metaphors reveal that targets experience deep psychological pain (they must live in a world that is unstable and crazy making, they experience psychological torture, and they are heartbroken) and a loss of important social networks (they lose beloved friends when they are driven from their jobs, their work feels like a dysfunctional family, and they experience guilt over their inability to defend coworkers).

Abuse, in turn, leads to costly organizational repercussions. Bullying destroys productive networks of communication (Lockhart, 1997) and increases the likelihood of nontargeted coworkers' departure (Vartia, 1996). Even less tangible negative effects are "opportunity costs of lowered employee commitment, such as lack of discretionary effort, commitments outside the job, time spent talking about the problem rather than working, and loss of creativity" (Bassman, 1992, p. 137). Finally, although there is scant evidence in the bullying literature (or our data) regarding the potential for bullied workers to respond with violence, workplace aggression research suggests active revenge could be a very real possibility. Perceptions and reports of unfair treatment are common precursors of workplace aggression, violence, and sabotage (Analoui, 1995; Hoad, 1993; Neuman & Baron, 2003). Certainly, if feeling like the unpopular kid at school is one factor leading to bloodshed among children (Garbarino & deLara, 2002), it is not unthinkable that a worker who feels continually abused, tortured, and isolated in an organization might respond with aggression.

Limitations, Future Directions, and Conclusions

We as researchers noted that participants appeared to have difficulty narrowing down and articulating their experience succinctly in the focus group format. We therefore complemented focus group data with more open-ended interviews in which participants controlled the pace and development of their story. Although focus groups may have curbed narrative development to some extent, we wonder whether the data produced through them were telling of some of the prohibitive structures that employees likely also encounter when voicing problems in the workplace setting. Specifically, in both focus group and organizational venues, employees have voice only among a cacophony of other voices, competing demands, and within short windows of time. Therefore, future research that combines focus group and participant observation data might examine how much the focus group structure provides a unique view into the difficulty employees have in articulating their story to organizational superiors, coworkers, or HR personnel.

Given the difficulty bullied workers illustrate in succinctly translating their experiences into words, future research would also do well to conduct a close narrative analysis of various target stories— both coherent narratives and those marked by hypertext—nonlinear discourse made up of pieces or fragments of information (Nelson, 1983). Such an analysis could examine the ways targeted persons frame themselves, their bullies, and witnessing coworkers, and the ways they define personal identities through the emplotment of their experience (Lawler, 2002). Furthermore, a close discourse analysis could compare stories told by those who are currently experiencing bullying and contrast them with stories told by those who have moved on. Doing so might serve to pinpoint junctures in which articulation of the experience is especially trying and difficult for targets and provide recommendations for the most effective ways to communicate complaints of workplace abuse.

Third, alternative representation practices could further develop the emotions associated with workplace bullying. Although metaphorical imagery is a powerful tool for analyzing the emotion of work life, the vividness of understanding emotion is limited by the printed page. During focus groups and interviews, we witnessed nonverbal facial expressions, changes in pitch, shortness of breath, and spontaneous weeping that intensely illustrated participants' depth of pain. To get at this feeling, future analyses should entertain various representational options, including performance and creative writing (Richardson, 2000; Tracy, 2004).

Last, we believe that future research should analyze the interweavings of race, gender, and age with workplace bullying. The similarities among workers' emotional experiences in this study are notable, despite differences that we often believe "make a difference." Participants ranged from a 26-year-old male to a woman in her 70s. Education ranged from a high school diploma to graduate degrees. Industries included service and sales persons, educators, engineers, and government workers. Both men and women participated. Even with this wide range of participants, group interactions were marked by multiple signs of agreement such as head nodding, murmured concurrence, and cascading stories in which one person's experience evoked, "yes, that's what happened to me." This suggests that the emotional experience of workplace bullying can be similar across workgroups, age, and sex. However, our sample, like that of most workplace-bullying research, was racially homogenous, and so future research should do more to analyze the ways that bullying and racial discrimination may be connected. Furthermore, although demographic differences did not emerge as salient factors in our study, past critical organizational communication research would certainly suggest that workplace mistreatment is affected by larger discourses of gender and race (Allen, 2001).

In conclusion, this study provides an important step in understanding the emotion and pain associated with workplace bullying. Whether empowering or disempowering, the metaphors pinpointed through this analysis provide targets with words to explain their situation to others— an important move considering that one of the main problems targeted employees face is that their plight is largely invisible. Similar to how the term *sexual harassment* allowed recipients of the behavior to better make sense of their situation (Kramarae, 1981), we learned that our respondents appreciated the terms *bully* and *target* in helping them to make sense of a situation for which many had previously found no words to adequately describe. People understand their lives through the language available to them (Kay & Kempton, 1984). Therefore, it is important for researchers to provide venues in which abused workers can make meaning of their experience and engage in analysis practices that articulate the devastating effects of bullying. Indeed, "people make sense of their lives through the stories that are available to them and they attempt to fit their lives into the available stories" (Richardson, 1995, p. 213). Metaphors act as mini stories and thus "act as a compass, which serves to orient us" (Hart, 2003, p. 1). Attending to the metaphors of abused workers serves not only to lay bare the feelings associated with workplace bullying but also to diagnose current interpretations and provide cues for potential intervention and change.

NOTES

1. Names used throughout the article are pseudonyms, and several identifying details of participants have been modified.
2. Within 5 months of beginning the data gathering for this project, we had been contacted by more than 15 journalists and included in 12 media stories on the topic. Furthermore, within 2 weeks of placing an advertisement calling for persons bullied at work, we received 20 telephone calls and more than 200 e-mails.
3. Self-help books include *The Bully at Work* (Namie & Namie, 2000a); *Brutal Bosses* (Hornstein, 1996); *Mobbing: Emotional Abuse in the American Workplace* (Davenport, Schwartz, & Elliott, 2002); *Work Abuse: How to Recognize It and Survive It* (Wyatt & Hare, 1997); *Stalking the Soul* (Hirigoyen, 1998); *Bullying in Adulthood* (Randall, 2001), and *You Don't Have to Take It: A Woman's Guide to Confronting Emotional Abuse at Work* (NiCarthy, Gottlieb, & Coffman, 1993).

REFERENCES

Adams, A., & Crawford, N. (1992). *Bullying at work: How to confront and overcome it.* London: Virago.

Alberts, J. K., Lutgen-Sandvik, P., & Tracy, S. J. (2005, May). *Workplace bullying: A case of escalated incivility.* Paper presented at the International Communication Association, New York.

Allen, B. J. (2001). Gender, race, and communication in professional environments. In L. P. Arliss & D. Borisoff (Eds.), *Women and men communicating: Challenges and changes* (pp. 212–231). Prospect Heights, IL: Waveland.

Analoui, F. (1995). Workplace sabotage: Its styles, motives, and management. *Journal of Management Development, 14,* 64–86.

Andersson, L. M., & Pearson, C. (1999). Tit for tat? The spiraling effect of incivility in the workplace. *Academy of Management Review, 24,* 454–471.

Aristotle. (1954). *Rhetoric* (W. R. Roberts, Trans.; compiled by Lee Honeycutt). Retrieved May 12, 2005, from http://www.public.iastate.edu/~honeyl/Rhetoric/

Baron, R. A., & Neuman, J. H. (1998). Workplace aggression—The iceberg beneath the tip of workplace violence: Evidence on its forms, frequency and targets. *Public Administration Quarterly, 21,* 446–464.

Bassman, E. S. (1992). *Abuse in the workplace: Management remedies and bottom line impact.* Westport, CT: Quorum Books.

Björkqvist, K., Osterman, K., & Hjelt-Back, M. (1994). Aggression among university employees. *Aggressive Behavior, 20,* 173–184.

Brodsky, C. (1976). *The harassed worker.* Lexington, MA: D.C. Heath.

Buzzanell, P. M., & Burrell, N. A. (1997). Family and workplace conflict: Examining metaphorical conflict schemas and expressions across context and sex. *Human Communication Research, 24*, 109–146.

Buzzanell, P. M., & Turner, L. H. (2003). Emotion work revealed by job loss discourse: Backgrounding-foregrounding of feelings, construction of normalcy, and (re)instituting of traditional male masculinities. *Journal of Applied Communication Research, 31*, 27–57.

Carey, J. W. (1994). The group effect in focus groups: Planning, implementing, and interpreting focus group research. In J. Morse (Ed.), *Critical issues in qualitative research methods* (pp. 225–241). Thousand Oaks, CA: Sage.

Charmaz, K. (2001). Grounded theory. In R. M. Emerson (Ed.), *Contemporary field research* (pp. 335–352). Prospect Heights, IL: Waveland.

Cialdini, R. B. (1984). *How and why people agree to things.* New York: Morrow.

Clair, R. P. (1993). The use of framing devices to sequester organizational narratives: Hegemony and harassment. *Communication Monographs, 60*, 113–136.

Cooper, C. L., Dewe, P. J., & O'Driscoll, M. P. (2001). *Organizational stress: A review and critique of theory, research, and applications.* Thousand Oaks, CA: Sage.

Cowie, H., Naylor, P., Rivers, I., Smith, P. K., & Pereira, B. (2002). Measuring workplace bullying. *Aggression and Violent Behavior: A Review Journal, 7*, 33–51.

Crawford, N. (2001). Organisational responses to workplace bullying. In N. Tehrani (Ed.), *Building a culture of respect: Managing bullying at work* (pp. 21–31). London: Taylor & Francis.

Davenport, N., Schwartz, R. D., & Elliott, G. P. (2002). *Mobbing: Emotional abuse in the American workplace* (2nd ed.). Ames, IA: Civil Society Publishing.

Deetz, S. A. (1984). Metaphor analysis. *International and Intercultural Annual, 8*, 215–228.

Deetz, S. A. (1992). *Democracy in an age of corporate colonization: Developments in communication and the politics of everyday life.* Albany: State University of New York Press.

Djurkovic, N., McCormack, D., & Casimir, G. (2004). The physical and psychological effects of workplace bullying and their relationship to intention to leave: A test of the psychosomatic and disability hypothesis. *International Journal of Organizational Theory and Behavior, 7*, 469–497.

Duffy, M. K., Ganster, D. C., & Pagon, M. (2002). Social undermining in the workplace. *Academy of Management Journal, 45*, 331–351.

Einarsen, S. (1999). The nature and causes of bullying at work. *International Journal of Manpower, 20*, 16–27.

Einarsen, S., Hoel, H., Zapf, D., & Cooper, C. L. (Eds.). (2003a). *Bullying and emotional abuse in the workplace: International perspectives in research and practice.* London: Taylor & Francis.

Einarsen, S., Hoel, H., Zapf, D., & Cooper, C. L. (2003b). The concept of bullying at work. In S. Einarsen, H. Hoel, D. Zapf, & C. L. Cooper (Eds.), *Bullying and emotional abuse in the workplace: International perspectives in research and practice* (pp. 3–30). London: Taylor & Francis.

Einarsen, S., & Mikkelsen, E. G. (2003). Individual effects of exposure to bullying at work. In S. Einarsen, H. Hoel, D. Zapf, & C. L. Cooper (Eds.), *Bullying and emotional abuse in the workplace: International perspectives in research and practice* (pp. 127–144). London: Taylor & Francis.

Einarsen, S., & Raknes, B. I. (1997). Harassment at work and the victimization of men. *Violence and Victims, 12*, 247–263.

Einarsen, S., Raknes, B. I., & Mattheisen, S. B. (1994). Bullying and harassment at work and their relationships to work environment quality: An exploratory study. *European Work and Organizational Psychologist, 4*, 381–401.

Farrell, A., & Geist-Martin, P. (2005). Communicating health: Perceptions of wellness at work. *Management Communication Quarterly, 18*, 543–592.

Ferraro, K. J. (1996). The dance of dependency: A genealogy of domestic violence discourse. *Hypatta, 11*, 77–91.

Field, T. (1996). *Bully in sight: How to predict, resist, challenge and combat workplace bullying.* Oxfordshire, UK: Success Unlimited.

Fineman, S. (1996). Emotion and organizing. In S. K. Clegg, C. Hardy, & W. K. Nord (Eds.), *Handbook of organization studies* (pp. 543–564). London: Sage.

Fraser, B. (1993). The interpretation of novel metaphors. In A. Ortony (Ed.), *Metaphor and thought* (2nd ed., pp. 329–341). Cambridge, UK: Cambridge University Press.

Freud, S. (1926). Inhibitions, symptoms, and anxiety. In J. Strachey (Ed.), *Standard edition* (Vol. 20, pp. 70–176). London: Hogarth.

Garbarino, J., & deLara, E. (2002). *And words can hurt forever: How to protect adolescents from bullying, harassment, and emotional violence.* New York: Free Press.

Glaser, B. G., & Strauss, A. L. (1967). *The discovery of grounded theory: Strategies for qualitative research.* Hawthorne, NY: Aldine.

Grant, D., & Oswick, C. (1996a). Introduction: Getting the measure of metaphors. In D. G. C. Oswick (Ed.), *Metaphor and organizations* (pp. 1–20). London: Sage.

Grant, D., & Oswick, C. (1996b). The organization of metaphors and the metaphors of organization: Where are we and where do we go from here? In D. Grant & C. Oswick (Eds.), *Metaphor and organizations* (pp. 213–226). London: Sage.

Harlos, K. P., & Pinder, C. (2000). Emotion and injustice in the workplace. In S. Fineman (Ed.), *Emotions in organizations* (pp. 255–276). Thousand Oaks, CA: Sage.

Hart, J. (2003). Organizational orienteering: Charting the terrain. *American Communication Journal, 6*(2), 1–9.

Hirigoyen, M. F. (1998). *Stalking the soul: Emotion abuse and the erosion of identity.* New York: Helen Marx Books.

Hoad, C. D. (1993). Violence at work: Perspectives from research among 20 British employers. *Security Journal, 4*, 64–86.

Hochschild, A. R. (1983). *The managed heart: Commercialization of human feeling.* Berkeley: University of California Press.

Hoel, H., & Cooper, C. L. (2001). Origins of bullying: Theoretical frameworks for explaining workplace bullying. In N. Tehrani (Ed.), *Building a culture of respect: Managing bullying at work* (pp. 1–20). London: Taylor & Francis.

Hoel, H., Einarsen, S., & Cooper, C. L. (2003). Organisational effects of bullying. In S. Einarsen, H. Hoel, D. Zapf, & C. L. Cooper (Eds.), *Bullying and emotional abuse in the workplace* (pp. 145–162). London: Taylor & Francis.

Hornstein, H. A. (1996). *Brutal bosses and their prey: How to identify and overcome abuse in the workplace.* New York: Riverhead Books.

Innes, B. (1998). *The history of torture.* New York: St. Martin's.

Janus-Bulman, R. (1992). *Shattered assumptions: Toward a new psychology of trauma.* New York: Free Press.

Kay, P., & Kempton, W. (1984). What is the Sapir-Whorf hypothesis? *American Anthropologist, 86*, 65–79.

Keashly, L. (1998). Emotional abuse in the workplace: Conceptual and empirical issues. *Journal of Emotional Abuse, 1*(1), 85–117.

Keashly, L. (2001). Interpersonal and systemic aspects of emotional abuse at work: The target's perspective. *Violence and Victims, 16*, 233–268.

Keashly, L., & Jagatic, K. (2003). By any other name: American perspectives on workplace bullying. In S. Einarsen, H. Hoel, D. Zapf, & C. L. Cooper (Eds.), *Bullying and emotional abuse in the workplace: International perspectives in research and practice* (pp. 31–91). London: Taylor & Francis.

Keashly, L., & Neuman, J. H. (2005). Bullying in the workplace: Its impact and management. *Employee Rights and Employment Policy Journal, 8*, 335–373.

Keashly, L., & Nowell, B. L. (2003). Conflict, conflict resolution and bullying. In S. Einarsen, H. Hoel, D. Zapf, & C. L. Cooper (Eds.), *Bullying and emotional abuse in the workplace: International perspectives in research and practice* (pp. 339–358). London: Taylor & Francis.

Kirby, E. L., & Harter, L. M. (2003). Speaking the language of the bottom-line: The metaphor of "managing diversity." *Journal of Business Communication, 40*, 28–54.

Koch, S., & Deetz, S. A. (1981). Metaphor analysis of social reality in organizations. *Journal of Applied Communication Research, 9*, 1–15.

Kramarae, C. (1981). *Women and men speaking.* Rowley, MS: Newbury House.

Lakoff, G., & Johnson, M. (1980). *Metaphors we live by.* Chicago: University of Chicago Press.

Lawler, S. (2002). Narrative in social research. In T. May (Ed.), *Qualitative research in action* (pp. 242–258). London: Sage.

Lee, D. (2002). Gendered workplace bullying in the restructured UK Civil Service. *Personnel Review, 31*, 205–227.

Lewis, D. (1999). Workplace bullying—Interim findings of a study in further and higher education in Wales. *International Journal of Manpower, 20*, 106–118.

Lewis, S. E., & Orford, J. (2005). Women's experiences of workplace bullying: Changes in social relations. *Journal of Community and Applied Social Psychology, 15*, 29–47.

Leymann, H. (1990). Mobbing and psychological terror at workplaces. *Violence and Victims, 5*, 119–126.

Leymann, H. (1996). The content and development of mobbing at work. *European Journal of Work and Organizational Psychology, 10*, 165–184.

Leymann, H., & Gustafsson, A. (1996). Mobbing at work and the development of post-traumatic stress disorders. *European Journal of Work and Organizational Psychology, 5*, 251–275.

Liebermann, M. (1991). *Art therapy for groups: A handbook of themes, games and exercises.* London: Routledge.

Lindlof, T. R., & Taylor, B. C. (2002). *Qualitative communication research methods* (2nd ed.). Thousand Oaks, CA: Sage.

Lockhart, K. (1997). Experience from a staff support service. *Journal of Community and Applied Social Psychology, 7*, 193–198.

Lutgen-Sandvik, P. (2003). The communicative cycle of employee emotional abuse: Generation and regeneration of workplace mistreatment. *Management Communication Quarterly, 16*, 471–501.

Lutgen-Sandvik, P. (2005). Water smoothing stones: Subordinate resistance to workplace bullying (Doctoral dissertation, Arizona State University, 2005). *Dissertation Abstracts International, 66/04*, 1214.

Lutgen-Sandvik, P., Tracy, S. J., & Alberts, J. K. (2005, February). *Burned by bullying in the American workplace: A first time study of U.S. prevalence and delineation of bullying "degree."* Paper presented at the Annual Conference, Western States Communication Association, San Francisco.

Marshak, R. J. (1996). Metaphors, metaphoric fields and organizational change. In D. Grant & C. Oswick (Eds.), *Metaphor and organizations* (pp. 147–165). London: Sage.

Matusewitch, E. (1996). Constructive discharge: When a resignation is really a termination. *Employment Discrimination Report, 6*(7), 1–5.

Meares, M. M., Oetzel, J. G., Derkacs, D., & Ginossar, T. (2004). Employee mistreatment and muted voices in the culturally diverse workforce. *Journal of Applied Communication Research, 32*, 4–27.

Meyer, A. (1991). Visual data in organizational research. *Organization Science, 2*, 218–236.

Miles, M. B., & Huberman, A. M. (1994). *Qualitative data analysis*. Thousand Oaks, CA: Sage.

Mischler, E. (1986). *Research interviewing: Context and narrative*. Cambridge, MA: Harvard University Press.

Morgan, G. (1997). *Images of organizations*. Thousand Oaks, CA: Sage.

Morgan, J. M. (2003). Moldy bagels and new toasters: Images of emotion in workplace relationships. *Iowa Journal of Communication, 35*, 207–232.

Namie, G. (2003). Workplace bullying: Escalated incivility. *Ivey Business Journal, 68*(2), 1–6.

Namie, G., & Namie, R. (2000a). *The bully at work: What you can do to stop the hurt and reclaim your dignity on the job*. Naperville, IL: Sourcebooks.

Namie, G., & Namie, R. (2000b). Workplace bullying: The silent epidemic. *Employee Rights Quarterly, 1*(2), 1–12.

Nelson, T. (1983). *Literary machines*. Swarthmore, PA: Author.

Neuman, J. H. (2004). The role of the workplace in workplace bullying. *Perspectives on Work, 40*, 7–32.

Neuman, J. H., & Baron, R. A. (2003). *Social antecedents of bullying: A social interactionist perspective*. London: Taylor & Francis.

NiCarthy, G., Gottlieb, N., & Coffman, S. (1993). *You don't have to take it: A woman's guide to confronting emotional abuse at work*. Seattle, WA: Seal.

O'Rourke, D. K. (2004). *How America's first settlers invented chattel slavery: Dehumanizing Native Americans and Africans with language, laws, guns, and religion*. New York: Peter Lang.

Ortony, A. (1975). Why metaphors are necessary and not just nice. *Educational Theory, 25*, 45–53.

Planalp, S. (1993). Communication, cognition, and emotion. *Communication Monographs, 60*, 3–9.

Randall, P. (2001). *Bullying in adulthood: Assessing the bullies and their victims*. New York: Brunner-Routledge.

Rayner, C., & Cooper, C. L. (1997). Workplace bullying: Myth or reality—Can we afford to ignore it? *Leadership and Organization Development Journal, 18*, 211–214.

Rayner, C., & Hoel, H. (1997). A summary review of literature relating to workplace bullying. *Journal of Community and Applied Social Psychology, 7*, 181–191.

Rayner, C., Hoel, H., & Cooper, C. L. (2002). *Workplace bullying: What we know, who is to blame, and what can we do?* London: Taylor & Francis.

Reason, P. (1994). Three approaches to participative inquiry. In N. K. Denzin & Y. S. Lincoln (Eds.), *Handbook of qualitative research* (pp. 324–339). Thousand Oaks, CA: Sage.

Richardson, L. (1995). Narrative and sociology. In J. V. Maanen (Ed.), *Representation in ethnography* (pp. 198–221). Thousand Oaks, CA: Sage.

Richardson, L. (2000). Writing: A method of inquiry. In N. K. Denzin & Y. S. Lincoln (Eds.), *Handbook of qualitative research* (2nd ed., pp. 923–948). Thousand Oaks, CA: Sage.

Richman, J. A., Rospenda, K. M., Flaherty, J. A., & Freels, S. (2001). Workplace harassment, active coping, and alcohol-related outcomes. *Journal of Substance Abuse, 13*, 347–366.

Salin, D. (2001). Prevalence and forms of bullying among business professionals: A comparison of two different strategies for measuring bullying. *European Journal of Work and Organizational Psychology, 10*, 425–441.

Sarri, R. C., & Sarri, C. M. (1992). Organizational and community change through participatory action research. *Administration in Social Work, 16*, 99–122.

Schneider, K. T., Hitlan, R. T., & Radhakrishnan, P. (2000). An examination of the nature and correlates of ethnic harassment experiences in multiple contexts. *Journal of Applied Psychology, 85*, 3–12.

Schön, D. A. (1993). Generative metaphor: A perspective on problem-solving in social policy. In A. Ortony (Ed.), *Metaphor and thought* (pp. 254–283). New York: Cambridge University Press.

Scott, J. C. (1990). *Domination and the arts of resistance*. New Haven, CT: Yale University Press.

Scott, M. J., & Stradling, S. G. (2001). Trauma, duress and stress. In N. Tehrani (Ed.), *Building a culture of respect: Managing bullying at work* (pp. 33–42). London: Taylor & Francis.

Sheenan, K. H., Barker, M., & McCarthy, P. (2004). Analysing metaphors used by victims of workplace bullying. *International Journal of Management and Decision Making, 5*, 21–31.

Smith, R. C., & Tuner, P. K. (1995). A social constructionist reconfiguration of metaphor analysis: An application of "SCMA" to organizational socialization theory. *Communication Monographs, 62*, 152–181.

Spradley, J. P. (1979). *The ethnographic interview*. New York: Holt, Rinehart and Winston.

Tattersall, A. J., & Farmer, E. W. (1995). The regulation of work demands and strain. In S. L. Sauter & L. R. Murphy (Eds.), *Organizational risk factors for job stress* (pp. 139–156). Washington DC: American Psychological Association.

Tepper, B. J., Duffy, M. K., & Shaw, J. D. (2001). Personality moderators of the relationship between abusive supervision and subordinates' resistance. *Journal of Applied Psychology, 86*, 974–983.

Tracy, S. J. (2004). The construction of correctional officers: Layers of emotionality behind bars. *Qualitative Inquiry, 10*, 509–533.

Vartia, M. (1996). The sources of bullying: Psychological work environment and organizational climate. *European Journal of Work and Organizational Psychology, 5*, 203–214.

Vince, R., & Broussine, M. (1996). Paradox, defense and attachment: Accessing and working with emotions and relations underlying organizational change. *Organization Studies, 17*(1), 1–21.

Waldron, V. R. (2000). Relational experiences and emotions at work. In S. Fineman (Ed.), *Emotion in organizations* (pp. 64–82). Thousand Oaks, CA: Sage.

Weiss, H. M., & Cropanzano, R. (1996). Affective events theory: A theoretical discussion of the structure, causes and consequences of affective experiences at work. *Research in Organizational Behavior, 17*, 1–74.

Williams, K. D., & Sommer, K. L. (1997). Social ostracism by co-workers: Does rejection lead to loafing or compensation? *Personality and Social Psychology Bulletin, 27*, 693–706.

Wyatt, J., & Hare, C. (1997). *Work abuse: How to recognize it and survive it*. Rochester, VT: Schenkman Books.

Yamada, D. (2000). The phenomenon of "workplace bullying" and the need for status-blind hostile work environment protection. *Georgetown Law Journal, 88*, 475–536.

Yamada, D. (2005). Crafting a legislative response to workplace bullying. *Employee Rights and Employment Policy Journal, 8*, 476–517.

Zapf, D., Einarsen, S., Hoel, H., & Vartia, M. (2003). Empirical findings on bullying in the workplace. In S. Einarsen, H. Hoel, D. Zapf, & C. L. Cooper (Eds.), *Bullying and emotional abuse in the workplace: International perspectives in research and practice* (pp. 103–126). London: Taylor & Francis.

Zapf, D., & Gross, C. (2001). Conflict escalation and coping with workplace bullying: A replication and extension. *European Journal of Work and Organizational Psychology, 10*, 497–522.

Zapf, D., Knorz, C., & Kulla, M. (1996). On the relationship between mobbing factors, and job content, social work environment and health outcomes. *European Journal of Work and Organizational Psychology, 5*, 212–237.

Zuboff, S. (1988). *The age of the smart machine. The future of work and power*. New York: Basic Books.

Sarah J. Tracy (PhD, 2000, University of Colorado, Boulder) is an associate professor and director for The Project for Wellness and Work-Life in the Hugh Downs School of Human Communication at Arizona State University. Her research interests include organizational identity, emotion labor, bullying, dirty work, and work–life balance.

Pamela Lutgen-Sandvik (PhD, 2005, Arizona State University) is an assistant professor in the Department of Communication and Journalism at University of New Mexico and studies employee advocacy, bullying, and injustice in the workplace.

Jess K. Alberts (PhD, 1986, University of Texas at Austin) is a professor in the Hugh Downs School of Human Communication at Arizona State University and conducts research in the areas of conflict, domestic labor, mediation, and humor.

Authors' Note: We thank the Office of the Vice President for Research and Economic Affairs at Arizona State University for a grant that helped fund this research. Furthermore, we are grateful to Editor James Barker and two anonymous reviewers for their suggestions on this article. Correspondence should be directed to the first author at Arizona State University, P.O. Box 871205, Tempe, AZ 85287-1205; e-mail: Sarah.Tracy@asu.edu.

Discussion Topics and Activities for "Nightmares, Demons, and Slaves"

1. Reflect on how the article might have stimulated personal, comparable memories of bullying, and how those memories might have been triggered (e.g., a participant's vignette, a coauthors' assertion, a particular metaphor).

2. Discuss how metaphor analysis was utilized in the research and its possible application and transfer to other qualitative studies.

3. Discuss how a qualitative study might be designed to explore bullying among children or adolescents, including the phenomenon of cyberbullying.

"They Think Minority Means Lesser Than": Black Middle-Class Sons and Fathers Resisting Microaggressions in the School

Quaylan Allen[1]

Urban Education 48(2), 171–197

© The Author(s) 2012 Reprints and permission: sagepub.com/journalsPermissions.nav
DOI: 10.1177/0042085912450575

uex.sagepub.com

ABSTRACT

The current literature on Black middle-class men is sparse, leaving little to be known about the raced, classed, and gendered experiences for many Black middle-class male students and their families. Employing qualitative methodology, this study uses critical race theory (CRT) to examine the educational experiences of Black middle-class high school male students through the counterstories of Black students and their fathers. This study highlights various microaggression events experienced by the male students as well as the forms of cultural wealth drawn upon by the fathers to divert the potential negative outcomes of school racism.

KEYWORDS

Black middle-class, Black males, Black fathers, critical race theory, microaggressions

INTRODUCTION

Though the literature on the Black male experience is growing, there is still a gap in the literature regarding the experiences of middle-class Black men. Relatively few studies have seriously examined the educational experiences of Black middle-class students in general (Allen, 2010b;

---

[1]Chapman University, CA, USA

Corresponding Author:

Quaylan Allen, PhD, Assistant Professor Chapman University, One University Drive, Orange, CA 92866, USA.

Email: qallen@chapman.edu

Ascher & Branch Smith, 2005; Ferguson, 2001; Hemmings, 1996; Horvat & Antonio, 1999; Lareau & Horvat, 1999; Ogbu, 2003; Tyson, 2002). The majority of research conducted on Black students has focused on the working-class, only peripherally mentioning the experiences of Black middle-class students, and rarely disaggregating Black underachievement by class. This presumes that Black schooling experiences are homogeneous and are consistent over time. Studies that focus on the raced and classed experiences of Black students, unfortunately, are really only looking at the raced and classed experiences of the working- and under-class. This lends itself to providing explanations of Black (under)achievement and solutions that lack nuance by class, location, and time.

The plight of the Black middle class may not be currently salient in public discourse, though it does not mean Black middle-class families are without their perils. Statistically speaking, the process of middle-class reproduction for Black families is a difficult one. More than 80% of the Black middle-class population is first-generation middle class (Billingsley, 1992; Landry, 1987; McAdoo, 1978), with most specifically identified as lower middle class (McBrier & Wilson, 2004; Pattillo-McCoy, 1999, 2000). Black families also have great difficulty transmitting middle-class status from generation to generation (Hertz, 2005; Issacs, 2007; Kearney, 2006), meaning that many Black middle-class families will have offspring who are downwardly mobile (Attewell, Lavin, Domina, & Levey, 2004).

It is possible that the difficulties of Black middle-class reproduction are emblematic of the achievement gap between middle-class Blacks and middle-class Whites, a gap that in many cases is greater than the gap between working-class Blacks and Whites (Belluck, 1999; Hallinan, 2001).

The research literature regularly speaks to the underrepresentation of Black men, including middle-class men, in gifted and talented programs and overrepresentation in lower-ability, remedial, or special education programs (Aud, Fox, & Kewal Ramani, 2010; Blanchett, Klingner, & Harry, 2009; Grantham, 2004; Mickelson, 2001; Oakes, 2005). In addition, Black men regardless of class status lag behind Black women in achievement scores and graduation rates (Hubbard, 1999; Roach, 2001; Trent, 1991). For these reasons research on Black middle-class men is quite pertinent to the larger investigation of Black educational achievement.

In this article I present narrative data on the school experiences of Black middle-class men, focusing on the school-based racial microaggressions as well as the intervention responses by the middle-class fathers. A brief discussion of critical race theory (CRT) and microaggressions as theoretical frameworks will be followed by a methodological summary. I will then present the study results, which include the experienced microaggressions of assumptions of intelligence and deviance and differential treatment in discipline. Also presented in the results include the intervention responses by the parents, drawing upon their cultural wealth to contest microaggressions and create opportunities for success. Finally, an analytical discussion of the results will be conducted along with concluding remarks.

THEORETICAL FRAMEWORK

Critical race theory. Employing critical race theory (CRT) as a theoretical lens, this study foregrounds the role of race and racism in the secondary schooling experiences of Black middle-class men. A product of the 1960s Civil Rights activities and formulated within legal studies, CRT is an interdisciplinary movement that puts the impact of race and racism at the center of any critical examination (Delgado & Stefancic, 2001). Though CRT has largely been used in legal studies (Crenshaw, Gotanda, Peller, & Thomas, 1995), it has become an equally useful analytic tool in the field of education. As Solórzano (1998) explains, "A critical race theory in education challenges the dominant discourse on race and racism as they relate to education by examining how educational theory, policy, and practice are used to subordinate certain racial and ethnic groups" (p. 122). The literature on CRT consistently identifies five foundational tenets of the theory.

1. Centrality and intersectionality of race and racism: As race and racism are endemic to American society, CRT places race, and its intersection with other identities (i.e., class, gender, sexual orientation, language, immigrant status, etc.), at the center of its analysis (Bell, 1992; Crenshaw, 1993).

2. Challenges dominant ideology: CRT seeks to challenge dominant claims of race and gender neutrality, objectivity, universalism, ahistoricism, colorblindness, and equal opportunity. Such claims within educational and other social institutions camouflage the self-interests and privileges of dominant groups and maintains the status quo of racial inequalities (Delgado, 1991; Ladson-Billings & Tate IV, 2006).

3. Centralizes experiential knowledge: CRT rejects master narratives that attempt to mask racial, sexual, and gender discrimination and privileges the lived experiences of people of color. Through counterstorytelling, narratives, biographies, and other qualitative methods, the lived experiences of people of color are recognized as valid and necessary to the analysis of race and racism (Delgado, 1995; Dixson & Rousseau, 2006; Miron & Lauria, 1998; Solórzano & Yosso, 2002). In addition, through counterstories CRT seeks to identify various forms of cultural wealth (Yosso, 2006) that people of color draw upon to resist racial injustices and create opportunities for success.

4. Commitment to social justice: CRT works to eliminate racial injustice as well as other forms of insubordination that pervade American society (Matsuda, 1991).

5. Interdisciplinary in nature: CRT analysis is applicable across disciplines, as race and racism are endemic to American society and should be studied and taught across disciplines (Crenshaw et al., 1995; Taylor, Gillborn, & Ladson-Billings, 2009).

At its axis, CRT analysis invariably works to uncover how race mediates the ways people of color experience subordination through social and institutional racism, and is a useful tool in analyzing the impact of racial microaggressions on Black males in schools.

Racial microaggressions. Using CRT as an analytical tool, this study seeks to examine how the daily and sometimes subtle experiences of racism adversely affect the schooling opportunities for Black middle-class men. Though overt racism is still very much prevalent in American society, it is often recognized through public discourse as socially unacceptable. It is the covert or subtle racism that often goes unnoticed but quietly demeans and denigrates people of color. Pierce et al. (Pierce, Carew, Peirce-Gonzalez, & Willis, 1978) defines microaggressions as

> subtle, stunning, often automatic, and non-verbal exchanges which are "put downs" of blacks by offenders. The offensive mechanisms used against blacks often are innocuous. The cumulative weight of their never-ending burden is the major ingredient in black-white interactions. (p. 66)

Though Pierce is speaking specifically about race, microaggressions affect all marginalized groups and are felt through environmental cues as well as verbal and nonverbal hidden messages that serve to invalidate one's experiential reality and perpetuate feelings of inferiority. For example, microaggressions taking the form of nonverbal or behavioral exchanges may include a White woman clutching her purse when a Black man walks by or a group of Black students being ignored or given "slow" service at a restaurant. Microaggressions also include verbal exchanges that aim to denigrate people of color (Solórzano, Ceja, & Yosso, 2000) such as, "She's so articulate," or "You're different from the others." Furthermore, microaggressions are impactful to marginalized groups, as they can psychologically and spiritually affect the ways they can experience successful opportunities in schools or in other settings (Franklin, 2004; Solórzano et al., 2000; Sue, 2004).

Sue et al. (2008, 2007), outline a taxonomy of racial, gender, and sexual orientation microaggressions that fall into three major categories: (1) microassaults, (2) microinsults, and (3) microinvalidations. Microassaults "are conscious, deliberate, and either subtle or explicit racial, gender, or sexual orientation biased attitudes, beliefs, or behaviors that are communicated to marginalized groups through environmental cues, verbalizations, or behaviors" (Sue, 2010, p. 28). These forms of microaggressions may be more blatant than others and may include outright name-calling (i.e., "nigger-boy") or environmental cues such as denigrating symbols (i.e., a noose).

Microinsults are subtler but still include the interpersonal and environmental messages that convey stereotypes and biases toward marginalized groups. Common microinsult themes include assigning degrees of intelligence to a person's race, treating one as a second-class citizen, pathologizing cultural values or communication styles, or assumptions of deviance (Sue, 2010, p. 35). For example, on high school and college campuses, many Black students experience invisibility, differential treatment by school teachers, and the feeling of being stereotyped due to pejorative perceptions of Black identity (Allen, 2010b; Henfield, 2011; Solórzano et al., 2000), which reflect some of the common microinsult themes.

Last, microinvalidations are the interpersonal and environmental messages that negate, nullify, or undermine the experiences, feelings, and realities of marginalized groups. Some examples of microinvalidations include feeling like a foreigner in your own country; encountering color-, gender-, or sexual orientation–blind individuals or policies; or encountering individuals who believe racism, sexism, and homophobia don't really exist (Sue, 2010, p. 37). Microinvalidations can be the most damaging as they devalue or invalidate the lived reality of racism, sexism, and homophobia for many people.

These categories are useful in understanding the various textures of microaggressions and the ways in which race is embedded in the fabric of one's life. Drawing upon CRT's use of intersectionality (Crenshaw, 1993), we must also consider how people may experience microaggressions at the intersection of race, gender, or sexual orientation. Intersectionality explains that race, gender, sexuality, and other identities cannot be examined in isolation as they intersect and influence each other. Thus, an examination of how individuals experience the world must be understood from the position at which these identities intersect. The same should be true for our understanding of microaggressions in that these subtle experiences of oppression may occur at a particular intersection. For instance, Black feminists have pointed out that masculinity for Black men is not always a privileged position (Collins, 2006; Mutua, 2006; Phillips, 2006). Black men often face a gendered racism where being a Black *man* is often a position of subordination. The race-gendered microaggression of racial profiling illustrates how Black men are targeted because they are Black *men* and not simply because they are Black or because they are male.[1] Therefore, in the case of Black men, microaggressions can be "race-gendered" (Mutua, 2006), occurring at this particular intersection.

In this study, I extend the discussion of racial microaggressions to include the everyday subtleties of race and racism middle-class Black families face in secondary education. Privileging the voice and the experiential knowledge of these students and their parents through counterstories and personal narratives is an important tenet of the CRT model, necessary to achieve social justice (Delgado, 1995; Montoya, 1995). Despite their middle-class status, these young Black men were not exempt from the experience of school racism and race-gendered microaggressions. However, what made some of these young men and their families unique was their ability to resist and circumnavigate the potential negative outcomes of these microaggressions.

METHOD

Background information. The findings presented in this article derive from a larger ethnographic study conducted at Central High,[2] a suburban school with a student population of more than 2,000 and located in a large Western U.S. city. Data were collected during the 2008–2009 school year using various interview strategies and field observations focusing on interactions between students, teachers, administrators, and the effects of school policy. The larger research project included 10 Black male students and their families, with 6 of them coming from middle-class households[3] and 4 from working-class households. Six teachers selected by the student participants were also included in the study. Though the project's emphasis was on middle-class men, including working-class students allowed me to observe how class mediated the experience of Black men in a particular schooling context. However, this article focuses specifically on the data and analysis pertaining to the Black middle-class families.

Research site. Central High School was a racially and economically diverse suburban school. At the time of my study the student population was 29% Black, 28% Asian, 19% Latino, 11% White, and 13% Other; almost half of the students qualified for free or reduced price lunch.[4] The surrounding community consists of a large number of new tract and custom homes, apartments, retail shops, a community college, a new public library, and other facilities. Residents were primarily middle-class families; however, the school catchment area also included students who were bussed from several neighboring communities that are more socioeconomically diverse.

Table 1   Descriptors of Middle-Class Male Students.

Student Alias	Grade	Parent alias
Jamal Baker	Sophomore	Mr. Baker
Sean Strauss	Junior	Mr. Strauss
Billy Anderson	Senior	Mr. Anderson
Mark Thomas	Sophomore	Mr. Thomas
Jayson Mensah	Senior	Mr. Mensah
Rodney Howard	Senior	Mr. Howard

Participants. Six Black middle-class male students and their fathers participated in the study (see Table 1). As the study's primary unit of analysis were Black middle-class men, purposive sampling (Merriam, 1988; Warwick & Lininger, 1975) was used to select this particular population. Selecting informants from a particular set of theoretical and intersecting categories was meaningful to how the identities of race, class, and gender influence the lived experiences of students within school structures.

Data collection and analysis. The students participated in three separate structured interviews, and the parents and teachers were each formally interviewed once. Taken together, the interviews became multivocal interpretations (Tobin, Wu, & Davidson, 1989) of the same phenomena and were an important source for discovering meaning behind the actions and behaviors of participants, particularly the students. Unstructured questions were used during observations and the researchers had casual interactions with the participants. All structured and unstructured interviews were recorded with a digital recorder and were later transcribed.

Observations were conducted within classrooms and other school spaces covering the full range of the school day and after-school activities. In the classroom, I often sat near the student, and when time permitted, asked questions about certain behaviors, practices, or feelings about their classroom experience. Occasionally, a teacher would ask me for help with checking classwork, placing my observations somewhere in the middle of the "detached" and "full participant" observational continuum (Graue & Walsh, 1998). After each observed class session, I asked each teacher and student whether behaviors I observed in the classroom were typical that day, to attempt to determine whether my presence and overt observations had an impact on classroom dynamics (Patton, 1990). I shadowed students in the hallways or during lunch (Solomon, 1992; Valenzuela, 1999), observing and noting the dynamics of their social groups, which provided points of reference for questions during later formal interviews.

Triangulation of analysis was built into the data collection process as multiple data sources (e.g., interviews, observations, document collection, etc.) were used to confirm or disconfirm any findings (Huberman & Miles, 1994; Patton, 1990). Data analysis itself followed a qualitative interpretive approach known as modified analytic induction (Erickson, 1986; Patton, 1990). Interviews and field notes were transcribed, the data corpus was read thoroughly and repeatedly to get a holistic sense of the phenomena, and Atlas.ti qualitative research software was used for coding and managing the data corpus. The data were bracketed into elements, which were analyzed independently for noncontextual meaning (Denzin, 1989). After coding and bracketing, the data corpus was again reviewed thoroughly to search for key linkages among the different forms of data and with a goal of developing an initial set of empirically grounded assertions. The data corpus was then reviewed again, as initial assertions were tested in light of confirming and disconfirming evidence. Assertions were then organized into major themes and subthemes, and the data were reconstructed and contextualized in light of its historical moment in time.

In addition to triangulating my data as they were collected, assertions were evaluated by identifying consistent interpretive patterns among student, parent, and teacher narratives and in field notes. Finally, I employed member checking (Lincoln & Guba, 1985) to obtain an additional level of validation, by asking participants for feedback on final themes identified and on my overall findings.[5]

In the next section, I will share my findings, which include Black male school encounters with racial microaggressions; racialized assumptions about intelligence and deviance and differential treatment in discipline will be highlighted. In addition, the cultural wealth used by the fathers to respond to these microaggressions will be presented.

SCHOOL ENCOUNTERS WITH RACIAL MICROAGGRESSIONS

The Black middle-class fathers in the study displayed orientations toward schooling and involvement practices that were consistent with school ideology and expectations (Allen, 2010a). The parents placed premium value on using education to achieve middle-class status, stressing meritocracy, accountability, and resiliency to their children as important parts of their socialization process (Allen, in press). Being highly involved in their sons' education, they worked diligently to make school and home life consistent, replicating instructional techniques used in the school within their own homes. They frequently activated their highly educated social networks, which included teachers from the school as well as educators within their own families, to provide their sons with opportunities to excel academically. They also closely monitored their sons' academic progress, using school-sanctioned outlets such as online grade checks and parent–teacher nights, a practice that schoolteachers praised. However, despite their parental involvement practices, these fathers were not naïve about the experience of racism they and their children would face in society. Through proactive racial socialization (Allen, in press; Caughy, O'Campo, Randolph, & Nickerson, 2002; Murray & Mandara, 2003), the parents gave forewarning to their sons that they would experience forms of racism, including racial microaggressions, in their own schooling. Racial microaggressions (Pierce et al., 1978; Solórzano et al., 2000) are the subtle forms of discrimination that serve to denigrate people of color. This includes microinsults, such as race-influenced ascriptions of intelligence or assumptions of deviance. The sons and the fathers in the study all spoke of microaggression events in their school, which included the negative and stereotypical views teachers and school administrators held of Black men that resulted in racialized assumptions of intelligence, deviance, and differential treatment.

Rodney, a senior, describes his observation of how school personnel regard Black deviancy and intelligence:

> I experienced it with this lady that actually came to our school. She was like a visitor from somewhere else and she had to visit the athletic director and, you know, you can tell she's one of those people that hasn't been around a lot of Black people, and you

know our school [has a large Black population] so she's holding her purse all close and stuff and she's looking around and you can see her eyes are all big and she's like wow, all these colored people. You could tell she was really nervous and I was the TA and I had to show her where the athletic office was and so I was walking with her and she was talking with me and she was like, "I can tell you're—what's your GPA?" I said 3.6. She said, "Yeah I can tell you have a really high [GPA] because of the way you talk and the way you carry yourself, you carry yourself so well!" And I'm like thank you but . . . it was just this realization of wow; this is how the world sees Black men. They don't think that we're smart or talk normal.

Similarly, Mark, a sophomore, explains that teachers are often apprehensive of him until they learn he is a high achiever:

Some of the teachers, like new teachers, they are kind of distant from me at first and then I think once they realize, if I'm in their class and they see my grades, then they're like, "This is a cool student," and that's when they start kind of warming up to me and having more of a relationship. But when they just walk around they don't have any interaction with me.

The fathers were also concerned with how teachers and administrators assumed deviance of their sons, observing how the pejorative perceptions of Black men influenced school approaches to campus safety. Mr. Mensah, the father of Jayson, describes how popular discourse on Black men created an administrative "witch-hunt" of Black male students:

I went to a meeting. They were talking about gang violence . . . and I heard the whole spiel, Glenpark police, Glenpark sheriff, the county sheriff, detectives, the whole nine yards and they're telling all the parents what to look for. The hats and if there are tattoos or the cuts in the eyebrows, and they're telling all these things to look out for and I'm sitting there and I just couldn't take in no more and I had to really calm myself because I was going to be yelling and my voice was shaking and I said, you know? I've sat here for 45 minutes to an hour and I listened to you and all you police and detectives say what to look for in the kids. . . . This witch-hunt, what you're doing, is kids. These are kids that live in $600,000 homes, million [dollar] homes. But because this is the fad to dress like this, now you're telling the parents to look at their kids as gang members and not as kids anymore, that can be changed or influenced. You're saying this is what you look for and when you find it call us so we can take your kids away. And I said because all you've done is you've told me to hold on to my kids that much closer because what you're trying to do is arrest them and get rid of them.

Mr. Mensah's commentary points to a unique intersection of race, class, gender, and youth culture for Black middle-class men in that their class status provides a certain element of economic privilege (i.e., living in $600,000 to million dollar homes), yet they are still subject to racial profiling based on race, gender, and culturally driven youth stylistic preferences. This was a matter of contention for the Black middle-class families who worked to provide opportunities for success for their sons yet also recognized the endemic nature of racism. In this particular situation, their class privilege could not shield their sons from the racial "witch-hunt."

Racial stereotypes, fear, and curiosity about Black men were understood as contributing to how student participants were treated differentially in matters of discipline. Sean, a junior, describes his observation of this type of differential treatment saying,

> It wasn't . . . like, they said, "Oh I hate you because you're Black," kind of thing, but being Black, I think I can tell when somebody has that type of feeling towards me. There will be times where I can do something and another race can do something, but I get in trouble for something and they wouldn't. I think it happens more than people think.

Likewise, Mark observes how teachers' misunderstanding of Black men leads to various forms of academic exclusion, explaining,

> Some of the teachers don't know how to deal with the Black kids . . . so instead of teaching them or working with them, they send them to some other class and write them off as ADD. They send them to OCS, suspend them. They do what they can to get them out of their hair not caring what happens in the long term.

Central High's suspension records evidence the consequences of disciplinary racial microaggressions; Black males accounted for almost 40% of student suspensions, a statistic unfortunately consistent with the larger research literature on Black male suspension rates (Mendez, Knoff, & Ferron, 2002; Monroe, 2005; Skiba, 2001). The students identified teachers most likely to suspend a Black male as White, novice teachers or substitute teachers who, as Jamal, a sophomore puts it, were not "outright racist, but I'm pretty sure they have their prejudices. Like you be in a class and the whole class will be talking and the subs [substitute teacher] will single out the black guy."

Parents were also observant of the differential treatment of their sons in the school. As many of the parents were involved in customizing their son's schooling, they often sat in on classes. In doing so, Mr. Anderson observed how his son Billy, a senior, was inexplicably singled out:

> I remember one time, I went to school and sat in his class and I was sitting there and kids were, I mean it was kind of bizarre because kids would get up in the middle of class

while the teacher was teaching, get up walk over, get some water, get up, walk over, start sharpening a pencil, and she didn't stop or anything. But then Billy did something and I don't remember what it was, but it didn't seem like it was that big of a deal and she kind of like lashed out at him and I was like wow . . . I wonder why that is.

Though Mr. Anderson's interpretation of his son's interactions with the school teacher could be explained in other ways (e.g., teacher incompetence) rather than a racially driven encounter, the endemicity of racism in school systems makes race a salient factor for Black parents like Mr. Anderson.

In this next section, I will describe how the fathers demonstrate agency, desiring to provide educational opportunity for their sons by responding to and resisting race-gendered microaggressions in the school. By resisting, the fathers were able to disrupt the racially stratifying nature of the school.

RESISTING RACIAL MICROAGGRESSIONS

In response to microaggression events, the middle-class fathers demonstrated agency by drawing upon various forms of cultural wealth as acts of resistance. Yosso (2006) defines cultural wealth as forms of cultural capital people of color often draw upon as a means to fight discrimination and experience opportunity. Two of the forms of cultural capital she identifies are relevant to this study: social capital and navigational capital. Yosso defines social capital as the networks of people and community resources that allow people of color to succeed within and outside of their communities. Navigational capital is defined as the ability to maneuver through social institutions that were not initially intended for the inclusion of people of color. The fathers in this study frequently drew upon their school-based social networks and their understanding of the school system to respond to and resist race-gendered microaggressions and create opportunity for their sons.

Observing the subtleties of racism in the school seemed to motivate the fathers to closely monitor their son's education. Black middle-class families are more likely to report racial discrimination and assume that Whites negatively stereotype Blacks (Feagin & Sikes, 1994; Hochschild, 1995; Sigelman & Tuch, 1997). Likewise, Black middle-class families often distrust schools, worrying that their children will be denied opportunity or labeled negatively (Beard & Brown, 2008). Thus, like other middle-class families seeking to shield their children from racism (Carter-Black, 2003; Hochschild, 1995; Tatum, 1987), the middle-class fathers in this study were proactive, relying on their social capital, particularly their relationships with the teachers to shield their sons from differential treatment in the classroom. Building and maintaining relationships with teachers allowed the parents to build better rapport, hoping that this rapport would help teachers see their sons beyond essentialized expectations of racial performance. Mr. Strauss, the father of Juan, describes this effort:

> He's one of those kinds of kids that also feels like when you say something funny, he can't control the laugh. And so he's the kind of kid that will sit in class and if somebody says something, he's going to laugh. He don't have to be the one that cracked the joke or start trouble, but he would always get in trouble because he's the loudest. And so I've had to go to every school and kind of explain to each teacher, each principal or each counselor, "okay, the one thing I do know is my son. He's not going to start any trouble." . . . He's always been a huge kid, and so they automatically assume he's going to be a trouble maker. And come to find out, he's going to be your best student . . . being African American and always the biggest kid in class, I think he automatically had that against him.

Other proactive parents sat in on their sons' classes observing student–teacher interactions, a practice common to middle-class families (Lareau, 2000a, 2000b). Mr. Mensah explains how he believes his presence in the classroom influenced the student–teacher interactions:

> I would go in and the kids would say, "Whose dad is that? Oh, it's Jayson's dad." And I would just stay there, but the teacher was the one that was on her best behavior. I would say [to the students], "How did the teacher act when I left?" "They [the teachers] treated us a little bit different when you was there."

For parents like Mr. Mensah, their presence in the classroom was a way to not only build teacher relationships and gain inside academic information but also keep teachers "in check" in regards to how they treated students in general and their sons in particular.

Furthermore, when events perceived to be race related specifically involved their sons, the fathers drew upon their navigational capital, which included their understanding of school process and hierarchy and their ability to navigate the institution in ways that disrupted racially stratifying practices. For example, during separate interviews with Mr. Mensah and his son Jayson, they describe what they believe to be a racially motivated outcome of an in-class altercation Jayson was involved in, an outcome that almost led to Jayson's suspension. Using both Mr. Mensah and his son Jayson's narrative to describe this event, a verbal argument between Jayson and two classmates occurred, which, by the vice principal's admission, should have been handled by the teacher but was instead interpreted as a violent event. Jayson felt the teacher's failure to intercede reflected her fear of students of color (the other students involved in the conflict were Asian males), which could be seen as a microinsult due to an assumption of criminality. Mr. Mensah was called in to meet with the vice principal and was informed that

Jayson would be suspended for 3 days, referring to the school's discipline rubric that assigns a 3-day suspension for classroom arguments involving physical threats. Mr. Mensah replied, "What would make you want to suspend Jayson for three days? Check the school records, he's never been in any trouble and you want to suspend him for three days? Of course [they made threats], they were heated. They said some things that they didn't mean. He's a kid!" Mr. Mensah continued, retorting, "Well, I've had enough. I'm going over to the school board right now," to which the vice principal responded by agreeing to remove the incident from Jayson's record as well as the other two students involved. Satisfied with the outcome but still disappointed with the disciplinary process, Mr. Mensah concludes the meeting by saying,

> You know what, Mr. Matthews? It's awful odd. I've watched these things happen. I've been around the school and I've come to meetings and I'm so frustrated I have to stay away and just hold my kids close to me. There's a perception out [there] Mr. Matthews, that most minority children, [people] think they're lesser than, and so do the teachers. They think [minority] means lesser than.

Mr. Mensah's narrative exemplifies how he actively resisted the outcome of the microaggression event, which began with the assumption of deviance by teachers and administrators and led to the criminalization of Black men through the discipline policy. In resisting the microaggressions, Mr. Mensah critiqued the vice principal for indiscriminately using a discipline rubric that would have suspended all three students for three days (missing three days of instruction) instead of using discernment to see the event as simply an argument between kids that should have been handled by the teacher. For Mr. Mensah, the fact that his son Jayson, who was a senior and had no discipline record beforehand, could have easily been relabeled as a *troublemaker* because of teachers' views on "minority children" was cause for him to maintain distrust of the school.

Mr. Mensah's criticism of the school discipline policy also highlights a key tenet of CRT that challenges dominant claims of race and gender neutrality, objectivity, universalism, and colorblindness (Delgado, 1991; Ladson Billings & Tate IV, 2006). The problem with the discipline rubric isn't the rubric in itself, but the fact that Black men are disproportionately sent to the disciplinary office (Skiba, Michael, Nardo, & Peterson, 2002), frequently because of racial incongruences or fear, ensuring that a large number of Black male students will encounter this disciplining system and experience some form of punishment, even for an argument. Furthermore, the use of the discipline rubric allows administrators to act as "objective" or "colorblind" disciplinarians, hiding behind an institutional set of so-called universal guidelines that can be applied to all cases across time. The "objectivity" of such educational policies is called into question by CRT, which argues against universalistic application of laws in favor of a particularistic approach, one that accounts for history and context (Delgado, 1991; Delgado & Stefancic, 2001; Ladson-Billings & Tate IV, 2006).

This is the exact argument Mr. Mensah alludes to when he questions the sensibility of his son being suspended for three days for an argument. A more particularistic approach would have considered the costs of three missed days of instruction, the role the teacher played in failing to employ effective classroom management strategies, and the role race played in escalating the event to the point of parental intervention. Still, the fact that Mr. Mensah and Jayson were able to provide counternarratives to the conflict, and Mr. Mensah was able to use his knowledge of school authority and rank to threaten to go to the school board demonstrates how the counternarratives and cultural wealth of people of color can resist school-based microaggressions and disrupt the stratifying nature of schools.

DISCUSSION

The Black middle-class students and their fathers in the study described various microaggressions encountered in school. This included pejorative views of intelligence, assumptions of deviance, and differential treatment in school discipline. In many ways, the racial microaggressions these students encountered were similar to the experiences of other Black students (Henfield, 2011; Lewis, 2003; Sue, Capodilupo, & Holder, 2008). Assumptions of intelligence and deviance and differential treatment in discipline, all exemplify how race functions as a social stratifying structure, exists as a barrier to social mobility for Black people, and stigmatizes Black male identity (Akom, 2008; Gerald, 1972; Grusky, 1994; Ogbu, 1994).

For example, teacher perceptions of Black male intelligence and deviance are often influenced by racist discourse about Black masculine performance and teachers regularly interpret the behavior of Black boys as aggressive, disrespectful, defiant, and intimidating even when such behaviors were not intended to be so (Davis, 2003; Ferguson, 2000; Lynn, Bacon, Totten, Bridges, & Jennings, 2010; Noguera, 2003). The imprecise interpretation of these behaviors results in discipline that is often unnecessary, unfair, and in many cases, harsher for Black boys than it would be for their White counterparts (Monroe, 2005; Skiba, 2001).

Moreover, on a theoretical level, the microaggressions of "colorblind" disciplining events within the school are important moments where "symbols of power and authority are perpetuated" (Noguera, 2008, p. 96). When Black male students are stereotyped by their teachers, racially profiled by administrators and experiencing racially differentiated discipline, they engage in conflict with White institutional hegemony and a racially stratifying system (Brown, 2003; Delgado & Stefancic, 2001; Essed, 1991; Feagin & Vera, 1995; Gibson, 2002; Noguera, 2008). The disciplining function of schools also become regulators of identity, defining what behaviors or performances of masculinity are "good" or "bad" in relationship to a bourgeois norm (Foucault, 1979; Haywood & Mac an Ghaill, 1996). Employing a Foucauldian analysis, Ferguson (2000) examines the role of school discipline:

So school rules operate as instruments of normalization. Children are sorted, evaluated, ranked, compared on the basis of (mis)behavior: what they do that violates, conforms to, school rules. Foucault argues that disciplinary control is a modern mode of power that comes into existence with the formation of the bourgeois democratic state as a technique of regulation particularly suited to a form of governance predicated on the idea of formal equality. (pp. 52–53)

Schools then become sites of identity regulation where the performances of Black masculinity are stigmatized as "different" through normalizing judgments. Those Black male students who do not perform "normal" school behavior are feared and, thus, deserving of punishment. In this sense, to succeed in schools Black male students must prove they are normal by self-consciously regulating their every action in ways that prove adaptation to institutionally generated norms. This situation also demonstrates how Whiteness is property (Harris, 1993) in that White male behavior is normalized, giving White male students the right of use and enjoyment of school spaces and the ability to perform masculinities in ways that are unchallenged, de-racialized, and with assumed innocence.

The observation of these normalizing practices and other racial microaggressions required the fathers to expend countless amounts of energy socializing their sons to prepare for such events (Allen, in press), monitoring their sons' education, and attempting to protect their sons from damaging experiences of racism (Day-Vines, Patton, & Baytops, 2003; Lareau, 2003). This form of parental overinvolvement holds the potential for these parents to experience racial battle fatigue, which is the psychological, emotional, and physical strain people of color experience when perpetually having to address racial microaggressions (Nunez-Smith et al., 2007; Smith, 2004; Smith, Yosso, & Solórzano, 2006).

Superficially, the experiences of these Black middle-class families may warrant the argument from some that the structure of race is a greater barrier than the structure of class (O'Connor, 2007), but this is not necessarily so. In many cases, middle-class parents have been able to employ their class power to divert racial injustice (hooks, 2000; Lacy, 2002), and such was the case in this study. Yet the implications of race and class must be seen not as either/or, but as both/and. They are categories that intersect and are indeed intertwined in ways that systematically marginalize people of color out of opportunity structures (Anthias, 2005; Faber, 2005). For the families in this study, race, class, and gender intersect in unique ways. Though their class status affords them opportunities and power within the school not easily accessible to their working-class counterparts, their sons are still Black men in school and were subjected to microaggressions rooted in racist ideologies. Thus, these middle-class fathers' ability to transcend race was made possible by their use of cultural wealth as resistance to the race-gendered microaggressions in the school.

Though the efforts of these fathers are commendable, it can also be argued that their responses to these racial microaggressions were singular acts, aimed solely at removing the danger of racism for their own children. So though these fathers' ability to navigate a racist school structure provides opportunity for their children, little is done, in the immediate sense, to actually change the racially stratifying structure of the school. However, in the larger sense, the success of these families in navigating the school structure could be interpreted as an opportunity for Black middle-class families to replicate their class status and use education as a means to obtain power, power that could be used to dismantle White hegemony in schools in meaningful and powerful ways. This was DuBois' (1903) thesis when he called upon the talented tenth, the Black educated, to engage in group leadership with the Black masses. For the middle-class families in this study, the outcome of educational attainment remains to be seen. Yet these fathers' ability to resist race and racism in the school greatly influences the social and economic trajectories their sons will ultimately travel.

CONCLUSION

This study documented the raced, classed, and gendered encounters that Black middle-class male students and their fathers had within the school structure and process. Despite the perceived privilege their class standing supposedly afforded, the families observed the endemicity of racism, experienced through subtle but potentially damaging racial microaggressions. Assumptions about intellectual inferiority, deviance, and differential treatment in discipline were just some of the microaggressions encountered by the male students, microaggressions that undermine the identity of Black men and put at risk their ability to use education for social mobility. To resist these microaggressions, the middle-class parents drew upon their cultural wealth, particularly their social and navigational capital, to create opportunity for their sons in light of racist encounters. The actions of these parents demonstrate the power of human agency to resist the racially reproductive nature of schools and provide models of parental intervention that may serve to improve the process of Black middle-class social reproduction.

DECLARATION OF CONFLICTING INTERESTS

The author(s) declared no potential conflicts of interest with respect to the research, authorship, and/or publication of this article.

FUNDING

The author(s) received no financial support for the research, authorship, and/or publication of this article.

NOTES

1. This statement does not let Black men off the hook and dismiss their part in the maintenance of patriarchy; it simply denotes that gender for Black men is not always a position of privilege.

2. The names of the school and participants are pseudonyms. Names have been changed to ensure confidentiality.

3. Race and gender were the primary criteria used to select the students, but to gain the particular interpretations this study sought, identifying socioeconomic class standing was critical. To identify the middle-class participants, I adopted a classification influenced by the work of Pattillo-McCoy (1999), whose seminal work concentrated on Black middle-class performances. Middle-class participants were identified through a combination of five criteria, which include (1) household income in relation to the state poverty line, (2) education level of parent(s), (3) occupation of parent(s), (4) residential location and ownership (i.e., property values, renting vs. owning), as well as (5) social groups the families were involved in (e.g., Jack and Jill, Mason's, college Greek organizations).

To ascertain class standing via household income, an income-based definition was used, which the U.S. Census Bureau (2008) refers to as the income-to-needs ratio. This is a family or person's income divided by their poverty threshold. The lower limit of the income-to-needs ratio for the economic middle-class definition is set at 200%, which means that a family at the lower-limit of the middle-class makes 200% more or double the poverty line. In addition to income, occupation and education were also used to identify class standing. Sociological studies on class categories along with research on the Black middle-class use white-collar and blue-collar occupations as a means to distinguish class standing (Collins, 1983; Durant & Louden, 1986; Frazier, 1962; Landry, 1987). In addition, the acquisition of a college education has typically been a strong indicator of middle-class status both ideologically and economically (Bourdieu, 1976; DuBois, 1903; Ginwright, 2002; Hochschild, 1995). Furthermore, superfluous data such as residential location and ownership and performances of middle-class life were utilized in defining class. For example, living in secluded communities and/or holding positions in social organizations such as college fraternities or churches (three fathers were church pastors) were used as part of middle-class identification.

4. Student demographic data collected from school documents. Citation withheld for school confidentiality.

5. For further detail on the research study methodology, please see Allen (2010a, 2012).

REFERENCES

Akom, A. A. (2008). Ameritocracy and infra-racial racism: Racializing social and cultural reproduction theory in the twenty-first century. *Race, Ethnicity & Education, 11*(3), 205–230.

Allen, Q. (2010a). *Black middle-class males, their parents, and their teachers: A process of social reproduction through education*. Ph.D. Dissertation, Arizona State University, Tempe. Retrieved from http://proquest.umi.com/pqdlink?did=203799 2971&Fmt=7&clientId=79356&RQT=309&VName=PQD

Allen, Q. (2010b). Racial microaggressions: The schooling experiences of black middle-class males in Arizona's secondary schools. *Journal of African American Males in Education, 1*(2), 125–143.

Allen, Q. (2012). Photographs and stories: Ethics, benefits and dilemmas of using participant photography with black middle-class male youth. *Qualitative Research, 12*(4), 443–458.

Allen, Q. (2013). Balancing school and cool: Tactics of resistance and accommodation among black middle-class males. *Race Ethnicity and Education, 16*(2), 203–224.

Anthias, F. (2005). Social stratification and social inequality: Models of intersectionality and identity. In F. Devine (Ed.), *Rethinking class: Culture, identities and lifestyles* (pp. xi, 229). New York, NY: Palgrave Macmillan.

Ascher, C., & Branch-Smith, E. (2005). Precarious space: Majority black suburbs and their public schools. *Teachers College Record, 107*(9), 1956–1973.

Attewell, P., Lavin, D., Domina, T., & Levey, T. (2004). The black middle-class: Progress, prospects, and puzzles. *Journal of African American Studies, 8*(1/2), 6–19.

Aud, S., Fox, M. A., & Kewal Ramani, A. (2010). *Status and trends in the education of racial and ethnic minorities*. Washington, DC: U.S. Department of Education.

Beard, K. S., & Brown, K. M. (2008). Trusting schools to meet the academic needs of African-American students? Suburban mothers' perspectives. *International Journal of Qualitative Studies in Education, 21*(5), 471–485.

Bell, D. (1992). *Faces at the bottom of the well: The permanence of racism*. New York, NY: Basic Books.

Belluck, P. (1999). Reason is sought for lag by blacks in school effort. *The New York Times*. Retrieved from The New York Times website: http://www.nytimes. com/1999/07/04/us/reason-is-sought-for-lag-by-blacks-in-school-effort.html?pagewanted=all&src=pm

Billingsley, A. (1992). *Climbing jacob's ladder: The enduring legacy of African-American families*. New York, NY: Simon & Schuster.

Blanchett, W. J., Klingner, J. K., & Harry, B. (2009). The intersection of race, culture, language, and disability. *Urban Education, 44*(4), 389–409. doi:10.1177/ 0042085909338686

Bourdieu, P. (1976). The school as a conservative force: Scholastic and cultural inequalities. In R. Dale, G. Esland, & M. MacDonald (Eds.), *Schooling and capitalism: A sociological reader* (pp. 110–117). London: Routledge and Kegan Paul.

Brown, T. N. (2003). Critical race theory speaks to the sociology of mental health: Mental health problems produced by racial stratification. *Journal of Health and Social Behavior, 44*(3), 292–301.

Carter-Black, J. (2003). The myth of "the tangle of pathology": Resilience strategies employed by middle-class African American families. *Journal of Family Social Work, 6*(4), 75–100.

Caughy, M. O. B., O'Campo, P. J., Randolph, S. M., & Nickerson, K. (2002). The influence of racial socialization practices on the cognitive and behavioral competence of African American preschoolers. *Child Development, 73*(5), 1611–1625.

Collins, S. M. (1983). The making of the black middle class. *Social Problems, 30*(4), 369–382.

Collins, P. H. (2006). A telling difference: Dominance, strength, and black masculinities. In A. D. Mutua (Ed.), *Progressive black masculinities* (pp. 73–97). New York, NY: Routledge.

Crenshaw, K. (1993). Demarginalizing the intersection of race and sex: A black feminist critique of antidiscrimination doctrine, feminist theory, and antiracist politics. In D. K. Weisberg (Ed.), *Feminist legal theory* (p. 383). Philadelphia: Temple University Press.

Crenshaw, K., Gotanda, N., Peller, G., & Thomas, K. (Eds.). (1995). *Critical race theory: The key writings that formed the movement*. New York, NY: The New Press.

Davis, J. E. (2003). Early schooling and academic achievement of African American males. *Urban Education, 38*(5), 515–537.

Day-Vines, N. L., Patton, J., & Baytops, J. (2003). Counseling African American adolescents: The impact of race and middle class status. *Professional School Counseling, 7*(1), 40–51.

Delgado, R. (1991). Brewer's plea: Critical thoughts on common cause. *Vanderbilt Law Review, 44*(11), 1–13.

Delgado, R. (1995). Legal storytelling: Storytelling for oppositionists and others: A plea for narrative. In R. Delgado (Ed.), *Critical race theory: The cutting edge* (pp. 64–74). Philadelphia: Temple University Press.

Delgado, R., & Stefancic, J. (2001). *Critical race theory: An introduction*. New York: New York University Press.

Denzin, N. K. (1989). *Interpretive interactionism*. Newbury Park, CA: Sage.

Dixson, A. D., & Rousseau, C. K. (2006). Are we still not saved: Critical race theory in education ten years later. In A. D. Dixson & C. K. Rousseau (Eds.), *Critical race theory in education: All god's children got a song* (pp. 31–54). New York, NY: Routledge.

DuBois, W. E. B. (1903). The talented tenth. In B. T. Washington (Ed.), *The negro problem: A series of articles by representative American negroes of today*. New York, NY: J. Pott & Co.

Durant, T. J., Jr., & Louden, J. S. (1986). The black middle class in America: Historical and contemporary perspectives. *Phylon, 47*(4), 253–263.

Erickson, F. (1986). Qualitative methods in research on teaching. In M. C. Wittrock (Ed.), *Handbook of research on teaching* (3rd ed.). New York: MacMillan

Essed, P. (1991). *Understanding everyday racism: An interdiscplinary theory.* Newbury Park, CA: Sage.

Faber, S. T. (2005). *Towards an intersectional analysis of gender and class on the basis of Bourdieu's sociology.* Paper presented at the Intersectionality Analysis Conference, Aalborg University, Aalborg, Denmark. January.

Feagin, J. R., & Sikes, M. P. (1994). *Living with racism: The black middle-class experience.* Boston, MA: Beacon.

Feagin, J. R., & Vera, H. (1995). *White racism: The basics.* New York, NY: Routledge.

Ferguson, A. (2000). *Bad boys: Public schools in the making of black masculinity.* Ann Arbor: The University of Michigan Press.

Ferguson, R. F. (2001). A diagnostic analysis of black-white GPA disparities in Shaker Heights, Ohio. In D. Ravitch (Ed.), *Brookings papers on education policy* (pp. 347–414). Washington, DC: Brookings Institution.

Foucault, M. (1979). *Discipline and punish* (A. Sheridan, Trans.). New York, NY: Vintage.

Franklin, A. J. (2004). *From brotherhood to manhood: How black men rescue thier relationships and dreams from the invisibility syndrome.* Hoboken, NJ: Wiley.

Frazier, E. F. (1962). *Black bourgeoisie: The rise of the new middle class in the United States.* New York, NY: Collier.

Gerald, B. (1972). Race, caste, and other invidious distinctions in social stratification. *Race & Class, 13*(4), 385–414.

Gibson, C. (2002). *Being real: The student-teacher relationship and African-American male delinquency.* New York, NY: LFB Scholarly Publishing.

Ginwright, S. A. (2002). Classed out: The challenges of social class in black community change. *Social Problems, 49*(4), 544–562.

Grantham, T. C. (2004). Multicultural mentoring to increase black male representation in gifted programs. *Gifted Child Quarterly, 48*(3), 232–245.

Graue, M. E., & Walsh, D. J. (1998). *Studying children in context: Theories, methods, and ethics.* Thousand Oaks, CA: Sage.

Grusky, D. B. (1994). *Social stratification: Class, race, and gender in sociological perspective.* Boulder, CO: Westview.

Hallinan, M. T. (2001). Sociological perspectives on black-white inequalities in american schooling. *Sociology of Education, 74*, 50–70.

Harris, C. I. (1993). Whiteness as property. *Harvard Law Review, 106*(8), 1707–1791.

Haywood, C., & Mac an Ghaill, M. (1996). Schooling masculinities. In M. Mac an Ghaill (Ed.), *Understanding masculinities* (pp. 50–60). Buckingham, UK: Open University.

Hemmings, A. (1996). Conflicting images? Being black and a model high school student. *Anthropology & Education Quarterly, 27*(1), 20–50.

Henfield, M. S. (2011). Black male adolescents navigating microaggressions in a traditionally white middle school: A qualitative study. *Journal of Multicultural Counseling and Development, 39*(3), 141–155.

Hertz, T. (2005). Rags, riches, and race: The intergenerational economic mobility of black and white families in the United States. In S. Bowles, H. Gintis, & M. Osbourne (Eds.), *Unequal chances: Family background and economic success* (pp. 165–191). New York, NY: Russell Sage.

Hochschild, J. (1995). *Facing up to the American dream: Race, class and the soul of the nation.* Princeton, NJ: Princeton University Press.

hooks, b. (2000). *Where we stand: Class matters.* New York, NY: Routledge.

Horvat, E. M., & Antonio, A. L. (1999). "Hey, those shoes are out of uniform": Black girls in an elite high school and the importance of habitus. *Anthropology & Education Quarterly, 30*(3), 317–342.

Hubbard, L. (1999). College aspirations among low-income African American high school students: Gendered strategies for success. *Anthropology & Education Quarterly, 30*(3), 363–383.

Huberman, A. M., & Miles, M. B. (1994). Data management and analysis method. In N. Denzin & Y. Lincoln (Eds.), *Handbook of qualitative methods* (1st ed.). Thousand Oaks, CA: Sage.

Issacs, J. B. (2007). *Economic mobility of black and white families.* Washington, DC: The Pew Charitable Trusts/Brookings Institution.

Kearney, M. S. (2006). Intergenerational mobility for women and minorities in the United States. *The Future of Children, 16*(2), 37–53.

Lacy, K. R. (2002). A part of the neighborhood?: Negotiating race in American suburbs. *International Journal of Sociology and Social Policy, 22*(1–3), 39–74.

Ladson-Billings, G., & Tate IV, W. F. (2006). Toward a critical race theory of education. In A. D. Dixson & C. K. Rousseau (Eds.), *Critical race theoy in education: All god's children got a song* (pp. 11–30). New York, NY: Routledge.

Landry, B. (1987). *The new black middle class.* Berkeley: University of California Press.

Lareau, A. (2000a). *Home advantage: Social class and parental intervention in elementary education.* London: Falmer.

Lareau, A. (2000b). Social class and the daily lives of children: A study from the United States. *Childhood, 7*(2), 155–171.

Lareau, A. (2003). *Unequal childhoods : Class, race, and family life.* Berkeley: University of California Press.

Lareau, A., & Horvat, E. M. (1999). Moments of social inclusion and exclusion: Race, class, and cultural capital in family school relationships. *Sociology of Education, 72*(1), 37–53.

Lewis, A. E. (2003). *Race in the schoolyard: Negotiating the color line in classrooms and communities.* New Brunswick, NJ: Rutgers University Press.

Lincoln, Y. S., & Guba, E. G. (1985). *Naturalistic inquiry.* Beverly Hills, CA: Sage.

Lynn, M., Bacon, J. N., Totten, T. L., Bridges, T. L., & Jennings, M. E. (2010). Examining teachers' beliefs about African American male students in a low performing high school in an African American school district. *Teachers College Record, 112*(1), 289–330.

Matsuda, M. J. (1991). Voices of America: Accent, antidiscrimination law, and jurisprudence for the last reconstruction. *The Yale Law Journal, 100*(5), 1329–1407.

McAdoo, H. P. (1978). Factors related to stability in upwardly mobile black families. *Journal of Marriage & Family, 40*(4), 761.

McBrier, D. B., & Wilson, G. (2004). Going down? Race and downward occupational mobility for white-collar workers in the 1990s. *Work & Occupations, 31*(3), 283–322.

Mendez, L. M. R., Knoff, H. M., & Ferron, J. M. (2002). School demographic variables and out-of-school suspension rates: A quantitative and qualitative analysis of large, ethnically diverse school district. *Psychology in the Schools, 39*(3), 259–277.

Merriam, S. B. (1988). *A case study approach to research problems: A qualitative approach.* San Francisco, CA: Jossey-Bass.

Mickelson, R. A. (2001). Subverting Swann: First and second generation segregation in the Charlotte-Mecklenburg school system. *American Educational Research Journal, 38*(2), 215–252.

Miron, L. F., & Lauria, M. (1998). Student voice as agency: Resistance and accomodation in inner-city schools. *Anthropology and Education Quarterly, 29*(2), 189–213.

Monroe, C. R. (2005). Why are "bad boys" always black? Causes of disproportionality in school discipline and recommendations for change. *The Clearing House, 79*(1), 45–50.

Montoya, M. E. (1995). Un/masking the self while un/braiding Latino stories in legal discourse. In R. Delgado (Ed.), *Critical race theory: The cutting edge* (pp. 529–539). Philadelphia: Temple University Press.

Murray, C. B., & Mandara, J. (2003). An assessment of the relationship between racial socialization, racial identity and self-esteem in African American adolescents. In D. A. Y. Azibo (Ed.), *African-centered psychology* (pp. 293–325). Durham, NC: Carolina Academic Press.

Mutua, A. D. (2006). Theorizing progressive black masculinities. In A. D. Mutua (Ed.), *Progressive black masculinities* (pp. 3–42). New York, NY: Routledge.

Noguera, P. A. (2003). The trouble with black boys: The role and influence of environmental and cultural factors on the academic performance of African American males. *Urban Education, 38*(4), 431–459.

Noguera, P. A. (2008). *The trouble with black boys: And other reflections on race, equity, and the future of public education.* San Francisco, CA: Jossey-Bass.

Nunez-Smith, M., Curry, L. A., Bigby, J., Berg, D., Krumholz, H. M., & Bradley, E. H. (2007). Impact of race on the professional lives of physicians of African descent. *Annals of Internal Medicine, 146*(1), 45–47.

Oakes, J. (2005). *Keeping track: How schools structure inequality.* New Haven, CT: Yale University Press.

O'Connor, C. (2007). Researching "black" educational experiences and outcomes: Theoretical and methodological considerations. *Educational Researcher, 36*(9), 541–552.

Ogbu, J. (1994). Racial stratification and education in the United States: Why inequality persists. *Teachers College Record, 96*(2), 264–298.

Ogbu, J. (2003). *Black American students in an affluent suburb.* Mahwah, NJ: Lawrence Erlbaum.

Pattillo-McCoy, M. (1999). *Black picket fences: Privilege and peril among the black middle class.* Chicago, IL: The University of Chicago Press.

Pattillo-McCoy, M. (2000). The limits of out-migration for the black middle class. *Journal of Urban Affairs, 22*(3), 225–241.

Patton, M. Q. (1990). *Qualitative evaluation and research methods* (2nd ed.). Newbury Park, CA: Sage.

Phillips, S. L. (2006). Beyond competitive victimhood: Abandoning arguments that black women or black men are worse off. In A. D. Mutua (Ed.), *Progressive black masculinities* (pp. 217–226). New York, NY: Routledge.

Pierce, C., Carew, J., Pierce-Gonzalez, D., & Willis, D. (1978). An experiment in racism: TV commercials. In C. Pierce (Ed.), *Television and education* (pp. 62–88). Beverly Hills, CA: Sage.

Roach, R. (2001). Where are all the black men on campus? *Black Issues in Higher Education, 18*(6), 18–21.

Sigelman, L., & Tuch, S. (1997). Metastereotypes: Blacks perceptions of whites' stereotypes of blacks. *Public Opinion Quarterly, 61*(1), 87–101.

Skiba, R. (2001). When is disproportionality discrimination? The overrepresentation of black students in school suspension. In W. Ayers, B. Dohrn, & R. Ayers (Eds.), *Zero tolerance: Resisting the drive for punishment in our schools* (pp. 176–187). New York, NY: New Press.

Skiba, R., Michael, R. S., Nardo, A. C., & Peterson, R. L. (2002). The color of discipline: Sources of racial and gender disproportionality in school punishment. *The Urban Review, 34*(4), 317–342.

Smith, W. A. (2004). Black faculty coping with racial battle fatigue: The campus climate in a post-Civil Rights era. In D. Cleveland (Ed.), *A long way to go: Conversations about race by African American faculty and graduate students*. New York, NY: Peter Lang.

Smith, W. A., Yosso, T., & Solórzano, D. (2006). Challenging racial battle fatigue on historically white campuses: A critical race examination of race-related stress. In C. A. Stanley (Ed.), *Faculty of color: Teaching in predominantly white colleges and universities* (pp. 299–328). Bolton, MA: Anker.

Solomon, R. P. (1992). *Black resistance in high school: Forging a separatist culture*. Albany: State University of New York Press.

Solórzano, D. G. (1998). Critical race theory, race and gender microaggressions, and the experience of chicana and chicano scholars. *International Journal of Qualitative Studies in Education, 11*(1), 121–136.

Solórzano, D., Ceja, M., & Yosso, T. (2000). Critical race theory, racial microaggressions, and campus racial climate: The experiences of African American college students. *The Journal of Negro Education, 69*(1/2), 60–73.

Solórzano, D. G., & Yosso, T. J. (2002). Critical race methodology: Counter-storytelling as an analytical framework for education research. *Qualitative Inquiry, 8*(1), 23–44.

Sue, D. W. (2004). Whiteness and ethnocentric monoculturalism: Making the "invisible" visible. *American Psychologist, 59*(8), 759–769.

Sue, D. W. (2010). *Microaggressions in everyday life: Race, gender, and sexual orientation*. Hoboken, NJ: Wiley.

Sue, D., Capodilupo, C. M., & Holder, A. M. B. (2008). Racial microaggressions in the life experience of black Americans. *Professional Psychology, 39*(3), 329–336.

Sue, D. W., Capodilupo, C. M., Torino, G. C., Bucceri, J. C., Holder, A. M. B., Nadal, K. L., & Esqulin, M. (2007). Racial microaggressions in everyday life: Implications for clinical practice. *American Psychologist, 62*(4), 271–286.

Tatum, B. D. (1987). *Assimilation blues: Black families in a white community*. Westport, CT: Greenwood.

Taylor, E., Gillborn, D., & Ladson-Billings, G. (Eds.). (2009). *Foundations of critical race theory in education*. New York, NY: Routledge.

Tobin, J. J., Wu, D. Y. H., & Davidson, D. H. (1989). *Preschool in three cultures: Japan, china, and the United States*. New Haven, CT: Yale University Press.

Trent, W. T. (1991). Focus on equity: Race and gender differences in degree attainment, 1975–76, 1980–81. In W. R. Allen, E. G. Epps, & N. Z. Haniff (Eds.), *College in black and white: African American students in predominantly white and historically black public universities* (pp. 41–60). Albany: State University of New York Press.

Tyson, K. (2002). Weighing in: Elementary-age students and the debate on attitudes toward school among black students. *Social Forces, 80*(4), 1157–1189.

U.S. Census Bureau, (2008). *Poverty thresholds for 2008 by size of family and number of related children under 18 years* (HaHES Division, Trans.). Washington, DC: U.S. Census Bureau.

Valenzuela, A. (1999). *Subtractive schooling: U.S.-Mexican youth and the politics of caring.* Ithaca: State University of New York Press.

Warwick, D. P., & Lininger, C. A. (1975). *The sample survey: Theory and practice.* New York, NY: McGraw-Hill.

Yosso, T. J. (2006). Whose culture has capital? A critical race theory discussion of community cultural wealth. In A. D. Dixson & C. K. Rousseau (Eds.), *Critical race theory in education: All God's children got a song* (pp. 167–189). New York, NY: Routledge.

Author Biography

Quaylan Allen is an assistant professor in the College of Educational Studies at Chapman University. His research focuses on race, class and gender in educational policy and practice, Black male educational outcomes and visual methods in educational research.

Discussion Topics and Activities for "They Think Minority Means Lesser Than"

1. Evaluate how the "Theoretical Framework" and "Method" sections of this report corroborate to address the researcher's central purpose of the study.

2. Locate passages in the article that exhibit low and high-level assertions supported with an evidentiary warrant (see Chapter 10).

3. Reflect on this study's possible transfer of findings to other school populations (e.g., Latino youths, LGBTQ youths), or what elements of Allen's research design might require adaptation to study a different demographic in the high school setting.

GLOSSARY

a priori—Determined beforehand, such as codes and categories formulated before fieldwork and data analysis

abduction—Examining an array of possibilities or explanations and selecting the most reasonable and credible one; exploring the possible links or causation between phenomena

access—The ability and permission to observe and/ or interview participants at a particular field site

action—A micro-unit of human activity consisting of a purposeful and meaningful behavior, including speaking and mental activity

action research—Collaboration between the researcher and participants working together systematically on a particular problem or issue to diagnose its sources, to develop specific action strategies for changing the current conditions, and to assess the efficacy of their efforts; also used by practitioners for self-reflection on their work and professional development

active role—Occasional researcher participation in the action of the field setting to provide firsthand knowledge of what participants are doing and experiencing

aggregate—A collective, composite representation of various data that have been brought together

analysis—The synthesis of data, reconfigured into new formulations of meaning as key ideas related to a specific line of inquiry

analytic and formal writing—Technical writing that illustrates how key factors interrelate and presents the patterned regularities of data through a sense of ordered management

analytic induction—A process by which answers to research questions are emergently constructed as more data are collected and systematically examined

analytic memo—A brief or extended researcher commentary stimulated by field notes or other data such as documents and interview transcripts; reflective narratives that expand and expound on observations to transcend description and venture into richer analytic meanings

analytic story-line—The narrative, processual description, or explanation of interactions or outcomes

angles—Cultural landscape positions held by the researcher such as insider or outsider, intimate or distant, emotionally invested or objectively detached; also micro-, meso-, and macro-perceptions of social life

anonymity—Keeping the actual name and identity of a participant or other entity unknown in a data corpus and research report

antecedent conditions—Preexisting or preestablished contexts and actions that are influenced and affected by mediating variables

argot—Vocabulary and communication patterns unique to a particular culture

argument—A central statement or key assertion about the study's investigation

artifact—Any object that can be touched and handled

assent—Agreement to participate, usually oral; minors assent to participate in a study

assertion—A declarative, summative statement that synthesizes various observations, supported by confirming evidence from the data corpus

asynchronously—Occurring at different times, such as an e-mail interview exchange between a researcher and a participant

attitude—The way we think and feel about ourselves, another person, thing, or idea; evaluative perceptions and sets of cumulative reactions, reflecting the beliefs learned through time; interrelated with a value and belief

autoethnographic, autoethnography—
An account written in the first person about the researcher's personal lived experiences with an emphasis on the cultural or social domains of the experiences

belief—Personal knowledge, experiences, opinions, prejudices, morals, and other interpretive perceptions of the social world; interrelated with a value and attitude

Belmont Report—A 1979 report published by the U.S. Department of Health & Human Services prescribing ethical guidelines and procedures for the protection of human subjects in research

boundaries—The parameters that limit the scope of a research study such as time, geography, and access

bracket—To set aside one's own worldview in order to understand and respect another's

CAQDAS—An acronym for Computer Assisted Qualitative Data Analysis Software

case study—A focused research study on one unit of interest—One person, one setting, one organization, one event, etc.

category—A label in the form of a word or phrase applied to a grouped pattern of comparable codes and coded data

causation—Explanation of or attribution to actions and reactions, describing how, why, or what kinds of certain actions happen; an assertion that one or more things directly caused other things

central research question—A primary question for inquiry, derived from the purpose statement, that serves as an axis for related research questions

citations—Information about a source or quote (e.g., author, year of publication, page numbers) within the main narrative

code—A word or short phrase that symbolically assigns a summative, salient, essence-capturing, and/or evocative attribute for a portion of language-based or visual data

codeweaving—Integration of the primary codes of interest into a brief narrative to analyze their interrelationship

collaborative and polyvocal writing—Includes multiple individual voices throughout the report; a democratic process among participants to provide voice and agency to the researched

complete role—The researcher as co-participant, personally immersed in the social world studied, living the same experiences as those observed for a lengthy duration

composite narratives—An amalgam of different yet related participant quotes or other data into a single representative passage

concept—A word or short phrase that symbolically represents a suggested meaning or idea broader than a single observable item or action

conceptual frames—The conceptual parameters of a study, such as a specific experience or phenomenon to be studied

conceptual framework—A set of epistemological, conceptual, and theoretical foundation principles for guidance throughout a research study

conference theme—An association's primary topic or focus during a gathering, with submissions and presentations often centered around the theme

confessional tale—The researcher's first-person account of the subjective experiences he encountered throughout the project; reveals emotions, vulnerabilities, uncertainties, fieldwork problems, ethical dilemmas, and data collection or analytic errors

confidentiality—Keeping information private, such as participants' identities and their related data

constructivist—An epistemological approach to research that is inductive and emergent; cumulative processes of knowledge building

content analysis—A systematic analysis of material that primarily counts the number of times particular words, images, ideas, themes, or concepts appear in a set of data; applied to assess any particular latent and manifest meanings to the material

control group—Participants not receiving an experimental condition for purposes of comparison to a treatment or intervention group

convenience sampling—Selecting participants with whom researchers have easy access

core category—In grounded theory, the central category derived from analysis that functions as an umbrella for all of the study's constituent elements

covert role—An undisclosed researcher identity to participants that provides access to hidden facets of social life when the phenomenon of interest cannot be studied as in depth through other methods

credibility—The audience's belief that the conduct, analytic processes, and outcomes of a qualitative study have generated findings that make sense and persuade readers of the researcher's efficacy

critical and advocacy writing—Thoughtful inquiry that surveys the manifest and latent meanings of people's discourse and the actions, reactions, and interactions that result in power imbalances; advocates productive solutions and emancipatory action

culture—Knowledge learned and shared that people use to generate behavior and interpret experience; a historically transmitted pattern of meanings embodied in symbols

data—Various forms of information collected for a research study

data corpus—The body of data; the total assembly of all empirical materials collected for a research study

datum—A piece of information; the singular form of data

deception—Deliberate action by a researcher to mislead or hide information from a study's participants, usually for covert investigation

deduction—Conclusion-making from evidence; a culminating process and product, derived from inductive, abductive, and/or retroductive thinking

descriptive and realistic writing—Straightforward reportage, factual storytelling of the participants' daily lives and critical incidents with neutral and objective writing to paint a vivid picture of reality for the reader

Descriptive Coding—Summarizing in a word or short phrase—most often as a noun—the basic topic of a passage of qualitative data

diagram—An active, visually illustrated representation of the participants' experiences or the phenomenon under investigation

digital culture—A conception of social life as one that is imbued with ubiquitous digital technology as part of daily living

disconfirming evidence—Data that negate the validity or truth value of an assertion

discourse analysis—Analysis of the contents and contexts of narrative and visual texts; a focus on selected nuances of language, conversation, and images to assess how elements such as vocabulary, grammar, intonation, topics, etc., work together to impart meaning about human relationships and ideas such as culture, identity, politics, and power

discussant—Person responsible for leading a feedback session at the end of conference paper presentations

documents—Forms of textual communication that reflect the interests and perspectives of their authors

dramatic writing—A play script that dramatizes the participants' and/or researchers' experiences in monologic or dialogic forms with theatrical elements such as scenery, properties, lighting, costumes, sound, and media to enhance the performance aesthetics of the research story

Dramaturgical Coding—Applies the basic conventions of dramatic character analysis onto naturalistic social interaction or onto a participant's stories contained in an interview

duoethnography—A report cumulatively composed by two or more researchers who exchange ideas, usually through e-mail; dialogue and responses to each other's ideas about a central topic, exchanging stories from personal experience, and citing the professional literature, as needed

dyadic analysis—The exchange and development of ideas between two researchers as co-analysts of data

Emotion Coding—Codes the emotions recalled, experienced by, or inferred about a participant as suggested by the data

emotional arc—A visual representation of the shifting trajectory of a participant's varying emotions experienced through a period of time

empirical materials—Participant-centered forms of data collected for a research study

epistemology—A theory of knowledge construction based on the researcher's worldview; how her lens on the world and angled ways of knowing it focus and filter the perception and interpretation of it

ethnography—A research methodology for the study and writing of a group of people constituting a culture

ethos—A culture's values system

evaluation research—Quantitative, qualitative, or mixed methods research that assigns judgments about the merit, worth, or significance of programs or policy

evidentiary warrant—The presentation of data that supports a study's assertions

exempt—An IRB status for a research study proposal that does not require institutional review or approval

expedited—An IRB status for a research study proposal that involves minimal risk for participants when selected criteria are met

eyeballing—Visual overview of data to collect first-impression readings and to detect initial patterns

fieldwork—The research act of observing social life in a specific setting and recording it in some way for analytic reference; placement and immersion among people in an environment for close examination

fieldwork observation log—A written record of the days and dates, time blocks, number of clock hours, locations, and general content observed at various fieldwork sites

filters—A set of personal values, attitudes, and beliefs about the world, formed by one's unique personal biography, learned experiences, and individual thinking patterns; consist of particular theoretical perspectives or standpoints within a discipline

focus group—A guided interview with two or more participants simultaneously as they engage in conversational interaction about a topic

found poetry—Poetic work whose words originate from participant interview transcripts or other written texts

front matter—The preliminary narrative of elements (e.g., rationale, literature review, conceptual framework) before the main findings and discussion in a written report

full review—An IRB status for a research study proposal that cannot be exempted or expedited and requires full board review, revision (if needed), and final approval

gatekeepers—People with the authority to grant permission and facilitate the researcher's entry into a particular field setting or to conduct a study at all, such as IRBs

generalizability—In quantitative research, findings from a particular group of study participants that can also be assumed to be found in the entire population the participants represent

genres—Methodological approaches for qualitative research and inquiry geo-identity—The qualities or personality of a particular space or environment

ground plan—A bird's-eye view drawing of the main field site to label and assess its accommodation of furnishings, spatial relationships, and foot traffic

grounded theory—A methodological approach to qualitative inquiry that inductively and systematically builds a theory through detailed coding, categorization, and analytic memoing of data

heuristics—Open-ended methods of discovery during inquiry

hierarchy—Interpretive ranking of qualitative data from most to least, strongest to weakest, etc.

highdeep thinking—Reflection on what actually happened that keeps researchers grounded in the realities of the setting while transcending them to higher or deeper levels of meaning

high-level inferences—Researcher interpretations that extend beyond particulars to speculate on what they mean in the more general social scheme of things—the meso or macro

hypothesis—A predictive statement field tested or put through field experimentation to assess its reliability and validity

identities—Conceptions of self and personal perceptions of personality attributes and characteristics

impressionist tale—First-person writing that helps the reader relive the researcher's field and/or personal experiences that are exceptional, memorable, striking, and vibrant rather than typical

In Vivo Coding—An analytic procedure that utilizes the participant's verbatim words from data as codes

induction—An open-ended investigation with minimal assumptions, leaving one's self open to emergent leads, new ideas, exploratory discovery, and decision making

infer—Reasoning from partial evidence to determine or embellish on what's currently happening, has happened, or might happen

influences and affects—The qualitative paradigm for the positivist cause-and-effect of quantitative research

informed consent—Permission granted by a participant to take part in a study after the researcher has explained its major parameters and conditions (e.g., compensation, the right to withdraw, assurances of anonymity)

Institutional Review Board (IRB)—A U.S. approval and oversight committee for research proposals that involve human subjects to ensure legal and ethical compliance

interaction—The collective back-and-forth sequences of action and reaction between individuals or between an individual and something else

intercoder agreement—Two or more researchers as analysts concurring on the coding and interpretation of data

interpretation—The personal, subjective way humans perceive and respond to social experiences and construct the meanings of action, reaction, and interaction

interpretive writing—A level of insightful thinking and understanding in research reportage; transcendence beyond the case to find broader application or meaning

interrelationship—Researcher-generated analytic connections between or among different things such as codes, categories, themes, etc.

interview—A method of data collection by posing questions or conversational topics to participants to gather their personal experiences, perceptions, histories, and other information for a research study

interview condensation—The reduction of a full-length interview transcript to focus on the more salient data presented and to eliminate extraneous and tangential comments unrelated to the research questions of interest

interview protocol—A prepared document of ordered tasks, questions, and topics that guides interviewers through all stages of their interactions with participants

jointly told tale—Reportage that brings the researcher and participants together as coauthors of an account

jottings—Brief, quickly handwritten or typed notes with descriptions of action and participant quotes; later used as an outline or template for elaborated field notes

key assertion—A central argument or all-encompassing interpretive claim about the researcher's fieldwork and data analysis

key linkages—Statements of connection or interrelationship between main assertions

keywords—A list of terms that identify and summarize the core subjects and contents of a research study

latent—That which is hidden within or inferred about something; subtexts interpreted by the observer

lenses—Significant demographic attributes such as the researcher's gender, age, race/ethnicity, sexual orientation, socioeconomic class, and/or occupation; the particular research methodology or disciplinary approach employed for a study

letters of information—Courtesy information for participants about the nature of and procedures for a research study; an IRB might require them

Likert scale—A continuum-scaled quantitative measure of affective reactions/responses and attitudes

literary narrative writing—Creative nonfiction that uses the power of narrative storytelling to recount the participants' perceptions and experiences

low-level inferences—Researcher interpretations that address and summarize what is happening within the particulars of the case or field site; the micro

macro-level—Analysis of the global, universal, or conceptual meanings suggested by social settings

mandated reporter—An individual with a legal obligation to report any suspicious or criminal activity to officials

manifest—That which is readily observable in something; its apparent and surface content

material culture—A conception of social life as one that commercially produces and values objects and artifacts for consumption and daily living

matrix—An intersection of lists, set up as rows and columns; a tabular display that summarizes and arranges data from a larger corpus by factors such as time, site, case, variable, etc.

mediating variables—Contexts and actions that influence and affect antecedent conditions, leading to specific outcomes

meso-level—Analysis of the cultural, national, or mid-range implications of social settings

meta-analysis—A systematic analysis of statistical data pooled from comparable quantitative studies

meta-ethnography—An analysis of the major findings and themes from a number of comparable ethnographic studies

meta-memo—An analytic memo that integrates the accumulated memos to date to compose an even richer composite of the field experience

metasummary—A qualitative analysis of the major outcomes from a number of comparable qualitative studies

metasynthesis—A qualitative analysis and integration of the major findings and themes from a number of comparable qualitative studies

method—How someone does something or solves a problem, often systematic in its approach

methodology—The purpose or rationale for a particular method; why someone does something

microanalysis—Repeated scrutiny of the nuances and details of short or small moments of data for in-depth analysis

micro-level—Analysis of the local and particular elements of a social setting

mixed methods—The intentional blending of qualitative and quantitative data collection and analyses for studies that will benefit from the combined outcomes

moments—A collection of short yet significant (as interpreted by the researcher) participant actions, reactions, and interactions in the data that merit focused analysis and discussion

multi-case sampling—The collection of participant data from two or more settings to explore variances and comparability

netnography—Ethnographic study of online/digital cultures and participants

networking—Developing relationships with fellow scholars, publishers, and others in a field, possibly resulting in future collaborations and professional opportunities

observer's comments (OCs)—Field note entries that document uncensored impressions of what's going through a researcher's mind, analytic jottings of observations in progress, or relevant sidebars or follow-up reminders; a forum for interpreting participant subtexts and researcher reflexivity on the social action witnessed

ontology—A theory of the nature of being

oral history—A form of semi-structured interviewing that solicits historic narratives and period detail from participants' lived experiences

outcomes—Interpreted, summative results of actions, reactions, and interactions

outliers—Discrepant data or extreme cases that vary from the typical or majority

paper presentations—A conference delivery format in which researchers share their studies' findings orally, usually from prepared texts and media presentations

paradigm—A set of assumptions and perceptual orientations shared by members of a research community (Donmoyer, 2008)

paradigmatic corroboration—A mixed-methods analytic comparison when quantitative outcomes harmonize with qualitative outcomes

participant check—Consultation with a participant on the researcher's analysis and interpretation of the data provided by the participant

participant compliance—A participant's self-initiated yet coerced agreement with the researcher on matters of perspective or protocol; telling the researcher what the participant thinks the researcher wants to hear

participant observation—The researcher's method for watching and listening to people act, react, and interact in natural social settings, most often during everyday matters but sometimes during exceptional circumstances

pattern—An action, phenomenon, or content arrangement that occurs more than twice in the data that the researcher establishes as repeated and regular

peripheral role—A fly-on-the-wall participant observation stance; unobtrusive, not participating directly in any activities; witnessing and documenting social life as it naturally occurs

phenomena—Plural of phenomenon

phenomenology—The study and description of lived experiences; the essences and essentials of experiential states, natures of being, and personally significant meanings of phenomena

phenomenon—An experience, event, or conceptual state of being

photo-elicitation interviews—Photographs or other digital images, most often created by participants, used as stimuli or question prompts during interviews

photovoice—A representational and presentational style of research that combines original participant photography with accompanying texts written by the participant

plot—The overall structure of a story

poetic inquiry—Research methodology that investigates human experiences through poetic representation

poetic writing—Use of the conventions of literary poetry to evocatively represent and present data

point of view—The researcher's perspective in writing (e.g., first person, third person)

positionality—The researcher's reflexive stance in relationship to participants

positivist—A research paradigm that adheres to experimentation and observation with statistical representation of data and outcomes

poster presentations—A conference delivery format in which researchers prepare and exhibit large displays for other conference attendees to view

power—A concept referring to hierarchical status, attributed dominance, and control by individuals, organizations, governments, etc.

precoding—Preparatory formatting of data into stanzas with tentative codes and jottings for further analysis

prewriting—Preliminary writing (e.g., field notes, analytic memos, interview transcriptions) before the more formal writing stage of a study

principal investigator—The lead researcher of a study, designated as the "PI" on an IRB application

Process Code—An action-oriented word or phrase in gerund ("-ing") form that symbolically represents a larger datum

Process Coding—An analytic procedure that utilizes gerunds ("-ing" words and phrases) as codes

properties—The constituent elements that attribute qualities to something such as a code, category, phenomenon, etc.

proposition—A predictive statement, usually with two primary elements, that proposes a conditional event

protocols—Specific procedures and methods for the conduct of a study

proverb—A statement of folk wisdom passed through the generations

pseudonym—A fictitious name that replaces a participant's actual name to help ensure anonymity

purpose statement—A focusing framework for an investigation that sums up in one sentence the study's primary research goal

purposive sampling—The deliberate selection of participants who are most likely to provide insight into the phenomenon being investigated due to their position, experience, and/or identity markers

qua—Latin for "in the role of"

qualitative research—An umbrella term for a wide variety of approaches to and methods for the study of natural social life through primarily (but not exclusively) nonquantitative data

quantitative research—An umbrella term for a wide variety of approaches to and methods for the statistical transformation and analysis of numeric data

quantitize—The transformation of qualitative data into numeric representations

rapport—The interpersonal and preferably positive relationship between a researcher and participant

rationale—A narrative overview of the professional and personal motives driving the study, brief references to key research literature, and the projected outcomes or benefits for the people involved

reaction—The individual's response to an action from either another person or thing or to one's own action

references—Bibliographic information about sources cited within a narrative, with author's name, title of work, publication year, publisher, etc.

reflection—Personal, mental immersion in the data, their meanings, and the study as a whole

reflexivity—Individual reflection on one's relationships with the data, the participants, and even with one's self as a researcher

related research questions—A recommended maximum of five questions derived from the central research question that drive specific lines of inquiry

relationships—The quality of social interactions with and perceptions of others

relevant text—Data excerpts for analysis that are directly related to the research questions of interest

research design—The overall framework and provisional plan for initiating and conducting a research study

ritual—A special, significant, or sacred moment of action that suggests meaningful importance, either to the participants or to the researcher

roles—The assumed or attributed actions, personas, and characteristics of individuals

roundtables—A conference format in which groups of researchers sit around large tables, briefly discuss their work, and engage in conversation about the aspects of their studies that overlap

routines—Actions that take care of the everyday business of living, symbolize our self-cultivated and socialized habits, and meet our human need to create a sense of order

rules—Frames for acceptable social conduct; formal regulations and laws; a personal code of ethics or a moral compass for action, reaction, and interaction with others

sample—The person or group of people who will contribute data in some way to the study

sampling—The parameters and procedures used for selecting the specific participants for a study

saturation—An intuitive feeling that nothing new about the site and its participants are being learned after an extended observation or analytic period

schema—A procedural routine or script in the brain to cognitively process information and to act or respond

scope of inquiry—The boundaries, parameters, and limitations of a specific qualitative study, including assumptions of transferability to other contexts

secondary data—Relevant data derived from other sources and not personally collected by the researcher for analytic purposes

semantic differential—A quantitative survey instrument that assesses participants' responses in the affective domain toward a particular concept

semi-structured interview—Interview with a degree of structure combined with flexibility to offer researchers significant latitude to adjust course as needed

session chair—Person responsible for all logistics (introductions, media, timekeeping, facilitation, etc.) at a conference session

significance—Meaningful importance to an individual or group; something that transcends the mundane of the everyday

significant trivia—Rich, small details of a social scene that embellish the written report

snowball sampling—The referral of additional participants by participants to take part in a research study

social desirability bias—Compliant actions on the part of a participant in order to appear in a positive manner to the researcher; a participant telling a researcher what the participant thinks the researcher wants to hear

socialization—Learned expectations, codes, and regulations for our daily conduct

society—A social organization of people who share a history, a culture, a structure, a set of social institutions, usually a language, and an identity (Charon, 2013)

standpoints—Philosophical, theoretical, epistemological, methodological, and other perspectives inherent in or assumed by the researcher

stanzas—Data divided into units with a line break between them when a noticeable topic shift occurs; used to better manage the data corpus and to parse the changes in a participant's narrative trajectory

status—A hierarchical level or position of authority in relationship to others

storyline—The units of action contained within a plot

styles—Forms of writing for qualitative reportage

subassertions—Constituent claims related to an assertion

subcode—A primary code followed with a supplemental tag for detail

subjectivity—The researcher's personal and unfettered perspective

survey—A highly structured questionnaire composed of closed or open-ended questions; often administered to large groups of people for quantitative and qualitative analysis

synchronous—Events happening at the same time or during the same period of time

synoptic—A view of the whole

synthesis—The combination of different things in order to form a new whole

theme—An extended phrase or sentence that identifies and functions as a way to categorize a set of data into a topic that emerges from a pattern of ideas

theoretical constructs—Phrases that serve as category-like, abstract summations of a set of related themes

theoretical sampling—Often employed later in a qualitative study; the search for participants who might be able to confirm or disconfirm the patterns and theories developed by the researcher to date; particularly useful in the development of grounded theory

theory—A generalizable statement with four properties and an accompanying explanatory narrative: (1) predict and control action through an if–then logic, (2) account for variation in the empirical observations, (3) explain how and/or why something happens by stating its cause(s), and (4) provide insights and guidance for improving social life

thick description—A written interpretation of the nuances, complexity, and significance of a people's actions

through-line—A thematic thread that weaves throughout a research endeavor or extended experience

transcript—The written documentation of the verbal exchanges from an audio or video recorded interview

treatment—An experimental condition applied to participants, most often for quantitative research studies

triangulation—The use of at least three different sources or types (e.g., participants, sites, methods) of data, collected for purposes of comparison, corroboration, and/or synthesis

trustworthiness—The perceived rigor and truth value of a qualitative study

unity—A design principle in which seemingly disparate things or elements harmonize when brought together

unobtrusive measures—Residual traces or artifact evidence of previous human presence and activity

unstructured interviews—Informal conversations and spontaneous questions with participants with little structure at all beyond the general scope of inquiry

utility—The usefulness and pragmatic value of research for other applications

value—The importance attributed to oneself, another person, thing, or idea; values are the principles, moral codes, and situational norms people live by; interrelated with a belief and attitude

Values Coding—Analysis of the values, attitudes, and beliefs suggested by a participant's interview transcript content or inferred from documents, artifacts, and visual materials

values system—An individual's composite and intertwined values, attitudes, and beliefs

verbatim—The authentic and unedited (i.e., word-for-word) documentation of a participant's speech and narrative

Versus Coding—Applied to data in which conflicts between and among participants are overtly evident or covertly implied; codes appear as binary or dichotomous terms in an X VS. Y format

vignette—A research-based account of fieldwork in the form of a brief literary narrative

visual analysis—A variety of methods for studying material products, landscapes, architecture, photographs, video, digital media, and artwork

visual culture—A conception of social life as imbued with visual images, primarily digitally mediated, as a ubiquitous form of communication

webinars—Online, interactive broadcasts of seminars, workshops, and professional development experiences

within-case sampling—Participants who are all drawn from a single site

working sessions—Conference sessions where groups of scholars who have already read each other's reports discuss the papers individually and/or collectively for continued development

write-up—The expanded, narrative set of field notes from jottings

REFERENCES

Abbott, A. (2004). *Methods of discovery: Heuristics for the social sciences.* New York: W. W. Norton.

Adams, T. E., Jones, S. H., & Ellis, C. (2015). *Autoethnography.* New York: Oxford.

Adler, P. A., & Adler, P. (1987). *Membership roles in field research.* Newbury Park, CA: Sage.

Almeryda, M. (Producer & Director). (2015). *Experimenter: The Stanley Milgram story* [Motion picture]. USA: Magnolia Pictures.

Altheide, D. L., & Schneider, C. J. (2013). *Qualitative media analysis* (2nd ed.). Thousand Oaks, CA: Sage.

Alvesson, M., & Kärreman, D. (2011). *Qualitative research and theory development: Mystery as method.* London: Sage.

American Educational Research Association. (2016). *Poster preparation instructions.* http://www.aera.net/ EventsMeetings/AnnualMeeting/ PresenterandParticipant Information/tabid/16170/Default .aspx#Poster

Andersen, M. L. (1993). Studying across difference: Race, class, and gender in qualitative research. In J. H. Stanfield II & R. M. Dennis (Eds.), *Race and ethnicity in research methods* (pp. 39–52). Newbury Park, CA: Sage.

Atkinson, P. (2015). *For ethnography.* London: Sage.

Auerbach, C. F., & Silverstein, L. B. (2003). *Qualitative data: An introduction to coding and analysis.* New York: New York University Press.

Back, M. D., Küfner, A. C. P., & Egloff, B. (2010). The emotional timeline of September 11, 2001. *Psychological Science 21*(10), 1417–1419. doi:10.1177/0956797610382124

Belcher, W. L. (2009). *Writing your journal article in 12 weeks: A guide to academic publishing success.* Thousand Oaks, CA: Sage.

Berbary, L. A. (2011). Poststructural writerly representation: Screenplay as creative analytic practice. *Qualitative Inquiry 17*(2), 186–196. doi:10.1177/ 1077800410393887

Berbary, L. A. (2012). "Don't be a whore, that's not ladylike": Discursive discipline and sorority women's gendered subjectivity. *Qualitative Inquiry 18*(7), 602–625. doi:10.1177/ 1077800412450150

Berger, A. A. (2012). *Media analysis techniques* (4th ed.). Thousand Oaks, CA: Sage.

Berger, A. A. (2014). *What objects mean: An introduction to material culture* (2nd ed.). Walnut Creek, CA: Left Coast Press.

Bernard, H. R. (2011). *Research methods in anthropology: Qualitative and quantitative approaches* (5th ed.) Walnut Creek, CA: AltaMira Press.

Birks, M., & Mills, J. (2015). *Grounded theory: A practical guide* (2nd ed.). London: Sage.

Bloch, K. B. (2014). 'Anyone can be an illegal': Color-blind ideology and maintaining Latino/ citizen borders. *Critical Sociology 40*(1), 47–65. doi:10.1177/ 0896920512466274

Boal, A. (1995). *The rainbow of desire* (A. Jackson, Trans.). New York: Routledge.

Bogdan, R. C., & Biklen, S. K. (2007). *Qualitative research for education: An introduction to theories and methods* (5th ed.). Boston: Pearson Education.

Bonilla-Silva, E. (2002). The linguistics of color-blind racism: How to talk nasty about Blacks without sounding 'racist.' *Critical Sociology 28*(1–2), 41–64. doi:10. 1177/08969205020280010501

Brinkmann, S. (2012). *Qualitative inquiry in everyday life: Working with everyday life materials.* London: Sage.

Brinkmann, S. (2013). *Qualitative interviewing.* New York: Oxford.

Brinkmann, S., Jacobsen M. H., & Kristiansen, S. (2014). Historical overview of qualitative research in the social sciences. In P. Leavy (Ed.),

The Oxford handbook of qualitative research (pp. 17–42). New York: Oxford.

Bryant, A., & Charmaz, K. (Eds.). (2007). The SAGE handbook of grounded theory. London: Sage.

Bryman, A. (2006). Integrating quantitative and qualitative research: How is it done? Qualitative Research 6(1), 97–113. doi:10.1177/1468794106058877

Butler-Kisber, L. (2010). Qualitative inquiry: Thematic, narrative, and arts-informed perspectives. London: Sage.

Chang, H. (2008). Autoethnography as method. Walnut Creek, CA: Left Coast Press.

Charmaz, K. (2008). Grounded theory. In J. A. Smith (Ed.), Qualitative psychology: A practical guide to research methods (2nd ed.) (pp. 81–110). London: Sage.

Charmaz, K. (2009). The body, identity, and self: Adapting to impairment. In J. M. Morse et al., Developing grounded theory: The second generation (pp. 155–191). Walnut Creek, CA: Left Coast Press.

Charmaz, K. (2014). Constructing grounded theory (2nd ed.). Thousand Oaks, CA: Sage.

Charon, J. M. (2013). Ten questions: A sociological perspective (8th ed.). Belmont, CA: Cengage Learning.

Chirkov, V. (2016). Fundamentals of research on culture and psychology: Theory and methods. New York: Routledge.

Churton, M., & Brown, A. (2010). Theory & method (2nd ed.). New York: Palgrave Macmillan.

Cigna. (2012). A healthier point of view: Living at a healthier weight (Publication no. 835420 b04/12). Cigna Health and Life Insurance Company.

Clarke, A. E., Friese, C., & Washburn, R. (Eds.). (2015) Situational analysis in practice: Mapping research with grounded theory. Walnut Creek, CA: Left Coast Press.

Clark-Ibáñez, M. (2008). Gender and being "bad": Inner-city students' photographs. In P. Thomson (Ed.), Doing visual research with children and young people (pp. 95–113). London: Routledge.

Coghlan, D., & Brannick, T. (2010). Doing action research in your own organization (3rd ed.). London: Sage.

Collins, S. G., & Durington, M. S. (2015). Networked anthropology: A primer for ethnographers. New York: Routledge.

Connolly, K., & Reilly, R. C. (2007). Emergent issues when researching trauma: A confessional tale. Qualitative Inquiry 13(4), 522–540. doi:10.1177/107780040 6297678

Corbin, J., & Strauss, A. (2015). Basics of qualitative research: Techniques and procedures for developing grounded theory (4th ed.). Thousand Oaks, CA: Sage.

Creswell, J. W. (2015). A concise introduction to mixed methods research. Thousand Oaks, CA: Sage.

Creswell, J. W. (2016). 30 essential skills for the qualitative researcher. Thousand Oaks, CA: Sage.

Creswell, J. W., & Plano Clark, V. L. (2011). Designing and conducting mixed methods research (2nd ed.). Thousand Oaks, CA: Sage.

Daiute, C. (2014). Narrative inquiry: A dynamic approach. Thousand Oaks, CA: Sage.

Department of Health, Education, and Welfare (DHEW) National Commission for the Protection of Human Subjects of Biomedical and Behavioral Research. (1979). The Belmont report: Ethical principles and guidelines for the protection of human subjects research. (DHEW Publication No. [OS] 78–0012). Washington, DC: Government Printing Office.

DeWalt, K. M., & DeWalt, B. R. (2011). Participant observation: A guide for fieldworkers (2nd ed.). Lanham, MD: AltaMira Press.

Dey, I. (1993). Qualitative data analysis: A user-friendly guide for social scientists. London: Routledge.

Dey, I. (2007) Grounding categories. In A. Bryant & K. Charmaz (Eds.), The SAGE handbook of grounded theory (pp. 167–190). London: Sage.

Donmoyer, R. (2008). Paradigm. In L. M. Given (Ed.), The SAGE encyclopedia of qualitative research methods (pp. 591–595). Thousand Oaks, CA: Sage.

Duhigg, C. (2016). *Smarter faster better: The secrets of being productive in life and business.* New York: Random House.

Duneier, M. (1999). *Sidewalk.* New York: Farrar, Straus and Giroux.

Eastman, J. T. (2012). Rebel manhood: The hegemonic masculinity of the southern rock music revival. *Journal of Contemporary Ethnography* 41(2), 189–219. doi:10.1177/0891241611426430

Ehrenreich, B. (2001). *Nickel and dimed: On (not) getting by in America.* New York: Henry Holt and Company.

Emerson, R. M., Fretz, R. I., & Shaw, L. L. (2011). *Writing ethnographic fieldnotes* (2nd ed.). Chicago: University of Chicago Press.

Emery, B., Friedman, L., Lauder, K., & Little, G. (Producers), & Alvarez, K. P. (Director). (2015). *The Stanford prison experiment* [Motion picture]. USA: IFC Films.

Erickson, F. (1986). Qualitative methods in research on teaching. In M. C. Wittrock (Ed.), *Handbook of research on teaching* (3rd ed.) (pp. 119–161). New York: Macmillan.

Evergreen, S. D. H. (2014). *Presenting data effectively: Communicating your findings for maximum impact.* Thousand Oaks, CA: Sage.

Fetterman, D. M. (2010). *Ethnography: Step by step* (3rd ed.). Thousand Oaks, CA: Sage.

Finley, S., & Finley, M. (1999). Sp'ange: A research story. *Qualitative Inquiry* 5(3), 313–337. doi: 10.1177/107780049900500302

Fishburne, L., & Benedetti, R. (Producers), & Sargent, J. (Director). (1997). *Miss Evers' boys* [Motion picture]. USA: Home Box Office.

Foster, E. (2002). Storm tracking: Scenes of marital disintegration. *Qualitative Inquiry* 8(6), 804–819. doi:10.1177/1077800402238080

Fox, M., Martin, P., & Green, G. (2007). *Doing practitioner research.* London: Sage.

Fox, R. (2014). Are those germs in your pocket, or am I just crazy to see you? An autoethnographic consideration of obsessive-compulsive disorder. *Qualitative Inquiry* 20(8), 966–975. doi:10.1177/1077800413513732

Franzosi, R. (2010). *Quantitative narrative analysis.* Thousand Oaks, CA: Sage.

Fredricks, J. A., Alfeld-Liro, C. J., Hruda, L. Z., Eccles, J. S., Patrick, H., & Ryan, A. M. (2002). A qualitative exploration of adolescents' commitment to athletics and the arts. *Journal of Adolescent Research* 17(1), 68–97. doi:10.1177/0743558402171004

Friese, S. (2014). *Qualitative data analysis with ATLAS.ti* (2nd ed.). London: Sage.

Galletta, A., & Cross, W. (2013). *Mastering the semi-structured interview and beyond: From research design to analysis and publication.* New York: New York University Press.

Gardner, H. (1999). *Intelligence reframed: Multiple intelligences for the 21st century.* New York: Basic Books.

Gee, J. P. (2011). *How to do discourse analysis: A toolkit.* New York: Routledge.

Geertz, C. (1973). *The interpretation of cultures.* New York: Basic Books.

Gibson, B., & Hartman, J. (2014). *Rediscovering grounded theory.* London: Sage.

Gibson, W. J., & Brown, A. (2009). *Working with qualitative data.* London: Sage.

Glaser, B. G., & Strauss, A. L. (1967). *The discovery of grounded theory: Strategies for qualitative research.* New York: Aldine de Gruyter.

Gobo, G. (2008). *Doing ethnography* (A. Belton, Trans.). London: Sage.

Goffman, E. (1959). *The presentation of self in everyday life.* New York: Anchor Books.

Goleman, D. (1995). *Emotional intelligence.* New York: Bantam Books.

Gorman, T. J. (2000). Cross-class perceptions of social class. *Sociological Spectrum 20,* 93–120. doi:10.1080/027321700280044

Grant, C. A., & Tate, W. F. (1995). Multicultural education through the lens of the multicultural education research literature. In J. A. Banks & C. A. M. Banks (Eds.), *Handbook of research on multicultural education* (pp. 145–166). New York: Macmillan.

Hacker, K. (2013). *Community-based participatory research*. Thousand Oaks, CA: Sage.

Hager, L., Maier, B. J., O'Hara, E., Ott, D., & Saldaña, J. (2000). Theatre teachers' perceptions of Arizona state standards. *Youth Theatre Journal 14*, 64–77. doi:10.1080/08929092.2000.10012518

Hammersley, M., & Atkinson, P. (2007). *Ethnography: Principles in practice* (3rd ed.). London: Routledge.

Hanauer, D. I. (2015). Being in the second Iraq war: A poetic ethnography. *Qualitative Inquiry 21*(1), 83–106. doi:10.1177/1077800414542697

Handwerker, W. P. (2015). *Our story: How cultures shaped people to get things done*. Walnut Creek, CA: Left Coast Press.

Heath, C., Hindmarsh, J., & Luff, P. (2010). *Video in qualitative research: Analysing social interaction in everyday life*. London: Sage.

Hitchcock, G., & Hughes, D. (1995). *Research and the teacher: A qualitative introduction to school-based research* (2nd ed.). London: Routledge.

Hlava, P., & Elfers, J. (2014). The lived experience of gratitude. *Journal of Humanistic Psychology 54*(4), 434–455. doi:10.1177/0022167813508605

Hochschild, A. R. (2003). *The managed heart: Commercialization of human feeling* (2nd ed.). Berkeley, CA: University of California Press.

Horn, M. J., & Gurel, L. M. (1981). *The second skin: An interdisciplinary study of clothing* (3rd ed.). Boston: Houghton Mifflin.

Jackson, A. Y., & Mazzei, L. A. (2012). *Thinking with theory in qualitative research: Viewing data across multiple perspectives*. New York: Routledge.

Jones, S. H., Adams, T. E., & Ellis, C. (Eds.). (2013). *Handbook of autoethnography*. Walnut Creek, CA: Left Coast Press.

Kelling, G. L., & Wilson, J. Q. (1982). Broken windows: The police and neighborhood safety. *The Atlantic*. http://www.theatlantic.com/magazine/print/1982/03/broken-windows/304465/

Kidder, T. (1989). *Among schoolchildren*. New York: Avon Books.

Kitchen, J., & Stevens, D. (2008). Action research in teacher education: Two teacher-educators practice action research as they introduce action research to preservice educators. *Action Research 6*(1), 7–28. doi:10.1177/1476750307083716

Knowles, J. G., & Cole, A. L. (2008). *Handbook of the arts in qualitative research: Perspectives, methodologies, examples, and issues*. Thousand Oaks, CA: Sage.

Knowlton, L. W., & Phillips, C. C. (2013). *The logic model guidebook: Better strategies for great results* (2nd ed.). Thousand Oaks, CA: Sage.

Koro-Ljungberg, M. (2016). *Reconceptualizing qualitative research: Methodologies without methodology*. Thousand Oaks, CA: Sage.

Kozinets, R. V. (2015). *Netnography: Redefined* (2nd ed.). London: Sage.

Krippendorff. K. (2013). *Content analysis: An introduction to its methodology* (3rd ed.). Thousand Oaks, CA: Sage.

Krippendorff, K., & Bock, M. A. (Eds.). (2009). *The content analysis reader*. Thousand Oaks, CA: Sage.

Lakoff, G., & Johnson, M. (2003). *Metaphors we live by* (2nd ed.). Chicago: University of Chicago Press.

Lancy, D. F. (1993). *Qualitative research in education: An introduction to the major traditions*. New York: Longman.

Leavy, P. (2015). *Method meets art: Arts-based research practice* (2nd ed.). New York: Guilford Press.

LeRoy, M. (Producer), & Fleming, V. (Director). (1939). *The wizard of Oz* [Motion picture]. US: MGM.

Lieberman, M. D. (2013). *Social: Why our brains are wired to connect.* New York: Crown Publishers.

Liebow, E. (1967). *Tally's corner: A study of Negro streetcorner men.* Boston: Little, Brown and Company.

Lincoln, Y. S., & Guba, E. G. (1985). *Naturalistic inquiry.* Newbury Park, CA: Sage.

Lindlof, T. R., & Taylor, B. C. (2011). *Qualitative communication research methods* (3rd ed.). Thousand Oaks, CA: Sage.

Madden, R. (2010). *Being ethnographic: A guide to the theory and practice of ethnography.* London: Sage.

Madison, D. S. (2012). *Critical ethnography: Methods, ethics, and performance* (2nd ed.). Thousand Oaks, CA: Sage.

Margolis, E., & Pauwels, L. (Eds.). (2011). *The SAGE handbook of visual research methods.* London: Sage.

Marín, G., & Marín, B. V. (1991). *Research with Hispanic populations.* Newbury Park, CA: Sage.

Marshall, M. N. (1996). Sampling for qualitative research. *Family Practice 13*(6), 522–525. doi:10.1093/fampra/13.6.522

McCammon, L. A., & Saldaña, J. (2011). Lifelong impact: Adult perceptions of their high school speech and/or theatre participation. Unpublished report.

McCammon, L., Saldaña, J., Hines, A., & Omasta, M.

(2012a). Lifelong impact: Adult perceptions of their high school speech and/or theatre participation. *Youth Theatre Journal 26*(1), 2–25. doi:10.1080/08929092.2012.678223

McCammon, L., Saldaña, J., Hines, A., & Omasta, M. (2012b). The reader's theatre script for "Lifelong impact: Adult perceptions of their high school speech and/or theatre participation." *Youth Theatre Journal 26*(1), 26–37. doi:10.1080/08929092.2012.678218

McCurdy, D. W., Spradley, J. P., & Shandy, D. J. (2005). *The cultural experience: Ethnography in complex society* (2nd ed.). Long Grove, IL: Waveland Press.

Mears, C. L. (2009). *Interviewing for education and social science research: The gateway approach.* New York: Palgrave Macmillan.

Merriam, S. B. (1998). *Qualitative research and case study applications in education.* San Francisco: Jossey-Bass.

Miles, M. B., Huberman, M. A., & Saldaña, J. (2014). *Qualitative data analysis: A methods sourcebook* (3rd ed.). Thousand Oaks, CA: Sage.

Miller, D. L., Creswell, J. W., & Olander, L. S. (1998). Writing and retelling multiple ethnographic tales of a soup kitchen for the homeless. *Qualitative Inquiry (4)*1, 469–491. doi:10.1177/107780049800400404

Morgan, D. L. (2014). *Integrating qualitative & quantitative methods:*

A pragmatic approach. Thousand Oaks, CA: Sage.

Morris, E. W. (2008). "Rednecks," "rutters," and 'rithmetic: Social class, masculinity and schooling in a rural context. *Gender & Society 22,* 728–751. doi:10.1177/0891243208325163

Morse, J. M. (2012). *Qualitative health research: Creating a new discipline.* Walnut Creek, CA: Left Coast Press.

Nathan, R. (2005). *My freshman year: What a professor learned by becoming a student.* New York: Penguin Books.

Neuendorf, K. A. (2017). *The content analysis guidebook* (2nd ed.). Thousand Oaks, CA: Sage.

Nordmarken, S. (2014). Becoming ever more monstrous: Feeling transgender in-betweenness. *Qualitative Inquiry 20*(1), 37–50. doi:10.1177/1077800413508531

Omasta, M. (2011). Artist intention and audience reception in theatre for young audiences. *Youth Theatre Journal 25*(1), 32–50. doi:10.1080/08929092.2011.569530

Omasta, M., & Adkins, N. B. (2017). *Playwriting and young audiences: Collected wisdom and practical advice from the field.* Chicago: Intellect.

Omasta, M., & Brandley, A. T. (2016). Student perceptions of high school theatre programs: An investigation of social issues and call for replication. *Youth Theatre Journal 30*(1), 50–67.

Park, H.-Y. (2009). Writing in Korean, living in the U.S.: A screenplay about a bilingual boy and his mom. *Qualitative Inquiry 15*(6), 1103–1124. doi:10.1177/1077800409334184

Pascoe, C. J. (2007). *Dude, you're a fag: Masculinity and sexuality in high school.* Berkeley: University of California Press.

Patton, M. Q. (2008). *Utilization-focused evaluation* (4th ed.). Thousand Oaks, CA: Sage.

Patton, M. Q. (2015). *Qualitative research & evaluation methods* (4th ed.). Thousand Oaks, CA: Sage.

Paulus, T., Lester, J. N., & Dempster, P. G. (2014). *Digital tools for qualitative research.* London: Sage.

Pezzarossi, H. L. (2015). A steely gaze: My captivation with the American tintype. In S. Brown, A. Clarke, & U. Frederick (Eds.), *Object stories: Artifacts and archeologists* (pp. 85–92). Walnut Creek, CA: Left Coast Press.

Pink, S., Horst, H., Postill, J., Hjorth, L., Lewis, T., & Tacchi, J. (2016). *Digital ethnography: Principles and practice.* London: Sage.

Plano Clark, V. L., & Ivankova, N. V. (2016). *Mixed methods research: A guide to the field.* Thousand Oaks, CA: Sage.

Poulos, C. N. (2008). *Accidental ethnography: An inquiry into family secrecy.* Walnut Creek, CA: Left Coast Press.

Prendergast, M., Leggo, C., & Sameshima, P. (Eds.). (2009). *Poetic inquiry: Vibrant voices in the social sciences.* Rotterdam: Sense Publishers.

Prior, L. (2004). Doing things with documents. In D. Silverman (Ed.), *Qualitative research: Theory, method and practice* (2nd ed.) (pp. 76–94). London: Sage.

Rallis, S. F., & Rossman, G. B. (2003). Mixed methods in evaluation contexts: A pragmatic framework. In A. Tashakkori & C. Teddlie (Eds.), *Handbook of mixed methods in social & behavioral research* (pp. 491–512). Thousand Oaks, CA: Sage.

Rapley, T. (2007). *Doing conversation, discourse and document analysis.* London: Sage.

Roulston, K., deMarrais, K., & Lewis, J. B. (2003). Learning to interview in the social sciences. *Qualitative Inquiry 9*(4), 643–668. doi:10.1177/1077800403252736

Rubin, H. J., & Rubin, I. S. (2012). *Qualitative interviewing: The art of hearing data* (3rd ed.). Thousand Oaks, CA: Sage.

Saldaña, J. (1997). "Survival": A white teacher's conception of drama with inner city Hispanic youth. *Youth Theatre Journal 11,* 25–46. doi:10.1080/08929092.1997.10012482

Saldaña, J. (2005a). *Ethnodrama: An anthology of reality theatre.* Walnut Creek, CA: AltaMira Press.

Saldaña, J. (2005b). Theatre of the oppressed with children: A field experiment. *Youth Theatre Journal 19,* 117–33. doi:10.1080/08929092.2005.10012580

Saldaña, J. (2010). Exploring the stigmatized child through theatre of the oppressed techniques. In P. B. Duffy & E. Vettraino (Eds.), *Youth and theatre of the oppressed* (pp. 45–62). New York: Palgrave Macmillan.

Saldaña, J. (2011a). *Ethnotheatre: Research from page to stage.* Walnut Creek, CA: Left Coast Press.

Saldaña, J. (2011b). *Fundamentals of qualitative research.* New York: Oxford.

Saldaña, J. (2015). *Thinking qualitatively: Methods of mind.* Thousand Oaks, CA: Sage.

Saldaña, J. (2016). *The coding manual for qualitative researchers* (3rd ed.). London: Sage.

Saldaña, J., & Otero, H. D. (1990). Experiments in assessing children's responses to theatre with the semantic differential. *Youth Theatre Journal 5*(1), 11–19. doi:[none]

Salmons, J. (2016). *Doing qualitative research online.* London: Sage.

Santos-Guerra, M. A., & Fernández-Sierra, J. (1996). Qualitative evaluation of a program on self-care and health education for diabetics.

Evaluation 2(3), 339–347. doi:10.1177/13563890 9600200307

Sawyer, R. D., & Norris, J. (2013). *Duoethnography.* New York: Oxford.

Scarduzio, J. A., & Tracy, S. J. (2015). Sensegiving and sensebreaking via emotion cycles and emotional buffering: How collective communication creates order in the courtroom. *Management Communication Quarterly 29*(3), 331–357. doi:10.1177/0893318915581647

Schreier, M. (2012). *Qualitative content analysis in practice.* London: Sage.

Schwartz, S. (2003). Wonderful. On *Wicked: Original Broadway cast recording.* New York: Universal Classics Group.

Seidman, I. (2013). *Interviewing as qualitative research: A guide for researchers in education and the social sciences* (4th ed.). New York: Teachers College Press.

Shaw, M. E., & Wright, J. M. (1967). *Scales for the measurement of attitudes.* New York: McGraw-Hill.

Smith, J. A., Flowers, P., & Larkin, M. (2009). *Interpretative phenomenological analysis: Theory, method and research.* London: Sage.

Speedy, J., & "The Unassuming Geeks." (2011). "All Googled out on suicide": Making collective biographies out of silent fragments with "The Unassuming Geeks." *Qualitative Inquiry 17*(2), 134–143. doi:10.1177/1077800410392333

Spencer, S. (2011). *Visual research methods in the social sciences: Awakening visions.* London: Routledge.

Spry, T. (2011). *Body, paper, stage: Writing and performing autoethnography.* Walnut Creek, CA: Left Coast Press.

Stake, R. E. (1995). *The art of case study research.* Thousand Oaks, CA: Sage.

Stanfield, J. H., II. (1993). Methodological reflections: An introduction. In J. H. Stanfield II & R. M. Dennis (Eds.), *Race and ethnicity in research methods* (pp. 3–15). Newbury Park, CA: Sage.

Stringer, E. T. (2014). *Action research* (4th ed.). Thousand Oaks, CA: Sage.

Sullivan, P. (2012). *Qualitative data analysis using a dialogical approach.* London: Sage.

Sunstein, B. S., & Chiseri-Strater, E. (2012). *FieldWorking: Reading and writing research* (4th ed.). Boston, MA: Bedford/St. Martin's.

Tashakkori, A., & Teddlie, C. (Eds.) (2010). *SAGE handbook of mixed methods in social & behavioral research* (2nd ed.). Thousand Oaks, CA: Sage.

Tavory, I., & Timmermans, S. (2014). *Abductive analysis: Theorizing qualitative research.* Chicago: University of Chicago Press.

Thomson, P. (Ed.). (2008). *Doing visual research with children and young people.* London: Routledge.

Tracy, S. J., Lutgen-Sandvik, P., & Alberts, J. K. (2006). Nightmares, demons, and slaves: Exploring the painful metaphors of workplace bullying. *Management Communication Quarterly 20*(2), 148-185. doi: 10.1177/0893318906291980

Urquhart, C. (2013). *Grounded theory for qualitative research: A practical guide.* London: Sage.

Vagle, M. D. (2014). *Crafting phenomenological research.* Walnut Creek, CA: Left Coast Press.

Van Maanen, J. (2011). *Tales of the field: On writing ethnography* (2nd ed.). Chicago: University of Chicago Press.

Vogt, W. P., Vogt, E. R., Gardner, D. C., & Haeffele, L. M. (2014). *Selecting the right analyses for your data: Quantitative, qualitative, and mixed methods.* New York: Guilford.

Wadsworth, Y. (2011). *Everyday evaluation on the run* (3rd ed.). Walnut Creek, CA: Left Coast Press.

Wagner, J. (1986). *The search for signs of intelligent life in the universe.* New York: Harper & Row.

Wallace, T. L., & Chhuon, V. (2014). Proximal processes in urban classrooms: Engagement and disaffection in urban youth of color. *American Educational Research Journal 51*(5), 937-973. doi:10.3102/0002831214531324

Watkins, R. K. (2012). The belly dancer project: A phenomenological study of gendered identity through documentary filmmaking. Unpublished dissertation, Arizona State University.

Weber, R. P. (1990). *Basic content analysis* (2nd ed.). Newbury Park, CA: Sage.

Wertz, F. J., Charmaz, K., McMullen, L. M., Josselson, R., Anderson, R., & McSpadden, E. (2011). *Five ways of doing qualitative analysis*. New York: Guilford.

Wheeldon, J., & Åhlberg, M. K. (2012). *Visualizing social science research: Maps, methods, & meaning*. Thousand Oaks, CA: Sage.

Whyte, W. F. (1993). *Street corner society: The social structure of an Italian slum* (4th ed.). Chicago: University of Chicago Press.

Wierzbicka, A. (2012). Is pain a human universal?: A cross-linguistic and cross-cultural perspective on pain. *Emotion Review 4*(3), 307–317. doi:10.1177/1754073912439761

Wilkinson, D., & Birmingham, P. (2003). *Using research instruments: A guide for researchers*. London: Routledge Farmer.

Willig, C. (2008). Discourse analysis. In J. A. Smith (Ed.), *Qualitative psychology: A practical guide to research methods* (2nd ed.) (pp. 160–85). London: Sage.

Wolcott, H. F. (1994). *Transforming qualitative data: Description, analysis, and interpretation*. Thousand Oaks, CA: Sage.

Wolcott, H. F. (2005). *The art of fieldwork* (2nd ed.). Walnut Creek, CA: AltaMira Press.

Wolcott, H. F. (2008). *Ethnography: A way of seeing* (2nd ed.). Walnut Creek, CA: AltaMira Press.

Wolcott, H. F. (2009). *Writing up qualitative research* (3rd ed.). Thousand Oaks, CA: Sage.

Yang, C., Brown, B. B., & Braun, M. T. (2013). From Facebook to cell calls: Layers of electronic intimacy in college students' interpersonal relationships. *New Media & Society 16*(1), 5–23. doi:10.1177/1461444812 472486

INDEX

a priori, 226

abduction, 9

abstracts, 310–312

access, 33

action
  action research, 155–156
  definition and overview, 12–15
  reflection on, 50–51

active role, 36

Adams, T. E., 15

adapting, 11–12

Adler, P., 36

Adler, P. A., 36

advertisements, analyzing, 70–72

affects, 239

aggregate, 194

Alberts, Jess K., 341, 355–387. *See also*
  "Nightmares, Demons, and Slaves" (Tracy,
  Lutgen-Sandvik, Alberts)

"All Googled Out on Suicide" (Speedy), 296–298

Allen, Quaylan, 341, 388–410

Altheide, David L., 83

ambiguity, of ethics, 206–208

American Educational Research Association (AERA),
  318, 325

analysis, 3–28
  analytic assemblage, overview, 213
  condensing large amounts of data, 4–7
  defined, 3
  developing fundamental skills for,
    overview, 3–4
  interpreting routines, rituals, rules, roles,
    relationships of social life, 15–23,
    16 (figure), 21 (figure), 22 (figure)
  leading an analytic life, 335–340
  noticing patterns in textual and visual materials,
    7–10
  qualitative research, defined, 4
  as through-line, 23–24
  understanding social processes, 12–15
  unifying seemingly different things, 10–12,
    10 (figure)
  See also field site analysis; interviews; material
    culture; presentations; synthesis of analysis;
    write-ups

analytic and formal writing, 284–286, 285 (figure)

analytic formatting, 121–126, 124 (figure)

analytic induction, 9

analytic memos, 54–57, 125–126, 255, 267–268

analytic story-line, 11

angles
  defined, 35
  for fieldwork, 34–36

Angrosino, Michael V., 341, 343–387. *See also*
  "On the Bus With Vonnie Lee" (Angrosino)

anonymity, 193

antecedent conditions, 238, 238 (figure)

"Anyone Can Be an Illegal" (Bloch), 292–294

APA manual style, 310

"Are Those Germs in Your Pocket, or Am I Just
  Crazy to See You?" (Fox), 289–290

argot, 158

argument, 306–307

artifacts
  analysis of, overview, 73–74
  analyzing belonging, 74–76
  defined, 73
  extensions of, 79–81
  Process Coding of, 78–79
  symbolism of, 76–77, 77 (figure)

assent, 193

assertions, 245–251, 247 (figure), 265

asynchronous interviews, 90

attitude
  analysis of values, beliefs, and, 64–66
  defined, 64
  in Dramaturgical Coding, 220
  materials and meanings of human production,
    66–67
  Values Coding for interviews, 128–129,
    128 (figure)

audio-recording
  for field notes, 45–47
  for interviewing, 102–103

autoethnography, 158–159

Back, M. D., 153, 154 (figure)

"Becoming Ever More Monstrous"
  (Nordmarken), 158

"Being in the Second Iraq War" (Hanauer), 300–302

Belcher, W. L., 306

belief

analysis of values, attitudes, and, 64–66
defined, 64
materials and meanings of human production, 66–67
Values Coding for interviews, 128–129, 128 (figure)
Belmont Report (U.S. Department of Health, Education, and Welfare), 191–192
belonging, 74–76
beneficence, in research, 192
benefit descriptions, for Institutional Review Board applications, 202
Berger, Arthur Asa, 76, 83
Biklen, S. K., 43
Bloch, K. B., 292–294
Bogdan, R. C., 43
boundaries, 97
bracket, 152
Brandley, A. T., 328–330

CAQDAS (Computer Assisted Qualitative Data Analysis Software), 268–271, 269 (figure), 270 (figure), 271 (figure), 331–332
Carless, David, 302
case studies, 148–150
categories
    core category, 11
    defined, 226
    for patterning textual and visual materials, 226–230, 263
causation, 237–238, 257, 259
central research questions, 175–177, 176 (figure)
Charmaz, Kathy, 11–12
Charon, J. M., 31, 258–259
Chhuon, V., 186–187, 187 (figure)
children, interviewing, 102
citations, 310
Clarke, A. E., 12
Clark-Ibáñez, Marisol, 148–150
clock hours, for fieldwork, 47–48
Cmap, 331
coding
    analytic synthesis and constructing theory, 262
    code, defined, 5
    codeweaving, 79
    Versus Coding, 222–224
    of data, overview, 216

Descriptive Coding and subcoding, 217–219
Dramaturgical Coding, 219–222
Emotion Coding, 129–131, 131 (figure)
of interview answers, 91
overview, 117, 120–121
Process Coding for interviews, 126–128
Values Coding, 128–129, 128 (figure)
In Vivo Coding and analytic formatting, 121–126, 124 (figure)
See also interviews
collaborative and polyvocal writing, 296–298
color, for slide presentations, 322
communication, research ethics and, 195
complete role, 36
composite narratives, 194
concepts
    analytic synthesis and constructing theory, 263
    defined, 235
    elements of theories, 259–260
    overview, 235–237
conceptual frames, 97
conceptual framework, 184–188, 187 (figure)
condensing, of data
    analytic synthesis and constructing theory, 262
    analyzing relevant text, 215–216
    codes and coding, 216
    Versus Coding, 222–224
    Descriptive Coding and subcoding, 217–219
    Dramaturgical Coding, 219–222
    overview, 215
    research-based found poetry, 224–225
    summarized, 273–275 (figure)
    See also synthesis of analysis
condensing, of interviews, 117–120
confessional tales, 287–289
confidentiality, 193–194, 194 (figure)
conflict of interest descriptions, for Institutional Review Board applications, 203
conflict-free research, 195–196
conflicts, in Dramaturgical Coding, 219
Connolly, K., 287–289
consent, 192–193
constructivism, 142–143
content analysis, 66–67, 153–155, 154 (figure)
convenience sampling, 96
conversation, for interviewing, 111–113, 111 (figure)
core category, 11

covert role, 36

Crafting Phenomenological Research (Vagle), 152

credibility, 271–273

Creswell, J. W., 286

critical and advocacy writing, 292–294

Critical Sociology, 292–294

Cross, W., 104–105

cultural shock, 11

culture

    defined, 30–31

    field site analysis and, 30–31, 31 (figure)

    See also material culture

dance, 303, 303 (figure)

data

    condensing large amounts of, 4–7

    data analysis methods, 181–182, 272

    data collection methods, 180–181, 272

    data corpus, 30

    datum, defined, 4

    guidelines for analytic synthesis of, 214–215 (*See also* condensing, of data)

    outliers, 235

    presenting data effectively, 328–333, 329 (figures), 330 (figure), 331 (figure), 332 (figure)

deception, 201–202

Dedoose Software, 269, 270 (figure)

deduction, 9

Dempster, P. G., 48

descriptive and realistic writing, 286–287

Descriptive Coding, 217–219

Dey, I., 255, 260

diagrams

    for data presentation, 331–333, 332 (figure)

    defined, 252

    diagrammatic displays, 252–255, 253 (figure), 267

digital culture, 63

digital object identifier (DOI), 172

digital recording, for field notes, 45–47, 46 (figure)

Digital Tools for Qualitative Research (Paulus), 83

disconfirming evidence, 245–246

discourse analysis, 66–67

Discovery of Grounded Theory, The (Glaser, Strauss), 150

discussants, 319

documents

analysis of, overview, 68–69

    analyzing attention, 70–72

    analyzing creators' identity, 72–73

    collecting materials, 69–70

    defined, 68

do-it-youself (DIY) transcribing, 114–115

Doodle, 102

Douglas, Kitrina, 302

dramatic writing, 298–300

dramatic/staged readings, 326, 326–327 (figure)

Dramaturgical Coding, 219–222

Dude, You're a Fag (Pascoe), 31

duoethnography, 296

dyadic analysis, 83

Eastman, J. T., 306–307, 308

Egloff, B., 153, 154 (figure)

Ehrenreich, Barbara, 36

elements, of studies, 303–312

elements, of theories, 260–262

Elfers, J., 152, 180

Ellis, C., 15

"Emergent Issues When Researching Trauma" (Connolly, Reilly), 287–289

Emotion Coding, 129–131, 131 (figure)

Emotion Review, 291–292

emotional arc, 130

"Emotional Timeline of September 11, 2001, The" (Back, Küfner, Egloff), 153, 154 (figure)

emotions, in Dramaturgical Coding, 220

empirical materials, 4

empirical observations, 257, 258–259

epistemology, 141–142, 184

Erickson, Frederick, 185, 245, 246–247, 251

ethics. *See* research ethics

Ethics Committees. *See* Institutional Review Boards (IRB)

ethnography

    autoethnography, 158–159

    defined, 31

    duoethnography, 296

    meta-ethnography, 171

    as qualitative methodology, 147–148, 148 (figure)

    See also write-ups

ethos, 21

evaluation research, 156–158

Evernote, 172

evidentiary warrant, 246, 307–308
Excel (Microsoft), 48, 124, 161 (figure), 172, 239
exemption, 198
expedited review, 198
experts, for research, 173
eyeballing, 226

Facebook, 64–66
Fasterplan, 102
Fernández-Sierra, J., 157–158
field notes
  front matter of, 39
  jottings and write-ups, 40–43, 41 (figure)
  observers' comments in, 43–44
  overview, 38
  setting for, 39–40
  technical matters of, 45–49, 46 (figure),
    49 (figure)
  time stamps for, 44–45
  for written documentation of analytic
    observation, 38–39
field site analysis, 29–62
  analyzing observations of social life in, 50–57,
    52 (figure)
  culture and, 30–31, 31 (figure)
  field notes used in, 38–45, 41 (figure)
  fieldwork, defined, 32
  method and methodology, 30
  observation settings for, 32–34,
    33 (figure)
  observers' frames for, 34–38, 35 (figure),
    38 (figure)
  overview, 29–30
  site selection, 178
  technical matters of fieldwork and field notes,
    45–49, 46 (figure), 49 (figure)
fieldwork
  defined, 32
  fieldwork observation logs, 48, 49 (figure)
filters, 34–36
Finley, Macklin, 294–296
Finley, Susan, 294–296
5 Rs (routines, rituals, rules, roles, relationships),
  15–23
  analytic synthesis and constructing theory,
    267–268
  in documents, artifacts, and visual materials,
    85–86

interpreting routines, rituals, rules, roles, and
    relationships of social life, 255–257
  overview, 15, 22 (figure)
  reflection on, 51–52, 52 (figure), 53
  relationships, 20–23, 21 (figure)
  rituals, 16–17, 16 (figure)
  roles, 19–20
  routines, 15–16
  rules, 17–19
  See also relationships; rituals; roles;
    routines; rules
focus groups, 93–94, 94 (figure)
Foster, E., 298–300
found poetry, 224–225, 262
Fox, R., 289–290
frames, of observers, 34–38
framework, analyzing. See qualitative
    methodologies; qualitative research design;
    research ethics
Fredricks, J. A., 284–285, 312
Friese, Susanne, 12
front matter, 39
full review, 199

Galletta, A., 104–105
gatekeepers, 33–34
Geertz, Clifford, 31
generalizability, 99
genres, 146–147, 162–163
geo-identity, 39
gerunds, for describing artifacts, 78–79
Glaser, Barney G., 150
Goffman, Erving, 19
Goleman, D., 129
Google Scholar, 336
ground plan
  defined, 40
  to present data, 328, 329 (figures)
grounded theory, 11, 150–151
Guba, E. G., 271

Hager, L., 72–73
Hanauer, D. I., 300–302
Handwerker, W. P., 259
Healthier Point of View, A (workbook), 70–72
Heath, C., 83
heuristics, 7
hierarchy, 233

highdeep thinking, 55
high-level inferences, 246
Hindmarsh, J., 83
Hines, A., 160, 162 (figure)
Hlava, P., 152, 180
"home," eight categories of "home" (theory
  example), 261–262, 264, 264 (figure),
  266 (figure)
Huberman, A. M., 97
human production, materials and meanings of,
  67–68
human subjects research, defined, 197–198. *See also*
  Institutional Review Boards (IRB)
Human Subjects Review Boards. *See* Institutional
  Review Boards (IRB)
hypothesis, 143–144

identities, 19, 72–73
if-then logic, 257–258
image conversion, to PDFs, 70
impressionist tales, 289–290
In Vivo Coding, 5–6, 121–126, 124 (figure)
induction, 9
infer (inference)
  defined, 51
  high-level inferences, 246
  low-level inferences, 246
influences and affects, 239
informed consent, 104, 201, 203, 204–205 (figure)
insight, theories and, 257, 259
Institutional Review Boards (IRB)
  defined, 196–197
  human subjects research, defined, 197–198
  informed consent, 204–205 (figure)
  IRB applications, 199–203, 199 (figure)
  review types and timelines, 198–199
INTERACT, 270, 271 (figure)
interaction, 12–15, 22, 50–51
intercoder agreement, 6
International Visual Sociology Association, 63
Internet resources, 336–337
interpretation, 142
interpretive writing, 291–292
interrelationship, 10
interviews, 89–116, 117–138
  asking questions for, 103–113, 103 (figure),
    105–107 (figure), 111 (figure)
  coding, overview, 117, 120–121

defined, 89
  Emotion Coding, 129–131, 131 (figure)
  interview condensation, 117–120
  interview protocol, 103–105, 105–107 (figure)
  participant selection for, 95–100, 98 (figure),
    100 (figure)
  preparation, scheduling, and arrangements for,
    101–103
  Process Coding, 126–128
  transcribing, 113–116, 115 (figure)
  types of, 89–94, 91 (figure), 94 (figure)
  Values Coding, 128–129, 128 (figure)
  In Vivo Coding and analytic formatting,
    121–126, 124 (figure)
investigators, for Institutional Review Board
  applications, 199–200
"Is Pain a Human Universal?" (Wierzbicka),
  291–292

jointly told tales, 296–298
Jones, Bill T., 303
Jones, Kip, 302
Jones, S. H., 15
jottings, 40–43, 41 (figure)
journal articles
  publishers of, 335–336
  researching, 170–174
  submission and publication, 312–313
  See also write-ups; *individual names of journals*
Journal of Adolescent Research, 284–285
Journal of Contemporary Ethnography, 306–307,
  308, 341
justice, in research, 192

key assertion, 246, 247 (figure)
key linkages, 246
keywords, 171–172, 310–311
Kidder, Tracy, 37–38
Kitchen, J., 155–156
Kozinets, Robert V., 21, 63
Küfner, A. C. P., 153, 154 (figure)

"Lady Who Blew Herself Up, The" (Hanauer),
  301–302
language
  for analyzing documents, 68, 69
  argot, 158
  consent for research and, 193

latent content, 66–67, 66 (figure)
layout, for slide presentations, 322
leading questions, 109
lenses, 34–36
Lester, J. N., 48
letters of information, 198
Lieberman, M. D., 13
"Lifelong Impact" study (McCammon, Saldaña, Hines, Omasta), 160, 162 (figure)
Likert scale, 160
"Limitations" section, of research reports, 168
Lincoln, Y. S., 271
LinkedIn, 333
literary narrative writing, 294–296, 294 (figure)
literary tales, 294
literature review, 170–174
logs, for fieldwork observation, 48, 49 (figure)
Long Run, The (Carless, Douglas), 302
low-level inferences, 246
Luff, Paul, 83
Lutgen-Sandvik, Pamela, 341, 355–387. See also "Nightmares, Demons, and Slaves" (Tracy, Lutgen-Sandvik, Alberts)

macro-level, 35
Madden, R., 261–262, 264
Maier, B. J., 72–73
Management Communication Quarterly, 341
mandated reporter, 203
manifest contents, 66–67, 66 (figure)
material culture, 63–88
    analysis of, overview, 63–64
    analyzing artifacts, 73–81, 77 (figure)
    defined, 63
    documents, 68–73
    5Rs in documents, artifacts, and visual materials, 85–86
    manifest and latent contents, 66–67, 66 (figure)
    materials and meanings of human production, 67–68
    values systems and, 64–66
    visual materials, 81–85, 82 (figure), 84 (figures)
    See also patterns, for textual and visual materials
matrices, 239–242, 240 (figure), 264
Mayo, Elton, 112–113
McCammon, L., 160, 162 (figure), 179

mediating variables, 238, 238 (figure)
mentors, for research, 173
meso-level, 35
meta-analysis, 171
meta-ethnography, 171
meta-memos, 57, 255–257, 267–268
metasummary, 171
metasynthesis, 171
method, 30
methodology
    defined, 30
    guidelines for analytic synthesis of, 215
    See also qualitative methodologies
microanalysis, 83
micro-level, 35
Microsoft
    Excel, 48, 124, 161 (figure), 172, 239
    PowerPoint, 323–326, 323 (figure), 331, 331 (figure)
    Word, 239–241, 240 (figure), 331
Miles, M. B., 97, 332
Miller, D. L., 286
minors, research consent and, 192–193
mixed-method research
    for analytic synthesis, 242–244, 265
    analyzing framework of research, 159–162, 161 (figure), 162 (figure)
    defined, 159
MLA manual style, 310
moments, 13
multi-case sampling, 96
My Freshman Year (Nathan), 147–148

Nathan, Rebekah (pseudonym), 147–148
Nazis, research ethics and, 191
netnography, 63
Netnography (Kozinets), 63
networked individualism, 21
networking, 333
Nickel and Dimed (Ehrenreich), 36
"Nightmares, Demons, and Slaves" (Tracy, Lutgen-Sandvik, Alberts), 341, 355–387
    Abstract, 355–357
    Workplace Bullying: Terminology, Characteristics, and Costs, 357–360
    Method, 360
    Data Collection Procedures, 361–362
    Grounded Metaphor Analysis, 362–363

What Bullying Feels Like, 363–364,
    364 (table)
Metaphors of the Bullying Process, 364–370,
    366 (figure)
Metaphors of the Bully, 370–371
Metaphors of Targets, 371–374
Discussion, 374
Theoretical Implications, 375–377
Practical Applications, 377–379
Limitations, Future Directions, and Conclusions,
    379–381
Nordmarken, Sonny, 158–159
NVivo, 332, 332 (figure)

objectives, in Dramaturgical Coding, 219
observation
    observers' comments (OCs), 43–44
    observers' frames for field site analysis, 34–38,
        35 (figure), 38 (figure)
    settings for field site analysis, 32–34,
        33 (figure)
    See also field site analysis
observation logs, for fieldwork, 48, 49 (figure)
O'Hara, E., 72–73
Olander, J. S., 286
Omasta, M., 160, 162 (figure), 197,
    328–330
"On the Bus With Vonnie Lee" (Angrosino),
    341, 343–354
    Abstract, 343
    A Life in Process, 343–346
    Bus Trip, 346–349
    The Meaning of the Bus, 349–350
    Discussion, 350–353
ontology, 141
open-ended questions, 176
oral history, 92
Otero, H. D., 243
outcomes, 238, 238 (figure)
outliers, 235

paper presentations
    defined, 317
    protocols and etiquette, 318–320
    roles of participants, 318 (See also write-ups)
    slide design, 321–322
    slide types, 323–326, 323 (figure)
paradigm, 143

paradigmatic corroboration, 161
participant check, 6
participant compliance, 109
participant incentive descriptions, for Institutional
    Review Board applications, 201
participant observation
    access for, 33
    defined, 29
    See also field site analysis
participant population description, for Institutional
    Review Board applications, 200
participant selection
    for interviews, 95–100, 98 (figure),
        100 (figure)
    qualitative research design, 178–180
    See also research ethics
participants, relationship to researchers, 205–206
Pascoe, C. J., 31
patterns
    analysis of, 7–10
    defined, 7
patterns, for textual and visual materials
    analytic synthesis and constructing
        theory, 263
    categories, 226–230
    overview, 225
    summarized, 275 (figure)
    themes, 230–235
    See also synthesis of analysis
Patton, M. Q., 23, 157
Paulus, T., 48, 83
PDF conversion, mobile apps for, 70
peers, for research, 173
peripheral role, 36
Pezzarossi, H. L., 81
phenomenology, 151–153
phenomenon, 11, 143
photo-elicitation interviews, 149
photos, for data presentation, 330–331
photovoice, 303
phrasing, of interview questions, 108–111
plot, 245
poetic inquiry, 224
poetic writing, 300–302, 300 (figure)
point of view, 308–309
positionality, 35, 35 (figure)
positivist, defined, 144
poster presentations, 324–325

power, 19

PowerPoint (Microsoft), 323–326, 323 (figure), 331, 331 (figure)

precoding, 217

preparation, for interviewing, 101–103

presentation modes, 182–183

Presentation of Self in Everyday Life, The (Goffman), 19

presentations, 317–334
  dramatic/staged readings, 326, 326–327 (figure)
  overview, 317–318
  paper presentations, 318–324, 323 (figure)
  poster presentations, 324–325
  presenting data effectively, 328–333, 329 (figures), 330 (figure)m 331 (figure), 332 (figure)
  professional networking, 333

prewriting, 304

principal/other investigators, for Institutional Review Board applications, 199–200

privacy descriptions, for Institutional Review Board applications, 203

procedure descriptions, for Institutional Review Board applications, 202

Process Code, 6–7

Process Coding, 78–79, 126–128

production, materials and meanings of, 67–68

professional association conferences, 182–183

professional associations, 337–338

professional development, 338

professional networking, 333

project title, for Institutional Review Board applications, 199

properties, 8, 257–259

proposal, for Institutional Review Board applications, 200

propositions, 237–239, 238 (figure), 263

protocols, 191

proverb, 260

"Proximal Processes in Urban Classrooms" (Wallace, Chhuon), 186–187, 187 (figure)

pseudonym, 58

publication
  of journal articles, 312–313
  qualitative research publishers, 335–336
  See also journal articles; *individual names of journals*

purpose statement, of research reports, 168–170

purpose-driven observation, 37–38

purposive sampling, 96–97

"Qualitative Evaluation of a Program on Self-Care and Health Education for Diabetics" (Santos-Guerra, Fernández-Sierra), 157–158

"Qualitative Exploration of Adolescents' Commitment to Athletics and the Arts, A" (Fredricks), 284–285, 312

Qualitative Inquiry, 286, 287–290, 294–302

qualitative methodologies, 141–164
  action research, 155–156
  autoethnography, 158–159
  case studies, 148–150
  content analysis, 153–155, 154 (figure)
  ethnography, 147–148, 148 (figure)
  evaluation research, 156–158
  on genres, 146–147, 162–163
  grounded theory, 150–151
  guidelines for analytic synthesis of, 215
  mixed methods, 159–162, 161 (figure), 162 (figure)
  phenomenology, 151–153
  rationale for, 145–146
  selected types, overview, 146–147
  theoretical premises of qualitative research, 141–145

qualitative research
  defined, 4
  example of, 144–145
  learning about, 335–339
  quantitative research compared to, 143, 159–162, 161 (figure)
  See also field site analysis; interviews; material culture; qualitative methodologies

qualitative research design, 165–190
  analyzing literature, 170–174
  conceptual frameworks, 184–188, 187 (figure)
  data analysis methods, 181–182
  data collection methods, 180–181
  overview, 165–166
  participant selection, 178–180
  presentation modes, 182–183
  research design, defined, 165
  research questions, 174–177, 176 (figure)
  researching and analyzing topic, 166–170, 168 (figure)

site selection, 178
timeline design, 183–184
quantitative research
for analytic synthesis, 242–244
analytic synthesis and constructing theory, 265
defined, 143–144
mixed-methods research, overview, 159–162,
161 (figure)
quantitize, defined, 160
questions (for interviews)
interview protocol for, 103–105,
105–107 (figure)
maintaining conversation for, 111–113,
111 (figure)
phrasing, 108–111
questions (for research), 174–177, 176 (figure), 215
Quirkos Software, 269, 269 (figure)

Rallis, S. F., 156
rapport, 206
rationale, 169–170
reaction, 13, 50–51
"Rebel Manhood" (Eastman), 306–307, 308
recording
for field notes, 45–47, 46 (figure)
for interviewing, 102–103
references, 310
reflection
on action, reaction, interaction, 50–51
analytic memos and, 54–57
defined, 50
on roles and relationships, 52 (figure), 53
on routines, rituals, rules, 51–52
reflexivity, 50
Reilly, R. C., 287–289
related research questions, 175–177, 176 (figure)
relationships
analytic synthesis and constructing theory,
267–268
defined, 20
in documents, artifacts, and visual materials,
85–86
interpreting, for analytic synthesis, 255–257
overview, 21 (figure), 22 (figure)
reflection on, 52 (figure), 53
research design
defined, 165
as preliminary report outline, 304–306
See also qualitative research design

research ethics, 191–209
analyzing ethical ambiguity, 206–208
ethos, 21
Institutional Review Boards (IRB),
196–203, 199 (figure), 201 (figure),
204–205 (figure)
overview, 191–192
researcher and participant relationships,
205–206
rules of research, 192–196
research questions, 174–177, 176 (figure)
research reports. See write-ups
ResearchGate, 333
respect for persons, in research, 192
risk descriptions, for Institutional Review Board
applications, 202
rituals
analytic synthesis and constructing theory,
267–268
artifacts used in, 74
defined, 16
in documents, artifacts, and visual materials,
85–86
interpreting, for analytic synthesis, 255–257
overview, 16–17, 16 (figure), 22 (figure)
reflection on, 51–52
roles
analytic synthesis and constructing theory,
267–268
defined, 19
in documents, artifacts, and visual materials,
85–86
interpreting, for analytic synthesis, 255–257
observer membership roles, 36–37
overview, 19–20, 22 (figure)
reflection on, 52 (figure), 53
Rossman, G. B., 156
roundtables, 317–318
routines
analytic synthesis and constructing theory,
267–268
artifacts used in, 74
defined, 15
in documents, artifacts, and visual materials,
85–86
interpreting, for analytic synthesis,
255–257
overview, 15–16, 22 (figure)
reflection on, 51–52

Rufus Stone (Jones), 302
rules
    analytic synthesis and constructing theory, 267–268
    defined, 17
    in documents, artifacts, and visual materials, 85–86
    interpreting, for analytic synthesis, 255–257
    overview, 17–19, 22 (figure)
    reflection on, 51–52

Saldaña, J.
    analysis, overview, 11
    analytic synthesis, 243, 253
    analyzing documents, artifacts, and visual materials, 82–83
    analyzing materials, 64, 72–73
    field notes, 39–40, 41–42
    field observation, 53
    interviews, 93, 97
    "Lifelong Impact," 160, 162 (figure)
    secondary data, 150–151
    "Theatre of the Oppressed," 169–170
    writing, 306
Salmons, J., 203
sample/sampling, 95, 179–180
Santos-Guerra, M. A., 157–158
saturation, 47, 99
scheduling, for interviewing, 101–103
schema, 15
Schneider, Christopher J., 83
scientific validity, for Institutional Review Board applications, 200
scope of inquiry, 168
screenplays, 302
searching, 171–172, 310–312
secondary data, 150–151
semantic differential, 243
semi-structured interviews, 92
session chair, 319
setting, of field notes, 39–40
significance, 17
significant trivia, 286
site selection, 178
slides
    design, 321–322
    types of, 323–326, 323 (figure)
snowball sampling, 97
social desirability bias, 109

social life, routines/rituals/rules/roles/relationships of. *See* 5 Rs (routines, rituals, rules, roles, relationships); relationships; rituals; roles; routines; rules
social media
    for interviews, 93
    for professional networking, 333
    values, attitudes, and beliefs, 64–66
social processes of human action, reaction, and interaction
    analytic synthesis, overview, 245
    analytic synthesis and constructing theory, 265–267
    assertions, 245–251, 247 (figure)
    diagrammatic displays, 252–255, 253 (figure)
    field site analysis of, 50–57, 52 (figure)
    summarized, 276 (figure)
    understanding, 12–15
    vignettes, 251–252
    See also field site analysis
socialization, 17
society, defined, 31
"Sp'ange" (Finley, Finley), 294–296
Speedy, Jane, 296–298
Stake, Robert E., 24
stakeholders/issues at stake/stakeholder perspectives, of Versus Codes, 223
standpoints, 34
stanzas, 123
status, 19
Stevens, D., 155–156
"Storm Tracking" (Foster), 298–300
storyline, 245
Strauss, Anselm L., 150
Street Corner Society (ethnography), 147
structured interviews, 90–91
subassertion, 246, 247 (figure)
subcode, 218
subjectivity, 35–36
subtexts, in Dramaturgical Coding, 220
superobjectives, in Dramaturgical Coding, 220
surveys, 90–91, 91 (figure)
symbolism, 76–77, 77 (figure), 121
synchronous interviews, 103
synoptic, defined, 246
synthesis of analysis, 213–244, 245–281
    analytic methods, summarized, 273–277 (figure)

CAQDAS (Computer Assisted Qualitative Data Analysis Software), 268–271, 269 (figure), 270 (figure), 271 (figure)
condensing large amounts of data, 215–225
credibility and trustworthiness of, 271–273
interpreting routines, rituals, rules, roles, and relationships of social life, 255–257
overview, 213–215, 245
patterning textual and visual materials, 225–235
synthesis, defined, 213
theorizing for, 257–268, 264 (figure), 266 (figure) (*See also* theory)
understanding social processes of human action, reaction, and interaction, 245–255, 247 (figure), 253 (figure)
for unifying seemingly different things, 235–244, 238 (figure), 240 (figure)
See also social processes of human action, reaction, and interaction

tabular displays, 239–242, 240 (figure), 264
tactics, in Dramaturgical Coding, 220
TagCrowd, 330
Tally's Corner (ethnography), 147
technical matters, of fieldwork and field notes, 45–49, 46 (figure), 49 (figure)
"Theatre of the Oppressed" (Saldaña), 169–170
themes
    defined, 230
    for patterning textual and visual materials, 230–235
theoretical constructs, 234
theoretical framework, 184
theoretical sampling, 97, 100
theory
    for condensing large amounts of data, 262–265
    constructing theories, 260–262
    defined, 257
    eight categories of "home" (example), 264, 264 (figure), 266 (figure)
    elements of theories, 259–260
    for interpreting routines, rituals, rules, roles, and relationships of social life, 267–268
    properties of theories, 257–259
    for understanding social processes of human action, reaction, and interaction, 265–267

"They Think Minority Means Lesser Than" (Allen), 341, 388–410
    Abstract, 388
    Keywords, 388
    Introduction, 388–389
    Theoretical Framework, 389–392
    Method, 393–395, 393 (table)
    School Encounters with Racial Microaggressions, 395–398
    Resisting Racial Microaggressions, 398–401
    Discussion, 401–403
    Conclusion, 403
thick description, 31
Three for All! (game), 4–7, 8–10
through-line, 23–24
time stamps, for field notes, 44–45
timeline, for Institutional Review Boards, 198–199, 200
timeline design, 183–184
titles of works, 310–312
topics
    researching and analyzing, 166–170, 168 (figure)
    summarizing, for transcripts, 116
Tracy, Sarah J., 341, 355–387. *See also* "Nightmares, Demons, and Slaves" (Tracy, Lutgen-Sandvik, Alberts)
Transana (video analysis software), 81, 82 (figure)
transcripts
    for condensing interviews, 117–120 (*See also* coding)
    defined, 114
    transcribing interviews, 113–116, 115 (figure)
treatment, 143
triangulation, 99
trustworthiness, 271–273
"Tuskegee Study of Untreated Syphilis in the Negro Male" (U.S. Public Health Service), 191

unity
    analysis and, 10–12, 10 (figure)
    defined, 10
    of seemingly different things, 235–244, 238 (figure), 240 (figure), 263–265, 275–276 (figure)
unobtrusive measures, 74
unstructured interviews, 92
Urban Education, 341
U.S. Department of Health, Education, and Welfare, 191–192

U.S. Public Health Service, 191
utility, 169

Vagle, Mark D., 152
value
    analysis of attitudes, beliefs, and, 64–66
    materials and meanings of human production,
        66–67
    Values Coding for interviews, 128–129,
        128 (figure)
    values system, defined, 64
Values Coding, 91
Van Maanen, John, 283, 284
verbatim, 47
Versus Coding, 222–224
video-recording
    for field notes, 45–47, 46 (figure)
    for interviewing, 102–103
videos, for data presentation, 330–331
vignettes, 247, 251–252, 265–267
visual analysis
    collaboration for, 82–83
    defined, 81–82
    evocation used for, 83–85, 84 (figures)
    software example, 81, 82 (figure)
visual culture, 63
V-Note software, 45, 46 (figure)
vulnerable participant information, for Institutional
    Review Board applications, 201

Wallace, T. L., 186–187, 187 (figure)
Washburn, R., 12
webinars, 337
What Objects Mean (Berger), 76

Wierzbicka, A., 291–292
within-case sampling, 95–96
Wolcott, Harry F., 64–65, 283, 284, 287
Word (Microsoft), 239–241, 240 (figure), 331
word clouds, 328–330, 330 (figure)
WordItOut, 330
Wordle, 330
working sessions, 318
write-ups
    about major elements of a study, 303–312,
        310 (figure)
    analytic and formal writing, 284–286,
        285 (figure)
    collaborative and polyvocal writing, 296–298
    confessional tales, 287–289
    credibility and trustworthiness of, 273
    critical and advocacy writing, 292–294
    dance and, 303, 303 (figure)
    defined, 42
    descriptive and realistic writing, 286–287
    dramatic writing, 298–300
    impressionist tales, 289–290
    interpretation for, 291–292
    journal article submission and publication,
        312–313
    literary narrative writing, 294–296, 294 (figure)
    overview, 40–43, 41 (figure)
    photovoice and, 303
    poetic writing, 300–302, 300 (figure)
    screenplays and, 302
    styles of presentation, overview, 283–284
"Writing and Retelling Multiple Ethnographic Tales
    of a Soup Kitchen for the Homeless" (Miller,
    Creswell, Olander), 286